THE CHRISTIAN MORAL LIFE

THEOLOGY IN GLOBAL PERSPECTIVE SERIES

Peter C. Phan, General Editor
Ignacio Ellacuría Professor of Catholic Social Thought
Georgetown University

At the beginning of a new millennium, the *Theology in Global Perspective* Series responds to the challenge to reexamine the foundational and doctrinal themes of Christianity in light of the new global reality. While traditional Catholic theology has assumed an essentially European or Western point of view, *Theology in Global Perspective* takes account of insights and experience of churches in Africa, Asia, Latin America, Oceania, as well as in Europe and North America. Noting the pervasiveness of changes brought about by science and technologies, and growing concerns about the sustainability of Earth, it seeks to embody insights from studies in these areas as well.

Though rooted in the Catholic tradition, volumes in the series are written with an eye to the ecumenical implications of Protestant, Orthodox, and Pentecostal theologies for Catholicism, and vice versa. In addition, authors will explore insights from other religious traditions with the potential to enrich Christian theology and self-understanding.

Books in this series will provide reliable introductions to the major theological topics, tracing their roots in Scripture and their development in later tradition, exploring when possible the implications of new thinking on gender and sociocultural identities. And they will relate these themes to the challenges confronting the peoples of the world in the wake of globalization, particularly the implications of Christian faith for justice, peace, and the integrity of creation.

Other Books Published in the Series

Orders and Ministries: Leadership in a Global Church, Kenan Osborne, O.F.M.
Trinity: Nexus of the Mysteries of Christian Faith, Anne Hunt
Eschatology and Hope, Anthony Kelly, C.Ss.R.
Meeting Mystery: Liturgy Worship, Sacraments, Nathan D. Mitchell
Creation, Grace and Redemption, Neil Ormerod
Globalization, Spirituality and Justice, Daniel G. Groody, C.S.C.
Christianity and Science: Toward a Theology of Nature, John F. Haught
Ecclesiology for a Global Church: A People Called and Sent, Richard R. Gaillardetz

THEOLOGY IN GLOBAL PERSPECTIVE SERIES

THE CHRISTIAN MORAL LIFE

Faithful Discipleship for a Global Society

PATRICIA LAMOUREUX
AND
PAUL J. WADELL

ORBIS BOOKS

Maryknoll, New York 10545

Founded in 1970, Orbis Books endeavors to publish works that enlighten the mind, nourish the spirit, and challenge the conscience. The publishing arm of the Maryknoll Fathers and Brothers, Orbis seeks to explore the global dimensions of the Christian faith and mission, to invite dialogue with diverse cultures and religious traditions, and to serve the cause of reconciliation and peace. The books published reflect the views of their authors and do not represent the official position of the Maryknoll Society. To learn more about Maryknoll and Orbis Books, please visit our website at www.maryknollsociety.org.

Published by Orbis Books, Maryknoll, New York 10545-0302.
Manufactured in the United States of America.

Library of Congress Cataloging-in-Publication Data

Lamoureux, Patricia.
    The Christian moral life : faithful discipleship for a global society /
Patricia Lamoureux & Paul J. Wadell.
        p. cm. — (Theology in global perspective series)
    Includes bibliographical references (p.   ) and index.
    ISBN 978-1-57075-881-2 (pbk.)
    1. Christian ethics—Catholic authors. 2. Catholic Church—Doctrines.
I. Wadell, Paul J. II. Title.
    BJ1249.L32 2010
    241'.042—dc22
                                                            2010011792

To Barbara, Damion, and Annie

Disciples Who Live Faithfully amidst Adversity

Contents

Foreword

by Peter C. Phan

Even a cursory glance at the developments in Roman Catholic moral theology in the last half century—from the decade before the Second Vatican Council (1962-65) to the first decade of the twenty-first century—will reveal enormous changes. To describe the difference between the two kinds of moral theology prevalent before and after the council, the "hermeneutics of rupture" is more helpful than the "hermeneutics of continuity." Part of the reason for this sea change lies with the council itself, which urges that moral theology "should draw more fully on the teaching of holy Scripture and should throw light upon the exalted vocation of the faithful in Christ and their obligation to bring forth fruit in charity for the life of the world" (Decree on the Training of Priests, *Optatam totius*, no. 16).

The authors of this volume, Patricia Lamoureux and Paul Wadell, unabashedly intend their work to be a response to the council's exhortation. A renewed moral theology, as the above-cited conciliar text indicates, must be biblically based, focus on the baptismal vocation, center on Christ as the model of Christian life, promote the virtue of love, and foster service to humanity and the world. To the letter, faithfully and splendidly, the book fulfills these five requirements. Its subtitle alone says in a nutshell what Christian life, as well as moral theology, is all about: *Faithful Discipleship*. Christian life is not about keeping a set of rules and norms but about *being a disciple* of Jesus—a lifelong and dynamic process—for which norms and rules are necessary and useful but without discipleship would lead to a deadly legalism.

There is another term in the book's subtitle that needs careful consideration, that is, *faithful*. To be a disciple of Jesus requires a new vision, or, as the authors put it elegantly, "to see truthfully and reverently." *Faithful* implies not only fidelity but also faith, which provides that reverent and truthful vision. What is specifically Christian in theological ethics is not a new superstructure of values or a different, larger set of norms added to the purely human ethics, but a new vision, making Jesus' way of seeing one's own, and acting accordingly.

To help us understand this new vision the authors present the central message of Jesus' ministry, namely, the reign of God, especially as contained in the so-called Sermon on the Mount. In this theological framework they then go on to discuss the staple themes of what was once known as "fundamental moral theology": sin, conversion, virtues, conscience, love, the Paschal Mystery, and the role of the Holy Spirit in Christian life.

All these themes are well-worn indeed. But an alert reader immediately senses that there is something—refreshingly—new in these pages, the proverbial new wine in new skins. The newness is conveyed by a phrase in the book's subtitle: *Global Society*. When Vatican II mandated a renewed moral theology, it was not yet fully aware of all the implications of globalization and religious pluralism for doing theological ethics. After all, it still spoke of it within the context of training of priests! The society in which theology is being done today has changed enormously. No one is more aware of this than our two authors, as is clear in their question: "What does faithful discipleship require of us in an increasingly global world characterized by religious, philosophical, political, cultural, and economic diversity?" In wrestling with this question, Pat and Paul humbly acknowledge that the European and American perspectives in which they have been trained as moral theologians are "glaringly inadequate." To expand their intellectual horizon they lead us into dialogue with the beliefs and practices of other religions. But they do not stop there. They also engage in conversation with novels, poems, biographies, movies, and works of art. These are not merely rhetorical props but rich resources for doing theology. What their collaborative effort produced is a work of art itself, lucid, engaging, passionate, beautiful. Do not take my word for it. Read it and see for yourself.

Preface

This book is a response to an exhortation. Over forty years ago bishops and theologians of the Catholic Church gathered in Rome for the Second Vatican Council. Although no single document of the council focused on Catholic moral teaching, the council did issue a challenge to Catholic moral theologians. Lamenting the state of the discipline, the council called for a thorough renewal of Catholic moral theology by making it much more focused on Christ, rooted in the scriptures, and connected to the sacramental and spiritual life of the church. "Special care," the council observed, "should be given to the perfecting of moral theology. Its scientific presentation should draw more fully on the teaching of holy Scripture and should throw light upon the exalted vocation of the faithful in Christ and their obligation to bring forth fruit in charity for the light of the world."[1]

In what follows, we have tried to honor that challenge by envisioning the Christian moral life as a call to faithful discipleship. The New Testament depicts Christianity as a new way of being, characterized by distinctive attitudes and practices. Those who were baptized in Christ were to model their lives on Christ by growing in the virtues of the gospel—virtues such as love and justice, compassion and generosity, patience and forgiveness, peace and reconciliation. Moreover, these early Christians realized that in their individual and communal lives together they were to continue what Christ began. To be a Christian was to be entrusted with the mission of proclaiming and witnessing to the reign of God. Thus, being a Christian did not take one out of the world or require turning one's back on the world; rather, to be a Christian was to live in the world in a special way by striving to re-present Christ to others.

What would this mean today? What does faithful discipleship require of us in an increasingly global world characterized by religious, philosophical, political, cultural, and economic diversity? In wrestling with that question throughout the book, we dialogue not only with Catholic and other Christian theologians in Latin America, Africa, and Asia, but also with the other major world religions. Each of us writes from the context of the United States, and our theological training has been largely informed by European and American theologians. But given the diversity of our world today and the challenges that beset us, that perspective alone is glaringly inadequate. One of the joys of working on this book has been having our own ideas and perspectives challenged, expanded, and immensely enriched not only by the wisdom of other

Christian theologians and a variety of Christian theologies, but also by the moral traditions and practices of Judaism, Buddhism, Islam, and other world religions. Just as Christian teaching and practice has always been impacted by the encounter with other cultures, religions, and social practices, today we ponder what it means to follow Christ in a world where many either are not Christian or understand the Christian life in light of the distinctive social and cultural contexts in which they live. This is one reason why Christian moral reflection must increasingly take the form of an ongoing dialogue or conversation in which each person learns from and is enriched by the other.

That is what we have attempted in this book. In chapter 1 we begin the conversation by proposing the call to discipleship as an overarching framework for the Christian moral life. In reflecting on why this might be an appropriate way for envisioning the Christian moral life, we explore what it means to be called and why we are called, as well as why calling gets to the heart of what it means to be human. We examine the place of call in the scriptures, particularly Jesus' call to his disciples. Moreover, we suggest that call is the foundation of the moral life, first because to be human is to be called to wholeness through goodness and love, and second because each day of our lives we are called out of our selves by the presence of another. We conclude the opening chapter by speaking of the church as a people called to a community of faithful discipleship by God. The mission of the church is to be the people of God in the world by working on behalf of God's plans and purposes for the world.

But that cannot possibly be done unless one learns to see truthfully and reverently, and that is the focus of chapter 2. We typically connect morality with laws, principles, and rules, and not with learning to see. But we cannot act rightly unless we first see rightly. It's no accident that so many of Jesus' miracles involved restoring sight to the blind. If my vision is faulty, if it's twisted by prejudice or self-centeredness or fear, then I cannot possibly act justly. We must learn to see truthfully if we are to live just and loving lives. This is why the Christian moral life is an ongoing training in vision. Just as the disciples only very gradually came to see clearly who Jesus was and what his mission was about, so too in our own journey of discipleship do we only slowly come to make Jesus' way of seeing our own. In chapter 2 we'll explore what makes seeing truthfully and reverently so difficult, and how we can move beyond fantasy and illusion to making Christ's way of seeing our own.

The central theme of Jesus' teaching and ministry was the reign of God. In chapter 3 we explore the meaning of the reign of God for the Christian moral life by noting some of its characteristics and by giving particular attention to the Sermon on the Mount. A life of faithful discipleship requires wholehearted commitment to the reign of God. And yet, because the reign of God that was initiated by Jesus is not yet completely present, a life of faithful discipleship is impossible without hope. What does it mean to live in hope or to be a people of hope? How should Christians think about hope? These too are some of the questions that are addressed in chapter 3.

One of the reasons that the reign of God is not yet completely present in our world is sin. There is a fundamental goodness to human beings, but there is also an undeniable brokenness. We are not yet who we are called to be and seldom are we who we ought to be. That is why the Christian moral life is a call to ongoing repentance and conversion. In the fourth chapter we'll probe this dimension of faithful discipleship by examining a Christian understanding of sin, different manifestations of sin, the effects of sin on our selves and on our world, and why it is we can do wrong so easily and frequently. But since the trajectory of the Christian life is from darkness to light or, as the paschal mystery suggests, from death back to life, we'll also consider conversion. What does it mean to be converted? How and why do conversions happen? In addressing these questions, we'll explore different kinds of conversion and why, in a life of faithful discipleship, conversion culminates with faith in Christ.

Disciples are called to become "another" Christ. But we can only grow in likeness to Christ by acquiring the virtues we see in Christ. In chapter 5 we will examine the role of the virtues in the Christian moral life. What is a virtue? Why do we need the virtues? And how do we become virtuous? We'll give particular attention to the cardinal virtues, four virtues that traditionally have been seen to be absolutely necessary for living a good human life. And we'll expand our understanding of these quintessential virtues by considering how some other traditions have identified key virtues for life. We'll conclude the chapter with an analysis of the theological virtues and the infused moral virtues. These virtues are crucial for the Christian moral life because if the goal of the Christian moral life is communion with God and the saints in heaven, we cannot possibly achieve that without these virtues.

If the virtues help us grow in faithful discipleship to Christ, conscience helps us in deciding how to live and act in ways that are faithful to Christ. No one gets through life without having to make difficult decisions. And sometimes no trouble-free choice seems possible. We may not be able to make perfect decisions, but we are called to make decisions in good conscience. In chapter 6 we'll look at the role of conscience in the Christian moral life by first considering what we mean when we speak of conscience, and then reflecting on some of the things that shape and influence our conscience. We'll also discuss what it means to take responsibility for one's conscience as well as the tremendous cost of forsaking, ignoring, or betraying one's conscience. We'll conclude the chapter by considering what it might mean to speak of a "Christian" conscience. If disciples are called to be of "one mind and heart with Christ," how does this impact our understanding of conscience?

There's no denying that love is the heart of the Christian moral life. After all, Jesus didn't request that we love one another or hope that we would—Jesus commanded it! In chapter 7 we'll consider why love is the central task of the Christian moral life (and indeed of any human life). We'll explore what we are doing when we love and what loving well requires. These are important matters because love involves much more than simply good intentions. I may intend to love my neighbor well (whether parent, spouse, friend, or stranger), but unless I know what this means, I can do tremendous harm. It's also important to distinguish the different types of love. I may love a good martini, but surely not in the way I love my friend. And so in chapter 7 we'll attend to the different kinds of love, always remembering that Jesus challenges us to extend the circle of love not only to every human being, but to all of God's creatures as well.

The exemplary act of love for Christians is revealed in Jesus' passion, death, and resurrection. In chapter 8 we'll turn our attention to the paschal mystery and its implications for a moral life of discipleship. We'll investigate how the death and resurrection of Christ is portrayed and understood in the Gospels and in the New Testament writings of Paul. Since the paschal mystery begins with Jesus' suffering and death, we'll probe the role of suffering in the moral life, particularly the relation between love and suffering, and why in light of Jesus' passion the virtues of patient endurance and compassion are key to a life of faithful discipleship. We'll conclude chapter 8 by attending to the transformative power of Jesus' resurrection and how that empowers us to think about the moral life in new and hopeful ways.

Jesus remained present to his disciples by sending the Spirit to be with them and to guide them. The same is true for his disciples today. To live the Christian moral life is to be guided by the Spirit. In chapter 9 we'll look at the role of the Spirit in the moral life, particularly in helping us discern what God's call and our response should be. This will lead to a discussion of the gifts of the Spirit, particularly the gift of wisdom, and how this gift helps us discern what we ought to do. In chapter 9 we'll also briefly consider the different ways that law has functioned in Christian morality, but focus most of all on the Evangelical Law or Law of the Spirit that Thomas Aquinas saw as the animating principle for the Christian life. For him, the Christian moral life culminates in the Spirit moving freely within us, guiding us to God through the decisions and actions of our lives. In the final section of the chapter we'll explore the role of prayer in moral discernment and why moral discernment requires a community.

Our exploration of faithful discipleship concludes by reflecting on what it might mean today to follow Jesus' command to "make disciples of all nations." How are Christians called to bring Christ to the world? If followers of Jesus are called to be both faithful disciples and good citizens, how are these roles related? How should Christians participate in society? In grappling with these questions, we'll discuss the value of public life for discipleship, the importance of the virtue of solidarity, and the relation between love and justice.

Writing this book has been a thoroughly collaborative endeavor. While each of us took primary responsibility for some of the chapters, we commented on, critiqued, and made extensive suggestions on what the other had written. When one of us is on the East Coast and the other nestled in northeastern Wisconsin, such a collaborative project can be challenging. But our process for writing the book hopefully models the form we believe Christian theology and ethics must take in a global world. At its best, Christian ethics is a collaborative enterprise in which we come to a better grasp of what is true and good by listening to and learning from others. Through such collaboration we may discover that we do not always agree with another's viewpoint or opinion, but we are always better for listening humbly and attentively to what the other has to say. In this respect, our hope is that readers will feel invited to this conversation and feel called to contribute to it and continue it.

Speaking of readers, since we want as many as possible to join us in exploring these different dimensions of the Christian moral life, we have tried to make the book both engaging and accessible. While what we offer grows out of extensive reading and research, our goal was to avoid an overly scholarly or academic tone to the book. We hope that the book would be useful in the classroom for undergraduates studying Christian ethics, for adult education groups, or for anyone interested in thinking about what it might mean to live a life of faithful discipleship in today's world.

Finally, a word of thanks. Many people have encouraged and sustained us in this project, but we are especially indebted to Peter Phan for inviting us to write for this series and for allowing us to collaborate on this book, and to Bill Burrows of Orbis Books for his patience and guidance in helping us see this book to completion.

1

The Call of Discipleship

"Come, Follow Me" (Mark 1:17)

W E ARE ALL SEEKERS, people who are searching for some measure of happiness and fulfillment. We may seek material possessions or prestige. Or we may be attracted to the moral qualities of someone we admire and whom we desire to know more intimately. Others may long to become a doctor, a nurse, a teacher, an actress, or a firefighter. People may desire to work in education, health care, or civil service not primarily for esteem, financial remuneration, or security, but out of a sense of vocation to care for others, to save lives, or to protect one's country. The calling we experience may be a yearning from within for something more. Or it may be part of a vision we have of something better than the existing reality. We may not know exactly what is the "better" or the "more" we are searching for, but we know that we have to follow our heart's desire.

There are also people who feel called to certain ways of life out of a need for self-fulfillment. In America, work has often been identified with the theme of personal advancement. Alexis de Tocqueville dwelled at length on the "restlessness of temper" with which the citizens of the new nation went about their business. Max Weber identified this kind of eagerness to achieve worldly advancement with the Reformed Protestant notion of calling. Weber chose Benjamin Franklin as the "ideal type" of what he labeled the Protestant ethic. But he could easily have pointed to American religious leaders such as Cotton Mather and Jonathan Edwards as well. For example, Mather wrote, "Every Christian should have a calling . . . some settled business wherein . . . he may glorify God by doing of good for others and getting of good for himself."[1]

For the Christian, part of the fundamental sense of self is the call to be Jesus' disciple. "Come, follow me" is an invitation offered not just to the first group of disciples, but to men and women throughout the ages. The Christian moral life begins with this awareness of being called to discipleship, and the ethical task is to respond appropriately. Throughout the book, we will explore what it means to follow Jesus in this time and place, in the midst of a pluralistic, multicultural, globalized world.

1

In this chapter, we focus on the notion of being called to discipleship and the relation of this call to the moral life. What does it mean to be called? Who are called? What are people called to? What response is expected of those who are called? In the first part, we will examine the notion of calling found in the Hebrew and Christian biblical stories. In the second section, we suggest a framework for the moral life that incorporates the insights gleaned from the biblical exploration. But first we begin with a fable about the calling of a young shepherd boy named Santiago. We meet him in Paulo Coelho's marvelous story, *The Alchemist*.

SANTIAGO'S CALLING

Santiago was going to be a priest. At least that's what his father wanted him to become. It would be a source of pride for his simple farm family to have a son as a clergyman. But ever since he could remember, Santiago wanted to travel. Since the only people who could afford to travel were shepherds, he bought a flock of sheep. With his father's blessing, Santiago set out on a journey to discover the world. One night this Andalusian shepherd boy had a dream about buried treasure in the pyramids of Egypt. In fact, he had the same dream twice. Santiago could not forget this dream nor could he resist the call to search for the buried treasure.

So, Santiago set off on a journey that took him from his homeland in southern Spain, across the Mediterranean Sea, to the Egyptian desert. Along the way the young boy met several people who encouraged him and pointed him in the direction of his quest. He met a gypsy woman who interpreted dreams. She said that Santiago should go to the pyramids of Egypt, for there he would find a treasure that would make him a rich man.

At one point, when he became disillusioned about the possibility of finding his way to the pyramids, he encountered an old man named Melchizedek who called himself king of Salem. The "king" told Santiago that his only obligation was to pursue his "Personal Legend," that is, the heart's desire, a persistent yearning for something good. It is important to be attentive to one's Personal Legend, the old man said, for it is also our mission on earth and the path God wants us to follow. At the core, it is a desire that originates in the soul of the universe. Because all things are united, everything in the universe conspires in helping us achieve it.[2]

At times, though, it seemed to Santiago that there were forces in the universe working against him. There were so many perils on his journey and obstacles to overcome—robbers, warriors, endless deserts, and people who tried to talk him out of continuing his quest. Santiago was constantly subjected to tests of persistence and courage. But he never stopped dreaming and he followed the advice of Melchizedek who told him to "follow the omens," the signs along the way that would help Santiago arrive at the treasure he was seeking.

As he continued his search for the buried treasure, Santiago met a camel driver who told the boy of the disasters he had encountered in his own life, and of the need to trust in the One who has created us all, who takes away our fears of the unknown. And in a desert oasis, Santiago fell in love with Fatima. He came to realize that love is the core of creation and existence, the transforming power of the world.

On the last leg of his journey, an alchemist who befriended Santiago helped him understand the language of the desert and the world. The alchemist taught Santiago that the principle governing all things is the Soul of the World. "When you desire something with all your heart," the alchemist said, "you are closest to the Soul of the World. It's always a positive, transformative force that permeates everything on earth." On their mutual trek through the desert, Santiago asked his guide: "Why don't people's hearts tell them to continue to follow their dreams?" The alchemist responded: "Because that's what makes a heart suffer most and hearts don't like to suffer."[3]

The alchemist offered bits of wisdom that helped the boy continue on his journey. He learned from the maker of gold not to be hasty or impatient. If he pushed forward impulsively, he would fail to see the omens left by God along his path, signs that indicated what he should do. Santiago learned that love is a universal language all people could understand in their hearts. And the alchemist taught him that there is only one way to learn, through action. What he meant was immersing oneself in the world that God created, for it is through visible objects that we come to understand the marvels of God's wisdom. Since Santiago was in the desert, he should immerse himself in it.

"How do I immerse myself in the desert?" asked Santiago.

"Listen to your heart. It knows all things because it came from the Soul of the World, and it will one day return there," the Alchemist responded.

"Why do we have to listen to our heart?" the boy asked.

"Because wherever your heart is, that is where you'll find your treasure.
. . .

"Unfortunately, very few follow the path laid out for them—the path to their Personal Legends, and to happiness. Most people see the world as a threatening place, and because they do, the world turns out, indeed, to be a threatening place. . . . Don't give into your fears," said the Alchemist. . . . "If you do, you won't be able to talk to your heart. . . . The one thing that makes a dream impossible to achieve is the fear of failure."[4]

So the boy trekked on toward the pyramids of Egypt, and when he finally reached them he fell to his knees and wept. He thanked God for making him believe in his Personal Legend, and for leading him to meet so many people along the way, especially the gypsy woman, the king, the camel driver, Fatima, and the alchemist. Then Santiago began digging and digging and digging for the treasure, but he found nothing.

All was not lost, though, for what started out as a journey to find worldly goods turned into a discovery of different riches. Santiago learned that the treasure was the journey itself, the people he encountered, the discoveries made, and the wisdom acquired. The story teaches that one must pursue one's dream, for a personal calling is God's blessing, the path that God chose for us here on earth. In following and fulfilling our personal calling, we become God's instruments; we help the Soul of the World; and we understand our purpose for being on this earth.[5]

Santiago was called to embark on a journey toward self-discovery. What started as a personal quest for buried treasure led to a series of encounters with people who guided him along the way and, ultimately, to following the alchemist, whose wisdom helped the young boy to discover life's real treasures. Paulo Coelho's fable presents the personal calling as a kind of religious beckoning—a call to be true to what God has envisioned for each person. We find this sense of being summoned by the sacred in the biblical call stories. But there is more that the Hebrew and Christian stories have to teach us about the meaning and implications of God's call.

BIBLICAL PERSPECTIVES

The Hebrew Story

In the beginning, God called creation into existence. The earth with its vegetation, the birds of the sky, the fish of the sea, the animals that roam the land, and humankind made in God's image are all called to life by God. Humankind is called into being for the purpose of "civilizing the earth," to have dominion over it.[6] This means that we are to be conscious of our responsibility for creation and for its future, to care for it, not to exploit it or to dominate others.

The biblical account of creation views the human person in the context of relationships. We are all creatures of God and stand in relation to God—as creature to Creator. And there is an essential equality and inherent dignity among people for all are created in God's image and likeness. When God called man and woman into being, human community was created. What we learn from the creation narratives is reaffirmed throughout the Bible; that is, a call from God is always a call to life and a call to relationship. From the beginning we are not meant to be alone. Rather, we are called to communion with one another. God stays bound to persons for their well-being by calling them into covenant relationship. The establishment of the covenant is a divine initiative and Israel is expected to respond appropriately.

The moral life of the believer in the Hebrew testament was wrapped up in the experience of covenant, of being called to a certain way of life. The understanding of what this meant concretely changed as various aspects of human life became important at different times in the history of the covenant people. For example, Abraham is called unexpectedly to leave his homeland. He is given a mission, to be father of a new people. Abraham responded faithfully by doing God's will and thus a great nation of twelve tribes was brought forth. The Abrahamic covenant represents the dependable graciousness of God— gracious because freely given, and dependable because it is based on God's solemn pledge. The covenant is the promise of God's unconditional love and ongoing presence. "I will be your God. You shall be my people" (Lev 26:12).

In the later Mosaic covenant, Moses is called to be God's agent of liberation and justice for the Israelites. He is called to a nearly impossible task by God—to deliver the people from slavery—and he reluctantly accepts. In the Exodus story (3:1-12), the call of Moses has a certain pattern to it that is used throughout the Bible as the model of a call of the great prophets and leaders. Moses was called and then led into the desert away from anything familiar in order to hear the voice of Yahweh, to know Yahweh's saving and caring love and protection, and finally to respond in faith, gratitude, and fidelity. The desert experience is important, for it is there that "God calls Moses to live the exodus personally, and there to experience God's powerful presence, to know him, the Holy One, the Liberator."[7]

The call to covenant relationship is marked by *hesed*, the Hebrew word for loving-kindness. It is a sign of God's fidelity, an active concern for the well-being of people, particularly the weak and needy. Doing justice is the way of showing loving-kindness even beyond one's own circle of acquaintances. While it is not restricted to any one kind of relationship, loving-kindness cannot be understood outside of some relationship. Because Yahweh is just, those who enter into covenant with God must also be just. The content of justice can be seen in Yahweh's way of caring for Israel. One of the characteristics of Yahweh's justice is concern for the widow, the orphan, the alien, and the oppressed (Deut 14:28-29). For the faithful Jew, compassion and charity were duties that were required if one was to be faithful to the covenant. The widow, orphan, and sojourner could not be neglected. Poverty became a social problem for Israel during the monarchy when the emergence of privileged classes came with the establishment of a royal court. The unity of the nation in the old days of tribal confederation was being undone and social inequality grew.

The prophetic movement arose as a *call* to conscience of the Hebrew people. The prophets reprimand the Israelites for their idolatry, indifference, and moral turpitude, and warn them that a relationship with a God of justice has

> *"He had told you, O world, what is good; and what does the* LORD *require of you but to do justice, and to love kindness, and to walk humbly with your God?"* (Mic 6:8)

consequences for their behavior toward others (Mic 6:6-8). The prophets issue a call to conversion; they call people back to covenantal relationship and to respond rightly to the depth of God's love. Jeremiah's prophecy of a "new covenant" (Jer 31:31-34), that the teaching of Yahweh "will be written on the heart," means that all people will know God and will be able to hear God's call.[8] No special training in theology or doctrine is necessary because the call is placed within the conscience or heart of each person. So a young shepherd boy, like Santiago, can hear a call to leave his father and mother, and everything familiar to him, in search of a buried treasure. And an old man like Abraham can hear a call to leave his homeland in order to found a new nation.

In sum, the Hebrew stories reveal a notion of *calling* understood in the context of covenant. Essentially, it is a story of God's commitment to humankind and the people's response to God's gracious and gratuitous call to relationship. The believer is called to live in a way that reflects the requirements of the covenant. This means that men and women are to be responsible to and for others, especially the poor and needy persons in society. They are to do justice, to love tenderly, and to walk humbly with God (Mic 6:8).

The Call to Follow Jesus

With the incursion of God into history in the person of Jesus Christ, a new and more decisive call was made. A central characteristic of the New Testament call stories is that discipleship begins with an invitation. No one is forced into following Jesus. One is invited to be part of a journey or an adventure that involves something promising but also baffling and challenging. It can be marked by misunderstanding, struggle, even defeat. As Santiago discovered in following his call, the old secure way of life must often be left behind. A follower of Jesus must be willing to venture into the unknown with all the risks and perils that inevitably arise on the journey.

While Jesus issued a general call to repentance and faith to all people, he called particular individuals to follow or to accompany him. There were those in the innermost circle who received more intensive teaching than others. Peter and the brothers James and John are at the center, with Peter as the chief spokesman. Sometimes Jesus expressly summons or commands a person to follow him; other times a group or crowd follow on their own accord. But there are also some occasions when Jesus follows another, and he responds to the call of the other, especially to someone in need. For example, before healing the official's daughter, "Jesus got up and followed him, with his disciples" (Matt 9:9); and Jesus followed the official to his home in order to heal his slave (Luke 7:6). Fundamentally, though, throughout his own life and ministry, Jesus shows how obediently and faithfully he follows the call of God.

When we consider all the various ways that men and women follow Jesus in the New Testament, we see multiple dimensions of discipleship. It is not limited to the twelve or to those explicitly called to be disciples; rather there are "circles of discipleship." Around the twelve is a wider circle of followers, including women who followed (Mary of Magdala and others) and women who stayed at home (Mary of Bethany). We can widen the circle to include those who followed Jesus secretly, such as the owner of the upper room and Joseph of Arimathea; blind Bartimaeus, who follows Jesus after he receives his sight; the poor, repentant sinners, and large crowds all follow Jesus. As biblical scholar James Dunn points out, what is striking about these circles of discipleship is how they overlap and intertwine, offering a caution against making a hard and fast distinction between disciples and followers, or designating different grades of discipleship.[9] Furthermore, within the New Testament as a whole, there are different and unique conceptions of, and various metaphors used to describe, what it means to follow Jesus, different essential characteristics and virtues emphasized in each tradition, as well as different views about the proper attitudes and actions to be taken vis-à-vis the world. We see, then, that there are many ways, not one way, to follow Jesus.[10] What it means for an individual will vary according to one's talents, circumstances, possibilities, and responsibilities. But for all those who respond to the call to follow Jesus, it will be a new way of life that requires faithfulness.

Faithful Discipleship

Faithfulness is the ground and fertile soil of discipleship. We are used to thinking, and rightly so, of the centrality of love, but in the Gospels faithfulness emerges as the first and pivotal virtue of a life of discipleship. While the love command is said to be the "greatest of all commands," it is Jesus' directive, "Don't be afraid," that is more basic to the discipleship stories in the New Testament.[11] The Markan Gospel illustrates most starkly the difficulty of faithful discipleship. In the face of trouble, the lure of wealth, the pursuit of honor, prestige, wrong ambitions, or the desire for other things, the faith of the inner circle of disciples falters. For example, Jesus rescues them from the storm and asks, "Have you no faith?" (4:40). They are associated with the faithless generation (9:19) and are concerned about social status (9:33-34; 10:35-41). Later, they do not watch and pray (14:38) and are asleep when Jesus comes to them in Gethsemane (14:50). Judas betrays Jesus (14:37-41); Peter denies knowing Jesus (14:68-72); and the disciples flee when Jesus is arrested (14:50).

The Markan portrait of these disciples may be surprising or even disturbing to people who expect disciples to be exemplary. While initially enthusiastic in responding to the call, followers of Jesus can be cowardly, something with which contemporary disciples can resonate. The early enthusiasm that generally characterizes a call experience commonly gives way to a period of testing. This may be referred to as a "desert experience," a time of difficulty or aridity that poses a challenge to faithfulness. When Santiago embarked on his trek through the desert, he was confronted with military battles, robbers, and people who tried to dissuade him from following the dream.

But he continued onward, even when the forces seemed to be working against him. Santiago's story exemplifies faithfulness, a kind of knowing or trusting in what cannot be seen or proven, but what is nevertheless accepted and believed. From a biblical perspective, faithfulness implies a way of life that reflects an awareness of and trust in God's presence, care, and abiding love. Remaining faithful in difficult and trying times is challenging even for the most committed of disciples. The journey of discipleship reveals our own imperfections and inadequacies as we falter in the face of struggles and setbacks. Because of human sinfulness and weakness, no one is protected from fallibility. Anyone can respond to Jesus' call to follow him, but no one finds it easy.

In contrast to Mark's portrayal of the disciples' weakness and timidity, there are some women whose faith appears to be stronger. For example, there are women who follow Jesus from the beginning of his ministry in Galilee to its end in Jerusalem; and after his death on the cross, Mary Magdalene, Mary (the mother of James and Joses), and Salome especially remain faithful to him. Too, in pressing Jesus to heal her demon-possessed daughter, the Canaanite woman in Matthew's Gospel shows how someone from the margin of society can be seen as a model of faith (15:21-28). The women characters in Matthew are portrayed as both models of faith and signifiers of the powerless in society. It is the "marginal one," the "outsider," the one whom society views as "unclean," who exhibits a persistent, vigorous faith, confident that God will be faithful to God's promises. The Canaanite woman is held up as a model of faith not simply as a woman and a Gentile, but as a despised Canaanite who calls Jesus forth to give her new life; in fact, she pushes Jesus to new possibilities. It is striking that the Canaanite woman initiates the action; Jesus responds or observes. She illustrates that we are not just passive recipients of a call, but true moral agents. Furthermore, the fact that Jesus interacts with this woman suggests that everyone is and can be called, even the so-called marginal and unclean person.[12]

What matters is not sex or numbers, not age or race, but a person's relation to Jesus.

The stories of these women followers of Jesus not only reveal the storyteller's intent to emphasize the importance of faithfulness for Christian discipleship, but also fill out the portrait of followers of Jesus in the New Testament.[13] It is the women, those among the least significant members of the community, who were entrusted with the first Easter encounter and the first mandate to proclaim it. The point is not that the women disciples are to be idealized as models of discipleship. Rather, the fact that it is the women who stay with Jesus to the end suggests the surprising openness of Christian discipleship to all people. An important lesson is that no one is excluded from discipleship, which is inclusive and demanding. What matters is not sex or numbers, not age or race, but a person's relation to Jesus. The standard used to assess faithful discipleship is whether a person is turning away from old ways of viewing the world, faithfully responding to the call, however it is experienced, and continuing on the quest despite the perils of the journey.

This is, indeed, a demanding standard. It is difficult, if not impossible, to stay faithful to the vocation to which we are called without the support and guidance of companions along the way. Just as Santiago needed a king, a camel driver, a soul mate, and an alchemist to help him find the treasure he was seeking, so too do we need others to guide and support us on the journey. New Testament stories of discipleship are not only about individual commitment or attachment to Jesus. Christian discipleship also involves communion with others who have responded to the gracious invitation and love of God.

Called to Community

While it is individuals who are called, the New Testament stories challenge a privatized view of Christian discipleship. To be a disciple is to be in union with Jesus and through Jesus with God, a union that is reciprocal and oriented toward community. The disciples live out their call not only by attaching themselves to Jesus, but also by living in fellowship with one another. The Johannine narrative captures this dual aspect of discipleship most clearly with the image of *abiding*. A discipleship community is characterized by the way its members abide in Jesus as the source of life. As an image of discipleship, abiding is most explicitly enunciated in the metaphor of the vine and the branches. Disciples are dependent on Jesus as the source of life as branches are attached to the vine in order to bear fruit. The fruit produced by abiding in love is predicated on the friendship between Jesus and his disciples. While the vine image expresses a personal relationship between the disciples and Jesus, it also includes the friendship and love among disciples and the union within the community of faith. Jesus is present in the community of disciples and its members live in him as branches of a vine. Thus, abiding encompasses the personal and communal aspects of discipleship: it is the intimacy of a personal relationship with Jesus (God abiding in each person and the individual abiding in God); and it reflects abiding in communion with other believers.[14]

The first Christians responded to the call to follow Jesus by abiding in him, but they also lived in fellowship with one another. This took the form of a distinctive way of life called *koinōnia*. That is to say, the "followers of the way" (Acts 2:42-47) gathered in communities, told stories about Jesus, supported one another through difficult times, rejoiced together, and celebrated the good news of Christ's presence among them. *Koinōnia* or "communion" is generally understood as central to the early Christian tradition, most aptly expressing the various New Testament images of church, such as the body of Christ and the household of God. As a community, the disciples have become the people of God, called to continue to share life in common and witness to the presence of God "to the end of the earth." This community is to be a new kind of family, "a new household of faith" where what matters fundamentally is doing the will of God and embracing the pattern of God's reign on earth in communion with others (Matt 4:22; 8:21-22). The Christian community is established by a baptism that requires faith and conversion. Through participation in a baptismal ritual, believers are called to a life in Christ that brings them into a new relationship with God. The journey of discipleship begins with baptism and initiation into the community of fellow believers.

We can glean three key insights from the New Testament discipleship stories. First, the call is a gracious invitation to begin a journey toward wholeness, to embark on a quest for true happiness and the fullness of life. We are not initiators of the call, but recipients, and our task is to respond graciously and gratefully. Second, the primary virtue required of disciples is faithfulness. To be faithful means to trust in God and to live in accord with God's commands. Third, the fundamental quality of discipleship is relationship with God through Jesus in community. The personal call to follow Jesus is an adventure we undertake with others. There are perils on the journey, and to remain faithful to the call we must be active participants in the community and its story. It is the Christian community that supports, challenges, and sustains a life of discipleship.

Now a question that remains is what does this view of discipleship have to do with the moral life? Isn't this what spirituality is about? Isn't morality concerned with doing the right thing and obeying certain rules or commandments? Sure it is, but not primarily. Choosing and acting rightly are integrally related to and flow from our character. That is to say, the kind of people we are and hope to become, as well as the quality of communities we create, provide the soil and foundation for the choices we make and the actions we perform. It is this view of the moral life that is closely related to discipleship, for it is about becoming people who take on the attitudes, virtues, and way of life of Jesus, whom we are called to follow. There is a close connection between morality and spirituality, for both disciplines are concerned with conversion, with leading a person to a deeper commitment to Jesus as Lord. Morality and spirituality can be viewed as twin aspects of our response to God's presence in our lives. In subsequent chapters we will discuss the role of conversion and spirituality in the moral life. But our aim here, and the focus of the next section, is to provide a framework for the moral life based on the gift-call-response dynamic we discovered in our biblical exploration of discipleship. We begin by examining the theological and anthropological underpinnings of this framework.

A FRAMEWORK FOR THE MORAL LIFE

Theological and Anthropological Underpinnings

Fundamentally, we all share in Santiago's experience of being lured toward something good and desirable. Whatever the sense of calling a person experiences, the common feature is that it comes primarily from within. It is an interior longing or desire to which one feels compelled to respond in order to be happy, to achieve self-fulfillment, integrity, and wholeness. The "treasure" we seek may differ, but the calling or desire for wholeness is an essential part of our humanity. The king in Coelho's novel described this longing as a Personal Legend. And the alchemist wisely advised Santiago to listen to his heart because it comes from the Soul of the World. The great medieval theologian Thomas Aquinas expressed a similar perspective, but in more theological language. Aquinas claimed that we are created with a basic drive by which we seek what is good for ourselves and resist what is harmful or detrimental; at least we have the capacity to do so. The fundamental desire is for the good. How one conceives of the good will differ, but the important point is that all people have this longing for goodness, which is also one's true happiness.

For Aquinas, to be human is to be needy and, therefore, to desire something to fill this neediness. The most general term Aquinas uses to explain this aspect of the human condition is "appetite." It is a fitting description, for we know what it means to hunger for something we lack. If we have not eaten for a long time, we have an appetite for food. If we have been confined to a bed for a long time due to illness, we yearn for the beauty of nature. If we are lonely and sad, we desire companions or activity. We want something because we think it will be good for us, but if we lack it we experience need. We sense our incompleteness and see before us something we think will ease it—that is why it strikes us as good. We want something because it appears to be at least a partial answer to our neediness. Moreover, the appetites are ways that we are called out of ourselves, whether it is in response to a meal, to beauty, or to another person.

What this reflection on appetites shows us is that we are all created to receive something. This is the heart of Aquinas's anthropology. We are not closed-off, self-sufficient individuals; rather, we are made to be receptive. This openness to goodness is the most basic and natural fact about us. We are made to be filled with the life our world offers, and ultimately to be filled with the vitality of God. This is true not only of humankind, but it is also true of the universe. Desire is an expression of a universal longing. Thomas paints a picture of all creation being touched, acted upon, and influenced by the multitude of goods in the world, whether that be another person, beautiful scenery, the power of a poem, or the magic of a wonderful meal shared with others.[15] Sebastian Moore describes this desire as the "allure of God" to enter more deeply into the mystery in which we are all engulfed. It is the relatedness that we have to all things in a universe in which everyone and everything is trying to realize itself. The experience begins with the sense of neediness and unfulfilled relatedness responding to the call of God. The more this emptiness is filled, the more we are capable of wider and deeper relationships.[16]

It is important to recognize, however, that there is a certain "inconsummation" or unfulfillment with which we must live. The human experience of the insufficiency of everything attainable reveals something important for the moral life. There is no fully consummate joy to be attained on earth. "All symphonies remain unfinished," as Karl Rahner stated. There is a longing that lies in the deep recesses of the soul that cannot be fully satisfied in this world. This insatiable desire is a "holy longing" because it is a "sacred energy given us by God and experienced in every cell of our being as an irrepressible urge to overcome our incompleteness, to move toward unity and consummation with that which is beyond us."[17]

Essentially, this basic drive or calling is for relationship. We are in need of others because we are relational beings who exist in an open and largely unfulfilled connection to humankind, to the universe, and ultimately to God. From a theological perspective, we are relational beings because we have been made in the image and likeness of a trinitarian God, who is the fullness of relatedness. As St. Augustine eloquently expressed it, the trinitarian God is a relationship of perfect mutual self-gift—the lover, the beloved, and the love among them. This relational anthropology is central to feminist theologies and ethics that tend to be critical of Western individualism. The notion of an isolated self apart from relationships and social location is rejected in favor of a pattern of mutual giving and receiving.[18] Relational anthropology is at the core of African culture as well. For the Africans, the person is a relational being and there is a dynamic structural unity and interdependence with God, community, and the family. One cannot flourish apart from these relationships because they are interrelated parts of a living organism.[19]

The theological anthropology of neediness and relatedness provides the condition of possibility for the gift-call-response framework of the moral life. Now we will examine the dynamic of the moral call that is woven into the very fabric of our everyday experience as relational beings in the world with others.

The Gift-Call-Response Dynamic of the Moral Life

As Enda McDonagh explains with his careful phenomenology of human experience, we are confronted with a moral call because of the nature of our life together. This call arises from the experience of the value of another person and the created order that beckons us, demands our attention, and makes an appeal to us. It is marked by the awareness that persons and their environment are valuable, part of God's wonderful creation, and as such they are to be appreciated and reverenced. It is the recognition and reverence for the gift of the other that is at the heart of the moral life of discipleship. So we can say that the moral life begins not so much in something we do but in response to God's initiative. It begins with the presence of the "other," whether another person, another creature, or the "otherness" of nature, calling us out of ourselves. Whatever the "presence" is, it calls for a response from us. This is the foundational moral experience, that of being confronted by the presence of the other who calls us out of ourselves, and calls for recognition, respect, and response.

The other is a gift-presence embodying a call because the person (or some other aspect of creation) is freely given, not a product of one's own manufacturing or achievement. The gift of the other implies an invitation to enter his or her world. It involves a call to move out of and beyond the narrow confinement of the self, beyond one's limited perceptions or biases, in recognition and exploration of diverse points of view. Thus, as gift, the encounter with the world of another has the *potential* for conversion.[20]

Ambiguous Dimension of the Call

Experience is quick to reveal that the other, as different, may be perceived as someone or something to be feared rather than as a complementary gift inviting acceptance and respect. There is an ambiguous character to the call-response dynamic. That the source of the moral call can be experienced as threat rather than as gift may be due to a fear of the other as taking over or upsetting one's controlled and controllable world. Or, a person or group may be seen as a threat because one cannot tolerate

> *It is the recognition and reverence for the gift of the other that is at the heart of the moral life of discipleship.*

the existence of those who challenge or call into question one's own viewpoint or values.[21] Of course, there are people who are actual threats to personal, communal, and societal well-being and they must be dealt with justly and mercifully. Even in these cases, however, the person has an inherent value and dignity as God's creation that is to be respected. If fear dominates, though, community tends to break down.

In reality, all of us are a mix of gift and threat. Even our personal call can be perceived either way. But if fear gets the best of us, it is difficult to respond to the call or to embrace the gift. For example, a person may have an experience of being called to marriage and parenthood. It may be something he dreamed about for years. Suppose he meets someone he comes to love and can envision as the mother of his children. He is ready to get married, everything seems right, but he is afraid to make a commitment. The unknown future is too scary. Maybe she is not the right one. Maybe he will get tired of her in a few years. Shouldn't he keep his options open? And so he never does get married; the dream remains unfilled. Fear dominates and the gift is rejected.

The temptation to turn gifts into threats is the heritage of sin. We come into the world prepared to be afraid. We strike out at others to defend ourselves from those who cause us to be fearful. We are the heirs of count-less generations of fear, suspicion, distrust, and mistreatment of the human race. We may be born into a family, community, or nation that has racial animosity. If so, it is likely that we will perpetuate this hostility through a lack of interracial friendships and effective segregation in housing or edu-cation. There is a pervasive inclination to limit our circle of caring to those who are like us. Yet we are capable of transcending our fears, of overcom-ing our evil heritage. It is possible to grow in reconciliation and love and to widen our circle of relationships. This capability is mobilized by an act of faith that sees the universe as basically trustworthy and that allows us to believe in the deep-down goodness of things despite ample evidence to the contrary.

God's call to us is related to God's will, so we have a basis for saying that we do not create the good, rather we respond to it as we perceive God's will revealed in the events of life, especially in the series of encounters we have with others. A central belief of the Roman Catholic tradition is that God addresses and calls us through revelation in time and space, in and through creation, directing people toward covenantal existence. While there may be immediate and personal revelatory experiences, generally the other is a source of that call, a medium of revelation in history. For the Christian believer the moral call arising from an encounter with the other is always also a call from God.

While belief has a religious dimension, it is also an essential component of the call-response dynamic of the moral life. That is, without belief in the value of life and all creation, there would be no moral grounding for their respect, reverence, and protection. Understood this way, faith is not a set of beliefs that takes the place of knowledge; but rather it is a basic trust or confidence that we have toward life. This attitude will affect our encounters with others, how we perceive the call, and how we respond. As Christians we believe that Jesus enables such faithfulness because he reveals to us the true nature of our life as brothers and sisters under the care of a gracious God. The moral challenge is to enable the sense of gift to triumph over the potential fear and move toward genuine communion and solidarity. This brings us to the question of what is the appropriate response to the gift-call of the other?

RESPONDING TO THE GIFT-CALL

Because we are relational beings in the world with others, the very presence of other persons and their environment demands a response. It cannot be avoided. Yet, we are free to determine how we will respond. For example, a homeless person standing on the street asks for help. We can ignore her, approach her, engage her in conversation, or offer a donation; but we cannot avoid some kind of response. While we are free to choose the kind of response we make to the other, it is impossible not to reply in some way. This is true not only of our life together as human beings, but also with regard to our interconnectedness with the environment and nonhuman life. The plants, the trees, the oceans, the air we breathe—all call forth from us some kind of response. It is in this broad sense that we can understand the moral life as a call-response dynamic.

The experience of the value of persons and their environment, the foundational moral experience, is the source of moral obligation and the primal data on which ethical reflection proceeds. If we value something, we normally seek its protection and try to promote its flourishing. We are led to ask: What does and does not befit persons? What response shows reverence and respect for the water, the air, and vegetation? For example, because persons are valuable, we ought to be faithful, loving, truthful, and just. In the Christian tradition, creation has an intrinsic value; therefore, we ought to care for and preserve it for future generations.

We might say that the foundational moral experience leads us to hold a set of moral presumptions with which we enter into moral reasoning about right and wrong. As we begin a process of moral discernment, we acknowledge these presumptions. Essentially we presume the goodness of created existence and the valuableness of the other. The dignity of the human person is not rooted in intelligence, utility, beauty, or productivity; rather it is based in the fact that we are made in the image and likeness of God. We will allow ourselves to be guided by efforts to know and to do those things that advance, or

> *The dignity of the human person is not rooted in intelligence, utility, beauty, or productivity; rather it is based in the fact that we are made in the image and likeness of God.*

at least keep us open to, these basic insights or presumptions.[22]

We can say, then, that morality is grounded neither in personal whim or sentiment nor in individual likes or dislikes, but in an objective source. The basis for moral obligation lies outside such a subjectivist posture. It is essentially located in the reality of another who confronts me as a person to be responded to by my valuing and promoting their well-being. In that response we learn that we do not create values, but must respect and appreciate them. Thus, moral objectivity is rooted in the very experience of being called forth by and responding to the other.

This call begins a process that can lead to moral growth and transformation, but such growth is always a matter of "more or less." There are many signs of limited moral sensitivity—racism, sexism, slavery, industrial pollution, disregard of worker safety, and destruction of ecosystems—that point to the need for continual moral development. As disciples of Jesus, we are never called to diminish life or to do harm to others; but rather we are called to bring life into being, to cherish it, and to promote the good of all aspects of the created order. Moral development is concerned with how one behaves with other human beings who are independent sources of value to be respected and reverenced, as well as with nonhuman sources of life from which we draw our sustenance. Hopefully, over time we grow in awareness of the reality that other human beings and the created order are not simply means to an end but ends in themselves. There is a formative aspect to the moral life of discipleship that begins with baptism. But moral formation is part of an ongoing journey of conversion to an ever-deepening life in Christ and in relationship with all creation.[23]

Essentially, disciples are called to respond as Jesus did, graciously and gratefully, to God's love as it is mediated to us through others. Our first moral response should be gratitude, thanksgiving, for the gift of another's presence in our lives. The close connection between morality and spirituality becomes evident, for both are modalities of our response to the presence of God and others in our lives. We do not earn or deserve these gifts of creation; they are freely given to us. Our primary response, then, ought to demonstrate our reverence and appreciation for the gifts.

One way that we show this reverence and appreciation is by love and care for God's creation. Other-centeredness becomes key for moral living. Broadly speaking, we behave appropriately when we are other-centered, and inappropriately when we are self-centered. We say "broadly speaking" because we do not want to deny a place for self-love in the Christian life nor to encourage a sort of "do anything to please" mentality that can be based on poor self-esteem. But a fundamental requirement for rightly responding to God's call is to acknowledge the unity of love of God and neighbor, a central theme throughout the Hebrew and Christian testaments. As Matthew 25 points out, love of God is mediated through love of neighbor, especially the "least among us." It is this biblical imperative that grounds Latin American liberation theology and ethics. It focuses on the call of the "neighbor par excellence"—the poor and needy person.

The Call of the Poor

The theology and ethics that have emerged from Latin America take seriously the invitation of the Second Vatican Council to interpret the "signs of the times" by reflecting on them critically in light of the gospel. As a biblically based ethic, the moral life is one of discipleship rooted in God's gratuitous call and the free response of human beings. It requires a comprehensive vision of faith as an overall attitude, and a commitment to God and to human beings. Faith has an active and social dimension that entails a discovery of the world of others and a decision to take up their cause, especially those who suffer from hunger and poverty.[24]

Latin American liberationists acknowledge the significant contribution of the council to the renewal of moral theology toward a more personalist, historical, and biblically centered approach. But in their view the council did not sufficiently shift moral theology's center of interest. That is, the locus can remain that of the more affluent and powerful persons in society. In contrast, the starting point of Latin American liberation ethics is the concrete situation and interests of the immense number of people who are poor, those who are from the "underside" of history and the world, from the outskirts of society, and from among the masses of an oppressed people. The poor person in need is the privileged expression of God's call to humankind.[25]

Liberation ethics claims a preferential, nonexclusive option for the poor, calling attention to those who are primary, but not the only ones who deserve love and concern. It does not exclude but presupposes a love for all persons. As Francisco Moreno Rejon states: "Reality is explicitly observed from the locus of the poor, and with the eyes of the poor. The concrete interests of the immense majority of poor are adopted, and an attempt is made to respond to the demands of God who has revealed a preferential love for the poor."[26] To state a preference for the poor as the locus of ethical reflection is simply to make explicit what is often implicit in ethical methodology. That is to say, people who have certain biases create the methodologies. The challenge is to recognize our preferences and determine if they are the proper ones. When liberation ethicists focus on the call of the poor, it is viewed as a call to conscience that comes primarily from the experience of the presence of Christ in suffering humanity. Thus, perspectives and experiences of impoverished, marginalized, and oppressed people of the world ought to influence the specific understanding of the call and the concrete form of response.

Throughout the centuries, people have responded to the call of the poor in different ways. Archbishop Oscar Romero responded by confronting the political powers that were sanctioning the killing and oppression of the people of El Salvador. St. Francis of Assisi responded by abandoning his wealth and starting the Order of Friars Minor that cared for the poor. Dorothy Day responded by establishing the Catholic Worker Movement and Houses of Hospitality for the forsaken in society. And Martin Luther King, Jr., answered his call to ministry by leading an oppressed people out of the manacles of segregation to freedom. He had a dream that brought him not to the pyramids of Egypt, but to the streets of Memphis and ultimately to his death.

The lives of these better-known disciples reveal a love for and commitment to the poor that significantly affected the way they responded to God's call. While they all heard and answered the call of the poor, they responded in different ways depending on the particular needs and circumstances of the time. We see again that there is no "one-size-fits-all" response to the call to follow Jesus. The challenge is to discover what such a way of life implies, entails, and requires in terms of attitudes, vision of life, and concrete day-to-day living. The stories of Oscar Romero, Francis of Assisi, Dorothy Day, and Martin Luther King, Jr., also show that if we listen and respond to God's call no matter how scary the future may be, God provides the strength and the grace for the journey. But we need to be willing to take the risk.

For Santiago, the grace came through his encounter with the camel driver who told him to trust in the Creator of the universe, and the alchemist who encouraged Santiago not to give in to his fears. God lavishly bestows the grace we need to continue on our quest, despite the perils of the journey. But are we open to receiving it? As a farmer prepares the field for the new crop, God will fertilize our efforts with love and care so that our work will be fruitful. We need others, though, to help us till the soil, plant the crop, patiently await its growth, and make it through the times of drought. Like the early followers of Jesus, contemporary disciples need a community of believers to accompany them on the journey. Before concluding this chapter, we offer a few brief comments on the qualities of a Christian community that can nurture and nourish the moral life of discipleship.

A Community of Disciples

As we learned from our biblical exploration, the early disciples not only attached themselves to Jesus, but also lived in fellowship with one another.

Followers of "the way," they joined in communion to support one another through difficult times and to rejoice and celebrate the good news of Christ's presence among them. Through baptism they were initiated into a community of disciples with a distinct way of life. This biblical view of Christian community is reflected in recent Catholic ecclesiology. John Paul II suggested the idea of the church as a community of disciples in his encyclical *Redemptor hominis* (par. 21). And in a revision of his now classic book *Models of the Church*, Avery Dulles, S.J., added the image of church as a community of disciples to the other models of institution, mystical communion, sacrament, herald, and servant. Each of these models has implications for the way members relate to one another and to the way the church engages the world.[27] Other examples of the more recent attention given to the church as a community of disciples are the U.S. bishops' pastoral letters *The Challenge of Peace* (1983) and *Economic Justice for All* (1986). Both documents begin with a lengthy biblical section that focuses on the call to discipleship not primarily as an individual, but as a communal endeavor. The task of the community of disciples is to struggle for justice, development, peace, and liberation in the world. This may involve suffering and renunciation as a prelude to a new life in the risen Christ.

A community of disciples comprises followers of Jesus who witness to the gracious love they have received from God and the way in which this love is offered to others. It is a church that should be a "discipleship of equals." Within the Christian community no structures of domination can be tolerated—no racism, classism, sexism, or any other obstacle to the kind of "abiding" that the Gospel of John emphasizes as characteristic of the Christian community. Where negative conditions for community may exist, followers of Jesus have a responsibility to do what they can to remove these obstacles to discipleship living. At a minimum, there must be genuine dialogue, respect for, and responsibility toward all God's creation.[28]

This ecclesiology is similar to the vision of church that emerged out of Asia in the 1990s. It is described as "a communion of communities," a church marked by solidarity among laity, religious, and clergy who recognize and accept one another as sisters and brothers. Too, it is a vision of church marked by the participation of all the faithful in accord with the gifts they have received from the Holy Spirit, and their faithful and loving witness to the presence of the risen Lord in the world. This also suggests a church "reaching out to people of other faiths and persuasions in a dialogue of love towards the integral liberation of all . . . a leaven of transformation in this world and . . . a prophetic sign daring to point beyond this world to the ineffable Kingdom that is yet fully to come."[29]

There is always a danger, however, that a community can become too homogeneous, composed of like individuals who set themselves over against other groups as rivals. If and when that happens, we need to remember H. Richard Niebuhr's caution that loyalty to the church community can be Christian only if it is loyalty to a more universal community. Niebuhr writes: "And even when I find that I can be responsible in the church only as I respond to Jesus Christ, I discover in him one who points beyond himself to the cause to which he is faithful and in which he is faithful to his companions—not the companions encountered in the church, but in the world to which the Creator is faithful, which the Creator has made his cause."[30] The Christian disciple is accountable not only to the community of faith but also to the universal community and to its Lord.

While the Christian community's way of life and values may at times conflict with those of society, it is necessary for followers of Jesus to engage the wider community, religious and secular. The question each of us must ask as we pursue a call to a particular vocation is how open we are to hearing the wisdom of those around us—family members, friends, colleagues in the workplace, and members of our own and other religious communities. If we think that no one can help us interpret or clarify our call because it is a personal revelation directly from God, then we forget the fundamental fact about human existence: we are relational beings and we need others to help us understand, interpret, and respond to the call to discipleship. Furthermore, while the call emerges from a personal center and from an individual's experience in a concrete historical situation, it is connected with other individuals and groups both near and far. The reality of globalization makes this all too clear. Natural disasters may evoke a feeling of moral obligation toward the victims, and people in distant lands that are suffering from hunger or poverty cry out for response. But whether we respond or not depends on how we view the people affected by the disasters. Are they gift to us or threat?

CONCLUSION

Christian disciples are people on the way, seeking the wholeness and happiness that comes from abiding in Jesus. The life of discipleship begins with the gracious invitation of God to embark on an exciting but perilous adventure leading to fullness of life. It is a personal call to faithfully follow Jesus by living in right relationship with God, others, and all creation. The discipleship journey is marked by a gift-call-response dynamic that provides a framework for the moral life. The moral call arises from the foundational experience of the value of the other who beckons for recognition, reverence, and respect. While the call is personal, it requires a community of fellow believers to provide nourishment, support, and encouragement. This is a community of disciples responsible not only to one another but also to the wider society. Otherwise followers of Jesus could perceive the world through the Christian community's limited perceptions, seeing only what they want to see, and going through life with blinders. A central aspect of the Christian moral life is learning to see rightly, viewing others and the world as gift, as valuable creations of God.

Throughout the book we will explore what it means to follow the way of Jesus, but in the next chapter we will focus on how a life of discipleship teaches us to see. Just as Santiago had a dream, a new vision of something wonderful that led him on a journey of self-discovery and to find the real treasure of life, so too are we led by a vision of what we perceive to be the good life. We need a vision that will enable us to notice new things about the living God. In so doing, we will find reality more surprising, more wondrous than we are capable of imagining. As Gregory of Nyssa said: "Concepts create idols, only wonder understands." Moral vision refers to our perspective on reality and it has repercussions for the way we relate to others, the choices we make, and the way we act in the world. Thus, we turn next to an examination of the meaning and importance of vision in the Christian moral life.

KEY POINTS

1. Each person has a "Personal Legend," a call to live authentically.
2. To respond to that call despite obstacles, even suffering, is an important aspect of living well.
3. For Christians, the call we hear and to which we must respond is a call from God to be faithful and committed believers.
4. A traditional term for those who seek to hear the call of God revealed in Jesus is *discipleship*.
5. The way of disciples, followers of Jesus, continues to be mediated to each of us through experiences of encounters with others, especially the weakest and poorest among us.

QUESTIONS FOR REFLECTION

1. What aspects of discipleship do you find most appealing and most challenging?
2. What is meant by the foundational moral experience?
3. How do you feel about the notion of following Jesus, or someone whose life inspires you? Does the notion of following limit your freedom or independence?
4. In U.S. society, individual rights are highly valued. Do you see a conflict between preserving individual rights and the biblical and theological view of the person as inherently relational and who flourishes in the context of community?
5. What are the moral presumptions you hold that ground your process of decision making?

SUGGESTIONS FOR FURTHER READING AND STUDY

Coelho, Paulo. *The Alchemist*. Translated by Alan R. Clarke. New York: HarperSan-Francisco, 1998.

Dunn, James D. G. *Jesus Remembered*. Grand Rapids: Eerdmans, 2003.

Howard-Brook, Wes, and Sharon H. Ringe. *The New Testament: Introducing the Way of Discipleship*. Maryknoll, N.Y.: Orbis Books, 2002.

Maguire, Daniel C., and A. Nicholas Fargnoli. *On Moral Grounds: The Art/Science of Ethics*. New York: Crossroad, 1991.

Matera, Frank J. *New Testament Ethics: The Legacies of Jesus and Paul*. Louisville: Westminster John Knox, 1996.

McDonagh, Enda. *Gift and Call: Towards a Christian Theology of Morality*. St. Meinrad, Ind.: Abbey Press, 1975.

O'Connell, Timothy E. *Making Disciples: A Handbook of Christian Moral Formation*. New York: Crossroad, 1998.

Wogaman, J. Philip. *Christian Moral Judgment*. Louisville: Westminster/John Knox, 1989.

Wright, N. T. *Following Jesus: Biblical Reflections on Discipleship*. Grand Rapids: Eerdmans, 1994.

2

The Christian Moral Life
and Learning to See

"Master, I Want to See" (Mark 10:51)

BRIAN FRIEL'S PLAY *MOLLY SWEENEY* tells the story of a young Irish woman who has been blind all but the first ten months of her life. "Molly wasn't totally sightless: she could distinguish between light and dark; she could see the direction from which light came," Friel tells us. "But for all practical purposes she had no useful sight." Her husband, Frank, arranges for her to have an operation that could possibly restore her sight. But he warns Molly "that if by some wonderful, miraculous good fortune her sight were restored, even partially restored, she would still have to learn to see and that would be an enormous and very difficult undertaking."[1]

Frank is right. Learning to see is "an enormous and very difficult undertaking," but not only for those who once might have been physically blind and had their sight restored. Learning to see is a difficult, arduous process for all of us, but perhaps especially for those who have always assumed their vision was fine. We think seeing clearly and truthfully is something that comes naturally to us, not a skill we only gradually—and often with great difficulty—acquire. And so we trust our perceptions more than we ought to, seldom stopping to consider how they might be twisted by self-interest, insecurity and anxiety, jealousy or envy, anger or self-righteousness. We assume that the way we see things is the way they really are; thus, it is only when reality snaps back at us that we realize how faulty our vision really was.

To be human is to exhibit all the symptoms of "blindsight," a condition, Friel says, in which we act as if we can see but in truth can see nothing at all.[2] It is an apt description for many of us but not one about which we can afford to grow complacent, because ignorance about our capacity to see the world truthfully and accurately can bring destructive consequences not only to ourselves but also to others. Cruelty, greed, thoughtlessness, and indifference testify to the costly consequences of not being able to see. In the moral life, unless we *see* rightly we cannot possibly *act* rightly. Virtue is inseparable from vision because everything we do is shaped by our perceptions.

It is customary to think that the most crucial matters in ethics involve freedom and intentions and decisions. Or when we begin discussing the moral life we typically turn to the language of principles, rules, obligations, duties, or laws. But we seldom think of morality as a matter of vision, as the ongoing discipline of learning to see truthfully in order to live justly. If you were enrolled in a course on the Christian moral life, would you expect the professor to say, "The principal business of ethics is learning to see! This is a course in having your vision corrected!" Would you stay in the class? Would you walk out thinking that is not what morality is about at all?

But the truth is that we can only choose and act within the world we can see.[3] And yet, seeing in the way that is necessary for goodness—the kind of seeing that would, for example, enable us to love well—is a skill learned over a lifetime. In the moral life, we do not see just by opening our eyes because we can open our eyes and miss what really matters. We must *learn* to see. We must adopt a way of life and habits of being that will teach us how to see. As the philosopher Martha Nussbaum wrote, we need "to be keen rather than obtuse."[4] But we are easily more obtuse than keen, not only because there are multiple obstacles to correct vision, but also because there may be many reasons we prefer not to see. Sometimes we refuse to see and develop all sorts of techniques for resisting corrected vision because it is to our advantage to be obtuse. This is especially true when our moral blindness profits us but unjustly harms someone else. To see what is real—to see without illusion and deception—is a rare and precious moral skill, but one we must learn if the harvest of our actions is to consist of love and justice and goodness, not harm and diminishment.

In this chapter we will examine the meaning and importance of vision in the Christian moral life. Even though we may not be accustomed to thinking of vision as a crucial element of the moral life, it must be central in any account of Christian ethics, because Christianity has traditionally described our highest possible happiness as the act of seeing and beholding God.[5] We are fulfilled and perfected as human beings, Christianity teaches, not when we think about God or talk about God, but when we *see* God, when we behold the perfection of goodness, love, and beauty that is God. None of us is born with the vision necessary to see and to enjoy God. In order to see God by being in the presence of God, our customary ways of seeing have to change. We have to discard ways of seeing and perceiving that lead us away from God and the good, and acquire the kind of vision that not only enables us to recognize God and the good but also teaches us to live accordingly. In the Christian moral life our happiness depends on learning "to see in a different way, with different eyes."[6]

And so we will explore what this conversion of vision might involve by first considering the contribution of Iris Murdoch, the English philosopher and novelist for whom learning to see was the often overlooked but absolutely necessary work of the moral life. We will examine why it can be so hard for us to see with truthful and reverent vision, and we will pay particular attention to what might most commonly skew our vision. This will draw us into conversation with Buddhism, because a central goal of Buddhism is to enable one to see without illusion.

In the second half of the chapter, we will probe how a Christian life of discipleship can be viewed as ongoing training in learning to see. If what distinguished Jesus was "his remarkable ability to see,"[7] then one goal of the Christian life must be learning to see as Jesus did. Theologian Arthur Sutherland wrote, "Jesus was blessed with perfect sight."[8] We who are prone to "blindsight" have our vision healed and restored when we strive to adopt the typically unnerving vision of Christ. Jesus might have had "perfect sight," but he saw in ways that can be immensely challenging, even frightening, for us. Nonetheless, our task in the Christian life is to grow in the vision of Christ, and we do so when we become part of the story Jesus disclosed to us in the Gospels. Thus, we'll conclude the chapter by probing how the teachings and example of Jesus, especially his parables, initiate disciples in ways of seeing that take us straight into what Jesus called the reign of God.

HUMAN BEINGS AS MASTERS OF ILLUSION

Iris Murdoch was a philosopher who is more popularly known for her novels. A prolific writer, Murdoch penned over two dozen novels and plays. But a consistent theme of all of her works is a human being's penchant for spinning illusions and seeking refuge in them. For Murdoch, "to be human is to create illusion."[9] Instead of respecting reality, we distort it to fit our needs. We bend the world to ourselves instead of letting it call us out of ourselves in reverence and love. We make ourselves the center of things and then see the world through a lens of gratification and consolation, not a lens of compassion or justice or humility.

For Murdoch, the "morally good life is one of seeing the world rightly and without self-delusion,"[10] but the person who does so is rare because our skill for creating delusion is polished and our need for doing so is deep. A typical example can be glimpsed in how we often go about love. At its best, love is a matter of being focused on the needs and well-being of another; at its best, to love someone is to seek his or her good. But for Murdoch, theologian Stanley Hauerwas writes, "most of our loving is more an assertion of self than a recognition of the other. We seldom love the other as he is; rather we love the other by imposing upon him our own preconceived image of who he is." Hauerwas explains: "We do not fall in love with a real person, but with the person we have created through our fantasy. Such love is a way of loving ourselves."[11] Any person who has been trapped in a manipulative, controlling relationship knows this to be true.

The Dangerous Seductions of Fantasy

To love someone not in light of her real distinctiveness, but only in terms of who we need her to be, is an apt example of what Murdoch calls *fantasy*. Murdoch says it is fantasy, and not malice, ignorance, or weakness of will, that is the "chief enemy of excellence in morality." She describes fantasy as "the tissue of self-aggrandizing and consoling wishes and dreams which prevents one from seeing what is there outside one." Fantasy is "the proliferation of blinding self-centred aims and images" that characterizes people, institutions, communities, movements, nations, and even churches that seek refuge in delusions fabricated by lies and self-deception.[12]

We see fantasy at work when nations embrace dangerous illusions about their importance and adopt distorted and self-serving views of the rest of the world. We see fantasy at work when communities become self-enclosed and suspicious rather than hospitable. We see the disastrous effects of fantasy unleashed on the environment when human beings see other species as having only utilitarian value. And we witness the toxins of fantasy when we see churches become self-righteous, dogmatic, and more legalistic and juridical than gracious and humane. Fantasies are not benign because nations, communities, institutions, and persons who fear the truth will do anything to maintain them.

Instead of being a way of engaging life and moving out toward others, fantasy turns us wholly in on ourselves. Fantasy is a strategy for escape, never engagement, and it is at work whenever we seek to evade truths that are hard for us to bear. Fantasy asserts itself when illusions we have about ourselves risk being exposed. Moreover, locked in fantasy, persons, communities, and institutions are too self-serving to do the good. Put more strongly, they are bound to do harm because they see everything in terms of their own needs, preferences, and desires. Driven by "the fat relentless ego,"[13] fantasy imprisons more than it liberates because it prevents people, communities, and institutions from engaging anything outside themselves truthfully. Fantasies may comfort us in deceptive ways, but they are highly destructive because they impede the growth and transformation that are necessary for life. Indeed, despite our tendency to associate fantasies with whatever might be exciting and energizing, in reality they are dull and dreary because they result in a world no bigger than ourselves.[14]

What Murdoch details philosophically, Christian theologians have described through the language of sin. As William Spohn wrote, "Moral blindness is the ordinary condition in humanity's fallen state."[15] Thus, it is not the case that we are born with unimpaired vision but lose it through poor choices and decisions; rather, we are born with an inability to see and that deficiency must be overcome in order for us to love well, live justly, and do good. In *People of the Truth*, Robert Webber and Rodney Clapp claim that "because of the Fall people can no longer see what is real. They live in unreality and illusion and are lost in the darkness of futility (Rom 1:20-21)."[16] That is a disturbing insight because it suggests that we have no natural capacity to see truthfully. If we are naturally skilled at anything, it is fabrication and deception. We are born not being able to see and remain trapped in unreality and illusion unless we find ways to have our faulty vision healed. Again, it is not so much that our lost sight needs to be restored, but that our original blindness needs to be overcome.

Obstacles to Correct Vision

Being and doing good requires learning to see the world justly and lovingly. It involves "the difficult task of developing a virtuous perception where one sees the world as it truly is."[17] But cultivating that kind of compassionate attentiveness is painstaking because there are many forces, both inside us and external to us, that teach us not to see. If anything, we are trained not to see, trained to nurture a moral myopia that prevents us from seeing clearly and justly. One monumental stumbling block is egotism, the stubborn tendency we have to make ourselves and our needs the center of the world. Few of us do this consciously or deliberately, which is why self-centeredness is doggedly hard to overcome. As Frederick Franck explains, there is "a tragic flaw in the human design, a defect in our makeup of which we are normally quite unaware. It consists, roughly, in the ego's narcissistic delusion that 'I am infinitely more real than you,' that my little *me* is more precious than anything else on earth and that this little me's observation point is the only valid one."[18] The whispered message of egotism is that I alone matter, that my needs, my desires, and my pleasures must always come first.

This is why a critical task in the moral life—and an essential one for overcoming fantasy—is learning to appreciate all that is other than our self. The "other" can be another person, people of another country or culture or religion, or all the other creatures and species of the earth. But our moral growth and development depend on our willingness to be lured from the entangling confines of egotism by the presence of an "other" who calls us out of ourselves and who frees us from fantasy by demanding our attention.

Morality begins in the discovery that something other than our self is real, and the whole quest of the moral life is to understand, deepen, and live from that discovery.[19] Put more strongly, we can only be moral when we learn to appreciate what is not our self, when we are able not only to acknowledge but also to attend to and revere all that is other, whether the other be God, a spouse, a stranger, or another species. Doing so decenters us because it draws us out of our self and reorients our attention away from our self and our own clamorous needs to the unique needs and well-being of others. And such decentering, Thomas Ogletree writes, is "not a threat to personal integrity, but . . . a summons to moral existence. Morality begins . . . precisely when my egoism has been called into question and I learn to take the other into account." "And egoism in this context," he explains, "refers not to selfishness in a crass sense, but to any process, however refined, in which I remain the decisive and controlling reference point for the meaning and value of the world."[20] In Murdoch's language, we move beyond the self-absorption of fantasy when we can "imagine the needs of other people, love unselfishly, lucidly envisage and desire what is truly valuable."[21]

To become good we must "pierce the veil of selfish consciousness and join the world as it really is."[22] But we can only do so when we move from the self-serving and falsifying world of fantasy to the creative, expansive, and truthful world of authentic imagination. Murdoch insists that the imagination, rightly understood and utilized, is the antithesis of fantasy. Imagination is fantasy's opposite because if fantasy distorts our perceptions and turns us in on ourselves, an authentic imagination cleanses and clarifies our perceptions and draws us out of ourselves into a deeper engagement with others and the world. If fantasy, according to Murdoch, is "mechanical, egoistic, untruthful," the imagination is liberating, "truth-seeking," and creative.[23] As William Spohn explains, fantasy "fabricates an image to evade reality," but imagination illumines and clarifies so that we not only are able to see more clearly and truthfully, but are also more lovingly engaged by life.[24] If fantasy deforms us by fostering in us the wrong sorts of attractions, attachments, and desires, an authentic imagination transforms us because it results in a more just, loving, and compassionate way of envisioning life.[25]

Fantasy and Fear

We can appreciate the distinction Murdoch makes between fantasy and imagination if we consider fear, another obstacle to seeing justly and truthfully. Throughout the Gospels, but particularly in the Gospel of John, Jesus counsels, "Do not be afraid." But aren't we often encouraged to adopt a posture of fear in our everyday lives? In *Following Jesus in a Culture of Fear*, Scott

Bader-Saye offers a catalogue of the many things that frighten us. Along with terrorism, school shootings, serial killings, and random murders, we're taught to fear strangers, the foods we eat and the air we breathe, the mysterious diseases we might possibly catch, and the viruses that could be lurking in our computers.[26]

Moreover, many have become experts at heightening, manipulating, and exploiting our fears. Businesses make money off of our fears by promising new and improved methods of securing us from the looming dangers of contemporary life. Politicians seek votes by playing on our fears. And advertising exploits our fear, whether it is the fear of getting old, the fear of being alone, the fear of being ordinary, or the fear of not having enough. We are "fed a steady diet of dread," Bader-Saye attests, and the result is "a culture where fear determines a disproportionate number of our personal and communal decisions."[27]

Fear shapes the way we see the world, and thus how we act. But fear, in Murdoch's analysis, can readily become another kind of fantasy if it is the primary lens through which we look at the world. If fear, rather than hope, trust, or love, colors our perceptions, then the abiding aim of our actions is self-preservation and our highest good is not love of God and neighbor (especially the neighbors who are strangers to us or threatening to us), but our own personal security. Fear constricts our world. It shrinks the boundaries of our world to whatever our safety requires. As Bader-Saye notes, fear can cause "a kind of contraction of the heart. By imagining some future evil, fear draws us in on ourselves so that we 'extend' ourselves to 'fewer things.'"[28]

That is the problem. The Christian moral life calls us not to contract our hearts in fear, but to enlarge them through love. Christianity summons us to extend ourselves outward on behalf of others. This is why virtues such as charity, justice, courage, hospitality, and generosity have always been fundamental elements of the Christian life. Jesus calls us to expand the horizons of our world, not to shrink them. But enflamed by fantasies, fear becomes an excuse for narrowing our care, for diminishing our compassion, and for shutting off our hearts. In a culture of fear, the very things that Christianity teaches us to disavow become virtues, and the virtues Christianity teaches us to embrace become suspect. As Bader-Saye notes, "Disordered and excessive fear has significant moral consequences. It fosters a set of shadow virtues, including suspicion, preemption, and accumulation, which threaten traditional Christian virtues such as hospitality, peacemaking, and generosity."[29] When our fears become excessive and unreasonable—or, in Murdoch's language, when our fears become fantasies—the result is either violence or self-imposed paralysis. That is why our fears must be met not by self-serving and falsifying fantasies, but by the creative imagination of love.

The Fantasy of Consumerism

A third obstacle to developing the moral vision necessary for love and justice and goodness is *consumerism*. Consumerism teaches that human beings are fulfilled not through personal relationships, not through intimacy, community, and faithful love, but through wealth and possessions. Consumerism and Christianity hold one belief in common. Both maintain that human beings are incomplete and unfinished, but where they differ is in their accounts of what will answer the deepest needs, longings, and desires of our hearts. In the gospel of consumerism, purchasing, accumulating, and consuming become our most sacred acts because these are seen to fulfill and complete us. Christianity, on the other hand, teaches that our restless hearts are quieted not in wealth and possessions, but in loving and in being loved by God and other persons. John Kavanaugh captures the dramatic difference between Christianity and the ideology of consumerism when he writes that consumerism "reveals our very being and purpose as calculable solely in terms of *what* we possess, measurable solely by what we have and take. We are only insofar as we possess. We are what we possess. We are, consequently, possessed by our possessions."[30]

As an ideology, consumerism trains us to desire and to relate to objects and possessions more than persons. This is why it diminishes us, why it makes us less instead of more. Consumerism fosters alienation between ourselves and others because it summons us to give our attention to material things rather than to persons. Our security, according to the ideology of consumerism, is not found in faithful friendships and marriages or in healthy communities, but in accumulating wealth and possessions. But an unhealthy consumerism also alienates us from ourselves because it teaches us to see everything, including ourselves, as commodities—to think of ourselves not as persons but as products. According to the gospel of consumerism, the most valuable people are the ones who can market themselves, the ones who can make themselves "desirable products" for others.[31]

In a scene from *Tuesdays with Morrie*, Mitch Albom's hugely popular account of his weekly visits to the bedside of his dying former professor, Morrie Schwartz, the dangers of a life of conspicuous consumption are memorably underscored. In one of his last conversations with his former student, Morrie illustrates how we are robbed of our authentic humanity by allowing ourselves to be held captive to the illusions of consumerism. Morrie tells Mitch, "It's all part of the same problem. . . . We put our values in the wrong things. And it leads to very disillusioned lives." The heart of the problem, Morrie continues, is that "We've got a form of brainwashing going on in our country. . . . Owning things is good. More money is good.

The Christian moral life calls us not to contract our hearts in fear, but to enlarge them through love.

More property is good. More commercialism is good. *More is good. More is good.* We repeat it—and have it repeated to us—over and over until nobody bothers even to think otherwise." Sounding much like Murdoch, Morrie says, "The average person is so fogged up by all this he has no perspective on what's really important anymore."[32]

That is the essence of consumerism. And it is a perfect example of what Murdoch means by fantasy because to immerse ourselves in lives of unhealthy consumption is to lose all sense of what really matters. "Wherever I went in my life," Morrie reminisces, "I met people wanting to gobble up something new. Gobble up a new car. Gobble up a new piece of property. Gobble up the latest toy. And then they wanted to tell you about it." These people felt compelled to speak about their new possessions because they were "so hungry for love that they were accepting substitutes. They were embracing material things and expecting a sort of hug back." "But it never works," the dying man tells Mitch. "You can't substitute material things for love or for gentleness or for tenderness or for a sense of comradeship."[33]

As Morrie Schwartz intimates, fantasies such as consumerism are dehumanizing because they deceive us about the kinds of desires and devotions that truly bring us to life and complete us. In order to be pried free from the captivating hold of an unhealthy consumerism, we need to develop new objects of attention. We need to cultivate interests, habits, and practices that redirect us away from the distorting and destructive effects of consumerism. Kavanaugh suggests that we will recover our lost humanity only through "a rediscovered interior life" of prayer, periods of silence and solitude, and time for contemplation. Too, restoring our lost humanity, he suggests, requires "a renewal of interpersonal relationships," so that we learn to find joy and satisfaction more in friendships rather than in possessions.

Overcoming the fantasy of consumerism also demands "reawakening to the joys of simplicity," so that we find freedom and liberation in having less instead of always accumulating more. It will involve "a rediscovery of our passion for justice," so that we experience deliverance through attending to the needs of others instead of by always first securing our own. And it will be complete, Kavanaugh insists, only by "a reopening of our hearts to the marginal people of our world," because contact with the poor, the disenfranchised, the unproductive, and the dying will reconnect us to our true humanity.[34]

In one of her philosophical essays, Murdoch wrote that "our ability to act well 'when the time comes' depends partly, perhaps largely, upon the quality of our habitual objects of attention."[35] In light of this analysis of consumerism, we know we will hardly act well "when the time comes" if our habitual objects of attention are the flaccid idols consumerism offers us. If what habitually has my attention are money, comfort, pleasure, and material things, I will not even notice, much less respond to, the needs of others. I will live in "blindsight" because I will focus my gaze on the superficial and ephemeral and not on the neighbors around me who depend on me and on whom I depend, and who are the true means to my liberation.

Buddhism and Learning to See

If a quintessential element in the moral life is learning to see, Buddhism has much to teach us. A central goal of Buddhism, particularly Zen Buddhism, is to see things "as they are in themselves, stripped of all delusion, of all fabrication and superstition."[36] The Zen master Thich Nhat Hanh writes, "In Buddhism, the most important precept of all is to live in awareness, to know what is going on."[37] In fact, for Buddhists, "The meaning of life is to see."[38] Moreover, truthful seeing leads to understanding and understanding to love. Seeing is not an end in itself for Buddhists because seeing is completed in just and loving actions. In *Being Peace*, Thich Nhat Hanh says, "The root-word *buddh* means to wake up, to know, to understand; and he or she who wakes up and understands is called a Buddha. . . . The capacity to wake up, to understand, and to love is called Buddha nature." Every person is called to become a Buddha because, Hanh explains, "In everyone there is the capacity to wake up, to understand, and to love," and "Someone who is awake, who knows, who understands, is called a Buddha. Buddha is in every one of us. We can become awake, understanding, and also loving." Too, waking up and seeing, understanding, and loving are ultimately one because if someone truly awakens from illusion she will see, and if she sees she will understand, and if she understands she will love. As Hanh writes: "When you understand, you cannot help but love."[39] For Buddhists, every human being is called to awakening or enlightenment, and enlightenment is essential if we are ever to recognize and overcome all the injustice that contributes to human suffering.

But, as with Murdoch's and Christianity's account of our human nature, Buddhism teaches not only that our ordinary condition is to live in illusion, not enlightenment, but also that we are addicted to *not* seeing. Our fundamental illusion—our most stubborn error of perception—is that we think of ourselves as autonomous, as completely separate and independent from others. Not realizing our connection with all other beings, we make ourselves the center of the universe and see everything else in terms of our needs and desires.[40] This core illusion expresses itself through the manifold instances of self-centeredness in which we are frequently trapped but habitually perpetuate: greed, obsessions about fame and celebrity, hunger for power, endless consumption, anger and aggressiveness, exploitative sex, anesthetizing distractions.[41]

From the perspective of Buddhism, these are not harmless developments for they deepen a blindness that leaves us tragically unaware of the suffering in the world, much of which is the result of our own self-centeredness and the indifference and carelessness it fosters.

For Buddhists, truthful seeing leads to understanding and understanding to love.

Errors of perception, chief among which is our chronic misreading of our true place in the universe and our tendency to make our own needs and desires sovereign, cause incalculable harm. For Buddhism, illusion leads to ignorance, and both give birth to disordered desires; and this, more than anything, is the cause of suffering. As Leo Lefebure writes, "For Buddhists, ignorance is not simply a lack of knowledge; it involves a fundamental warping of our relationships with all other beings and causes tremendous suffering."[42]

Thus, Buddhism teaches that if we are to become good our vision has to be rehabilitated. We have to unlearn ways of being that teach us not to see, and to learn habits, practices, and ways of being that enable us to see clearly, reverently, and compassionately. For Buddhists, the central practice for rehabilitating one's vision is meditation. Meditation redirects and trains our attention so that we eventually break through illusion and see things—both ourselves and other beings—as if for the first time. Meditation fosters the awakening that Buddhism teaches is necessary for understanding, and it does so by teaching one the difference between merely *looking at* and *seeing*. When I "look at" something instead of see it, I remain distant and detached from what I am observing. I stand apart from something, or over against it, and fail to see the connection between myself and another being. But when I *see* instead of look at, the distance I set between myself and another being is overcome.

To see is to become one with what we see, so much so that any distinction between ourselves and what we behold disappears. As Frederick Franck writes, "for the very moment I SEE, I become so identified with what I see that I *become* what I see and the split between subject and object is suspended. There is no longer an 'I vs. a Thou,' no longer self and other." Moreover, he continues, "What in primitive societies is called the Evil Eye may well be that not-yet-human, the not-yet-human-eye. Even if it be wreathed in smiles, it *looks at* me, does not *see* me."[43]

We can appreciate the importance of this teaching of Buddhism when we consider that any mistreatment of another human being, whether it is expressed in manipulation or exploitation, abuse or torture, cruelty or violence, is the result of *looking at* them instead of truly *seeing* them. Similarly, our careless disregard for other species and for the goods of the earth, especially the idea that other species and resources exist solely for our benefit, results from looking at them instead of really seeing them. Each of these behaviors reflects a "not-yet-human" way of seeing. If we really saw other human beings, as well as any other creatures, we could not harm them because we would realize the intimate and unbreakable connection between them and ourselves. In other words, when we are able to look at all beings, both human and nonhuman, with a vision of solidarity and compassion, we will have become enlightened. We will have become Buddhas.

From Murdoch and Buddha to Jesus

Some ways of seeing are clearly better than other ways. As our discussion of the thought of Iris Murdoch has shown, we typically view the world through the distorting and falsifying lens of fantasy. Because fantasy places the self at the center of the world and makes everything an object to serve our needs, it leads to behavior marked by thoughtlessness and carelessness—behavior that inevitably brings harm because its fundamental aim is the gratification of the imperial self.

Of course, the "self" can be an individual, but it can also be a community, an institution, or a nation. Consequently, if individuals, communities, institutions, and nations are to be agents of good in the world, they need to acquire the kind of moral vision necessary for compassion, justice, and love. For Murdoch, "the moral task that confronts us is one of purifying ourselves of distorting and self-serving illusions and coming to live in obedience to the good as it appears before us in a true vision of the world."[44]

If Buddhism teaches that we are purified of illusion through meditation, Murdoch says that we break the tantalizing spell of fantasy by regular encounters with "the Good," particularly as it manifests itself through beauty.[45] The path of moral rehabilitation begins when our attention is drawn away from the self and toward "the Good." For Murdoch, the Good is a transcendent reality that calls us out of ourselves and teaches us to see the world as it really is. The Good, especially as it is expressed in beauty, is powerfully attractive. The more our attention is drawn to it—the more we are lured by it—the more our vision of the world not only is transformed but expands. We begin to see other people and things differently, but we also begin to notice many things we previously had overlooked.

Murdoch holds that the most powerful manifestation of goodness and beauty comes through great art.[46] But Murdoch also speaks of art in a much broader sense when she writes of one encountering the beauty of nature or the beauty of another human being, perhaps especially in her need and vulnerability. No matter how we encounter beauty and goodness, they have the power to help us break through the veil of selfishness at the heart of fantasy in order to see the world justly and kindly and humbly.

But we can also be lured from fantasy and illusion through the everyday experiences of our ordinary lives. Our days are filled with revelatory moments, moments that awaken us by opening our eyes, moments that draw us out of ourselves and compel us to see differently. Revelatory moments can happen in all sorts of ways. Our eyes can be opened and our vision cleansed on a service trip to another city or country. Revelation can come to us when we volunteer at soup kitchens or homeless shelters, when we step out of our typically rushed routines to take time to tell a story to a child or, perhaps even better, listen to a child tell a story to us. Our eyes can be opened and our "blindsight" overcome when we risk sitting in silence, take time to pray or to play, or notice the very people we commonly take for granted. Revelatory moments occur "whenever something startles us out of our usual ways of seeing and shows us how poorly we have been seeing and how self-serving our vision often is."[47] Some of these revelatory experiences have profound and lasting effects on our perceptions.

A memorable example is given in the life of Thomas Merton, the Trappist monk and famous author whose life journey took him to the Abbey of Gethsemani in rural Kentucky. There, until his death in December 1968, Merton penned a multitude of works that made him one of the most esteemed spiritual writers of the time. In *Conjectures of a Guilty Bystander*, Merton recounts a trip he took to Louisville, roughly fifty miles from Gethsemani. Standing at the corner of Fourth and Walnut, then the center of downtown Louisville, Merton had an unexpected epiphany. He realized for the first time the deep interconnectedness that exists between all human beings. He felt deeply, almost mystically, the kinship he held with every man, woman, and child walking past him at the corner of Fourth and Walnut, and it drew him out of himself in love. Merton wrote:

> In Louisville, at the corner of Fourth and Walnut, in the center of the shopping district, I was suddenly overwhelmed with the realization that I loved all those people, that they were mine and I theirs, that we could not be alien to one another even though we were total strangers. It was like waking from a dream of separateness.[48]

Instead of seeing himself as a monk removed from the world, Merton discovered that the monks "are in the same world as everybody else, the world of the bomb, the world of race hatred, the world of technology, the world of mass media, big business, revolution, and all the rest." Even more, he did not see himself as holier or better than anybody else; rather, about everyone who passed him that day he said, "they are all walking around shining like the sun." At the corner of Fourth and Walnut in Louisville, Merton was liberated from a fantasy he never realized he had, the fantasy of separateness. His revelation led him to declare about every person who walked by him, and any person anywhere, "There are no strangers!" With great poignancy and emotion,

Merton describes the radical difference it would make if every person learned to see every other human being as Merton saw them that afternoon.[49]

> Then it was as if I suddenly saw the secret beauty of their hearts, the depths of their hearts where neither sin nor desire nor self-knowledge can reach, the core of their reality, the person that each one is in God's eyes. If only they could all see themselves as they really *are*. If only we could see each other that way all the time. There would be no more war, no more hatred, no more cruelty, no more greed. . . . I suppose the big problem would be that we would fall down and worship each other. . . .
>
> I have no program for this seeing. It is only given. But the gate of heaven is everywhere.[50]

THE CHRISTIAN MORAL LIFE AND LEARNING HOW TO SEE

To see one another, and indeed every creature and species, as God does is the unsurpassable, if forever out-of-reach, goal of the Christian moral life. Short of the beatific vision in which we see God as God is and see everything else in God's light, our moral vision, even at its finest, will be dramatically different from God's way of seeing.

Nonetheless, Christians are called to grow in the goodness of God by being increasingly attentive and attuned to Christ. If Murdoch says we overcome the enervating effects of fantasy through attentiveness to "the Good," for Christians "the Good" has a name. For Christians, God is the fullness and perfection of goodness—indeed, the very definition of goodness—and God's goodness entered our world in the incarnation of Christ. In his study of the ethics of the Catholic theologian Hans Urs von Balthasar, Christopher Steck notes that for von Balthasar, "We 'see' (perceive, understand, feel) well by seeing as Christ does and by entering his sensibility." We move from the "blindsight" of sin to a truthful and reverent vision capable of goodness when we "perceive what God has done for us in Christ Jesus," contemplating that divine act of love over a lifetime, and letting it reorder not just our vision, but our entire lives.[51]

If what becomes of us is ultimately determined by what most habitually has our attention, then we can only grow in the love and goodness of God when Christ stands at the center of our lives. It is by watching, listening to, learning from, and walking in the ways of Christ that we not only gradually break free from decrepit ways of seeing but also gradually take on the "scandalous" vision of Christ. To do this we must, as baptism symbolizes, join our life story to the story of Christ, and allow his story to illumine our own.

Sacred Stories

Each of us not only is a story—or really a blend of many stories—but we also choose a story to guide our lives and to help us order and make sense of the multiple narratives that shape us. Stephen Crites calls these "sacred stories" because our sense of self, our understanding of the world and our place in it, as well as what we should seek and aspire to, are all fundamentally informed by these more normative narratives.[52] The "sacred stories" that guide our lives shape our perceptions and our imaginations by employing images and metaphors that teach us to see and think and evaluate in particular ways. They provide an overarching framework for our lives by presenting us with goods to pursue and goals to accomplish. And it is under the influence of these master narratives that we come to understand what is good and what is evil, what actions are right and what actions are wrong, as well as what we should love, desire, and cherish.

Of course, as we saw with consumerism, some stories are not worthy of us because they skew our vision and foster the wrong sorts of desires. Some stories conceal and distort more than they reveal and illumine. Embracing them as the master narratives of our lives will corrupt and diminish us. We are often unaware of how our "sacred story" might be forming us until it collides with another narrative that not only offers a drastically different way of imagining our lives in the world but also exposes our "sacred story" as seriously lacking.

In the Christian life, this is the unsettling but ultimately liberating impact of scripture. There are many ways to approach the Bible, but one way is to see it as the collection of narratives, metaphors, and images that correct our faulty vision and teach us to see in ways befitting the goodness of God. Referring especially to the revelation that comes to us in Christ, H. Richard Niebuhr wrote, "Revelation means this intelligible event which makes all other events intelligible."[53] It is in light of Christ, Niebuhr suggested, that we learn to see ourselves, other persons, and the world rightly because for Christians Christ is the illuminating center of reality.

Christians do not think, reason, imagine, and perceive apart from the narratives, metaphors, images, and events of the Bible but rather through them. Every human being reasons, imagines, perceives, and evaluates through the narratives, metaphors, and images in the "sacred stories" that have claimed their lives. And every major religion has sacred stories or texts that its adherents embrace in order to understand who they should be and what they should do in life. Christians find their sacred stories in the Bible, because the scriptures present the texts that best enable them to make sense of their lives and to overcome what Niebuhr called "evil imaginations of the heart." "Evil imaginations of the heart" are those ways of seeing and imagining that foster egotism and illusion and "lead to confusion and disaster." In many respects, Niebuhr's account of "evil imaginations of the heart" parallels Murdoch's analysis of fantasy because, like fantasies, "evil imaginations of the heart" result in the "impoverishment and alienation of the self, as well as the destruction of others."[54]

Examples of "evil imaginations of the heart" are plentiful. All injustice issues from an evil imagination of the heart, whether it is the injustice wrought by greed, maliciousness, thoughtlessness and indifference, or violence. Biblical revelation exposes the evil imaginations of the heart and helps us be purified of them by showing us how our familiar ways of looking at the world are lacking, even harmful, and by teaching us new ways of seeing. As William Spohn says of the New Testament, "The New Testament writers attempt to convert the imaginations of Christians by parables, metaphors, and stories. They want their readers to see life in a new way and to act in radically different ways."[55] And because Christians believe that how the scriptures teach us to see is trustworthy, they do not view the narratives of scripture as remote to their lives, but precisely as the stories that must govern their understanding of reality and their sense of what being in the world involves.

Moreover, Christians insert their stories into the stories of God, because they want to make those stories their own. They want to absorb the viewpoints and perspectives, the values and vision of the scriptures; indeed, they want the biblical narratives to provide the stories, images, and metaphors in light of which they comprehend everything.[56] As George Lindbeck summarizes, "A scriptural world is thus able to absorb the universe. It supplies the interpretative framework within which believers seek to live their lives and understand reality."[57]

Learning to See

It is striking that so many of Jesus' miracles involve restoring sight to the blind—people like Bartimaeus, who when Jesus asked him "What do you want me to do for you?" unhesitatingly responded, "Master, I want to see" (Mark 10:51). But what distinguished Bartimaeus from so many other characters in the Gospels is that at least he was aware of his blindness. Bartimaeus knew he could not see and begged Jesus to restore his sight. In the Gospel of Mark, Bartimaeus is a model of discipleship because as soon as Jesus gave him sight, Bartimaeus "followed him on the way" (10:52).

Most of the other characters we meet in the Gospels are not as keenly aware that their vision is impaired or as ready as Bartimaeus to confess their need for a healing. Like ourselves, most of them assume there is nothing wrong with their ways of seeing, so if something Jesus says or does offends them, they are ready to judge and dismiss him instead of examining their own hearts. Consequently, they continually misperceive what Jesus and his mission are about.

Among the most severely obtuse are Jesus' closest intimates, the twelve apostles. Among all those who follow Jesus, the apostles are the "inner circle." They witness firsthand Jesus' teachings and miracles, and are with him throughout his ministry in Galilee. And yet, no matter how much time they spend with him or how often he pulls them aside to explain yet again what he has just done or what his mission is about, "they remain stupidly uncomprehending."[58] The apostles stumble all over themselves in trying to understand Jesus, so that Jesus' exasperation with them steadily increases; in fact, Jesus' dismay with the apostles becomes a background chorus to the Gospel of Mark.

Ironically, even the unclean spirit whom Jesus expels from a man early in that Gospel (2:23-26) seems to understand Jesus better than the twelve that Jesus personally selects to follow him. For example, in Mark 8:17-18, just after Jesus multiplied the loaves and fishes and fed them to the crowd, he says to his baffled intimates, "Do you not yet understand or comprehend? Are your hearts hardened? Do you have eyes and not see, ears and not hear?" Because of their persistent failures of perception, the apostles—the very ones who are "insiders" to Jesus and his message—become "outsiders" in the Gospel of Mark.[59]

But before we start congratulating ourselves on not being dense like the apostles, we must remember that for Mark they represent all potential followers of Jesus. To take up the journey of discipleship is to experience the same confusion and bewilderment and constant misunderstanding of Jesus and his message that we witness in his closest followers. To follow Jesus is to misunderstand because what Jesus reveals about the ways of God is so startlingly opposite of the ways we ordinarily see, think, and imagine. In this respect, all Christians are like Peter, the paradigm of gospel blindness. Like Peter, we are ready to confess that Jesus is the Messiah, but balk at the fact that this Messiah must suffer and die (Mark 8:31-33). And we are especially troubled to hear that any follower of his must walk the same path (8:34-35). Nonetheless, to be a follower of Jesus is to be called to a community that sees and thinks differently, a community that is "the light of the world" (Matt 5:14) only because it has abandoned former ways of seeing and embraced the radical vision of the reign of God.

Parables—Being Shocked into New Ways of Seeing

How then does Jesus teach us to see? How do the Gospels expose the deficiencies and distortions in our typical ways of seeing in order to train us in the vision of the reign of God? Put more strongly, if our normal ways of seeing *keep us from seeing*, how is our "blindsight" overcome? Of all the many ways that

Jesus challenges our customary logic and perceptions, none is more provocative and disturbing—and hence potentially redemptive—than his parables.

Parables are designed to offend our sensibilities by pointing out the vast difference between our ways of viewing things and God's. The strategy behind every parable is to clash with our sense of what is proper and expedient, and to do so by confronting us with the wildly different ways of God. By turning our lives inside out, parables shock us into new ways of seeing, thinking, and evaluating. Sallie McFague says that instead of reassuring or comforting us, parables have an "unnerving, distasteful, disturbing quality in them" because they are "an indirect assault on the accepted, conventional way of viewing reality, 'the way things are.'" She goes on to explain:

> A parable is an assault on the social, political, economic, mythic structures we human beings build for ourselves for comfort and security. A parable is a story meant to invert, to subvert, to throw wide open these structures and to suggest, always indirectly, that "God's ways may not be our ways." We do not like parables because all the efforts we have made to "put things in place," to understand our world and be comfortable in it, are undercut in them.[60]

Consider a parable that grates on every fair-minded person, the parable of the workers in the vineyard (Matt 20:1-16). Like every parable, it works with an easily understandable incident from everyday life, then shatters it. And, like every parable, it begins in a rather pedestrian fashion. The parable tells the story of a landowner "who went out at dawn to hire laborers for his vineyard" (v. 1). The workers agree to the usual daily wage, so the landowner sends them to his vineyard to begin their day's work. A few hours later, the owner again goes to the marketplace and sees other potential laborers. He promises to pay them fairly, and so they accept his terms and go to work. Twice more that day, once at noon and again at three o'clock, the owner does the same. He finds potential workers; they agree to a wage; and they're sent off to work. But then near the end of the day, at five o'clock, "he found others standing around, and said to them, 'Why do you stand here idle all day?' They answered, 'Because no one has hired us'" (vv. 6-7). So he hires them as well to work in his vineyard for the little time that is left in the day.

So far in the story there is nothing to predict what is about to happen. Everything sets up the reader to expect a conventional conclusion. Since we enter the parable with our own sense of what is fair and right, we fully expect the owner to pay the workers in proportion to the hours they worked; after all, equal pay for equal work, right? We think it only fair that those who worked the whole day would receive more than the stragglers who did not begin work until five in the afternoon. But, of course, this is not what happens.

At the end of the day, the owner gathers all of the workers. But instead of first paying those whom had worked the entire day (which is what everyone expects), he begins with the ones from the last group and shockingly pays them a full day's wage. Witnessing this, the workers who had spent the entire day in the vineyards are certain they will receive abundantly more. But the owner gives them not a cent more than what they had agreed on; thus, equal pay for unequal work.[61] Understandably, they're miffed, and the listener shares their chagrin. They protest to the owner: "These last ones worked only one hour, and you have made them equal to us, who bore the day's burden and the heat" (v. 12). By every standard of fairness they are right. It doesn't seem fair that the workers from the last group who hardly broke a sweat should be paid the same as those who toiled the entire day. Who among us with any sense of justice would not feel the same? But to their complaints the owner replies, "My friend, I am not cheating you. Did you not agree with me for the usual daily wage? Take what is yours and go. . . . Are you envious because I am generous?" (vv. 13-14, 15). The parable ends with a perfect description of how the logic of the reign of God subverts the logic of the world: "Thus, the last will be first, and the first will be last" (v. 16).

The story of the workers in the vineyard reveals the typical pattern in a parable: orientation, disorientation, then reorientation.[62] When the parable begins, it seems so ordinary and conventional because it fits our understanding of the world and seems to comply with our customary ways of seeing and thinking. We know what it is to put in a good day's work and to expect a just wage. But then, without warning, the parable completely confounds and disorients us by calling into question basic elements of our moral universe that we thought were permanently fixed. The parable of the workers in the vineyard does not ask us just to be a little bit looser and more flexible when it comes to thinking about fairness; rather, it dismisses the category of fairness altogether and replaces it with generosity. As William Spohn comments, "The parable does not critique our usual assumptions about what is fair and unfair; it subverts them. If life cannot be analyzed along the lines of fairness, our moral compass has lost magnetic north."[63]

And that is what the parable intends. It wants to disassemble the framework of our world in order to call us into a very different, and initially quite alien, world. Having broken open and subverted our world, the parable works to reorient us to God's world by showing us "that things really are not at all what they seem to be."[64] What we took to be reasonable and sensible in our world simply does not fit the world of the reign of God, a world governed not by strict criteria of fairness, but by lavish and extravagant generosity. As long as we remain in the moral universe of fairness, the parable of the workers in the vineyard can only shock and offend us.

However, if we move into the moral universe of the reign of God, and replace the logic of fairness with the logic of generosity, instead of resenting the generosity of the owner, we rejoice at the good fortune of those who were unexpectedly rewarded. In more theological language, if we move from a universe governed by fairness to a universe governed by grace, we will begin to see and think and judge quite differently. Our vision will not be the same because it has been reoriented away from the "wisdom of the world" to the joyfully disturbing and liberating wisdom of God. As Spohn summarizes, "Different conduct is appropriate in a world framed by fairness than would fit a world framed by generosity. . . . In a word, the world according to God is not fair; it is gracious. Those who want to enter it have to read the world and themselves in a new way and act accordingly."[65]

As we have discussed, anxiety, fear, the need for security, and cravings for personal gain often cloud our vision of life. Instead of seeing the world through a lens of justice and love and generosity, we tend to view life through a lens of self-interest and self-satisfaction. One reason parables aggravate us—and why we like to distance ourselves from them—is that they show us ourselves in ways we would rather not see, and typically by unmasking some of the pretensions we have about ourselves. This is why Spohn claims that "we do not interpret parables so much as they interpret us. They make us recognize more about ourselves than we care to."[66] Parables give us new ways of seeing, thinking, and understanding, but only by first showing us how blind and misguided we were before. They shock us into new ways of seeing and acting, but often by undermining our assumptions about our own goodness and righteousness.

Consider the parable of the rich fool from the Gospel of Luke (12:16-21). Jesus tells this story immediately after warning a crowd, "Take care to guard against all greed, for though one may be rich, one's life does not consist in possessions" (12:15), advice that surely is pertinent for anyone who understands planning for the future strictly in economic terms. Throughout the Gospels Jesus warns people about the dangers of wealth, and about trying to secure their lives with wealth and possessions instead of with the providential love and care of God. The parable of the rich fool is hardly the only time Jesus speaks of wealth and possessions as obstacles to entry into the kingdom of God. Most of us can recite by memory Jesus' famous pronouncement that it would be easier for a camel to slip through the eye of a needle than for the rich to enter the kingdom of God (Mark 10:25).

The parable of the rich fool focuses on a man whose harvest was so plentiful he did not have room enough to store it all. Instead of exhibiting generosity by sharing his good fortunes with those who did not have enough, the man decides to hoard everything that he has. But the only way he can preserve his abundant harvest is by tearing down his barns and building bigger ones. In the rich man's logic, he is only doing what is prudent. By building barns large enough to store everything he has, he is securing his future against the unexpected. He is not being selfish; he is exhibiting foresight and good planning. The rich man congratulates himself on a wise handling of his estate, and, viewed through the logic of scarce resources and an uncertain future, he is surely correct. In fact, most of us would praise the rich man for using his wealth so thoughtfully. At this point in the story the parable reinforces conventional understandings of what we should do with our property and possessions, and what it means to plan well for the future. Too, given the principles of liberal capitalism and the importance we put on the right to private property, what the man does with his harvest seems not only utterly reasonable, but also nobody's business but his own. Who are we to say what anyone ought to do with what is rightly his?

It is here that the parable subverts the logic of good economic planning by revealing how fragile anyone's hold on life truly is. The man thinks that by amassing resources for the future he will be secure against any potential misfortune; he believes his wealth will protect him from all possible adversity. But the one thing no amount of wealth and good planning can save him from is his own death, and that is where the parable ends. Immediately after the man basks in his assumed invulnerability, Jesus announces: "But God said to him, 'You fool, this night your life will be demanded of you; and the things you have prepared, to whom will they belong?' Thus will it be for the one who stores up treasure for himself but is not rich in what matters to God" (Luke 12:20-21).

The man may be rich, but he is also foolish because given the choice between trusting in God or trusting in wealth, he chose the latter. The parable suggests that he is most accurately described not as wealthy but as a fool, because he did not realize how impotent money and possessions are when confronted with the reality of death. They may be able to protect people from certain contingencies, but they cannot save them from their own mortality.

In deciphering this parable, Allen Verhey says the man's anxiety flowed from his misplaced priorities. "He was a fool because he was anxious about his possessions, and he was anxious about his possessions because he thought life consisted in the abundance of possessions. He was a fool because he thought money the measure of value and the guarantee of security."[67] What he took to be careful, prudent planning was in reality woefully miscalculated because it could not keep at bay the very thing that most threatened the man's craving for security—his own death.

The parable turns our ordinary ways of seeing and reasoning upside down because it suggests that the man would have been far wiser, and far more secure if, instead of spending his time tearing down smaller barns in order to build bigger ones, he had followed Jesus' admonition: "Be not anxious." His obsession with piling up wealth against an unknown future blinded him to what he really ought to have done; thus, instead of exhibiting foresight, he was really afflicted with "blindsight." The man was not nearly as wise and prudent and careful as we initially judged him to be. The parable suggests that instead of being anxious, he should have been generous. And if he had risked being generous he not only would have been freed from anxiety but would have also discovered that his wealth could not protect him anyway. As Verhey writes, "He was not a fool just because he was rich. He was a fool because his attempt to secure his own life and identity by his possessions made it impossible for him to be generous."[68]

That is Jesus' counsel about money. In the economic logic of the reign of God, we are not to hold on to our money but to give it away. The first law of the economics of the reign of God is to be extravagantly generous, to share without restraint, to give with no thought of tomorrow. As Jesus said in commenting on this parable, "If God so clothes the grass in the field that grows today and is thrown into the oven tomorrow, will he not much more provide for you, O you of little faith?" (Luke 12:28).

To anyone schooled in the logic of liberal capitalism, Jesus' announcement that we should find our security in God and trust God to provide sounds not only ridiculously sentimental but also dangerously irresponsible. We find it hard to fault the rich man because our thinking on these matters is so much like his own. Given the individualism of liberal capitalism, like the rich man we are taught to think only of ourselves; after all, if we do not, who will? Contrary to Jesus' instructions, we are taught not "to guard against greed" (Luke 12:15) but to foster it. And in a culture of capitalistic consumerism, Jesus strikes us as hopelessly out of touch when he declares that "one's life does not consist in possessions" (12:15). But the parable's startling ending exposes the rich man's (as well as our own) fatal misperception. Instead of being wise, as we initially take him to be, he was a fool "because he wanted to be on his own, looking out for number one, as though there were only one, himself. He was a fool because he had no sense of community, surely no sense of a community with the poor."[69]

The parable of the rich fool is a powerful and quite relevant example of how parables radically subvert our customary ways of perceiving, reasoning, and evaluating and expose them not only as sorely lacking but also as wholly at odds with the ways of God. By throwing up for grabs everything we take for granted, they invite us to re-envision and reimagine the world in more truthful and gracious ways.

Perhaps no parable is more instructive for showing us how Jesus challenges us to take on the vision of the reign of God than the parable of the Good Samaritan (Luke 10:29-37), probably the most famous parable in the Gospels. This parable has been called "a classic paradigm of perception and blindness"[70] because it tells the story of three men, each of whom encounters the same situation, but who respond in decidedly different ways on account of how they perceive. Jesus tells the story in response to a man—a scholar of the law—who inquires about exactly who the "neighbor" is that we are summoned to love. Does the circle of love encompass everyone or can our love be choosy and selective?

In response to the man's reasonable inquiry, Jesus tells the story of a man on his way from Jerusalem to Jericho who was robbed, stripped and beaten, and left half-dead on the side of the road. Two people pass by, first a priest and then a Levite, and they both see the man; however, instead of coming to his aid, they do nothing. In fact, Jesus says they "passed by on the opposite side" (vv. 31-32), which suggests that they went out of their way to remove themselves from what they saw. They saw, but their vision was monstrously faulty because they saw in a way that allowed them to pass the afflicted man by. They saw, but remained emotionally detached from what they beheld. Nothing of the man's plight, nothing of his suffering, broke through to them. As William Spohn comments, the robbed and beaten man "enters their field of vision but not their field of compassion. They cannot afford to perceive his full reality because his condition is threatening. They screen him out before his desperate situation can complicate their journey."[71]

But a third man, a Samaritan, also passes by and, like the previous two travelers, sees the man. What distinguishes him, however, is the way he sees. Jesus says the Samaritan "was moved with compassion at the sight" (v. 33). He sees differently than the priest and Levite because he looks at the wounded man not through a vision of self-protection or expediency but with compassion and mercy. In one respect, only the Samaritan truly sees because only he is open to taking in and being moved by what he beholds. He allows himself to be affected by the plight of another's suffering; in Murdoch's language, he risks a compassionate and sympathetic imagination, and this different way of seeing impels him to respond. He cleans and bandages the victim's wounds, and then takes him to an inn and cares for him. Before leaving the next day, the merciful Samaritan leaves money with the innkeeper for the wounded man's care. How is it that three people can "see" the same situation but respond so differently? "Compassion was the ingredient missing from the sight of the priest and the Levite," Spohn writes. "The Samaritan sees the man as a fellow human being in terrible trouble. . . . The priest and the Levite did not let themselves be affected by his plight. Any inchoate feelings of pity or shock were neutralized by wariness, disgust, or fear—or perhaps they felt nothing at all."[72]

The parable of the Good Samaritan shocks us into new ways of seeing in at least two ways. First, it suggests that compassion is necessary for seeing and acting rightly. The Samaritan comes to the aid of a stranger in need—indeed, he allows the need of another to redirect his path. But he responds to the robbed and beaten man because he does not allow himself to remain emotionally detached. Because of his compassion, he does not see this victim of violence as a stranger he can ignore, but as a fellow human being, as someone with whom he is connected and to whom he is responsible.

Spohn says that the parable of the Good Samaritan "shows that compassion is the optic nerve of Christian vision."[73] If we have compassion, we are much more likely to see as we ought to see. Compassion itself is a way of seeing that focuses our vision on the sufferings and afflictions of others, but in a way that we cannot, like the priest and Levite, act as if those sufferings and afflictions have nothing to do with us. A vision inspired by compassion calls us not only to identify with but also to enter into the experiences of others, especially their sufferings. In this respect, the parable of the Good Samaritan reveals how costly certain ways of misperceiving can be on others, especially those most in need. If I do not see the connection that I have with every other human being, and the obligations I have toward them, someone will suffer.

Second, the parable tests and corrects our vision by blowing open who in our lives we think merits the title of "neighbor." The priest and the Levite had obviously established boundaries around their love so that some were included in their circle of love but others, like this victim of violence, were not. Being observant Jews, they knew the command to love one's neighbor but also thought that some human beings were "non-neighbors" and, therefore, need not be recipients of their love. They knew that the law obliged them to love but also thought that love could be exclusive. Jesus praises the Samaritan because he realized that God's love excludes no one and is extended to all, particularly those most desperately in need of compassion and love. The Samaritan did not put boundaries around his love because neither does God. He put into practice the love that is revealed in God, a love that is compassionate, vulnerable, and merciful.

In many respects, the kind of merciful, compassionate vision that Jesus articulated through the story of the Good Samaritan expressed in words what he regularly enacted in his life. Like the Good Samaritan, Jesus habitually "trespassed" the conventional boundaries of love by reaching out to all the excluded members of society. One aspect of Jesus' ministry that made him a scandal to his contemporaries, especially the religious leaders, was that he welcomed and embraced the very people everyone else was taught to avoid. Jesus did not shun the "untouchable" members of his community; rather, he brought them into the community, even if they were known to be sinners. We see this particularly in Jesus' stubborn insistence to sit down at the table with anybody. If no one else would gather tax collectors, prostitutes, lawbreakers, and recognized sinners around the same table, he would. As Donald Senior comments,

> Jesus eats with the poor and sinners. He is a friend of tax gatherers and prostitutes and other unsound members of first century Jewish society. The gospel evidence is exceptionally rich here. Jesus invites sinners to his home and shares a meal with them (Lk 15:1-2). He enjoys table fellowship with the very people whom Jewish law banned as "unclean" (cf. Mk 2:15).

Furthermore, Senior notes, "This emphasis on table fellowship is notable in a semitic culture where sharing a meal was considered more of a sharing of life than simply a casual association."[74]

In the time of Jesus, to share a meal with someone was to identify with that person. It was to *see* him or her not as stranger, not as sinner or lawbreaker, but as neighbor. And it was to set one's self not above them, but side by side with them. When Jesus extends table fellowship to the typically invisible members of his society, he establishes community with the very persons who are never allowed to belong. "In the culture of the Middle East," Elizabeth Johnson writes, "sitting down at table with someone and breaking bread sets up a real bond of kinship. Not done lightly, this action makes people into friends, colleagues, 'family.'"[75] Put more strongly, "A meal shared with Jesus, it seems, is a place where just about anyone might be found—except those too proud or fussy to join the company. Some may exclude themselves, but Jesus excludes no one."[76]

Re-imagining Jesus

Throughout this chapter we have emphasized the importance of the teaching and example of Jesus for training us to see in ways that enable us to imitate the redemptive goodness of God in our lives. Our discussion of the importance of vision in the Christian moral life would not be complete, however, without also critiquing some of the ways that Jesus has traditionally been envisioned. As our analysis of the parables made clear, any honest reckoning with Jesus exposes the distortions in our customary ways of seeing and calls for a conversion of our habits of perceiving, reasoning, and imagining. But it is also true that the ways in which we see Jesus can become skewed so that we are not seeing the Jesus of the Gospels, but a Jesus that reflects our own biases and preferences, or a Jesus whose radical message has been distorted by social and cultural ideologies. When this occurs, Jesus is no longer the Christ, the liberator and redeemer, but just another consoling fantasy.

In her groundbreaking book *She Who Is*, Elizabeth Johnson points out that many feminist theologians maintain that "of all the doctrines of the church Christology is the one most used to suppress and exclude women." Something is seriously amiss if the Jesus who came to liberate and redeem is used to reinforce patterns of exclusion. Johnson argues that this is exactly what happened when the liberating and subversive Christ of the Gospels was suppressed and replaced by a Christ reinterpreted to conform to the norms and patterns of a patriarchal culture. Seen through the lens of patriarchy, Jesus' ministry of inclusion and his socially unconventional acceptance of women are blurred, and his proclamation of justice is blunted. From the perspective of patriarchy, which is itself a pernicious fantasy, what matters most about Jesus is not his gospel message, but that he is male. But, Johnson observes, this flagrant misreading of Jesus has had dismal social, economic, and political consequences for women. "In particular, when Jesus' maleness, which belongs to his historical identity, is interpreted to be essential to his redeeming christic function and identity, then the Christ serves as a religious tool for marginalizing and excluding women."[77]

Today we see consequences of this patriarchal reading of Jesus in some churches' exclusion of women from certain forms of ministry (such as ordination in the Roman Catholic Church). Once the fact of being male is viewed as one of the most important elements of Jesus' identity, then it is easy to conclude that men can more fully represent Christ than women. Most seriously, Johnson writes, "if maleness is essential for the christic role, then women are cut out of the loop of salvation, for female sexuality is not taken on by the Word made flesh. If maleness is constitutive for the incarnation and redemption, female humanity is not assumed and therefore not saved."[78]

In order to avoid such a catastrophic heresy for Christian theology, Johnson says we must re-envision who we take Jesus to be. She suggests retrieving "Sophia," a title and image of Jesus that the first Christians frequently employed. Sophia means wisdom, and along with "Messiah," "Lord," and "Son of Man," it was one of the titles the early church used to express their understanding of Jesus. In the Old Testament, Sophia is "a female personification of God," and the Bible depicts Sophia as one who "creates, redeems, establishes justice, protects the poor, teaches the mysteries of the world, and most especially gives life."[79] The New Testament links Jesus with Sophia when it speaks of him as "the image of the invisible God, the first born of all creation" (Col 1:15), and as the one "through whom all things are and through whom we exist" (1 Cor 8:6).

Similarly, Jesus embodies Sophia when "he calls out to the heavy burdened to come to him and find rest (Mt 11:28-30); he makes people friends of God (Jn 15:15), and gifts those who love him with life (Jn 17:2)."[80] Indeed, Johnson attests that "Jesus was so closely associated with Sophia that by the end of the first century he is presented not only as a wisdom teacher, not only as a child and envoy of Sophia, but ultimately even as an embodiment of Sophia herself."[81]

Why does thinking of Jesus as Sophia matter? Because as an antidote to patriarchal distortions of Jesus, it allows women to speak of "Jesus as Liberator, not in a generic sense with regard to the poor but specifically with regard to women. He brings salvation through his life and Spirit, restoring women to full personal dignity in the reign of God, and inspiring their liberation from structures of domination and subordination."[82] But seeing Jesus as Sophia also matters because "then it is not unthinkable—it is not even unbiblical—to confess Jesus the Christ as the incarnation of God imaged in female symbol." Johnson elaborates:

> Whoever espouses a wisdom Christology is asserting that Jesus is the human being Sophia became; that Sophia in all her fullness was in him so that he manifests the depth of divine mystery in creative and graciously saving involvement in the world. . . . Wisdom Christology reflects the depths of the mystery of God and points the way to an inclusive Christology in female symbols.[83]

"Who do you say that I am?" It is a question Jesus asked his disciples and a question with which every follower of Jesus must grapple. And it is a question that the churches must continually address. "Who do you say that I am?" The question surfaces anew as Christianity expands into other cultures and as Christians grapple with the meaning of Jesus in non-Western societies. Who is Jesus for Africans, Latin Americans, or Asians? As Christianity continues to engage, challenge, and be challenged by cultures across the world, what new images of Jesus will emerge?

Some Asian women theologians, for example, "given their poverty and oppression by colonialism, neocolonialism, military dictatorship, and over-arching patriarchy," emphasize images of Jesus as "liberator, revolutionary and political martyr," because these images of Jesus strengthen them "in their own struggle for freedom, even to the shedding of their blood for their people." Others have developed an Asian christology that sees Jesus as "the Minjung within the Minjung." *Minjung* is a Korean term that refers to all of the oppressed, all those who are exploited, dominated, and discriminated against economically, socially, and politically. To speak of Jesus as "*the* Minjung *within* the Minjung" refers to how Jesus enters into the lives and experiences of the most oppressed and marginalized persons.[84]

Other metaphors for Christ in Asian cultures speak of him as the Eldest Son and Ancestor. Both reflect the emphasis Confucian cultures place on honoring one's parents (filial piety) and on having respect for one's ancestors. In this respect, Asians can embrace Christ as the "eldest son" who came into the world to do the work of the father.[85]

CONCLUSION

"Sometimes I think the people we'll see in heaven are the people we don't see now." A friend said that not too long ago and it's a fitting way to bring this chapter to a close. Jesus may have been "blessed with perfect sight" but, as our analysis has shown, what was true with Jesus certainly isn't true with us. The Christian moral life can fittingly be described as an ongoing initiation into new ways of seeing because none of us possesses the vision necessary for grasping and imitating the goodness of God.

Acquiring such a vision is a lifetime project but not one any of us can afford to avoid, because the consequences of our inability to see are costly for ourselves and for others. If we are to move beyond the falsifying distortions of fantasy and into the compassionate, merciful, and penetrating vision of Jesus, our customary ways of seeing and perceiving have to be radically rehabilitated. We have to "unlearn" so many of the ways we have been trained to see in order to grow in the unsettling but liberating vision of God, a way of seeing, imagining, and perceiving that is revealed to us in Jesus' parables.

Initially, the way of seeing that Jesus invites us to assaults our customary estimation of what is fitting and reasonable; in fact, Jesus' perspective can seem downright foolish, even irresponsible. Nonetheless, to make his way of seeing our own is the aim of the Christian moral life because it is in and through Christ that we enter into the presence of God and achieve fullness of life in seeing and praising God. To leave behind the "blindsight" of sin and fantasy for the beatitude of seeing God, we must enter the reign of God. To understand what that might mean—and to appreciate its promise—is what we will explore in chapter 3.

KEY POINTS

1. In the Christian moral life, learning to act rightly depends on learning to see rightly. Thus, a life of discipleship must include learning to "see" as Jesus did.
2. We do not naturally see as we need to see. Our ability to see is weakened by what the philosopher Iris Murdoch called *fantasy* and by what Christians call *sin*. Some examples would be egotism, excessive fear and anxiety, and unhealthy consumerism.
3. Learning to see is also a central teaching of Buddhism. In Buddhism, truthful seeing leads to understanding and understanding leads to love.
4. Jesus' parables expose the shortcomings in our customary ways of seeing and "shock" us to see in new and better ways.
5. It is important to have our understanding of Jesus tested and challenged by others, particularly people who think of Jesus quite differently.

QUESTIONS FOR REFLECTION

1. Does it make sense to you to think of the Christian moral life as a matter of learning to see?

2. Why do you think it is so difficult to see other persons and the world truthfully and justly?
3. How would you describe Iris Murdoch's analysis of fantasy? Do you agree with her? What, for you, would be some examples of fantasy?
4. How does excessive consumerism affect our moral vision? What could we do to counter it?
5. What can Buddhism teach us about learning to see truthfully and justly?
6. What is a parable? Why do we find Jesus' parables unsettling and disturbing? Why might they be important for a life of discipleship?
7. Can you think of other ways that Jesus teaches us to see?

SUGGESTIONS FOR FURTHER READING AND STUDY

Franck, Frederick. *To Be Human against All Odds.* Berkeley, Calif.: Asian Humanities Press, 1991.

Friel, Brian. *Molly Sweeney.* New York: Penguin, 1995.

Hanh, Thich Nhat. *Being Peace.* Berkeley, Calif.: Parallax, 1987.

Johnson, Elizabeth A. *Consider Jesus: Waves of Renewal in Christology.* New York: Crossroad, 1990.

Lefebure, Leo D. *The Buddha and the Christ: Explorations in Buddhist and Christian Dialogue.* Maryknoll, N.Y.: Orbis Books, 1993.

Murdoch, Iris. *The Sovereignty of Good.* London: Routledge & Kegan Paul, 1970.

Spohn, William C. *Go and Do Likewise: Jesus and Ethics.* New York: Continuum, 1999.

Steck, Christopher. *The Ethical Thought of Hans Urs von Balthasar.* New York: Crossroad, 2001.

3

The Treasure We Seek—The Reign of God and the Moral Life

"The Kingdom of God Is at Hand" (Mark 1:15)

Santiago, the Andalusian shepherd boy we met in chapter 1, had a vision of buried treasure in the pyramids of Egypt. It was a dream that led him to leave everything—family, community, even his sheep—in order to discover that what he believed would bring him happiness. The young boy did not know exactly what he was seeking, or precisely where it could be found. But the vision so dominated his imagination that he was compelled to embark on a quest to find the treasure, and to continue on the journey despite the many hardships he encountered along the way.

Like Santiago, contemporary disciples are beckoned on a journey inspired by a vision of something good that will lead to a happy and joyful life. It is a quest for a treasure that is the reign of God. This is the central theme of Jesus' teaching and preaching. It is the horizon within which everything is apprehended, and the good Jesus seeks and serves. So following Jesus means primarily, but not exclusively, being committed to God's reign, the highest good that men and women ought to aim for and to seek. The reign of God provides the goal and motivation of the moral life, but as we learned in the previous chapter we need to see rightly if we are to act rightly. We need to see truthfully, if we are to live justly. That is because we can only choose and act within the world we see. If we have a distorted vision of the reign of God, then the good we seek and the happiness we pursue may lead to personal and social harm.

A prime example of the harmful consequences that can result from a distorted vision of God's reign is seen in the film *Kingdom of Heaven*. Directed by Ridley Scott, it starkly shows how the Crusaders, both Muslim and Christian, used the image of the kingdom to justify the slaughter of the inhabitants of the Holy Land.[1] The film is a Crusade-era epic that takes place between the second and third Crusades, a time when relative peace existed in the Holy Land, where religious faith could be expressed openly and freely. The first Crusade established the Christian kingdom of Jerusalem, which lasted until 1187, when the Muslim leader Saladin captured the city. This fictional account of a brutal and vicious period of history focuses not only on the conflict between Christian and Muslim armies, but also on the debates over what God's kingdom is like and what God's will requires. The Christian warriors known as the Knights Templar are confident that God will give them victory over the Muslim infidels. The Muslim leader, Saladin, believes that killing a Christian infidel is not murder but the path to heaven. There are Crusaders on both sides of the religious divide who believe that God's will is to destroy the enemy and in so doing bring about the kingdom of heaven.

But Scott offers another perspective, one that is in stark contrast to a kingdom brought about by violence, hatred, and revenge. Viewed through the eyes of Balian, a young French blacksmith who becomes a Christian Crusader, the kingdom of heaven is "a kingdom of conscience or nothing." Balian begins his political life in search of forgiveness for his own past sins by making a pilgrimage to the Holy Land. The peace and reconciliation he seeks in his personal life extends to the kind of kingdom he hopes to see established in Jerusalem. For Balian and some other Crusaders, the hoped for kingdom of heaven (Jerusalem) will be a place where Christians, Muslims, and Jews can live in harmony and peace.

The movie challenges us to examine our perceptions of God's reign. Is it a kingdom of conscience as Balian believed? Is it a territory that can be brought about by human agency, or is it all God's doing? And the film raises another crucial moral issue, that of motivation. Both Muslims and Christians act with complex and mixed motives, fighting for religious convictions, political power, and economic gain. The story summons us to examine our motivations to determine if what we are doing is really God's will or not. The film is a telling reminder of how the images of the gospel can become "evil imaginations of the heart" to those who are dominated by self-serving and egoistic dispositions.

With these questions in mind, we will examine the meaning and relevance of God's reign for the moral life. We begin by identifying some essential characteristics drawn from the words and deeds of Jesus, particularly the parables. We have introduced the parables in chapter 2 in relation to moral vision. But here we consider some stories that help illumine the characteristics and way of life that the reign of God requires. Then we will examine the Sermon on the Mount found in Matthew's Gospel. The sermon is the cornerstone of Jesus' ethical teachings about God's reign, and it provides key aspects of the morally exigent character of the kingdom that Jesus proclaimed. While there are several virtues commended by the sermon, it is permeated by the virtue of hope. In fact, hope is integral to the experience of God's reign. Moreover, without hope, why bother to continue seeking the treasure?

In the third section, we will explore the meaning of this virtue and its significance for the moral life. Finally, we will suggest a way to discern how to live rightly in God's presence by engaging both the analogical and dialectical imaginations. The analogical imagination helps us determine how to be faithful to Jesus' command to "Go and do likewise" (Luke 10:37). And the dialectical imagination helps us to identify and correct negativities of the existing social order that are opposed to the values of the reign of God.

ESSENTIAL CHARACTERISTICS OF GOD'S REIGN

In Hebrew thought, the "kingdom of God" is a biblical term that describes God's active rule or sovereignty in the world and history.[2] This understanding was part of ancient Israel's faith that emerged from the experience of being in covenant relationship with Yahweh and experiencing God's care, protection, love, forgiveness, and compassion. God's saving power is revealed in events such as the liberation from slavery in Egypt, guidance during the period of wandering in the wilderness, the gift of land, and the protection from surrounding nations.

Because of repeated failures of its political and religious leaders, Israel projected its hope in the final and decisive coming of God in the future when God's eternal reign would be established through a Davidic messiah, a priestly ruler, or through direct divine intervention. There is a longing for the Messianic rule, especially in times of need and struggle. The Israelite people dream of a time when the fullness of God's reign will be manifested, when all creation will acknowledge Yahweh as Lord and join in the eternal chorus of praise. When the glory of God is fully revealed, there will be the resurrection of the dead and the last judgment, where the righteous will be vindicated and the wicked punished. All people will live in right relationship with God and with one another. These were the hopes and desires of the Israelite people. Throughout many severe catastrophes that swept over Israel, the current of Messianic ideas and this vision of hope for a better future permeated the Jewish imagination and were stronger than ever during Jesus' life and ministry.[3] With the incursion of God into history in the person of Jesus Christ, a new covenant and a more decisive call was made.

God's Reign Has Arrived

Jesus begins his public ministry with a bold and radical proclamation: "The time is fulfilled, and the kingdom of God is at hand; repent, and believe in the gospel" (Mark 1:15). This passage summarizes the central theme of Jesus' teaching and preaching. It is a declaration with an implicit Messianic claim:

the time of waiting has come to an end, and God's reign has broken into history. The hope for the glory of God to be revealed has been inaugurated. Jesus understood God's reign to be breaking into history through his life and ministry, and he invited his audience to respond appropriately to that fact. This is the main point of Jesus' parables of the treasure in the field and the costly pearl.

> The kingdom of heaven is like treasure hidden in a field, which a man found and covered up; then in his joy he goes and sells all that he has and buys that field. Again, the kingdom of heaven is like a merchant in search of fine pearls, who, on finding one pearl of great value, went and sold all that he had and bought it. (Matt 13:44-46)

Like the kingdom, the treasure and the pearls are found and acquired here and now, not in some future yet to come. And when that treasure is discovered, there is nothing else so important and no joy so great. The parable of the costly pearl suggests that the reign of God is priceless; it can only be attained if we spend all that we have upon it. Thus, it makes sense for the merchant who is sure about the pearl's value to make such an effort to attain it.

But the parable can also expose our lack of dedication to a life of discipleship and the reign of God. Jesus may be important in our lives, but we can also have other allegiances and commitments that compete with a life of discipleship. Does our hesitancy to commit ourselves wholeheartedly mean that we do not value God's reign so highly? Without selling everything, the merchant will not gain the pearl. Are we willing to do the same in our own lives for the sake of the reign of God?

Both parables challenge us to think about how we will respond when we discover the treasure we are seeking. And these parables become terribly unsettling if we let them shock us into new awareness of our own compromises, cowardice, and timidity. On the other hand, the parables are good news, too, for if the man and the merchant could muster the courage to lose all for the sake of the treasure in the field and the fine pearl, maybe we can do the same.

The Lucan parallel to the Markan summary of Jesus' central message about God's reign also makes it clear that it is a present experience and not simply a future hope. As Luke tells the story, Jesus enters the synagogue in Nazareth to announce his mission. Reading from the book of the prophet Isaiah, he says:

> "The Spirit of the Lord is upon me, because he has anointed me to preach good news to the poor. He has sent me to proclaim release to the captives and recovering of sight to the blind, to set at liberty those who are oppressed, to proclaim the acceptable year of the Lord." And he closed the book, and gave it back to the attendant, and sat down; and the eyes of all in

the synagogue were fixed on him. And he began to say to them, "Today this scripture has been fulfilled in your hearing." (Luke 4:16-21)

In this passage, Jesus declares that the justice and liberation Isaiah promised as God's final messianic future is now at work. Something was happening here and now that his audience expected would occur only in an age to come. It is invading the world in every relationship and circumstance of our lives. Jesus is God's envoy, the one who will restore justice and side with the poor and weak against those who oppress them. The whole ministry of Jesus is geared toward promoting justice in the biblical sense of establishing right relationships. For example, the exorcisms and healing miracles demonstrate that God's rule affects all human relationships, and it aims to repair the brokenness of human existence (Matt 12:27; Mark 9:38; Luke 5:12-14).[4]

Jesus stresses that God's rule aims primarily at the restoration of Israel to the covenant ideal. Like the covenant, it is an experience of being in loving relationship with God and one another; and it is characterized by steadfast love, justice, and fidelity, with a concern for the well-being of all people, particularly the weak and needy. God's reign is experienced as the power that can give freedom, wholeness, meaning, and authenticity to our lives.

But it is never presented simply as a private affair between God and the individual. It includes the entire social order because its outreach embraces the whole of reality.[5] Also, like the covenant, the reign of God is a gift gratuitously offered to people that demands a response. As Rudolf Schnackenburg states, "The reign of God is an event that is to occur for people, a good offered to them, a privilege that is also a challenge. It is never something of which they can dispose or that they can compel and insist upon."[6]

God's Reign Is Gift and Task

In his preaching and teaching about God's reign, Jesus emphasizes that it is an unmerited and gracious gift from God, who offers unconditional love and liberation to all. It cannot be brought about simply by faithful adherence to the law, as some rabbis believed. Nor can it be forced into the present by violence, as the Crusaders supposed. As John Fuellenbach states, the kingdom that Jesus preached is God's gift and power, and "its final coming is totally up to God; it will come as God sees fit. It cannot be foretold nor calculated. No human initiative can bring it about, for it is God's own powerful and sovereign act."[7] It is the power of God that enables the "blind to receive their sight and the lame walk, lepers are cleansed and the deaf hear, and the dead are raised up, and the poor have good news preached to them" (Matt 11:4-5). Jesus tells the parable of the sower to help his listeners grasp this reality.

The parable of the sower is a story about a farmer who scatters seed that falls on four different types of ground (Mark 4:3-8). Some seeds fall on rocky ground and, because there is not sufficient depth for them to take root, they wither in the sun. Other seeds fall among thorns that eventually destroy them. But other seeds fall upon good soil and bring forth much grain. Eventually, there is a rich and abundant harvest.

People of Jesus' day would be familiar with the process of plowing and the type of ground on which seed is sown—rocky, among thorns, or on rich soil. And they would be aware of the usual results of planting in one or another type of ground. This story could generate feelings of joy, hope, discouragement, or frustration, depending on one's experience. However, the parable can also lead us to understand something significant about God's presence in the world and about ourselves that we do not immediately perceive or think is applicable.

As Joachim Jeremias explains, the parable presents us with stark contrasts. The beginning of the story describes the many frustrations the farmer experiences, which contrast significantly with the end of the parable when the good soil and the ripening field produce a rich harvest. The "harvest's yield signifies the eschatological abundance of God, surpassing all human measure." It may seem like the farmer is engaged in futile labor, with the newly planted seeds being scorched by the sun and choked by the thorns. But the parable is full of hope and joyful confidence. God's reign will bring with it a harvest of reward beyond all asking and understanding. "In spite of every failure and opposition, God brings from hopeless beginnings the glorious end that has been promised."[8]

The parable of the sower is about the concealed presence of God. It indicates that the future reign draws near, even under difficult conditions. The parable is concerned not with a wholly present or future concept of God's reign, but with that polarity between beginning and end, between sowing and harvest, the time in-between the present and full future revelation of God's glory. Like the rich harvest that the good soil yields, the reign of God is coming by God's power. It will appear in splendor, as surely as harvest time follows the sowing.

The farmer experiences frustration and disappointment when the newly planted seeds are scorched by the sun and choked by the thorns. But he patiently tends to his crops, and then unexpectedly there is abundant harvest. So, too, must disciples lovingly and patiently tend to daily affairs with trust and hope that God will bring the good work to fruition. The growth of God's reign in the world is beyond our understanding or control. Yet, we can recognize its progress and play a part in its flourishing. It is both gift and task.

God's reign is experienced as the power that can give freedom, wholeness, meaning, and authenticity to our lives.

This means that, although the reign of God comes about principally through the love and power of God, it nonetheless requires our active cooperation and contribution in response to God's free gift. Our primary response to the reign of God is shown through gratitude, love, and reverence for God. But Jesus teaches about other ways we are to respond to God's presence in the world. We see this in the parable of the talents (Matt 25:14-30), a story that vividly portrays God's expectation that men and women are to be active agents in furthering the reign of God.

The parable is a story about a rich man who, before setting out on a journey, entrusts to his servants a sum of money according to each one's talents. Two of the servants invested the money and doubled what they had been given. But the servant who had received the one talent went and hid the money in the ground. The two faithful servants who wisely invested the money are rewarded with increased responsibility. But the servant who hid the money in the ground out of fear of losing it, and consequently being punished by his master, was sent away "into the outer darkness; where men will weep and gnash their teeth" (v. 30).

As Joachim Jeremias notes, the parable's emphasis lies on the reckoning with the third servant who acts with an excess of caution. He gives the lame excuse that he made no use of the money entrusted to him because he feared that if he failed in his business transactions, he would incur his master's anger and punishment.[9] Like the servants in the parable, we will have to account for the way we have used the gifts God entrusted to us and the opportunities God made available to us. Have we used our talents on behalf of the reign of God? Have we cooperated with God in working for justice and peace?

The parable of the talents makes very clear that we will be held accountable by God for what we did with the gifts God bestowed on us. Moreover, the whole thrust of Jesus' preaching and ministry indicates that we will be judged especially on how we used our gifts to aid the poor and needy. As discussed above, Jesus began his public ministry by proclaiming his mission to preach good news to the poor, to proclaim release to the captives, recovering sight to the blind, and liberation to the oppressed. That is the work of the reign of God and each of us is called to partake of it.

A Reign of Justice and Inclusiveness

More than anything, Jesus' words and deeds reveal that God's presence in the world is experienced when people are treated with dignity and respect, and when they are given the freedom to participate fully in the community. This is dramatically displayed in the Gospels when Jesus associates with sinners and outcasts, especially when he shares table fellowship with them.

Consider the story about the conduct of those who had been invited to a banquet.

> When you give a dinner or banquet, do not invite your friends or your brothers or your kinsmen or rich neighbors, lest they also invite you in return, and you be repaid. But when you give a feast, invite the poor, the maimed, the lame, the blind, and you will be blessed, because they cannot repay you. You will be repaid at the resurrection of the just. (Luke 14:12-14)

In this parable, Jesus is not teaching about social etiquette but about the character of the reign of God. In the act of kindness to the neglected ones, there is a taste of the fullness of blessedness that is to be perfected at the resurrection of the just. And in inviting not his dearest friends and family members, or his rich neighbors, but "the poor, the maimed, the lame, the blind," the banquet host imitates the character of God. An important insight gleaned from the parable is that Jesus' proclamation of God's reign is not just for a particular people, Israel, but for the Gentiles as well. It is offered to all humankind; it is for all those who fulfill the conditions for entry into the kingdom without regard to origin or status. In this respect, the parable challenges us to widen our circle of love and caring to include all people, especially those who are poor and marginalized by society.

Another story that illustrates this essential characteristic of God's reign is the parable of the sheep and goats (Matt 25:31-46). This is an imaginative scene that reflects Jesus' concern for preparing oneself to enter the reign of God. When the last day arrives, when the Son of Man comes in glory surrounded by all the angels, all the nations will be assembled before him. They will be separated one from another as a shepherd separates sheep from the goats. The sheep will be placed on the right and the goats on the left. Those on the right will be called "blessed" and invited to enter the fullness of God's presence because they fed the hungry, gave them drink, welcomed the stranger, clothed the naked, cared for the sick, and visited the imprisoned. When these acts of love and mercy were done for the poor and needy, they were done also for God. Those on the left, the "cursed" who ignored their hungry and suffering brothers and sisters also ignored God. Just "as you did it not to one of the least of these, you did it not to me" (v. 45). Thus, they will go off to eternal punishment, while the righteous will enter eternal life.

As John Donahue, S.J., points out, the scene of judgment and the separation of the sheep from the goats disclose the transcendent values that should have been operative in the world prior to the judgment, as well as the actions that should have characterized our relationships with others. During the in-between time of the present and future fulfillment of God's rule, we ought to provide food for those who are malnourished and hungry; we ought to

provide housing for the homeless; we ought to care for the sick and welcome the stranger. God's presence will be experienced when acts of mercy
and loving-kindness are shown to those most in need. Indeed, the essence of
faith and discipleship is serving those in need, and the gospel boldly identifies
service to the needy with love for Christ.

Put differently, there is an imperative to act as God acts toward the poor;
and through such actions we not only come to know something of who God is
but also become more faithful disciples of Jesus Christ. In short, we participate
in the reign of God—we truly enter it—by habitually practicing the works of
mercy Jesus describes in the parable of the last judgment. The end time has
been inaugurated by the life and ministry of Jesus. The day of judgment is
already upon us. As disciples of Jesus, we are summoned to live not in light of
the evil of the present world, but in light of the fullness of the reign of God.[10]

In the parables of the banquet and the sheep and the goats, we find both
present and future imagery. What matters in the reign of God is the love,
compassion, and justice extended to all people, especially the poor and needy.
In Jesus' actions, the future of God's reign becomes visible and effective in
the present, and human beings are called to share in it and further it. As John
Fuellenbach states, "The transforming power of God's final intervention is
now breaking into the world."[11] But, as we have stressed, the reign of God that
entered the world in Jesus has not been fully and perfectly realized. It is "here,
but not yet." Thus, it has an eschatological dimension.

The Eschatological Reign of God

When Jesus prays, "Thy kingdom come" (Matt 6:10), he is praying for the
full establishment of something that has already begun but will only be con-
summated in the future. That is to say, the future fulfillment of God's reign
is experienced already, but in an anticipatory and incomplete way. The early
Christians testified to God's presence in their midst, but they were also aware
that God's glory had not yet been fully and perfectly realized. We, too, are
well aware of the violence and poverty that exist in the world, and so many
other calamities that testify that God's reign is not here in all its fullness.
As one humorist expressed it, the lion may lie down with the lamb, but the
lamb is not going to get much sleep. The point is, something of the presence
of a new age is to be found in the midst of the old. In the midst of suffering,
there can be an experience of love and caring, of hope and new possibilities.
In the midst of violence and war, there can be movement toward peace and
reconciliation. Because we are living in the in-between times, we will not
experience the fullness of peace, nor can all our hopes and dreams be completely or perfectly realized. Yet something of the future fulfillment of God's

glory is already operative in this present age. This is what is meant by the eschatological reign of God.

> *God's presence will be experienced when acts of mercy and loving-kindness are shown to those most in need.*

Eschatology provides a vision of how a disciple and the Christian community should understand their lives in the world and their responsibilities to society. An eschatological vision of the reign of God challenges us to do all we can so that our lives together in the world—including the institutions, structures, and practices of societies—better approximate the fullness of the reign of God.

But transforming the world according to the reign of God is not only an always incomplete task but also frustratingly difficult. And that is because even though the new reality of the future reign is already operative in this present age, we live in a world that, despite the prevalence of goodness and grace, is also clearly marred by sin. The ethical question then is determining what is possible in the ambiguous in-between time when "the new is overlapping the old." Human betterment and progress in the world are possible, but these will always be impaired by finitude and sin. Thus, eschatology creates a tension between the present social order and the coming fullness of God's rule. And it is amid this tension that men and women live out their call to discipleship.[12]

Before turning to Matthew's Sermon on the Mount, which provides further guidance for living amid the tension of the in-between times, let us summarize the essential characteristics of God's reign. First, it has been inaugurated by Jesus. It is a present reality and no longer remains only a future hope. Second, the presence of God is both gift and task. As the fulfillment of the covenant, it is God's gratuitous gift to humankind that demands a response. Third, God's reign is a relational reality of justice marked by inclusiveness, with a special concern for the poor and marginalized. Fourth, it is an eschatological reign that has a "here, not yet" quality. God's presence is experienced whenever and wherever there is freedom, wholeness, liberation, and justice, but not fully or completely.

THE SERMON ON THE MOUNT

The Sermon on the Mount in Matthew's Gospel is the keynote of Jesus' ethical teachings that provides guidance for righteous living.[13] It must be seen in the eschatological context discussed above. While the sermon illustrates the radical moral demands God's reign makes on people and calls for new ethical attitudes, it is not simply a perfectionist ethic or an impossible ideal. Rather, it is presented as something Christian disciples can and should put into practice.

The sermon is a motivating and empowering force for people who have opened their hearts to receive God's power and presence. The primary focus of the sermon is not on particular acts of righteousness, but on a way of being and living that gives witness to God's presence in the world. At the core, it calls for new ethical attitudes and "more abundant justice." It requires single-minded devotion to and love of God along with love of neighbor.[14]

The sermon begins with eight beatitudes that call disciples to live their lives in light of the kingdom of heaven (Matt 5:3-12). Each one announces a blessing of participation in God's reign and presents a moral and spiritual challenge. True happiness or blessedness is promised to those who practice righteousness. But the beatitudes call into question much conventional wisdom about happiness and how to achieve it.[15]

The Beatitudes: Blessings for Righteousness

Seeing the crowds, Jesus went up on the mountain, and when he sat down with his disciples, he taught them about the reign of God. The "poor in spirit" are blessed and "will inherit the kingdom of heaven" because they recognize their own poverty in the face of God's greatness and loving care. Their happiness is based not on money and possessions, but rather on dependency upon God. We should be clear that Matthew does not deny that the "poor in spirit" are also the needy ones of Israel. Economic destitution, here as elsewhere in the Bible, is an evil to be corrected.[16] Those who mourn are fortunate because they can acknowledge their own emptiness before God. They will be comforted. The gentle and meek, those who are open to another's perspective and are not manipulative or controlling of others, will inherit the land. Those who hunger and thirst for righteousness, seek justice, and offer forgiveness will be satisfied. The merciful, those who are compassionate and concerned about others, are fortunate because God will show mercy to them. The pure of heart, those who are focused on the good of others without seeking to advance themselves, will see God. The peacemakers, those who seek harmony, cooperation, and justice, are blessed and will be called children of God. And those who suffer persecution because they do what God requires are fortunate because the "kingdom of heaven" belongs to them. They will receive a reward; God will reverse the intolerable situation in which they now find themselves.[17]

Although the beatitudes describe various kinds of individuals who are blessed and the rewards they are promised, righteousness characterizes the conduct that is described in every instance. The kingdom of heaven is the ultimate blessing for those who are righteous.[18] Furthermore, God's reign is nurtured and sustained by those who are dependent upon God's presence and loving care, and those who are merciful and forgiving. And it is the righteous who seek goodness, justice, and peace, and are willing to undergo persecution.

Guidance for Righteous Living

Following the beatitudes, Matthew's Sermon on the Mount offers a series of moral imperatives to help guide the disciple in righteous living (5:21-48). They are presented in the form of antitheses, all with the same pattern, in which Jesus presents his interpretation of certain commands. First, Jesus introduces a portion of the law with a formula such as "you have heard that it was said." Then he introduces his interpretation of the law with a counterstatement, "but I say to you." For example, the commandment not to commit murder includes a prohibition against anger; the command to fulfill one's oaths to the Lord is made superfluous by the call to honesty; and the law of retaliation becomes a call to nonviolence. These antitheses are invitations for disciples to seek the deepest meaning of God's commands in order to produce a more abundant righteousness, not to live simply by the letter of the law.[19] Let us look more closely at a very challenging command: love of enemies.

> You have heard that it was said: "You shall love your neighbor and hate your enemy." But I say to you, Love your enemies and pray for those who persecute you. . . . For if you love those who love you, what reward have you? Do not even the tax collectors do the same? And if you salute only your brethren, what more are you doing than others? Do not even the Gentiles do the same? (vv. 43-47)

Now this does seem like an impossible ideal! Does Jesus really expect us to love the person who spreads lies about us and ruins our reputation? Are we supposed to love the man or women who is abusive or manipulative? Is it realistic to think that the Muslim and Christian Crusaders could love one another? And what about the terrorists who planned and carried out the attacks on the World Trade Center in New York City? Are we expected to love these enemies who perpetrated such violence, and those who continue to plot further terrorist attacks? According to the command to love the enemy, the answer to all these questions is yes. But how are we to do this?

The first step toward loving those people we consider our enemies is to give them the same basic respect that must be afforded to every person. As we discussed in chapter 1, the entry into the moral life is the experience of the value of the other—all others. We are called to view the other as gift, not threat, and to foster attitudes and actions that enhance human welfare. Jesus summons us to greater righteousness by calling us to see even those we consider our enemies as gifts.

This does not mean we have to befriend or live with people who denigrate or dehumanize us. The reign of God is about respecting human dignity. It is the experience of freedom, wholeness, liberation, and justice. So, the command to love the enemy cannot require us to negate these kingdom values. But since all people have an inherent human dignity that deserves respect, then we owe even the enemy that minimum response. This means we ought to wish them no harm. We ought to listen respectfully and seek to understand the other's point of view. And Jesus commands that we pray for the enemy.

Disciples are urged to love their enemies, but are not told exactly what kind of actions in which to engage to reflect this love. As Lisa Sowle Cahill maintains, the sermon requires loving actions, but these actions are not defined in any precise way. The purpose of loving even the enemy is to go beyond merely self-gratifying relationships and to reflect God's mercy and compassionate action. Specific commands such as "turn the other cheek" (Matt 6:39) are not to be taken literally, but rather are examples of righteousness that stand in tension with the usual ways of living and thinking. It is to act as God does, with inclusive forgiveness and mercy.

The Lord's Prayer, which Matthew places within the sermon, especially associates the fullness of the eschatological reign with forgiving as God does (Matt 6:9-13). Being forgiven by God depends on one's forgiveness of the neighbor. The Golden Rule, to do unto others as you would have them do unto you (Matt 7:12), urges us to identify with the other's needs and to act toward them in such a way as we would expect to be treated. As Cahill states, "The morally right act is simply but radically the act that demonstrates the forgiving attentiveness to the needs of others disclosed by Jesus as the will of God."[20]

Forgiveness then is not just a single act, but is indeed a way of life lived in fidelity to God's reign. And like other virtues, forgiveness has to be practiced so that it allows God's gracious love to transform the hatred we may feel in our hearts into mercy and compassion. This does not mean that people who have inflicted harm on others do not deserve just punishment, or that amends do not have to be made for the wrong done to others. But forgiveness, along with justice, is required to achieve the righteousness that the sermon commends. This entails unlearning all those things that divide and destroy relationships and learning to see and live as a people who are forgiven and are forgiving.[21]

Cahill also points out that although the Sermon on the Mount does not suggest a social ethics in any direct way, righteousness does have a social dimension. Individuals are called to conversion in societies whose members have responsibilities to others. The way of life that the sermon acclaims is not brought about in the first instance by sociopolitical transformation, but by a new and transformed heart. Yet, to act righteously is to challenge the societal structures that perpetuate injustice and enshrine exclusiveness.[22] In the life of Dietrich Bonhoeffer, we see both the personal and social dimensions of righteousness, and thus someone whose whole life radiated a resilient commitment to the reign of God.

Dietrich Bonhoeffer: An Example of Righteous Living

Bonhoeffer's life exemplifies the transformative power of the Sermon on the Mount. He believed that the sermon was the core of discipleship and the only power strong enough to make Christianity a vital force against injustice.[23] Moreover, Bonhoeffer did not view the beatitudes as a set of unachievable ideals, but rather as a benchmark of how the disciple should respond to the call of Christ. Following the beatitudes and accepting "costly grace," disciples can become the "salt of the earth" and the "light of the world" (Matt 5:13-16). Bonhoeffer describes the "cheap grace" that occurs when people falsely believe that they are forgiven without repenting and feel assured that God will protect them without following the way of Jesus. These pseudo-disciples proclaim that they are Christians without evidence of it making any difference in their lives.[24]

When most Christians supported Hitler's anti-Semitism and discriminatory policies, Dietrich Bonhoeffer criticized the Nazi leader's claim for absolute authority and his diabolical trampling of basic human rights. Why was Bonhoeffer able to see things more clearly than other Christians? How was he able to act courageously when others were silent? One significant factor is the experience of conversion that the Sermon on the Mount initiated in Bonhoeffer's life. Bonhoeffer's understanding of discipleship prompted him to begin a daily practice of meditating on the sermon.[25] The turning point occurred in 1930 when he was studying at Union Theological Seminary in New York. In a letter to a friend, Bonhoeffer discusses how he was all caught up in ambition, not interested in anything but work. Then something happened, something that changed his life. He describes it this way.

> For the first time I discovered the Bible. . . . I had often preached . . . but I had not yet become a Christian. . . . I had never prayed, or prayed very little. . . . Then the Bible, and in particular the Sermon on the Mount, freed me from all that. Since then, everything changed. . . . It was a great liberation. It became clear to me that the life of a servant of Jesus must belong to the Church, and step-by-step it became plainer to me how far that must go.[26]

Later on, when Bonhoeffer returned to Germany, he became the sole faculty member in an underground theological seminary free from Nazi domination.

With the sermon as guidance for his life, Bonhoeffer protested Nazi anti-Jewish policies, sought opposition to Hitler and the rise of fascism, smuggled Jews out of Germany into Switzerland, and urged the church to act in opposition. Taking the Sermon on the Mount seriously for Bonhoeffer meant love for all people, including the Jews. And it meant taking seriously Jesus' teachings on peace-making, which provided further grounds for opposing Hitler's bellicose and anti-Jewish policies. Bonhoeffer was arrested in 1943 when money used to aid escaping Jews was traced to him. The following year, after a plot to assassinate Hitler failed, he was moved to the concentration camp at Flossenburg, where he was executed on Easter Sunday, April 9, 1945, for conspiracy.

The impact the sermon had on the life of this courageous disciple influenced his vision of the world; it helped him to see the injustices that others overlooked; and it contributed to actions that ultimately led to his death. Most of us will not be involved in such heroic deeds and will not suffer such a death. But the beatitudes and moral imperatives in the sermon do have the potential to transform our minds and hearts so that our words and deeds better reflect the reality of the presence of God in our midst. And this is not a possibility just for Christians: "Mahatma Gandhi, a Hindu, observed that the vision and values contained in the Sermon on the Mount have had significant influence on other cultures, even those that do not at all consider themselves Christian."[27]

In sum, the Sermon on the Mount is essentially about becoming righteous and acting righteously. It presupposes conversion in order to more fully become beatitude people who live in hope of the promised blessings. The hope that is expressed in the beatitudes is for blessings or reward not simply in the afterlife, but in the here and now. However, the beatitudes do reflect the eschatological dimension of God's reign. They presuppose that blessings will occur for the poor in spirit, the merciful, the pure of heart, the gentle and meek, and the peacemakers. Those who suffer persecution will experience liberation. Those who mourn the loss of a loved one will be comforted. When Jesus prays "Thy will be done on earth as it is in heaven," he reveals the promise of the eschatological reign of God. God wills that humankind be blessed, that all creation flourishes, that there is abundant justice for all men and women. But for that to happen, we have to live in hopeful anticipation that love can overcome hate, that peace can replace violence, and that forgiveness can triumph over revenge. But what does it mean to live in hope and to be people of hope?

THE VIRTUE OF HOPE

As a characteristically human endeavor, hope implies a trustful movement toward the future from something negative to something more positive—a movement toward something one does not already possess. For example, a woman undergoes the pains of labor in hopeful anticipation of the new child that will be born. Students suffer through seemingly endless exams in order to receive the diploma that will open doors to graduate school or a desired profession. A young boy leaves his homeland in hopes of finding a buried treasure in the pyramids of Egypt. And disciples seek the reign of God hoping to discover happiness and fullness of life. As Josef Pieper states, from a theological perspective "hope is a reaching out for anything that is perceived as good, and for the anticipated fulfillment that the possession of something good brings."[28]

For Christian disciples, the good we seek is the reign of God. Too, hope is grounded in what Christians believe that God wills men and women to be and to do in order to experience true happiness. Unfortunately, we sometimes misinterpret what God's will is, as did some of the Crusaders in the film *Kingdom of Heaven*. While the specifics have to be determined in concrete situations, what God wills always is a way of living and acting that establishes a person in the stable pursuit of the truly good that is the reign of God. That is what is meant by hoping and praying for the will of God to be done.

Hope is based in the belief that either the present situation or the future can be better. So hopeful people exhibit a certain defiance and courage in pursuing the good. Furthermore, there is a confidence that whatever trials or tribulations one encounters, the good being pursued is worth the struggle. And hope nourishes a feeling of being part of something greater, something more human and lasting. The hoped-for reality must be perceived as attainable within a realm of possible options; otherwise it would be a utopian vision unconnected with reality, something that is not possibly achievable.[29]

The Christian understanding of hope focuses on a future good since we are not yet united with God in the face-to-face vision of eternal life. In this regard, hope is concerned with a difficult good. To desire and to seek the good that is promised as the supreme goal of our existence often involves making difficult choices and taking risks. It requires courage to continue in the face of struggle and humility to rely on God alone for ultimate fulfillment. As Anthony Kelly points out, an eschatologically focused theology refines and inspires hope in two ways. First, eschatology makes clear that hope is not simply an optimistic feeling. Nor is it like apocalyptic predictions that aim to offer detailed knowledge of the future. Hope looks beyond any clear and definite description of the last things to yield to a God "who by the power at work within us is able to accomplish abundantly far more than we can ask or imagine" (Eph 3:20-21).[30] And with this confidence, hope is expressed by patient endurance in the midst of life's struggles and sufferings. We have a glimpse of this view of hope in a poem by an Asian poet entitled "Unfinished Work."

We never finish our work
Here on earth, however good
Everything seems in our lives.
As long as people oppress one another,
Prophets are shouted down,
Statesmen are ignored and pushed aside,
We will calmly do our work.
We will run to get warm,
Sit in the shade to cool down,
And eventually things will get better,
We hope for the best.[31]

The poem expresses hope for a better life, but it does not commend passivity. In the midst of suffering, people work, they run to get warm, and they rest in the shade to cool down. The poem emerges from a hopeful imagination that envisions liberation from the present experience of injustice. It reflects something of the "vision quest" of Asian women who yearn for a "community of harmonious life on earth," where greed, hatred, and all forms of oppression are destroyed. Their hope is based on a remembrance of creation's original wholeness as well as the promise and present experience of God's reign.[32] Their focus is not only, or even primarily, on the injustice and oppression that violates God's reign. Rather, their hope is rooted in those goods that point to what the reign of God is like.

For example, for many Asian people rice is a powerful symbol of life and hope because it is their staple food. Rice means sufficient life, and abundance of rice brings about abundance of life. The struggle for life is like the great effort to obtain rice. As South Korean poet and human rights activist Kim Chi Ha symbolically expresses it, "Rice is heaven."[33] To conceive of rice as heaven is to imagine how good life could be for everyone if they had abundant nourishment. Despite the injustices he has endured, Kim Chi Ha lives in hope because he believes it is possible to create a more just society. He struggles to achieve a difficult but attainable good.

While for Christians Christ is always at the center of hope, how it is experienced and expressed will vary due to the ever-changing human condition and the circumstances of our lives. Consequently, it is necessary to re-imagine Christian hope in every age and context in which people are confronted with despair, loss, or meaninglessness. To remain hopeful in the midst of injustice and to discern how to live rightly in the in-between times of the reign of God requires engaging both the analogical and dialectical imaginations. These are the two "classic" languages of Christian theology.[34] We need to train our eyes to notice those things that Jesus paid attention to and critique those aspects of human experience that are contrary to the values of God's reign. The analogical imagination attends to the similarities or resemblances we see in our world to the reign of God, while the dialectical imagination stresses the differences or contradictions. Thus, we'll conclude this chapter by discussing how we can relate the promise of the coming reign of God both analogically and dialectically to historical forms of human life in the secular world.

ANALOGICAL AND DIALECTICAL IMAGINATIONS

The analogical imagination bridges moral reflection and the words and deeds of Jesus. It provides the cognitive content for obeying the command, "Go and do likewise."[35] If the analogy is a good one, it often conveys meaning better than literal language and tends to be more memorable. That is why to speak of rice as heaven is so meaningful to Asian women. We can understand this importance by analogy when we ask about comparisons, seeking to clarify one thing in terms of another. For example, we come to know something of the love of God by considering personal experiences of love, such as love of parents, spouses, friends, and the beauty of creation. Creativity is required to think analogically because the old and the new situation are both like and unlike each other. In short, there must be a fundamental harmony between the original and the new, but, at the same time, the new is not simply a copy of the old.

We see analogical reasoning at work in the parables that Jesus uses to describe the reign of God. The reign of God is compared to a mustard seed that a person plants in the garden; yeast that is mixed with wheat flour until the whole batch of dough is leavened; a treasure buried in a field; or a merchant searching for fine pearls. The parables help us to know what God's presence is like by comparing one thing in terms of another. We move analogously from the parables of Jesus to our own lives, trying to imagine actions that will be appropriate to a contemporary problem or situation and at the same time remain faithful to the story of Jesus. Engaging the analogical imagination, the new actions will be partly the same, partly different, but basically similar to the relevant portion of the story of Jesus.[36]

While the analogical imagination stresses the similarities in patterns of behavior, the dialectical stresses the differences. Where the analogical imagination begins with experiences of manifestations of God's graciousness and goodness in ordinary life, the dialectical imagination exposes the profound alienation of humanity from God. The dialectical imagination highlights the "not yet" character of human experience, pointing to what is not like God's reign. God's reign is not like the evil desires to murder, slander, or steal that come from the heart (Matt 15:18-20); it is not like the people of little faith

(Matt 17:17-20); it is not like the people who judge others without taking "the log out of their own eye" (Matt 7:1-5); it is not like the Pharisees who held to strict obedience of the Sabbath law while ignoring the hungry and needy (Matt 12:1-14); it is not seeking "an eye for an eye and a tooth for a tooth" (Matt 5:38); it is not hating the enemy (Matt 5:43). And it is not forsaking the poor and oppressed in this life.

The dialectical imagination makes clear the negation of God's reign that is evident when loving kindness, generosity, mercy, forgiveness, and abundant justice are not shown to those who are in need. The film *Kingdom of Heaven* engages the dialectical imagination by contrasting the brutality of some Crusaders with the noble aspirations of Balian. The slaughter of the inhabitants of the Holy Land and the violent means the Crusaders used to destroy the enemy show how far they were from the peaceable kingdom. Their brutal actions were dialectically opposed to the love of enemy that Jesus commends.

Liberation theologians from Africa, Asia, and Latin America, as well as feminist scholars, focus on the social aspects of the dialectical imagination. They argue that racism, sexism, and all forms of oppression embedded in social structures must first be identified and denounced before announcing the good news of God's presence in our midst.[37] In every situation where there is poverty, inequality, and denial of people's basic human rights, the dialectical imagination stands in judgment. And it provokes a crucial ethical question: What liberating actions can be undertaken so the reign of God can be truly "good news," especially for the poor? It is in the experience of liberation from situations of injustice, dehumanization, or marginalization that the power of God's reign can best be understood and lived.[38]

Jürgen Moltmann argues that because of the distorted perceptions we all have, it is necessary to engage both the dialectical and analogical imaginations. To put it in classical terms, we need to employ both the *via positiva* and the *via negativa* to gain fuller understanding of the ethical implications of God's reign. We need some experience in our lives and in our world of likeness to the reign of God in order to have any possibility of knowing it, recognizing it, and promoting it. But we also need to recognize the painful and scandalous difference between so many of the practices of the world and what is envisioned in the reign of God.[39]

As Moltmann points out, there is a danger in a purely analogical way of thinking and knowing, whereby "like is only known by like." When such a pattern of reasoning and imagining dominates, the result is not justice but further fragmentation and division. An example of this is a world of rich for rich, poor for poor, whites for whites, blacks for blacks, Asians for Asians, Hispanics for Hispanics, and all men and women for themselves. Without the revelatory power of the dialectical imagination, we are left with a closed, sterile, and ultimately suffocating society where people mutually endorse one another's thoughts and identify with them to the exclusion of others.[40] Such a society is the antithesis of the reign of God.

Moreover, without the challenge and correction the dialectical imagination provides, the analogical imagination risks leading either to the divinization of human beings or to the humanization of God. When similarities between God and ourselves are emphasized—and the radical differences overlooked—God easily becomes nothing more than a flattering projection of ourselves or a product of our limited imaginations. So we create God in our own image, as male, female, white, or black. Like the beautiful youth Narcissus, wherever we turn—to other people, to nature, or to God—we see nothing more than our own beguiling reflection.[41]

With the dialectical imagination, we creatively seek to achieve unity in diversity, not in uniformity. Disciples are called to witness to the reign of God in our midst by gathering people around the table and inviting everyone without exception to it, by offering hospitality to the stranger, feeding the hungry, healing the sick, and liberating the oppressed. We are called to proclaim the good news in a world of frequent bad news. One very important way to do so is by offering hospitality to the stranger.

Offering Hospitality to the Stranger

As Thomas Ogletree explains, to offer hospitality to the stranger is "to welcome something new, unfamiliar, and unknown into our world."[42] Extending hospitality can mean providing shelter and food to people who may be traveling through an unfamiliar area or environment. They may be refugees or other displaced people who are forced to leave their homeland. Hospitality designates opportunities to discover a world different from our own. Listening to the stories of people from a different land or culture can expand our vision and imagination, for we are invited to view the world from a new perspective. The stranger may challenge or threaten our values and attitudes, but she may also enrich and transform them. This presupposes that we perceive her as an equal, as a person of value who shares our common humanity.

However, there is some inequality of power in the relationship between the vulnerable person who is in a strange place and the one who offers hospitality. The stranger needs our recognition and the service we can provide. We are "at home" in our world; she is in an unfamiliar place and does not know what the future holds in store for her. But this relationship begins to change when we listen to the stranger's stories, for she commands a level of knowledge and authority that enriches and sometimes even surpasses our own. Equal dignity emerges in a concrete way as interactions unfold over time, and as we come to recognize that in some respects she is the expert and we are the novices. The point is that when we extend genuine hospitality to the stranger we must not only welcome the other into our world, but also be willing to enter into hers. As Ogletree states:

> Hospitality to the stranger points toward an ongoing dialectic of host and stranger. It expresses a fundamental recognition of the world's plurality. The point is not that I have no world of my own, or that my world is unworthy of vigorous defense and advocacy. It is that I can have my world in a moral way only as I learn to relate it positively to the contrasting worlds of others.[43]

Those who are different can complement one another, and they can clash. In this way of perceiving, we look at what is different in others, not what is like ourselves, and we try to understand the divergence. Perhaps this means changing something about ourselves—it could be the way we see the world, the attitudes we hold, or our behaviors. In so doing, we are willing to undergo the pains and joys of these changes in order to enter more deeply into the life of the other. Recognizing and appreciating another in his or her difference is the gateway to mutual understanding and to the formation of "community in the diversity and diversity in the community."[44] The dialectical imagination, the "not yet" of God's reign, provides the basis for critiquing the negativities of the existing social order. The analogical imagination provides the basis for hope that something new can happen because it shows us what actions and attitudes reveal God's presence in the world. The eschatological reign of God calls us to continue to hunger for justice, peace, and righteousness and to hope for a "new heaven and a new earth" to be realized in history.

CONCLUSION

Balian, the French blacksmith and Christian Crusader, was right: the reign of God does pose a challenge to conscience. As the law of God written on the heart, conscience is a dynamic quest for the good. The presence of God that is within summons us to create more loving and just personal and social relationships. We are summoned to personal decision and conversion, but not as isolated individuals without responsibilities to others in society. We are responsible for creating a world that better reflects the values of God's reign, to show mercy and loving-kindness, and to render justice to the poor and needy. We are called to reflect God's compassion and forgiveness by loving the enemy.

God wills a way of living and acting that establishes a person in the stable pursuit of the truly human good that is the reign of God. When this happens, there are signs of the kingdom of heaven on earth. Such reflections remind us that the call to discipleship, despite the challenges and hardships it sometimes entails, is always a call to become more human, not less. Put more strongly, if we understand the reign of God we know that God never wills the denial or diminishment of anyone's humanity. The God who created us and everything that lives always calls us to life.

Living amid the tension of the in-between times when God's reign is here, but not yet, requires an ability to discern what is like and what is contrary to God's presence. The glory of God is present in the world, but so is human sinfulness. Personal and social evil have not been totally eradicated. Jesus' proclamation that the "kingdom of God is at hand" is immediately followed in Mark's Gospel by the command to "reform your life and believe in the Gospel." Responding to the call to follow Jesus requires an ongoing process of conversion, turning away from sin, and embracing a life of faithful disciple- ship. The presence and power of God in our midst can bring about a reversal, a reshaping of the self, the community, and the world. Living a converted life means venturing forth on the path of discipleship, one that will be filled with joy, peace, and love, but will also be riddled with pain, struggle, confusion, and marred by sin. In the next chapter, we will examine some manifestations of sin and the process of conversion.

KEY POINTS

1. The eschatological reign of God is the highest good that Christian disciples ought to aim for and to seek.
2. Like the covenant, God's reign is a gift gratuitously offered to people that demands a response. It is both gift and task.
3. Matthew's Sermon on the Mount offers a series of moral imperatives that provide guidance for righteous living.
4. Jesus' words and deeds reveal the values, attitudes, and way of life that is both like and unlike the reign of God.
5. Hope is a central virtue that permeates Jesus' teaching and preaching about the eschatological reign of God.

QUESTIONS FOR REFLECTION

1. Which of the essential characteristics of God's reign is most apparent to you in contemporary society? What aspect seems to be missing or lacking?
2. Do you think that the Sermon on the Mount is too difficult or idealistic? How does it provide guidance for the moral life?
3. Which of the sermon's imperatives do you find most personally challenging?

4. Do you prefer the analogical or the dialectical imagination (or a combination) to discern a fitting response to God's reign? What are your reasons?
5. Why is the virtue of hope central to the reign of God? How can the Christian community be a sign of hope in the world?

SUGGESTIONS FOR FURTHER READING AND STUDY

Bonhoeffer, Dietrich. *The Cost of Discipleship*. New York: MacMillan, 1963.

Braaten, Carl E. *Eschatology and Ethics: Essays on the Theology and Ethics of the Kingdom of God*. Minneapolis: Augsburg, 1974.

Cahill, Lisa Sowle. *Love Your Enemies: Discipleship, Pacifism, and Just War Theory*. Minneapolis: Fortress, 1994.

Fuellenbach, John. *The Kingdom of God: The Message of Jesus Today*. Maryknoll, N.Y.: Orbis Books, 2002.

Harrington, Daniel, S.J., and James Keenan, S.J. *Jesus and Virtue Ethics: Building Bridges between New Testament Studies and Moral Theology*. Lanham, Md.: Sheed & Ward, 2002.

Jeremias, Joachim. *Rediscovering the Parables*. New York: Charles Scribner's Sons, 1966.

Kelly, Anthony. *Eschatology and Hope*. Maryknoll, N.Y.: Orbis Books, 2006.

Moltmann, Jürgen. *God for a Secular Society: The Public Relevance of Theology*. Minneapolis: Fortress, 1999.

Ogletree, Thomas W. *Hospitality to the Stranger: Dimensions of Moral Understanding*. Philadelphia: Fortress, 1985.

Pieper, Josef. *Hope*. Translated by Mary Frances McCarthy, S.N.D. San Francisco: Ignatius, 1986.

Schnackenburg, Rudolf. *God's Rule and Kingdom*. Translated by John Murray. Montreal: Palm, 1963.

Spohn, William C. *Go and Do Likewise: Jesus and Ethics*. New York: Continuum, 1999.

Stassen, Glen H., and David P. Gushee. *Kingdom Ethics: Following Jesus in Contemporary Context*. Downers Grove, Ill.: InterVarsity, 2003.

Viviano, Benedict T., O.P. *The Kingdom of God in History*. Wilmington, Del.: Michael Glazier, 1988.

4

Starting Over Again and Again:
Sin and Conversion in the Christian Life

"Repent, and Believe in the Gospel" (Mark 1:15)

WHO WE ARE NOW is not who we should be. But we cannot by ourselves become the people we ought to be. A fairly depressing assessment perhaps, but that's how Christianity sees us. There is a fundamental goodness to human beings, but we are also wounded, misguided souls with a penchant for mischief and a weary yet predictable talent for losing our way. We are loved and blessed by God, but we cling to behavior that cannot help but harm us. We're desperately in need of healing—in need of rescue and restoration—but remain mired in patterns of self-sabotage and deceit instead of opening ourselves to the love and mercy that can make us whole.

No one knew this better than Heather King, a California writer who "grew up not believing in much of anything," spent twenty years in an alcoholic fog and a string of empty sexual relationships, and became a waitress only because that left her with more time to drink.[1] In *Redeemed: A Spiritual Misfit Stumbles toward God, Marginal Sanity, and the Peace That Passes All Understanding*, King tells the story of her own death and resurrection. For two decades her life was a self-destructive odyssey she did not know how to escape. Spending her days and nights in Boston bars, and often waking up with men she didn't remember meeting, King knew she had to change. But she didn't change. She "stayed stuck for two decades" because, as she writes, "I was in the grip of a compulsion that was stronger than my will to change—so much stronger, in fact, that it almost killed me."[2]

King recognized that she was up against an adversary she was powerless to defeat single-handedly. She knew she was sick and needed to be healed. She knew something was really, really wrong with her—her alcoholic binges, her sexual liaisons, her increased isolation, her wasted talents and gifts—but she could not rescue herself. Her deliverance would come not through her own agency or efforts, and certainly not in some dramatic act of will and steely resolve. Rather, her path back to life would commence when she was willing to claim an identity all of us would prefer to keep hidden—the identity of a sinner in need, the identity of a self lost and broken and defeated. As King recollects, her road to recovery began when she could acknowledge "that I'm a sinner from the ground up—I'd sell my mother's soul for a drink, some sugar, fifteen minutes of sex."[3]

"I'm broken and I need help." Those were words of hope, not despair, for Heather King because they opened her to grace and to the God whose love can work marvelous transformations in ourselves. But we have to risk this openness—this unnerving vulnerability—because we cannot rescue ourselves from the plight in which we find ourselves, and we cannot make ourselves whole. What King discovered about her own deliverance is something that is true for all of us: "I don't have to try harder, I have to resist less."[4] Christianity teaches that there are problems in each of us that cannot be overcome by our own efforts alone. We need to change. We need to abandon attitudes, habits, and behaviors that leave others, as well as ourselves, diminished and depleted. We need radical reversals in the desires we cultivate and the things we pursue if we are not to deprive ourselves of what is best and most promising for our lives. We need a change of heart. We need conversion.

But we cannot be the principal agents of our own restoration. We cannot rescue, redeem, and restore ourselves. Our journey from death back to life requires that we link our lives to a God bold and daring and recklessly loving enough to enter our world, become one of us, and go to work restoring and renewing us. "People in trouble are always the interesting ones," King writes, and those are the people to whom Jesus was relentlessly drawn. Jesus spent much of his time with sinners, misfits, and seasoned reprobates. As the Gospels testify, he was justifiably infamous for sharing meals with people who could not disguise the mistakes they had made, the messes they were in, or the fact that they could not deliver themselves. And, as one whose life for twenty years had been a nightmare of self-inflicted abuse, King could not disguise the darkness in which she had entrapped herself. Her deliverance began when she found a group to support her in her decision not to drink, when she encountered a priest who told her, precisely at the moment when she felt most lost and confused, "You're very dear to God," and when she decided to give Jesus a try. As she wrote: "A guy who hung out with lepers, paralytics, the possessed: this is someone I can trust."[5]

King's *Redeemed* is a story of conversion, a story of a woman whose self-destructive ways finally convinced her that she was damaged and broken in ways she could not fix. It is a profoundly Christian story because Christianity teaches that there is something fundamentally wrong with ourselves and our world—something radically awry—that needs to be made right. Christians call this defilement, this inescapable defect, and all the misery that flows from it, sin. Sin is the abyss in which we place ourselves through actions that increasingly distance us from the good. Sin names the attitudes, perceptions, practices, and behaviors that make us strangers to happiness and our lives together bleak.

In Jesus God entered our world and became one of us to rescue us from the prickly entanglements of sin and to help us turn from sin to life. That is the trajectory of the Christian life, a trajectory from darkness to light, a trajectory from the dissipating powers of sin to the restorative powers of goodness and grace, a trajectory (as the story of Heather King illustrates) from death back to life. We cannot make the journey from sin to life apart from Christ not only because Christ alone can deliver us from sin, but also because our true self is found not in the illusory autonomy of sin, but in faithful discipleship with Christ.

To be a Christian is to answer the gospel's call to repentance and conversion; indeed, the Christian life *is* a life of ongoing and forever incomplete repentance and conversion. But we can pursue such a life only as disciples to Christ, as men and women whose lives together are marked by continual openness, deepening surrender, and resilient commitment to Jesus, his proclamation, and his mission.

In this chapter we'll explore the trajectory of the Christian life by looking first at a Christian understanding of sin, investigating not only what sin is, but also why it is both hopelessly destructive and remarkably foolish. We will examine different manifestations of sin, how we assess our responsibility for sin, and why it is we are ineluctably prone to sin in the first place. Second, we'll consider conversion. If conversion signals a fundamental redirection of one's life, what initiates such a full-fledged change of one's self? What does genuine conversion involve? And are there different kinds of conversion? Finally, we will reflect on the meaning and importance of faith, a virtue we considered in chapter 1 but that deserves further consideration here because of its close association in the Christian life with conversion. We will think about what is involved when we say "I believe" and why for Christians faith is intimately connected to Christ and a life of discipleship. Moreover, we shall discover that the object of conversion concerns not only our own well-being but the welfare of the world as well. This is why a conversion to Christ is always simultaneously a conversion to our neighbors, especially those in greatest need. In the words of Heather King, the objective of conversion is "to get in good enough shape so I can help someone else."[6]

SIN

In *God, Christ and Us,* English theologian Herbert McCabe says something at least mildly startling that should guide our analysis of sin: "The gospel is not about being good; it is about being rescued. It is not about being safe; it is about being saved."[7] His point is that the enduring focus of the Gospels is not on the moral achievements (or failures) of human beings but on the abiding love, mercy, and forgiveness of God that, as the death of Jesus testifies, works to overcome all that we do to separate ourselves from God. The Christian story begins not with a word about sin but with God's abundant and extravagant love for us. This has to be at the forefront of any analysis of sin.

The central message of the Gospels—and the core of Christianity—is that God is in love with us and, like any great lover, God wants what is best for us and works to make it happen. In fact, McCabe elaborates, "God loves his human creatures so much that he wants them to be, not only happy, flourishing, fulfilled human beings, but living in his friendship, sharing his own divine life."[8] The first truth about us then is not that we can be greedy, selfish, malicious creatures who know well how to bring chaos and misery into the lives of others and into our world. The first truth about us is that we are loved and cherished by a God who wants to share life with us, a God who wants nothing less than an intimate communion of friendship with us. This is why God can never be content with or indifferent to the estrangement effected by sin. It is why in the Christian story sin does not conquer, love does. And it is why in Jesus we encounter a God whose love, mercy, and forbearance are greater than even our most lamentable misdeeds.

Sin is real and horrible. Sin is toxic and virulent. Sin thwarts life and promotes death. But sin, for all its pervasiveness, pales before the love and goodness of God. As Servais Pinckaers observes, in the Gospels "it is never sin, but always grace, the proclamation of God's mercy, that predominates,"[9] and that is why even amid our failures we can live in hope. Sin may be a common fact in the world, and a fearfully destructive one, but it is neither the first nor the last word about life. That belongs to the language of love, the language of grace and forgiveness. Thus, for Christians the proper starting point and context for talking about sin is God's love and forgiveness, Jesus' ministry of reconciliation, and the gospel's summons to repentance and conversion.[10]

Christians do not soft-pedal sin. Rather, they locate sin in a narrative that proclaims that in God we discover that ultimate power belongs, not to sin and darkness and death, not to defeat and viciousness and annihilation, but to grace, love, mercy, and forgiveness. As the Irish theologian Vincent MacNamara says, "The ground of our being is mercy and love."[11] Or as Paul famously observed when writing to the Christian community in Rome, no matter how much sin might increase, grace will always surpass it (Rom 5:20). And the reason is that in the death and resurrection of Jesus, God has already defeated sin. Sin may be prevalent—and sometimes may seem to be stronger than goodness and mercy and love—but the cross testifies that in the death and resurrection of Jesus the stranglehold of sin was broken.

This is why Christian reflection on sin properly begins at the foot of the cross. There we see the horror and sorrow of sin, but also the unbreakable hope from which we live. At the foot of the cross, a narrative of sin and despair becomes, thanks to love, a narrative of hope and redemption. This is why "no genuinely Christian reflection on the reality of sin can even begin without at least an implicit recognition that the power of sin over the world has been shattered by the life, death, and resurrection of Jesus Christ."[12] Put differently, Christians cannot think properly about sin without simultaneously thinking about the priority of the grace, mercy, and love that frees us from sin. For Christians, sin presumes the forgiveness that enables us to live in hope.

How Should We Talk about Sin?

Today the language of sin can seem quaint and archaic, a relic from a less enlightened age. Indeed, many of us live in societies that have expunged sin from their cultural vocabulary. We speak of crimes and misdemeanors, of wrongs and transgressions, of mistakes and failures. But seldom do we hear people explain their misdeeds in the language of sin. That may be because sin is a religious concept that is intelligible only if we see ourselves as creatures given life by God and who cannot live apart from God. Many people no longer view their lives that way. They may see a relationship with God as a possible option, but not as a requirement of our nature. They are more likely to think of themselves as independent, autonomous beings that may choose to enter into relationship with God. But they would not see being dependent and indebted to a Being apart from whom we cannot live as the most illuminating truth about us.

But Christianity does. Christianity holds that men and women are inherently religious beings—creatures fashioned from the love and goodness of God—who find happiness and fulfillment only in God. It teaches that we thrive and flourish as persons not when we separate ourselves from God, the only genuine source of life, but when we acknowledge our absolute dependence on God and live in friendship with God. The language of sin can only rightly be spoken by someone who believes that the most fundamental and inviolable truth of our nature is that we are made for God and can live only by participating in the life and love and goodness of God. This is why, for Christians, sin never makes sense, and why no matter how familiar we may become with sin, it is never something good for us. Sin can never be embraced as a truly life-giving option because it rejects the very thing that constitutes us as persons. To enter a life of sin is to step outside of the relationship that gives us life. It is to disavow the core truth of our

> *The gospel is not about being good; it is about being rescued. It is not about being safe; it is about being saved.*

existence, namely, that we are creatures made in the image and likeness of God who find life only in fellowship and communion with God and one another.

It is not surprising then that the Bible depicts sin not primarily as the breaking of a law but as the violation of a relationship.[13] The dominant biblical view of sin sees it, not in juridical terms, but as a weakening of the covenant that Israel had with God. The covenant established a special relationship between God and Israel, a relationship rooted in love and marked by affection, but one that also carried certain obligations and responsibilities. If God loved and was faithful to Israel, the Israelites were to show their love and faithfulness to God by observing the commandments through which they could abide in harmonious relationship with God and with one another. From this perspective, sin involved less the breaking of a law and more the betrayal of a relationship. Put differently, if we think of the Ten Commandments as the habits and practices that enabled the Israelites to live in covenant life with God and one another, then the essence of sin lay not in violating the law but in violating the relationship to which God had called them.

As Richard Gula writes, "Sin in the Bible is not merely breaking a law. Sin is breaking or weakening the God-given bond of love."[14] The commandments established the terms of the covenant and the conditions that made covenant life with God and others possible. Consequently, to neglect, ignore, or break the commandments was not only to weaken one's relationship with God and others in the covenant community but also to spurn the love that was the foundation of the covenant. In more contemporary language, to sin is to weaken, betray, or even rupture the friendship with God to which we are called—a friendship that is meant to be the heart and center of our lives.[15]

There are other ways that the Bible talks about sin. It sometimes speaks of sin as an act that "misses the mark" (*hamartia*) in the way that an archer's wayward arrow misses the target—or that we miss opportunities to do what is good and to avoid what is evil.[16] It also describes sin in terms of injustice (*adikia*), whether expressed in neglect of others (particularly the poor), selfishness and greed, lying and deceit, or coldness and indifference. In each instance we shirk the obligations we have toward others because we make ourselves sovereign and our own needs supreme. In this respect, sin reflects the dismaying human tendency to put ourselves first, to turn in on ourselves and away from others, and eventually to "cease to pay attention to, or care about, anyone outside ourselves."[17]

Seen through the lens of injustice, sin nurtures the self-absorption by which we grow increasingly oblivious to the needs of others and indifferent to their well-being. The Bible also presents sin as lawlessness (*anomia*) and rebellion. And it sees sin not only in our actions but also in our hearts. Disordered actions flow from disordered and conflicted hearts. If we think of the heart as the very core of a person, then our sinful acts reveal something wrong in the center of our being, something fearfully amiss deep down within us.[18] This is why the Bible exposes sin not only as an external transgression but also as a debilitating quality of soul or a perverse quality of character. Sin may be revealed in our actions, but it is rooted in our hearts.

Besides presenting sin as an act and as a description of a person's character, the Bible also depicts sin "as a universal human condition, a pervasive and tragic fact of our creaturely existence" that no one escapes.[19] As Psalm 51 memorably states, we are flawed and broken from birth, turned toward sin before we've uttered our first breath. Indeed, even in our mother's womb we are marked by sin and cannot escape its dominion by ourselves. What we need is a "clean heart" and a renewed spirit, but the malignancy of sin runs deep and is so much part of the fabric of our being that we cannot give that new heart to ourselves.

Finally, the Bible depicts sin as a hostile, malevolent power that opposes God, is hostile to human well-being, and seeks dominion over us and our world. Sin is in us, but it also surrounds us and is more powerful than we are. Sin wants to defeat us; indeed, since sin brings death, its ultimate aim is to destroy us. Kevin O'Shea provides a graphic description of this final dimension of sin when he speaks of it as "a virus of evil" that "dynamically unfolds itself and tightens its grip on humanity and on the world in an escalating fashion down the ages of history."[20]

Some Initial Conclusions about Sin

How then should we understand sin? First, perhaps sin can best be understood as any thoughts, attitudes, actions, habits, and ways of being that reflect an egregious misunderstanding of who we are. Sin is rooted in a false estimation of who we are—really, it is a case of mistaken identity—because every sin manifests a refusal to accept who we truly are, not gods and sovereigns, but creatures. Every sin sustains this false identity because to sin is to attempt to free ourselves from our dependency on God and one another. To sin is to strike out on one's own; it is, as an act of futile rebellion, an attempt to flourish and succeed without God.

This is vividly demonstrated in the story of the first human couple. As recounted in the Book of Genesis, God gave the first human couple everything they could possibly need. Brought to life in a world that was emphatically good, there was no reason for them to be discontent because in a paradise of delights nothing was missing and nothing was amiss. But paradise wasn't enough for them. Resenting that they were creatures and not gods, they rebelled against God, and from that single act of defiance evil and death entered the world and paradise was lost.

The story of the first couple's rebellion reminds us that all sin begins in deception. To sin is to fall for the lie. Adam and Eve fell for the serpent's lie when it told them that if they ate the forbidden fruit they would not die, as God declared, but would become gods (Gen 3:5). They let themselves be deceived because they were seduced by the serpent's retort that they need not remain creatures, but could become the equal of the Creator. Thus, humanity's first false step on the path to happiness occurred when they tried to live apart from the very relationship that gave them life.

But it really is no different for us. The sin of the first human couple gets replayed throughout our lives when we, like them, think things will go better for us apart from God. The first couple's temptation is the human temptation. We assert ourselves against God (as well as against one another) and live not as we truly are (dependent, limited, and needy creatures), but as if we were the center of everything. This is one reason pride has often been called the root of sin. Adam and Eve disobeyed God because they believed they knew best what was truly good for them. Not wanting to be subject to God, they envisioned themselves as equal to God, even rivals to God.

Today, however, some theologians—particularly feminist, Hispanic, and Latin American theologians—question the claim that pride is always the root of sin. Feminist theologians suggest that for many women not pride but a lack of proper self-respect and healthy love for self is the basis for sin. Similarly, Ishmael Garcia argues that, while pride may be the root of sin for oppressors, for people who are oppressed it is much more likely that sin is expressed by too readily accepting the status of victim and too regularly adapting to the unjust situations in which one finds oneself. For many of the poor of the world, sin begins not in pride but in a failure to abjure the injustices inflicted upon them and in accepting the oppressor's assessment of themselves as being without worth and dignity. As Garcia writes, "Within oppressed groups, sin manifests itself through decisions to adapt, justify, and contribute to the perpetuation of those practices and structures that keep them in a state of oppression. If the powerful value themselves more than they are entitled to, the poor tend to engage in self-deprecation and self-hatred." He explains further, "They sin when they adapt to the paternalism their oppressors exercise over them, and conform themselves to the few menial activities they are entrusted with, that is, when they make oppression agreeable and part of God's will for humanity." In short, "To choose to remain silent when we are abused is a sin; not to struggle to avoid the many pains that are part of it is a sin. It makes us alien to God's will and perpetuates our mutual dehumanization, that is, the dehumanization of ourselves and of our oppressors."[21]

Second, in addition to expressing a grievous misunderstanding of who we are, sin also displays a costly misunderstanding of what constitutes a good and happy life. Theologian William Mattison suggests that sin "impedes our ability to live truly happy lives. It manifests a false estimation of how to live a good life."[22] This is exactly what the life of Heather King prior to her conversion illustrates. As King's narrative testifies, often when we sin we do not seek to do harm; rather, we pursue something that we (mistakenly) judge to be good. Or we seek good things but in the wrong ways. For instance, to be ambitious and to strive to succeed in life is good. We should use our gifts and talents to accomplish important goals for our lives. But if we are so driven by ambition that we begin to treat others unfairly, or lie and cheat to get ahead, then we allow our thirst for success to matter more than justice and truthfulness.

Similarly, money and material possessions are necessary for a good life, but they are not the purpose of life. If I allow them to become the overriding desire of my life, I am likely to become greedy and unmindful of others. Thus, sin typically reflects disordered loves and desires. I give some things disproportionate attention in my life while ignoring other more important matters. I cultivate attractions for things that are obviously enjoyable (sports, movies, television), but at the expense of goods that matter so much more (friendship, availability to others, time for reflection, prayer). Herbert McCabe summarizes well this very typical way that sin plays out in our lives:

> I am talking about real sin in the proper sense, which is to choose some perfectly genuine but minor good of this life, like wealth, at the expense of really important goods, like being just or faithful or compassionate. Sin lies in desiring the minor good and failing to desire the great good. When we sin we are not necessarily lusting after evil. But we are always failing to be passionate enough about the things that really matter to us. Real sin is to act in ways that amount to rejecting the whole idea that what matters above all in human life is charity. It is to seek what we want by opting out of the Kingdom of God (the kingdom of charity), for the sake of a trivial good.[23]

Third, sin is inherently self-defeating. There is an essential absurdity to sin because to embrace sin is to live and act in ways that violate the very meaning of our being. There may be some pleasure in sin (sin would not lure us if it were not in some way enticing), but there is never logic or real happiness because when we sin, we freely and deliberately assent to our own demise. In other words, when we sin we not only damage others, but also surely damage ourselves. Josef Pieper captures the baffling self-sabotage at the heart of every sin when he asks: "How could a human being possibly and with full deliberateness undertake an act of resistance to the very meaning of his own existence?"[24] But we do it all the time and often quite skillfully.

There is an essential craziness to sin, because to sin, as Heather King's conversion story dramatically demonstrates, is to become actively involved in our own destruction. Sin never makes sense because it represents a way of being that frustrates our growth and fulfillment as persons. Sin doesn't give, it always takes, and it takes by stealing life from us a little bit at a time. Sin doesn't affirm, it only negates and denies by leaving us further and further estranged from the very habits, activities, and ways of being that bring happiness. This is why sin, left unchecked, bottoms out in despair.[25] Russell Connors and Patrick McCormick offer a poignant account of the debilitating effects of sin on us:

> Instead of setting persons and communities free, sin distorts and crushes the lives of sinners, enslaves their wills, hardens their hearts, and darkens their intellects. Not just an act of defiance against God or even a rejection of the call to love one another, sin is fundamentally an act of self-annihilation, a rejection of the vocation to become fully human persons, resulting in the ultimate crippling of the sinners.[26]

When we sin we are cruel to ourselves.[27] This is why Catholic theology has traditionally spoken of sin as both "contrary to nature" (*contra naturam*) and "contrary to reason" (*contra rationem*). Sin is contrary to nature because human beings are fulfilled in goodness and love, in justice and generosity, in virtuous acts such as forgiveness and hospitality, and not in envy, greed, lust, or bitterness. Most seriously, sin is contrary to nature—and thus truly against our best interest—because with sin we increasingly distance ourselves from the God whose love and friendship is our happiness.

When we sin we violate the deepest inclinations and needs of our nature because we say no to the very things that are good for us. We say no to self-giving love. We say no to honesty and truthfulness. We say no to lives of faithfulness and responsibility. We say no to justice and compassion. With sin we are forever saying no to what is best for us, and in this respect are habitually willing our non-being.[28] This is one reason sin alienates us not only from God and from other persons but also from ourselves. And it is why sin brings never contentment and peace but only further discontent and dissatisfaction.

Likewise, sin is contrary to reason because it is thoroughly irrational to live and act in ways that diminish our freedom, bring chaos to our lives, our relationships, and our world, and eradicate our integrity. And it is thoroughly irrational to live and act in ways that turn us away from God, the very one whose goodness and love will complete us. This is why "we can never sin with the unreserved power of our will, never without an inner reservation, never with one's whole heart."[29]

We cannot sin *wholeheartedly* because even in the depths of self-deception we inwardly know that what we are about to do will only cause us harm. The liar cannot be completely at ease with lying because no matter how seasoned she is at lying, she knows with every lie she is making it impossible for people to trust her. The man who commits adultery cannot celebrate his feats because he knows (even if his spouse never discovers his unfaithfulness) that he has become the sort of person who will not allow faithfulness to a promise to supersede sexual pleasures. How could such a man ever really love himself? How could he truly want his good? In exchange for a fleeting relationship, a relationship that must remain hidden and secret, he destroys the truly promising good of his life. These examples demonstrate that although sin victimizes others, it is equally true that with sin we make victims of ourselves by denying ourselves the very things that make for a genuinely good human life.

Fourth, our reflections on sin have underscored that although sin may be intensely personal, it is hardly private. What we do hurts others. Put differently, there is a *transcendent* dimension to sin because sin affects our relationship with God; but there is also an *immanent* dimension to sin that is seen in the ways that sin damages our relationships with others, our communities, and our societies.[30] We can appreciate the relational dimension of sin when we consider how gossip not only weakens relationships, but also diminishes the trust necessary for good relationships and for healthy community living. The same is true for lying, dishonesty, or any kind of deceit. Similarly, sins such as pride and greed put the egoistic needs and desires of the self above anyone else, and thus sow seeds of injustice by neglecting the common good. Thus, even though sin is principally an act against God, its immediate target is nearly always another human being. When we turn away from God, we inevitably turn against one another.

In recent decades theologians have given more extensive attention to the immanent dimension of sin by exploring how sin impacts, not only the most immediate relationships of our lives, but also the structures, institutions, and practices of our societies as well. This corporate manifestation of sin is typically referred to as *social sin*, a term that emerged out of the liberation theologies of Latin America, particularly after the 1968 Medellín conference in Colombia. To speak of social sin is to protest an overly individualistic or privatized notion of sin, as if the repercussions of sin hardly trickled beyond ourselves. It is also to affirm that Jesus' proclamation of the reign of God called not only for personal conversion but also for a radically transformed social order characterized by justice. Social sin opens our eyes to how the decisions we make and the practices we adopt can contribute to social and economic practices that are unjust.

In the past there was too often a tendency to narrow the focus of sin to strictly personal behavior. If people went to church, were faithful in their marriages, and kept the law, they were deemed morally upright. However, such a restricted understanding of sin not only made it easy to overlook the social reality of sin, but also made it easy not to feel any responsibility for changing it.[31] This privatized understanding of morality failed to acknowledge that the faithful churchgoer and dutiful spouse often lived—and flourished—in societies whose economic and social practices facilitated the prosperity of the fortunate while neglecting and ignoring the rights and needs of the poor.

Social sin is manifested in structures, policies, and practices that privilege the prosperous at the expense of the poor. Social sin is at work in laws, social structures, and economic systems that embody and promote "the narrow self-interest of individuals and power groups within a society," while violating the rights of those on the margins of society.[32] Simply put, social sin is the institutionalized injustice that allows some to prosper at the inordinate expense of others. What makes this even more nefarious is that such blatantly immoral practices are typically both legally protected and socially accepted.[33]

Broadly speaking, social sin refers to "the injustices and dehumanizing trends built into the various institutions" of society.[34] We see social sin at work in tax policies that favor the already too wealthy over the middle class and poor. We see it in practices specifically designed to protect the interests of the powerful and in institutions and policies that violate human rights and victimize the oppressed. Social sin is institutionalized injustice. Examples of it abound in racism, sexism, clericalism, militarism, chronic poverty and destitution, and unjust war.

Today a growing number of people add ecological degradation to the list of social sins. If sin is behavior that unjustly harms, then we must recognize sin in habits of consumption that deplete natural resources and harm the earth. If sin brings disorder to relationships and communities, then surely many of the habits and practices of our societies have brought disorder to the habitats of other species. And if sin is rooted in disregard for the needs and well-being of others, it is clear that making human needs and desires supreme has resulted in unjust behavior not only to future generations but also to other creatures and species and to the earth itself.

Despite the pervasiveness of social sin, it is notoriously difficult to overcome, first because too many people benefit from it (even though many more suffer from it), and second because no single person is responsible for it. Those who benefit from it will do what they can to keep the existing structures, policies, and practices in place. They are unlikely to work to change unjust social practices not only because they prosper from them, but also because they are typically far removed from the harmful effects these practices have on others. What might crush and oppress others can seem not only benign but also perfectly proper to them because they have distanced themselves from the consequences that social sin has on those whom such policies disadvantage or exclude. But even when we recognize the injustice wrought by social sin, it is hard to undo because social sin points to "a surplus of evil beyond what can be ascribed to individuals." Social sin precedes us, shapes us, surrounds us, and surpasses us. Even though it is the result of human decisions, the cumulative effects of those decisions cannot be traced to any single individual.[35]

Nevertheless, the complex nature of social sin does not free us of responsibility. We may not have initiated the institutions, structures, and practices that perpetuate injustice, but as social beings—and morally responsible ones—we are implicated in them and, therefore, cannot be absolved of responsibility for them.[36] I may not have created a particular social injustice, but I can profit from it and collaborate with it. I can work to protect it from being exposed, and I can even work to increase it. And even if I do not actively sustain it, I may do nothing to expose and denounce it, and thus remain an accomplice in its existence.

Social sin may be bigger than any one of us, but it is the work of human hands. We add to this surplus of evil when we cooperate with sinful structures, work to sustain them, or fail to speak out against them. We are morally culpable for social sin because even though none of us single-handedly creates the world's injustice, we often contribute to its increase in our societies, in the workplace, and in our churches. Even though no one of us is solely accountable for the evil of the world, we are nonetheless, to some degree, responsible for it either through actions that reinforce it or through the silent indifference that fails to challenge it. "Even if we are not the persons or generation who created and developed these unjust policies and structures," Connors and McCormick write, "we are certainly the ones who maintain and cooperate with them. And while it is certainly true that we have been born into a world already governed and influenced by unjust social systems, . . . it is also true that these injustices, embedded as they are in our world and our hearts, could not continue to exist without some help from us."[37]

Categories of Sin

Thus far we have described sin and explored some of the effects of sin on ourselves, on others, and on societies and our world; however, we have not distinguished between different kinds of sin or levels of sin. All sin is wrong, but all sins are not equally serious. It takes little thought to know that there is a substantial moral difference between a single lie and a lifetime of falsehood and deceit. Similarly, no one would put a momentary act of selfishness on the same level as habitual indifference to others. We all sin, but we may not all sin grievously. This is why traditionally theologians have distinguished between *venial* sins and *mortal* sins. Venial sins refer to acts that fall short of the good, and indeed are wrong, but they are not grievously wrong. If we recall that every sin harms our relationship with God and with others, venial sin strains those relationships, while mortal sin ruptures them.[38]

What accounts for the difference? First, the object of venial sin does not involve serious evil but something of lesser account. For instance, an act of thoughtlessness toward a spouse is wrong, but it certainly lacks the moral significance of adultery or abuse. Second, we are less fully invested in acts of venial sin. They are failures, but smaller failures that do not deeply engage us and do not represent who we want to be.[39] With venial sin, I recognize my act of thoughtlessness, but I don't endorse it; rather, I immediately regret the act and do not intend to repeat it because I do not want to become that sort of person. This is why Richard Gula says that "venial sin is acting inconsistently with our basic commitment to be for life and love. Venial sin does not spring from the deepest level of our knowledge and freedom so as to change our fundamental commitment to be open to God, others, and the world."[40]

With venial sin it is not so much that we deliberately embrace evil, but rather that we fall short of who we want to be. We want to be considerate of others, but sometimes we aren't. We want to be generous, but occasionally we are selfish. We want to be patient with the shortcomings of others, but now and then we are not. When we sin venially we miss opportunities for growth in goodness, thoughtfulness, generosity, and love. We "miss the mark" of what we genuinely want to achieve in our lives. Harm results from venial sins as people are hurt, disappointed, and let down, but typically the harm is slight and its effects short-lived precisely because we do not want such behavior to become a permanent part of ourselves.

Nonetheless, it would be wrong to be overly casual about venial sins—first because that could signal a complacency that is dangerous in the moral life, and second because indifference to the lesser transgressions of our lives makes it more likely that we will develop them into habits. A single outburst of anger is not serious, but exploding every time someone irritates us or a situation frustrates us is. The path to more serious sin is typically the result of becoming lax about the more ordinary failures of our lives. Not trying to grow in the moral life, failing to do the good I can do, and too readily accepting my imperfections lessens my sensitivity for the good, weakens my sense of responsibility toward others, and makes me much more comfortable with wrongs I think I want to avoid.[41]

Some sins, however, are not only regrettable; they are lethal.[42] As the word suggests, *mortal* sin refers to actions, habits, and ways of being that bring death to our relationship with God, death to our relationships with others, and death to our own souls and spirits. There are some acts, but especially habits and ways of being, whose cumulative effects are so morally and spiritually corrupting that they permanently separate us from our true good and turn us toward evil as if it were our good. Mortal sin reminds us to take evil seriously. It calls our attention to habits of being and acting that are toxic for our souls. And it reminds us that if we give ourselves over to evil, it will ruin us.

At its most extreme, to settle into a state of deadly sin is to be so habitually given over to evil that it is difficult for us not to do what is wrong. It is not that we have completely lost our freedom to sin, but that we have so consistently misused it that we cannot, without grace, redirect it to the good. To speak of mortal or deadly sin is to recognize that we can live "contrary to nature" or "contrary to reason" for so long that from the innermost center of our lives, we regularly choose evil over good exactly because evil has become our good. As Vincent MacNamara reflects, "We must be talking then about someone who is attached to wrongness in the depths of the heart, who has, so to speak, settled for it."[43] As MacNamara intimates, the real danger of mortal sin occurs when we have so regularly embraced corrupting choices and actions that we no longer realize their destructiveness.

Traditionally, three things are required for a sin to be mortal. First, the sin must involve a grave matter, something truly seriously evil that will result in serious harm. Second, the sin must be done with full knowledge and understanding of its evil; in short, a person must clearly understand the seriousness of what he or she is about to do. And third, it must be done with full consent; in other words, it must be fully and deliberately embraced. But in practice the three criteria were often not weighed equally. In determining whether a sin was mortal or not, the dominant focus was on the gravity of the act itself and not on the degree of understanding or consent of the person. Consequently, certain acts in themselves were viewed as mortally sinful irrespective of the number of times they were committed, how much they truly reflected a person's life and character, or how fully invested a person was in the act.

The benefit of this approach was that it underscored the damage and harm involved in certain acts regardless of how well an individual grasped the gravity of what he or she was about to do. On the other hand, by focusing so exclusively on the act itself apart from the person, one could in theory commit mortal sins rather frequently. Moreover, such an act-centered morality led to a legalistic and individualistic understanding of sin in which the focus was not on the good one ought to do but on how easy it was to sin lethally.

Recent accounts of mortal sin have tried to address this imbalance by focusing, not as much on the gravity of the act, but on how fully committed a person is to the harm she is about to do and how adequately she understands it. Too, does the act accurately reflect the overall direction of her life? Is it a true portrayal of her character? Is she engaged with evil in such a radical way that it definitely has had deathly consequences for her relationship with God, her relationship with others, and her own soul?

In reacting against an approach to mortal sin that placed primary emphasis on the act, many theologians began to give more attention to the agent. In this respect, the key criterion becomes whether the evil done flows from the core of a person and expresses the kind of person he or she wants to become. For these theologians, to sin mortally is to make a clear choice—a *fundamental option*—for evil. Bernard Haring, for example, argued "that there can be no mortal sin without a fundamental option or intention that turns one's basic freedom towards evil."[44] For Haring and others, mortal sin requires that we consciously intend to direct our lives away from God and the good to evil, inasmuch as through such a decision or series of decisions we opt to make ourselves and our needs primary, irrespective of the cost to others. We choose to live lives that are unloving, selfish, and void of compassion. We choose to harden our hearts, to be cold and uncaring, and to do evil whenever it suits our purposes.

Moreover, in this view to sin mortally requires that we intend such a fundamental orientation of our lives to endure so that we remain permanently disposed to wrong, and so that such a disposition pervades all of our choices and actions. With such an understanding, people can sin mortally only if they are fully and completely engaged with what they do. And they can sin mortally only if, through their actions, they truly intend to be permanently alienated from God. In light of these qualifications, many theologians today think of mortal sin not so much as a single act but as an enduring way of being. Reflecting this view, Connors and McCormick write:

> All of this suggests that in its fullest sense, wickedness and mortal sin actually refer to a fundamental option against God, a decision to reject God, not just in this act or moment, not merely in this habit or area of our lives, but with our whole being. Indeed, wickedness and mortal sin are better understood as decisions that become ways of being. True mortal sin is an abiding choice to set and hold the course of our lives *away* from God, a decision to become and remain someone who is dead to God, neighbor and self. Wickedness is a way of being that permeates every part of our lives: our deeds, affections, attitudes, beliefs and desires.[45]

Of course, one critique of such an approach is that it makes sinning mortally both difficult and rare. Another critique is that focusing on a person's depth of engagement in an act risks overlooking the blatant evil at stake in particular acts irrespective of what a person ultimately intends by those acts. Whether or not a murderer intends a particular killing to signal permanent rupture in his relationship with God does not detract from the horror and viciousness of his deed. Whether or not an adulterer wants her infidelity to symbolize a heartfelt rejection of God does not reduce the harm the deed brings to others.

In light of this, some theologians suggest a third category of sin, namely, *serious* sin. These would be deeds and actions that are clearly much more heinous and harmful than venial sins, but which do not imply everything that is involved in mortal sin.[46] They are seriously wrong and can be quite destructive in their effects, but do not constitute a fundamental option against God. They may seriously damage our relationship with God but do not destroy it. Such sins are undeniably evil and corrupting, but they are not lethal.

One way to mediate these two approaches to mortal sin is to focus neither on the act itself nor on how invested we might be in the act, but on habits and patterns of acting in our lives. The real peril of sin is ordinarily found not in isolated acts of wrongdoing but in repeated patterns of wrongdoing that weaken our consciences, leave us untroubled by the evil we do, and ratify habits whose cumulative effect is to deaden us to all that is good.

It may be possible to destroy our souls and to kill our relationship with God through a single and fully intentional act of malicious evil. It may be possible to completely reshape our whole moral being and our whole orientation in life through a single act of momentous evil. But it is more likely that we turn away from God and the good not in a single instant, but through a prolonged series of choices that little by little, and in ways we hardly notice, leave us strangers to God. As Richard Gula suggests, mortal sin typically "comes as a result of frequent failures to love and to do the good within one's reach. This increasing laxity deadens the person's sensitivity to the good and responsibility to others. A point finally comes where a particular act embodies more clearly than others the erosion of bonds of love."[47]

Gula's insight confirms that, in assessing what constitutes mortal sin, the focus generally should be not on single acts but on patterns and habits of acting in our lives. What we do over and over again, all things considered, has much more impact on who we become than single lapses into sin. Repeated sins lead to habits of sinning, and once they take hold of us, habits of sinning make messing in evil second nature to us. Once that occurs we find ourselves sinning quite regularly and with a certain amount of ease. But when patterns of sinning take hold of us and facilitate a progressive moral decline that we do not reverse through contrition and repentance, the end result (whether we explicitly intend it or not) will be death to our souls. If a particular act symbolizes and embodies the lethal effects of mortal sin, it is only because it has "already been prepared for and preceded by a prehistory of moral decline," writes Thomas Kopfensteiner. "The sinful act becomes nothing other than the confirming evidence of our moral deterioration."[48] The seeds for that definitively lethal act were amply sown through countless other sinful acts, perhaps none of them especially serious in itself, but whose inevitable destiny was a fatal blow to our souls.

Once habits of sinfulness become second nature to us, we no longer realize their destructive effects. There is no more dangerous predicament than to have become so accustomed to sin (and accomplished in it) that we are completely unaware of what we are doing to ourselves. Habits of sinfulness lock us into self-destructive ways of being. Habits of sinfulness work the wrong kind of transfiguration in us. Instead of cultivating our inclinations to love and goodness and holiness, they make us accomplished in the very things that bring sadness and dissolution.

Unless broken by repentance and contrition, the sin that keeps reproducing itself becomes a fatal addiction, an ongoing conversion unto death. As Thomas Aquinas noted, we "choose readily those things which habit has made congenial."[49] If sin becomes habitual in us—truly second nature for us—we come to find pleasing the very things we should disdain. The utmost peril of habitual sinning is to begin to find wickedness more agreeable and attractive than goodness. It is to find delight in malice, delight in deceit, delight in greed, and delight in vindictiveness. Such a person is truly in a state of mortal sin because they have, through the choices they have made and the habits they have nurtured, come to love what will ultimately destroy them.

Original Sin

We have explored the meaning of sin, some different manifestations of sin, the destructiveness of sin, and different categories of sin. But we have yet to explore why we sin in the first place. Why do human beings go wrong? Why do we become so good at doing harm? Why are we experts of self-sabotage, skilled agents of our own demise? Why do we settle into habits guaranteed to prevent our fulfillment as persons? Why do we hurt one another, fail at love, and distance ourselves from happiness? Why does evil conquer our hearts and reign in our world? Christianity attempts to answer these questions through its teaching of original sin. The doctrine of original sin is not rooted in a pessimistic view of human beings; rather, it is meant to help us "make sense out of the actual world in which we find ourselves."[50]

Original sin calls our attention to a sobering but undeniable fact: We are not born into a neutral world in which the good is easily done; nor are we born into a world unscathed by evil. Quite the contrary, we are born into a world that is already weakened and damaged by sin, a flawed and fallen and disordered world in which there sometimes seems more darkness than light. Original sin means we enter a world that is enmeshed in evil, a world whose structures and institutions, histories and traditions, social, economic, cultural, and ecclesiastical practices are so commonly tangled up in wrongdoing that it becomes everyone's inheritance. Original sin means that evil precedes us and awaits us and surrounds us. It is part of the air we breathe, part of the fabric of life. Thus, when we sin we do not originate evil but add to what is already there. When we sin we do not stain a previously innocent world, but contribute to a legacy of misdeeds that did not begin with us and surely will not end with us. Original sin reminds us that the world may be graced and blessed, but it is not perfect. It confirms what we already know: Every one of us entered a world in which nothing is quite as it should be.

But it is not only our world that is flawed and broken and misshapen, for we ourselves are as well. Original sin means all is not well with us because even though the energy of grace is at work in us, there is also the dissipating energy of sin. We feel the downward pull of original sin when we hurt the people we really do want to love. We feel its power when we close our minds to what we know is true and our hearts to what we know we should love. We know the power of original sin when we make promises we fail to keep, when we allow anger to embitter us, or when we peevishly resent another's success. We feel it at work in us when we refuse to forgive even though our refusal leaves us lonely and sad. We can think of original sin as a force that pulls us off center, a force that lures us away from the good and keeps us consistently off balance. It is as if we are bound to fall short, bound to fail, bound to do less than the good we really want to do, and bound to make the same mistakes as those who came before us.

Original sin points to the fact that none of us is who we ought to be. We live with divided and conflicted hearts. We are flawed, broken, and wayward creatures who are not born healthy and whole, but infirm. Original sin is a power resolutely at work in us that drags us down and thwarts our efforts to love and live justly. Seen in light of original sin, we are creatures born with a malignant and debilitating spirit that may not completely corrupt us, but that surely leaves us weakened and infirm and affects every dimension of our being. Seen in light of original sin, we are inherently maladjusted. We are graced and blessed, and fashioned in the image of God, but nonetheless never quite who we ought to be. There lives in each of us a bent toward disorder that manifests itself (often quite successfully) in our attitudes, in our perceptions and beliefs, in our judgments and evaluations, and in our actions.[51] Anyone who has ever had a single regret knows that this "bent toward disorder" is real. Too, it is a disordering that so deeply infects us that we cannot free ourselves.[52] We need to be rescued, healed, and restored. And that, from a Christian perspective, is what conversion is all about.

CONVERSION

Our analysis of sin has shown that what Heather King discovered about herself is certainly true for all of us: We are sinners from the ground up who spend a good bit of our lives clinging to behavior that is harmful. And so we need to change. We need, in the language of the paschal mystery, to die to our old and unpromising self in order to be resurrected as a new person into a new way of life. We need a radical transformation in our attitudes, desires, and behavior. We need conversion, a fundamental reorientation of our lives that begins in our hearts and is expressed in everything about us. But we cannot fix ourselves. We cannot make ourselves whole. All the classic stories of conversion testify that conversion does not begin with us, but depends on and is made possible by grace. With conversion, the initiative is with God, a God who acts on us and with us to help us recover from ways of being and living that slowly deplete us, and a God whose love and mercy rehabilitates and heals. With conversion, the initiative is with a God who wants not only to rescue us but also to make us new creatures. In this section we'll explore the gift of conversion by first reflecting on what conversion means and what might bring it about.

Conversion—What Does It Mean?

In its most basic sense, conversion means to "turn around." But that implies turning away from something and toward something, a movement that signals a sharp change of focus or direction in one's life.[53] To convert is to "reverse one's direction in life, to change one's devotion or loyalty or to repent or rethink one's way of life as one lives before and in relation to God."[54] When we undergo a conversion in the most complete sense of the word, we abandon well-established patterns of thinking and perceiving and valuing and relating, forsaking those for new ways of thinking and seeing and valuing and relating that seem clearly superior and more promising.

As theologian Bernard Lonergan writes, "What hitherto was unnoticed becomes vivid and present. What had been of no concern becomes a matter of high import." Moreover, the "convert apprehends differently, values differently, relates differently because he has become different."[55] As Lonergan's comments attest (and Heather King's story of conversion so powerfully displays), to convert is not to change in partial or superficial ways. On the contrary, to convert, in this most complete sense, is to embrace a fundamental reorientation of one's whole life, a rethinking of life that is so comprehensive that it results in a completely new thrust to one's existence.

To convert is to become someone new. It is to abandon a former identity and way of being in order to grow into a new identity and way of being. It is to abandon former loyalties, devotions, loves, and commitments for the sake of new ones. It is to strip away old habits and inclinations in order to acquire new ones. A conversion is a fundamental transformation of the self that goes deep, impacting everything about us.

There are observable differences in the lives of people who have undergone conversions. What once was on the periphery of their lives moves to the center. What once was scarcely noticed or appreciated becomes for them a burning concern.[56] As John E. Smith says, it is "as if a new being now dwelt where another had lived before." A conversion entails a complete rethinking of one's life, a total reassessment of life in light of new beliefs and convictions, but especially in light of new loves and devotions. At its core, conversion signals "a change of heart, a change in nature, a change in the self sufficiently deep and lasting to bring about a change of conduct and bearing in the world."[57]

A conversion can also be described as a "horizon shift." Horizons represent the field of vision out of which we view the world. Horizons, however, "are not only visual, they are also moral or ethical," and in that respect delineate the moral landscape of our lives.[58] The moral horizons in which we find ourselves reveal what we care about and value, our interests and devotions, and our fundamental concerns and commitments. They illumine what we think is true and worthwhile. We also think, reason, and deliberate from within the parameters of our horizons.

Moreover, our moral horizon calls some things to our attention, but screens out other things. As Kenneth Melchin explains, "Horizons mark the difference between what we care about and value, and what we deem secondary, irrelevant, and inappropriate." Conversion occurs when we recognize the limitations of our own horizon. It occurs when an encounter with a different horizon not only exposes how insufficient our horizon might be but also reveals values, goods, and possibilities we had not previously considered but now recognize as superior. From this perspective, moral and religious conversion takes place when we "break through constricting horizons to broader, more comprehensive understandings of life."[59]

As we saw in chapter 2, it is the hoped-for effect of Jesus' parables on us. Such "breakthroughs" in our moral horizon lead to new cares, concerns, and commitments, indicating that we have abandoned our previous horizon in order to embrace a new one. Put simply, conversion indicates not that our customary horizon has evolved or developed, but that it has been transcended. And as John Haughey notes, "This means that the whole way one perceived reality, the principles and judgments one took to deal with the reality one found oneself in, has changed."[60]

Perhaps the most famous example of a "horizon shift" is the story of the conversion of Saul that is recounted three times in the Acts of the Apostles (9:1-22; 22:3-16; 26:2-18). A devout Jew and member of the Pharisee party (26:5), Saul is en route to Damascus in search of Jews who had become followers of Jesus. His intent is to "bring them back to Jerusalem in chains" (9:2). But on the way Saul is knocked to the ground and blinded by a light "brighter than the sun" (26:13), and hears a voice saying to him, "Saul, Saul, why are you persecuting me?" (9:4). When Saul asks who it is that is speaking to him, he is told: "I am Jesus, whom you are persecuting" (9:5). He is told to go into Damascus and wait there for instructions. Three days later a disciple named Ananias, who had been told in a vision to go to Saul, comes to him and prays over him. "Immediately things like scales fell from his eyes and he regained his sight. He got up and was baptized, and when he had eaten, he recovered his strength" (9:18-19). Saul's transformation is so complete, and represented such a total about-face in his life, that his name is changed to Paul and he who once persecuted Christians becomes not only a devout and passionate follower of Christ but apostle to the Gentiles.

The Swiss theologian Karl Barth offers a helpful analysis of Christian conversion that is reflected in the story of the conversion of Paul. Barth describes conversion as being roused and awakened by God. We do not wake ourselves up (because the hold of sin is too strong for us to break) but are stirred by the grace and power of God. Moreover, this being awakened represents, not a slight adjustment or a modest improvement in our lives, but a radical alteration in our being and acting. Being awakened by grace—like Saul being knocked to the ground—means letting go of a former way of life in order to embrace a totally different one. As Barth suggests, "It is not a question of a reformed or ennobled life, but a new one."[61]

For Barth, *conversio* always implies *renovatio*, a turning about that entails an expansive overhaul of our lives. The whole of one's being is taken up in conversion so that nothing is left unaffected by it. And, for Barth, Christian conversion is rooted in and sustained by the liberating awareness that God is *for us* and because God is for us we can be *for God*. This is the truth we are awakened to in Christian conversion, and awareness of this truth frees us to live in radically new and creative ways. Knowing that God is for us enables us to repent and renounce our former way of life in order to become part of the bold enterprise of living for God through discipleship to Christ.

Finally, for Barth, Christian conversion is not a single moment but an ongoing way of life that is centered in Christ. Indeed, a life of conversion is also always a life in and with Christ (*participatio Christi*) because Christ is both the perfect revelation of God being for us, as well as the perfect revelation of what it means to be for God.[62] And because conversion means following the teaching and example of Jesus, it affects not only our relationship with God but also our relationship with every other human being. Through the grace of conversion we are awakened to see others as sisters and brothers to us, as fellow friends on their way to God.

Conversion—Why Does It Happen?

There is no single reason for conversion and no single way conversions happen. The story of the conversion of Paul tells us that sometimes conversions catch us completely by surprise. There is no indication that Paul expected the overpowering experience he had on the road to Damascus, no indication that he in any way anticipated such a dramatic and lasting change to his life. But oftentimes conversions are neither so dramatic nor so unexpected; rather, they are preceded and facilitated by a series of events, each of which represents perhaps minor turning points in a person's life, but the cumulative effect of which is the thorough remaking of the person.

The path to conversion can begin in a feeling of dejection or sadness, in a sense of disillusionment and disenchantment, or in the growing awareness that all is not well with us and something has to change. Such feelings prompt us to search for something new. It can take root at moments of restlessness and dissatisfaction, at times when we are keenly aware that something is missing in our lives, or when we realize we are unhappy and have been for a long time. The seeds of conversion can be sowed as the result of a crisis or a major loss in our lives. Or the path of conversion can commence when we feel broken, lost, and powerless, or when we feel empty, vulnerable, and lonely, but perhaps therefore also susceptible to change. At such moments we may not know exactly how to change, but we know our lives cannot remain the same. At the heart of each of these stimulants for conversion is a conflict between the self I am and the self I want to become, and a conflict between the life I have and the life I (perhaps fearfully) desire.[63]

Each of these elements is present in one of the most memorable narratives of conversion in Christianity, the story of Augustine's conversion as recounted in his *Confessions*. For the first thirty-three years of his life, Augustine was a seeker. These years can be read as the ongoing quest of a restless and confused man who was looking for happiness and peace. Augustine sought contentment through sexual pleasures, through a string of love affairs, and in a relationship with a woman with whom he lived for fourteen years and had a son. After reading Cicero, Augustine turned to philosophy for guidance, but he sometimes even consulted astrologers for advice! And yet, all these attempts at happiness not only fell short but also left Augustine miserable and confused. At one point in the *Confessions*, Augustine describes himself as an "unhappy beast," as someone "wrapped around in a fog" and "floundering in the mud," and as little more than a "runaway slave."[64]

Nonetheless, when Augustine wrote the *Confessions* ten years after he became a Christian at Easter in 387, he realized that even though he may have been frantically running from God, God's grace was always at work in him. In recollecting events of his life, Augustine saw them as examples of God's providence, instances when God worked through ordinary events and experiences in his life to slowly guide him to God. Augustine's conversion did not occur in a single dramatic instant but through a series of events, each of which gradually brought him to the moment where he could commit his life to God.

Throughout the *Confessions*, Augustine marvels at how God's love and mercy and wisdom were working in his life in ways he did not realize at the time. For instance, Augustine abandoned his teaching job in Carthage, because his unruly students were more than he could control, in order to accept a position in Rome, where he heard the students were better behaved. But in Rome he discovered that even though the students were better behaved, they frequently failed to pay their tuition. Frustrated and disillusioned, he left Rome for a third teaching position in Milan. In looking back at this time in his life, Augustine realized that God's grace was at work in the changing circumstances of his life because it was in Milan that he met Ambrose, the bishop who was so instrumental in Augustine's decision to become a Christian.

Augustine's conversion was truly a "work in progress," a transformation that occurred over the course of many years. And the agents of conversion were many. In reconsidering his life, Augustine saw how God worked to guide him to Christ through the Manichees, a group with which he was connected for many years, but finally spurned. Similarly, God worked through his friends, especially his friend Alypius; through his mother, Monica; through the writings of Plato; through his spiritual mentor, Simplicianus; and even through a drunken beggar who, with his few coins and his bottle of wine, struck Augustine as much happier than he was. And in the culminating scene of his conversion, God worked through a little child who playfully kept repeating, "Pick it up and read, pick it up and read." Heeding the voice of the child, Augustine picked up the New Testament, opened it at random, and his eyes fell to a passage from Paul that extolled him to "put on the Lord Jesus Christ" (Rom 13:14).[65]

Some Initial Conclusions about Conversion

What does our analysis of conversion, both what it is and what might bring it about, suggest about the nature and experience of conversion, and about what it might mean to live a converted life? First, as the story of Augustine illustrates, even though conversions are often associated with dramatic, overpowering, or critical moments in our lives, the radical transformation they achieve is typically not instantaneous but rather an ongoing process that occurs over a lifetime.[66] This is especially true if conversion's goal is the total transfiguration of one's life in the love and goodness of God. We see this even with the conversion of Paul. Although it is true that his conversion began in an unforgettable moment en route to Damascus, Paul spent the rest of his life working out the implications of that moment. Having been "knocked down" and "awoken" by Christ on his way to Damascus, Paul still had to struggle to conform his thinking, perceiving, evaluating, and acting—indeed his whole life—to Christ.[67]

The total remaking of the self involved in Christian conversion has to be the task of a lifetime. This is why conversion is fittingly thought of as an ongoing journey—a journey in which we gradually, and often with great difficulty, abandon old habits and practices as we try to acquire new ones. Genuine

Christian conversion does not occur in a moment but is rather an ongoing and forever unfinished way of life in which we labor (with God's help) to grow in the virtues of Christ. To be converted is to take up a way of life whose cumulative effect is to make us a "new creation" in Christ.

In this respect, conversion is a way of life we enter into, a transformed and transforming way of life, but one whose goal is never perfectly achieved. In fact, it is probably best not to speak of one's self as being converted, but as always in the process of being converted. As Connors and McCormick remind us, "The call to conversion asks everything of us, and it takes a whole life to give that gift. It takes us a *whole* life to answer the call to give ourselves completely to God, to achieve our full dignity as loving human persons, to live out our vocations as disciples."[68]

Second, there are various stages or dimensions to conversion. In other words, the total remaking of the self that is the objective of Christian conversion happens incrementally as various parts of ourselves are gradually transformed. In his noteworthy analysis of conversion, Bernard Lonergan says that the goal of conversion is self-transcendence in love: a radical "being-in-love that is without conditions or qualifications or reserves," because such "unconditional being-in-love" is the absolute and unsurpassable fulfillment of the person, a fulfillment that brings a deep and abiding peace and joy.[69] Indeed, for Lonergan, human authenticity is a matter of achieving self-transcendence in love.[70] And yet, this self-transcendence in love is not where conversion begins; rather, it is reached through a series of conversions, each of which transforms us in important ways and each of which prepares us for the perfection of conversion in unrestricted love.

For Lonergan, conversion unfolds in three stages. First, there is an *intellectual* conversion that occurs when, instead of just experiencing life, we become concerned about questions of truth and meaning.[71] Not only do we want to understand, but we also want to know if what we think and experience is true. We discover in ourselves—or perhaps have awakened in ourselves—a passion to know and to understand, a passion to discover what is true and real. Even in this initial phase of conversion some kind of self-transcendence occurs because we are drawn out of ourselves in the quest to know what is true and, in seeking what is true, we acknowledge something independent of ourselves.

But not only do we want to know what is true, we also want to know what is good. Thus, the second stage of conversion for Lonergan is *moral* conversion. Here our concern shifts to what is genuinely of value, to what is worth pursuing, to what is so replete with goodness that it demands a response of our whole being.[72] Too, we not only want to know the good, but we also want to enact and embody the good. That is why this second stage of conversion brings about self-transcendence through moral responsibility. Our desire to know and to do what is good draws us out of ourselves in just and responsible action.

The horizons of our world expand because we are no longer concerned only for ourselves, but also for the needs and well-being of others. In this second phase of conversion, conscience is awakened in us.

Finally, these conversions that awaken in us a love for what is true and a love for what is good culminate in *religious* conversion, which Lonergan defines as being in love with God "without limits or qualifications or conditions or reservations. It is with one's whole heart and whole soul and all of one's mind and all of one's strength." This final phase of conversion is not something we can achieve on our own. It is God's gift, testimony of God's love for us and at work in us, and the goal of all previous conversions. Moreover, being in love with God wholeheartedly leads to a radical reevaluation of every aspect of our lives, including a radical reevaluation of our previous ways of knowing and valuing. As Lonergan explains, "So far from resulting from our knowledge and choice, it dismantles and abolishes the horizon within which our knowing and choosing went on, and it sets up a new horizon within which the love of God transvalues our values and the eyes of that love transform our knowing."[73]

Third, conversions lead to new and better ways of living, but also challenging, risky, and very demanding ways of living. Because we typically think of conversion as leaving something bad (or at least deficient) behind for the sake of something better, we can assume that conversions always bring peace, comfort, and security to our lives. We contrast the previous life of disorder and dissolution (sin) with the new life of integrity and tranquility (grace). But as Sallie McFague argues in her essay "Conversion: Life on the Edge of the Raft," the classic conversion stories suggest otherwise. Conversions are unsettling because they take us out of our previous "world" and insert us into a new one. Even more, conversions subvert and even explode our previous world by revealing it as lacking, distorted, and typically dangerously false. Everything we did to make ourselves comfortable and secure in our previous world is broken apart in conversion. We are not only asked to leave that previous comfort and security behind, but also are asked to become part of something new without understanding what it might ask of us, how it might change us, or where it might take us. McFague compares conversion to Gospel parables and says just as "a parable . . . is an indirect assault on the accepted, conventional way of viewing reality," a conversion is an assault on our previous assumptions, convictions, values, and perceptions.[74] This is one reason we often do our best to avoid conversions. Despite their promise, we fear their costs. Every conversion leads to a thorough reorientation of our lives, but not without first demanding an equally comprehensive *disorientation* from all that we previously cherished and embraced.

Fourth, although our analysis of conversion has focused on Christian conversion, it is important to recognize that it is a central element in all religions. For example, although there is no account of sin in Buddhism similar to what we find in Christianity, Buddhism nonetheless astutely appreciates the harm and suffering that are the result of ignorance and illusion.[75] As we recall from chapter 2, for Buddhists the human condition is one of ignorance and illusion, and this ignorance and illusion distort our understanding of ourselves and our place in the world, distort our relations with others and creation, and breed greed, egoism, and selfishness.

> *"Religious conversion [is] being in love with God . . . with one's whole heart and whole soul and all of one's mind and all of one's strength."*

For Buddhists the most trenchant example of ignorance and illusion is "the positing of an independently existing self," Leo Lefebure explains. "This false, clinging self makes itself the center of its universe, is addicted to its desires, and thus traps itself in an endless cycle of suffering."[76] Conversion occurs when one is "awakened" from ignorance and illusion and awakened from the falsifying dream of having a self. And one moves from ignorance and illusion to enlightenment by embracing Buddha's teaching of the Four Noble Truths, particularly the Fourth Noble Truth, which lays out the Noble Eightfold Path that outlines the behavior, habits, and practices by which one breaks free of illusion and is enlightened.[77]

Similarly, although Islam does not believe human beings are sinful by nature, it does hold that we are "naturally limited, weak, and subject to temptation." These weaknesses, limitations, and temptations can lead to sinful behavior, the most typical of which is disobedience or a failure to submit to Allah. For Muslims, the surest way to gain strength over one's weaknesses and shortcomings—and thus the path to conversion—is by faithfully adhering to the Five Pillars of Islam: the profession of faith, prayer, almsgiving, the fast of Ramadan, and the pilgrimage to Mecca.[78]

FAITH

If conversion signals a significant turnabout in one's life, in the Christian life to convert is to turn away from sin to the God who has turned toward us in Christ. And it is to reorient the whole thrust of one's life based on hearing the good news announced by Christ—his proclamation of the reign of God—and responding to it with repentance (*metanoia*) and faith. But, as Peter Phan notes, in the gospel to repent does not mean to be filled with guilt, sorrow, or shame; rather, to repent is to completely rethink and reassess one's life in light of Jesus and his message.[79] In the gospel, repentance is conversion because it is to change the way one thinks and feels about everything in light of one's encounter with Christ. It is a response to the love of God manifest in Jesus, a response that simultaneously reverses the direction of one's life in such a radical and drastic way that one dies to a former way of being in order to take up an utterly new way of being.

This does not mean that the fundamental reorientation of one's life is instantaneously achieved, for the turning of the self to Christ is continuous and ongoing, and marked by both progress and decline. However, it does mean that repentance, which begins a life of conversion, and the faith that sustains it, aims for the total re-creation of ourselves in Christ. Faith then is the virtue most expressly linked to conversion because it is through faith that we sustain, nurture, and deepen the remaking of ourselves in Christ that repentance begins. As Paul wrote to the Christian community at Corinth, "we walk by faith, not by sight" (2 Cor 5:7), an image that suggests that we grow in the Christian life in the measure that we believe in Christ and his message, commit to it, and strive to follow it in our lives.

What Does It Mean to Say, "I Believe"?

To believe is a basic human activity. In fact, to be human is to believe because each of our lives is shaped and guided by a cluster of beliefs, things we hold to be true even if they cannot be absolutely verified. We have beliefs about the meaning of life, beliefs about whether or not there is purpose to our existence, beliefs about happiness and what is most important in life, as well as beliefs about good and evil, suffering and death, and whether or not there is a God. We believe certain things about important persons in our lives, about the work we do, and about the tasks either we have accepted or that have been entrusted to us.

Our beliefs testify to what we think about the way things are or perhaps should be. No person is really without faith because each of our lives is constructed around certain beliefs that guide us and hold our lives together. It is in light of these beliefs that we understand ourselves, explain who we are and what we do, and move through life. Everyone "walks by faith" inasmuch as we define and lead our lives through our most consistent convictions and beliefs, the totality of which form our characters and, to a certain extent, determine the kind of persons we shall become. Moreover, sometimes the most important differences between ourselves and others, particularly in terms of how we view life, understand ourselves, and think about the future, reflect our very different (and often incompatible) beliefs. Thus, the question is not, Do we believe?, because all of us believe in something. Rather, the question we need to consider most carefully is What do we believe?, or perhaps Whom do we believe?[80]

So if to be human is to believe—to put faith in something—what does it mean to say, "I believe"? In a careful analysis of belief, Josef Pieper suggests that to believe is to give unqualified assent and unconditional acceptance to something that we cannot know on our own. It is to adhere to something as true even if we cannot be absolutely sure that it is. In this way, a deep and resilient faith combines assent and affirmation with doubt, questioning, searching, and even moments of disillusionment. Belief must leave room for doubt and questioning if it is to be a genuinely *living* faith, one that holds tight to what it believes to be true amid struggle and uncertainty, and also one that is able to grow, deepen, and mature. Doubt is not incompatible with assent any more than questioning is incompatible with acceptance. In fact, the strength of one's faith can sometimes be determined in light of one's willingness to be honest about doubts and uncertainty while yet believing. A faith that stands fast when darkness seems stronger than the light is solid, vital, and resilient.[81]

Pieper further develops his understanding of faith when he says that to believe is to accept "a given matter as real and true on the testimony of someone else." In short, "the reason for believing 'something' is that one believes 'someone.'"[82] Both are essential elements to faith. The "something" of faith, namely, the content of our belief, must be something that truly matters to us, concerns us, and is important to us. We will hardly believe "someone" if the "something" to which they testify is silly, trivial, useless, or patently false.

The "something" of faith must be truly good for us, something that answers our deepest needs and longings, and that will fulfill and complete us. But even if it is, we will hardly accept it as true if we do not find the "someone" who testifies to it to be compelling and authentic, one whose very presence elicits assent. Put differently, we believe the "something" of faith to be good for us because of the goodness we see in the "someone" who proclaims it. Ultimately, then, we are drawn to believe out of love. Belief is inseparable from love because we believe "something" in light of the love and devotion we have for the "someone" who proclaims it on our behalf.[83]

Faith in the Christian Life

We can appreciate how Pieper's study of belief both illumines and enriches our understanding of faith in the Christian life. For a Christian to have faith is for him or her to assent to the testimony of Jesus, first because they believe it presents the most truthful and compelling account of the way things are, and second because they are drawn by love to the one who proclaims it. The heart of Christian faith is wholehearted assent and adherence to the teaching, example, and way of life of Jesus, precisely because one finds him to be authentic, genuinely authoritative, and incomparably good.

Nonetheless, there is one decisive difference between Christian faith and other acts of believing. Ordinarily we distinguish between the "something" of faith and the "someone" who testifies. The message and the messenger are closely related but nevertheless distinct. But that is not the case in Christian faith. Christians believe in Christ not only because they are convinced that what he says is true, but also because they believe that the message he proclaims is absolutely inseparable from the messenger who proclaims it. For Christians, the "something" of faith is fully revealed in, and identical with, the "someone" who testifies to it.[84] Jesus not only preaches the love, goodness, justice, compassion, and incalculable mercy and faithfulness of God, but is that love, goodness, justice, compassion, mercy, and faithfulness *in person*. This is why in the Christian life both conversion and faith are indelibly connected to Christ. To convert is to assent to Christ—to center one's whole life on Christ—because in Christ God's truth, wisdom, love, and goodness entered the world. Put differently, for Christians both *what* they believe and *who* they believe in are one, and this is why the "focal point" of Christian conversion, as well as the "focal point" of a life of faith, is always Christ.[85]

The assent of faith, however, is not merely intellectual assent. On the contrary, to give assent to Christ entails the wholehearted dedication of ourselves to Christ. Faith in the Christian life implies more than intellectual and moral acceptance of the teaching and example of Christ, which might suggest that we could understand and appreciate the teaching and example of Christ but nonetheless go forward in life on our own. But if we think of faith as a habitual way of being, then it not only affects every dimension of our lives, but also demands the ongoing commitment of ourselves to the person of Christ. To "walk by faith" in the Christian life is to "walk with" Christ. It is to link our lives to Christ. It is to see our lives so intimately entwined with his own that we cannot be ourselves apart from him. It is to realize, as Gustavo Gutiérrez memorably put it, that "our center of gravity" is found not in ourselves but "outside ourselves" in Christ.[86] This means we become most fully ourselves to the degree that we grow in and with Christ. It means we secure our most authentic and promising identity when we become an *alter Christus* or another Christ in the world.

Thus to turn toward Jesus in conversion and to adhere to him in faith is to enter a lifelong relationship with him, which Christians call discipleship. To be a disciple is to see oneself as an *apprentice* or student of Jesus who grows in the attitudes, feelings, dispositions, and virtues of the Christian life not only by closely observing the behavior of Jesus but also by sharing his life.[87] Faith demands a life of discipleship because one turns toward Christ in order to become like Christ, and one becomes like Christ only by intimately sharing life with him.

The aim of a life of faith is for the apprentice to learn so well from the "master" that she can re-present Christ to the world through her whole manner of living, and thus be the "real presence" of Christ to others. In this way, to "walk in faith" is to so thoroughly absorb everything about Christ that one can continue his mission in the world. This is why a conversion to Christ is always also a conversion to his ministry, and why to "walk in faith" with Christ is to see ourselves as called to share in and carry forward his ongoing work of redemption and liberation.[88] We see this in the Gospels when Jesus called disciples not only that they might learn from him and have fellowship with him, but also that they might carry forward his mission of proclaiming and establishing the reign of God.

As we have mentioned already, this life of discipleship begins at baptism. Baptism is the fundamental sacrament of conversion and the fundamental sacrament of faith because to be baptized is so thoroughly to align one's life with Christ that one is said to "put on Christ" and to make his life the normative model of one's own. To be baptized is to set out on a journey in which one follows, learns from, and imitates Jesus in order increasingly to be conformed to him. It is to see the overarching project of one's life as the ongoing configuration of one's self to Christ. In other words, to be baptized is to confirm that one's fundamental identity is as a disciple.

Moreover, even though we might be baptized as individuals, we are always baptized into a community of fellow disciples—a church—whose members pledge to help one another grow together in the ways of Christ. Through baptism every Christian becomes part of a new community and a new way of life whose aim is to be faithful to the ways of Christ in order to witness something new and hopeful to the world. A genuine life of faith and discipleship is one in which disciples of Christ in their life together strive to imitate Christ by being a people of justice and love, of truthfulness and faithfulness, of mercy and compassion, and of forgiveness, reconciliation, and peace. As Ishmael Garcia writes, "The church was founded by Jesus for the purpose of showing the world a different way of living together as a community of mutual support and care for all God's people."[89] This does not deny that the church itself stands always in need of further conversion and renewal, or that the church should ever think of itself as anything other than a "holy penitent."[90] But it does mean that even as it struggles and falls short—even as it sins—the church realizes that its fundamental vocation is to be Christ's body in the world.

Finally, to turn toward Christ in a life of faith is always also to turn toward one's neighbors. There is no such thing as a private conversion or a purely personal conversion because genuine conversion always has social and communal implications. There is no such thing as a Christian conversion and life of faith that does not result in deeper concern for and greater attentiveness to one's neighbors. If the focal point of a life of faith is Christ, it must also be one's neighbors, because the only way to imitate and be faithful to Christ is to show to others the abiding interest, love, and concern that Christ extended to all.

In the Christian life, we do not convert only for our own sake, but also for the sake of those Jesus summons us to love. This is why a life of faith, like a life of hope and love as well, should always make our world bigger, never smaller. It is why a life of faith should expand the parameters of our world so that we begin to live more and more for the sake of others. If we truly "walk by faith," we will be drawn out of ourselves in love and service to others. If we truly "walk by faith," we will inevitably transcend ourselves through love because faith expresses itself most powerfully not through words, but through acts of generosity, justice, fidelity, and service, and perhaps especially through acts of solidarity with the most overlooked and forgotten members of society. Thus, to "walk by faith" demands that we not be silent before injustice, that we not be afraid to be prophetic when necessary, and that we be willing to speak out against evil in all its dehumanizing forms.

CONCLUSION

To be a Christian is to be on a journey from death back to life. We began this chapter with words of Heather King taken from her memoir, *Redeemed*: "I'm broken and I need help." Those words capture our attention—and perhaps unsettle us—because we surely can make them our own. The Christian understanding of the person is that every last one of us is broken and needs help. Born into a world where nothing is quite as it should be, we know what it is to lose our way, to fall short, and to make plentiful wrong turns on the path to goodness and life. And so we need to be redirected. We need to turn our lives around. We need to refocus and recenter our lives by turning away from habits and practices that harm others and diminish ourselves, and toward ways of being and acting that not only replenish us but also fulfill us. We need to turn toward the God who continually turns toward us in grace, Christ, and the Spirit.

The Christian moral life is a life of ongoing conversion. Indeed, to be a Christian is forever to be turning toward Christ because in him we find our path back to life. To take up this path is to embrace a life of faith, a life in which we assent to everything Jesus is about, and express this assent by committing ourselves to Christ. Conversion leads to faith and faith is lived through discipleship. The Christian moral life is a life of walking with Christ and learning from Christ. It is a life in which we try to absorb everything about Christ not only so that we can become like him in goodness and love but also so that we can re-present him to others.

That is the trajectory of the Christian life, the movement from sin to Christ to the neighbor. It may not be an easy life to embrace, but as the stories of Paul, Augustine, and Heather King dramatically illustrate, to "walk by faith" places us on a remarkable journey, one marked by challenge, adventure, and surprise. Too, it is a journey that is immensely rich in hope because while making it we discover what the life of Jesus reveals: Because God is for us, we can be for God. To be for God is to acquire the qualities of character befitting the saints. In the Christian moral life that is what the virtues are about, and they will be our focus in chapter 5.

KEY POINTS

1. A key teaching of Christianity is that, despite the pervasiveness of sin, God's love and mercy are deeper, stronger, and more pervasive.
2. Sin refers to ways of thinking, acting, and living that are harmful for ourselves, for our relationships with others, and for our relationship with God.
3. Today many theologians distinguish the different kinds of sin and levels of sin by talking about venial sin, serious sin, and mortal sin. They also emphasize that the effects of sin are both personal and social.
4. Conversion describes a fundamental and thorough change in one's life that results in decidedly different beliefs, values, priorities, attitudes, and actions.
5. Conversions can occur for different reasons, in different ways, and at different times in our lives.
6. In the Christian life, conversion leads to faith in the person and message of Jesus, and to a life of discipleship.

QUESTIONS FOR REFLECTION

1. What did you learn from the story of Heather King?
2. How would you define sin? How does the Bible speak of sin? And why do you think we seldom use or hear the language of sin?
3. What makes sin ultimately self-defeating?
4. What is social sin? What would be some examples of social sin?
5. What makes a sin mortal or deadly?
6. What is conversion? What can lead to a conversion? Why do we sometimes fear conversion? And can you identify moments of conversion in your own life?
7. What does it mean to have faith?
8. In the Christian life, what does faith involve? And what are some practical consequences of faith?

SUGGESTIONS FOR FURTHER READING AND STUDY

Conn, Walter E., ed. *Conversion: Perspectives on Personal and Social Transformation.* New York: Alba House, 1978.

Connors, Russell B., Jr., and Patrick T. McCormick. *Character, Choices and Community: The Three Faces of Christian Ethics.* New York: Paulist, 1998.

Gula, Richard M., S.S. *Reason Informed by Faith: Foundations of Catholic Morality.* New York: Paulist, 1989.

Haring, Bernard. *Free and Faithful in Christ: Moral Theology for Clergy and Laity*, vol. 1. New York: Seabury, 1978.

King, Heather. *Redeemed: A Spiritual Misfit Stumbles toward God, Marginal Sanity, and the Peace That Passes All Understanding.* New York: Viking, 2008.

Lonergan, Bernard J. F., S.J. *A Second Collection.* Edited by William F. J. Ryan, S.J., and Bernard J. Tyrrell, S.J. Philadelphia: Westminster, 1974.

Mattison, William C., III. *Introducing Moral Theology: True Happiness and the Virtues.* Grand Rapids: Brazos, 2008.

McFague, Sallie. "Conversion: Life on the Edge of the Raft." *Interpretation* 32, no. 3 (1978): 255-68.

Melchin, Kenneth R. *Living with Other People: An Introduction to Christian Ethics Based on Bernard Lonergan.* Collegeville, Minn.: Liturgical Press, 1998.

Pieper, Josef. *Faith, Hope, Love.* Translated by Sr. Mary Frances McCarthy, S.N.D., Richard Winston, and Clara Winston. San Francisco: Ignatius, 1997.

5

The Virtues—How to Be Good at Being Human

"Make Every Effort to Supplement Your Faith with Virtue" (2 Peter 1:5)

WHAT MAKES FOR A GOOD LIFE? What would it mean to live in a way that is truly becoming of a human being? What do we need—and what do we need to become—in order to find happiness? These questions drive the study of ethics because a central concern of ethics is helping us discover what a good human life looks like and what we have to do to achieve it. Ethics should help us plan our lives as well as possible so that at their end we are not haunted by the awareness that we never really understood, much less accomplished, what human beings are called to become. To raise these questions is to suggest that some ways of being human are better than other ways. To ask them is to argue that there is a purpose and meaning to life to which we need to devote ourselves in order to find freedom and fulfillment. Human beings flourish when they participate in ways of living that enable them to actualize their distinctive human potential. They prosper when they discover the overriding goods for our lives. This is why the fundamental business of ethics is to help us learn how to be good at being human.[1]

And we cannot become good at being human without the virtues. A virtuous person knows what counts as a good human life and a good human being. Such a person has wisdom about life because she or he knows the habits and skills we need to foster not only to make good on the distinctive promise of human life but also to confront and overcome everything that threatens our achieving it. It is through the virtues that we live in ways that are truly becoming for human beings; it is through the virtues that we flourish together and grow in happiness.

In this chapter we'll examine the role of the virtues in the moral life by first exploring what counts as a good life and what might best constitute happiness. Second, we will describe what virtues are, why we need them, and how they are acquired. Third, we'll give special attention to the cardinal virtues, four virtues that traditionally have been seen to be especially important for life. But we will also explore how other traditions have identified some core virtues thought to be necessary for life.

Finally, we will look at what happens to the virtues when we consider them not in general, but in the Christian life. If the meaning of the virtues is determined by the overarching goal of our lives, what happens to them when the excellence we hope to achieve is found in the love, goodness, and beauty of God? Are ordinary virtues sufficient for this? Moreover, Christianity teaches that nothing less than a life of friendship with God will content us. If this is true, what form must the virtues take if we are to enjoy the intimate communion with God for which we are made? These are the questions we'll grapple with as we explore the role of the virtues in a life of discipleship.

GOODNESS, HAPPINESS, AND THE VIRTUES

Human beings are attracted to the good. If I think something is good for me, I desire it and look for ways to make it my own or to enjoy it because I sense it will contribute to my well-being. The "good" can be a beautiful sunset, a well-paying job, or long life with the person I love. We cannot help but love the good because the good represents what befits us and ultimately completes us. I may be confused about what is truly good for me (or about how I should pursue it), but I cannot help being lured by it. This is one way an ethics of virtue is different from an ethics of obligation or duty. An ethics of virtue respects the fundamental inclinations of our lives. No one has to tell us that we have an "obligation" or "duty" to seek the good; in fact, to speak that way is silly since it ignores a basic truth about who we are. Just as no one has to "order me" to enjoy a juicy steak, Beethoven or the Beatles, a walk on a beach, or a conversation with a friend, no one needs to order us to love and to be attracted to the good. In the moral life, the good is like gravity; it's an attractive force impossible to resist. As Raymond Devettere writes, "Seeking what is good for us is natural—the desire for the good is rooted in human nature. What gets ethics going is our natural instincts, desires, and impulses for something good that we need and do not have."[2]

But in addition to the particular goods that entice us (a party, a good meal, solitude and prayer), there is a distinctive good that represents the perfection and fulfillment of our selves—if we possess it. Whatever this good is, achieving it allows us to judge the whole of our lives as good.[3] And the reason is that in the measure we grow in and are formed in this good, we achieve the excellence for which we are made. There may be many things that I desire in life. I can desire a meaningful and successful career. I can desire good friendships, a healthy marriage, and a rich family life. But if I seek all of these things while neglecting the good that would allow me to enjoy the excellence and perfection proper to human beings, then I will miss happiness because I will have failed to achieve the very thing that will complete me as a person. This is why Jean Porter says, "In its most proper sense, 'goodness' applies to *perfected* being, to whatever is, insofar as it is what it ought to be."[4] This means one thing for a juicy pear, another for a well-trained German shepherd, and something entirely different for human beings. But whether talking about pears, German shepherds, or persons, something is good in the measure that it attains the excellence that makes it fully what it is uniquely meant to be.

The Connection between Happiness, Goodness, and the Virtues

There are different ways to talk about the definitive good of human beings. A common way is to speak of it as our *telos*, a Greek word that can mean "complete," "final," "goal," "end," or "perfection." The *telos* represents "an ideal of human excellence and perfection"[5] that best expresses what it would mean for us to fulfill the utmost possibilities of our being. It is the most fitting and comprehensive good for human beings, the good that not only means complete well-being for us but also allows us to achieve the distinctive promise of our lives. But because the perfection represented by the *telos* always surpasses us, "it can never be fully actualized." Rather, as Joseph Kotva writes, "The telos is always in front of us, always calling us forward to a fuller realization of the human good."[6] Moreover, the *telos* is commonly described as the "final" or ultimate goal of our lives not only because nothing else surpasses it, but also because it represents "whatever is needed to make a life go well."[7]

The *telos* obviously represents human fullness and flourishing, but what precisely is it? Aristotle argued that the greatest good of a good life is *eudaimonia*, a word that often is translated as "happiness" but whose meaning is both far richer and more complex than how we ordinarily think about happiness. Aristotle maintained that the one thing every person seeks is happiness. It is the ultimate end or final goal of our lives inasmuch as we do not seek happiness as a means to something else but instead desire happiness for its own sake. As Devettere comments, "There is nothing better, nothing more good, than happiness. When we have happiness our greatest human desire is satisfied. Beyond happiness there is nothing to seek."[8]

But by *eudaimonia* Aristotle did not mean "some sort of temporary contentment or momentary feeling of elation,"[9] which is how we often think of happiness today; nor did he equate happiness with pleasure, because pleasures come and go while genuine happiness endures over time. Rather, *eudaimonia* refers to the best possible life for human beings, a life so complete and satisfying that nothing necessary for human flourishing is missing. *Eudaimonia* is a life well lived in every respect, but particularly lived in a way that enables us to achieve the excellence proper to human beings. Thus, we can speak of *eudaimonia* as happiness, but only if we understand happiness as "the fullest possible enjoyment" of the goods that fulfill and perfect us as human beings.[10]

What would such a life look like? What would it involve? To answer these questions we have to ask, What makes a human life good? The answer is many things. If we were to judge our lives as truly satisfactory, they would have to include the most fundamental and important goods of life. If we were to list what we might need to enjoy the best possible life for human beings, what would we include? A moment's reflection suggests that no single good would suffice. For human beings, a life of *eudaimonia* demands a rich variety of goods. We would obviously want a sufficient amount of material goods. We would also include education, satisfying work and financial security, opportunities to develop our talents, good health, time for leisure and relaxation, and a good reputation.

But since human beings are social creatures, we would also want this best possible life to include a loving and supportive family, loyal and trustworthy friends, healthy communities and societies, and a chance to contribute to something greater than ourselves. And since human beings are religious and spiritual creatures, *eudaimonia* would also have to include opportunities to develop our spiritual lives and to grow in our relationship with God. We see then that *eudaimonia*, far from being a single or exclusive good, embraces all the goods and activities that collectively enable us to prosper as human beings. Put more strongly, *eudaimonia* cannot be a single good because our nature is such that no single good is enough to satisfy or complete us. Some goods may matter more to us, and some things are decidedly more valuable than others, but human well-being requires multiple goods and activities, all of them "pursued and enjoyed in an orderly and harmonious way."[11]

Our analysis of the *telos* and *eudaimonia* suggests that we cannot think of either as something irretrievably fixed, static, or inflexible, as if a life of well-being demands that we all live in exactly the same way. Any understanding of human excellence must be flexible enough to honor the important differences that exist among ourselves and others. We will not prosper or be happy if we have to deny our uniqueness—if we have to suppress all those things that make us who we are, and not somebody else. Even though we cannot enjoy *eudaimonia* without certain fundamental goods and activities, we do not all have to pursue them in exactly the same way. Any credible account of human flourishing has to be expansive enough to allow our individual personalities, temperaments, interests, and talents, as well as our social and cultural backgrounds, to influence our pursuit of *eudaimonia*. Thus, although any life of well-being will include a diversity of particular goods, each of us will pursue those goods in different ways and in different modes of life.

Monks and the married will obviously go about *eudaimonia* in significantly different ways, as will people living in Montana or Manhattan or Malaysia. And what certain goods and activities mean to us, as well as the place they have in our lives, can change as we grow and develop, and especially as we move through the different stages of our lives. As we age, our priorities shift and our interests get redirected. For example, a woman or man about to retire will no longer be concerned about success in their careers, but they will likely greatly value friendship, time for reflection, and new opportunities to serve. They will seek *eudaimonia*, but in ways different from how they understood and sought it as adolescents or young adults. Thus, any account of the *telos* and *eudaimonia* must be substantive enough to offer us guidance on what an authentically good human life would entail; however, as Joseph Kotva concurs, "it need not be so definite that it eliminates all but a few ways of living."[12]

Thus far we have examined the *telos* or ultimate goal of our lives through the concept of *eudaimonia*; and we have understood *eudaimonia* as the best possible life for human beings—one that allows us to achieve our distinctive and most complete excellence. And we have suggested that a life of *eudaimonia* must include the fundamental goods and activities of human beings and must satisfy our most basic needs and inclinations. But our account of *eudaimonia* remains incomplete because we have not yet pinpointed the kinds of activities and projects that most fully constitute us as human beings.

If there is something distinctive about what enables us to fulfill the utmost potential of our being, what might it be? What is it that we can do well that other creatures cannot? What activities and ways of life are uniquely becoming for us? Knowing what these are is essential for knowing happiness. As Jean Porter notes, "But no matter how perfection is understood, it will necessarily involve some degree of proper development and exercise of the capacities distinctive to us as creatures of a specific kind—that is just what perfection is."[13]

Our happiness then depends on actualizing our distinctively human potential. Aristotle, for example, said that everything has its own special function or purpose (*ergon*). A thing's proper function is whatever activity makes it what it uniquely is, and not something else. The proper function of human beings is whatever distinctive activity or activities bring us to our highest possible excellence or perfection as human beings. A life of *eudaimonia* has to be one by which we can develop the characteristics, habits, and activities that best represent who we ought to become; and, for men and women, these are the virtues. The supreme excellence of human beings is found in goodness because goodness perfects us, and goodness comes to us through the ongoing exercise of each of the virtues. Each of the virtues activates a particular dimension of goodness and, therefore, is intrinsic to happiness. As Aristotle and Aquinas argued, human beings achieve their most fitting excellence through the development and exercise of all the virtues.[14] And that's because the virtues are the qualities of character and habits of being and acting through which we reach what is truly good for us by perfecting our most distinctive capacities.

We can see then that the *telos*, *eudaimonia*, and the virtues are intrinsically connected. We participate in our *telos* and know *eudaimonia* through a virtuous life. But this means, importantly, that the virtues are not a means to the end of *eudaimonia*, which would suggest that happiness comes after virtue or is the reward of virtue. Rather, a life of happiness is constituted by the virtues because the virtues are the habits of being and acting that develop us in all the various dimensions of goodness.

Stanley Hauerwas and Charles Pinches capture the relationship between *eudaimonia* and the virtues when they insist that "we cannot see happiness as some ideal final state, realizable only in the distant future. For happiness is not so much the end, but the way. Happiness comes as we acquire and live the virtues."[15] This suggests that we participate in *eudaimonia* now, however imperfectly or incompletely, in the measure that we grow in goodness through the virtues. Again, the virtues are not the means to happiness, but the very form and substance of happiness.

How can we summarize this account of human happiness? First, linking *eudaimonia* to the virtues reveals that there is an integral moral dimension to human happiness. Human beings are inherently *moral* beings; in fact, as Jean Porter stresses, "what it means to be human *is* just to be a moral being, capable of a unique kind of excellence."[16] This is why a distinctively human account of happiness involves more than satisfying fundamental human needs and inclinations, or all the other things we have in mind when we imagine our lives to be fulfilled.

For men and women, a life of virtue is a life of happiness because through the virtues we embody and express the distinctive manifestations of goodness that will perfect us as inherently moral beings. This is why we cannot simply equate human happiness or *eudaimonia* with ordinary understandings of well-being.[17] If the possession and exercise of the virtues constitute happiness, then possessing all the goods we ordinarily see as elements to a life of well-being will not be enough to make us happy. Happiness is attained through a virtuous life and not through wealth, possessions, education, or good careers alone.

At the same time, we should not radically separate the life of virtue from the various elements of a life of well-being, as if a life of virtue somehow lifted us above the earth and beyond our bodily needs. We attain and exercise the virtues as bodily, mortal, finite, earthbound creatures, creatures that must take their human needs and inclinations seriously. Thus, even though we do not want to say that having and enjoying certain particular goods is sufficient for happiness, neither should we say that possessing those goods and enjoying them rightly have no role in our happiness. Why is this?

First of all, a virtuous life should be a truly human life, a life that honors and respects our most basic needs and desires. Second, the only way to acquire, exercise, and flourish in the virtues is in an orderly, reasonable, but also joyful pursuit of the goods that make for human well-being. In this respect, acquiring and exercising the virtues is not something other than a life spent seeking and enjoying fundamental human goods; rather, a life of virtue *is* the pursuit and enjoyment of those goods in a reasonable and authentically human way.

As Porter suggests, "the virtues are nothing other than ordered ways of pursuing, preserving, and enjoying the functional capacities proper to the human creature, and as such they cannot be acquired and exercised except in and through the pursuit and use of discrete goods."[18] For example, human beings have "functional capacities" for friendship, for conversation, for study, for leisure, and for prayer. A life of virtue is not something other than these activities, but is pursuing and enjoying them in a balanced and intelligent way. If this were not the case, a life of virtue would hardly appear an attractive and inviting life, much less a good life. What makes it attractive is not that it ignores or neglects our human nature, but that it fulfills it. And it does so by showing us how to seek and enjoy these basic goods (wealth, possessions, food and drink, friendship, marriage and family life) in a way that is truly good for us as human beings—that is, in an ordered, reasonable, and joyous way of life.

VIRTUES

If a life of happiness is a life of virtue, it is important that we understand what the virtues are. In *Character, Choices and Community*, Russell Connors and Patrick McCormick offer a good working definition of the virtues when they describe them as "those good moral habits, affections, attitudes and beliefs that lead to genuine human fulfillment, even perfection, on both personal and social levels."[19] Their description suggests that virtues are first of all habits. Habits are affections, attitudes, beliefs, or actions that we display not occasionally or sporadically, but regularly and consistently.

Each of us has certain capacities, inclinations, and dispositions. For instance, I may have a natural inclination for kindness; but I do not yet have the virtue of kindness until I have acted kindly often enough to transform that inclination into a true quality of character. Or a person may have the capacity to be an excellent athlete, but to actually become one she must practice often enough in order to hone that capacity into a genuine habit for excellence.

In the moral life there is a crucial difference between "simply performing actions and actually having a habit," William Mattison explains. "A habit is an abiding disposition that inclines one to exercise a specific capacity in a certain manner. It is a change of who one is, with a resulting change in what one does."[20] Put differently, habits are *acquired* qualities of character. Habits capture what our most consistent attitudes, intentions, affections, beliefs, and actions make of us. They express how we are ineluctably formed by the things we most consistently feel, think, and do. If I have a tendency to be jealous of another person's success and repeatedly affirm that tendency, then I shall have become someone who can be counted on to be jealous and resentful. On the other hand, if I try to resist and uproot that tendency by developing instead a capacity for graciousness, then eventually I will find myself increasingly less inclined to be jealous precisely because I have acquired the habit of graciousness. Graciousness is no longer something I may occasionally show but is genuinely part of who I am.

Thus, habits form us in two ways. They form both *who we are* and *what we do*. They give us our character, our unique and abiding moral identity, and they give us our most expected ways of being and acting.[21] Habits form who we are because the more often we endorse certain attitudes and feelings, and the more often we act in certain ways, the more deeply do those attitudes, feelings, and actions become genuine characteristics of ourselves. This is why we become what we most consistently think, feel, and act. Those thoughts, feelings, and actions are not something other than who we are, but genuinely express who we are. By developing certain capacities, inclinations, and dispositions into habits, some attitudes, feelings, beliefs, intentions, and actions become second nature to us. People expect us to think, feel, act, and respond in certain ways, so that when we fail to do so they tell us it was "out of character" for us.

Similarly, habits form what we do because our actions flow from and express our character. Ways of acting follow upon ways of being. If I have done something so often that it truly becomes part of who I am, then because it is who I am I will continue to act accordingly. Joseph Kotva captures well the relationship between our character and our actions when he says, "In simplest terms, 'being' precedes 'doing,' but 'doing' shapes 'being.' That is, who we have become, including our states of character, precedes and informs our choices and actions. But our choices and actions help shape who we are and thus our future choices and actions."[22]

There is a circular relationship between our actions and our moral agency or character. If we regularly perform certain actions, then the quality or "character" of those actions becomes part of us. If I act justly occasionally, I am hardly a just person. But if I commit myself to acting justly regularly, then I will become a just person—someone who can be counted on to act justly—because the character of that act of justice has become a true characteristic of my self. This is true with any of the virtues. We are not virtuous when we do what is right and good occasionally or haphazardly, but only when we do what is right and good characteristically and skillfully. Virtuous people are skilled in goodness because they have sought and practiced the good often enough so that the good they do is a genuine expression of who they are.

This analysis of virtues as habits leads to four important conclusions. First, as suggested above, because virtues are habits they represent things we consistently think, feel, act, and intend. If I am fair, honest, and truthful only when it suits me, I have not yet acquired the virtues of fairness, honesty, and truthfulness. Such acts may be good, but they are not yet virtuous. They become virtuous acts—and I a virtuous person—only when I am regularly fair, honest, and truthful. In short, "the virtues are not a matter of whim or caprice, but of stability; they are relatively stable aspects of one's character."[23]

Second, because the virtues are habits, they are acts we do not only consistently but also spontaneously, joyfully, and with a certain amount of ease. The more practiced we become at something, the less we have to think about doing it and the easier it is for us to do it well. If someone is truly a "virtuoso" in music, he doesn't have to think about playing an instrument well because he has mastered the art of playing it. Playing well is so second nature to him that what took years of practice and discipline can appear to others as deceptively easy. The music seems to flow from him because it really has become part of who he is, part of his identity or character. In the same way, a person skilled in the virtue of love has "practiced" all the dimensions of love so often that she really does seem to love spontaneously, joyfully, and with much greater facility than most of us.

Third, virtuous acts must be done for virtuous reasons or intentions.[24] If a philanthropist gives money to charities out of a desire for acclaim and recognition, the act may do good, but it is not virtuous. If will be virtuous only if it is motivated by a genuine desire to do good for others. Or if a teacher works hard to improve her skills only because she wants tenure and not because she cares for her students, her teaching may be excellent, but she would not be a virtuous teacher.

Fourth, the virtues are habitual ways of being and acting, but this does not mean that a virtuous person always does the same thing in exactly the same way. Such mindless behavior would be rote and mechanical, not virtuous. Moreover, describing virtues as "second nature" does not make them thoughtless or impersonal acts—things we do so automatically that we hardly have to invest ourselves in them. Quite the contrary, we are completely invested in virtuous acts precisely because they genuinely express what we care about and who we have become.

This is why it is helpful to think of the virtues not only as habits but also as skills, specifically skills that enable us to achieve excellence in goodness in whichever way it can best be done. Gilbert Meilaender writes that a virtuous person "has not just mastered a technique; he has acquired a skill which permits him to respond creatively to new situations or unanticipated difficulties."[25] His comment suggests that we will excel in goodness not only when we perform it consistently or habitually, but when we also do so with insight, perceptiveness, and intelligence.

Virtuous people are skilled in goodness because they have sought and practiced the good often enough so that the good they do is a genuine expression of who they are.

Any virtuous action must be informed with what Lee Yearley calls "intelligent awareness."[26] An act done with "intelligent awareness" reflects careful attention to the context, circumstances, and unique features of a situation, and also the special needs and circumstances of persons. If we return to our example of the virtuous lover, what makes her so adept at loving is that she does not love in a rote or mechanical way; rather, her love displays insight and ingenuity, as well as perceptiveness and keen attention, to the needs of distinct persons.

Why Do We Need the Virtues?

In order to know why we need the virtues, let us return to the definition of the virtues offered by Connors and McCormick. If you recall, they spoke of the virtues not only as "good moral habits, affections, attitudes and beliefs" but also as ones "that lead to genuine human fulfillment, even perfection, on both personal and social levels."[27] Thus, a first reason we need the virtues is that the virtues help us achieve excellence, particularly the excellence that results in human flourishing and fulfillment. It is through them that we achieve our special *telos* as human beings. If the *telos* represents the fullest possible realization of the definitive human goods, then the virtues are the qualities of character and action that enable us to achieve and enjoy these goods. Or if we think of *eudaimonia* as the best kind of life for human beings, then it is only through the virtues that we can know and participate in that life.[28]

The virtues are skills that suit us for life because apart from them we cannot "live a life characteristic of flourishing human beings."[29] This is why we should never think of the virtues as confining or repressive, or of virtuous people as uptight and overly cautious. Rather, virtues are the attitudes, intentions, feelings, and actions that enable us to have rich and authentically good human lives. Far from oppressing us, the virtues are supremely liberating because through them we grow more deeply in our most exquisite excellence as individuals and as communities. It is no wonder then that a traditional way of describing the virtues has been to speak of them as truly rational acts and to see a life of virtue as a supremely wise or reasonable way to live. It is reasonable to live virtuously because it is only through the virtues that we can enjoy the happiness that most befits us as human beings.

A second reason we need the virtues is because it is through them that we move from *who we are now* to *who we are called to be*.[30] The utmost fulfillment of our lives is found in goodness; however, unlike other species who naturally or instinctively achieve their proper good, our moral development is largely the handiwork of our own agency. We'll qualify this statement when we turn to a Christian understanding of the virtues and consider the necessity of grace for us to enjoy a supernatural happiness that is found only in God. But even when aided by grace, human beings have an active and decisive role in their moral development that other creatures lack because of our ability to reason, deliberate, imagine, and choose.

Other creatures and species will, under ordinary circumstances, become what they are meant to become. But with us it is different. Depending on how we use our freedom, depending on the desires we endorse and the loves we pursue, we can live in ways that turn us away from our true good. We can live in ways that leave us a lifetime away from where we ought to be. Through the attitudes we adopt, the intentions we embrace, and the habits we develop, we can move toward, and participate more deeply in, the unique human good embodied in a life of virtue. But we can also neglect or deny that good, and thus become agents of our own demise and corruption. Our lives are ours to make. What becomes of us is in our hands inasmuch as whether we achieve excellence in goodness or not will be determined by the cumulative result of the choices we have made and the habits we have nurtured over a lifetime.

It is important to understand, however, that we move from who we are now to who we are called to become through the virtues precisely because the virtues shape our character by transforming us in goodness. The movement involves not a change of place but a change of self. If excellence for human beings is found in all the various ways goodness can be embodied and expressed, then we move toward that goodness in the measure that we become proficient in the virtues, each of which instantiates a unique quality of goodness. Every habit changes us because every habit brings a different quality to ourselves. Vices change us in harmful and destructive ways. Virtues change us in promising and healthy ways. We need virtues because it is only through them that we can develop and excel in the ways most fitting to human beings.

Finally, a third reason we need the virtues is that they give us the skills we need to deal successfully with all the opportunities and challenges we will encounter over the course of our lives. We saw this vividly displayed in *The Alchemist*, as Santiago battled with so much adversity on his journey to the pyramids in Egypt. And just like Santiago, virtue ethics envisions each of us as on a journey. The goal of the journey is to reach the special good that counts as excellence for human beings (for Christians this will be God). But the goal is not easily achieved because along the way we encounter obstacles, challenges, and setbacks. In order to reach our goal, we have to keep moving forward. But sometimes it is difficult to do so because much happens that leaves us disheartened.

As we move through life we meet all kinds of persons. Many help us and want what is best for us. But others (as we saw in *The Alchemist*) deceive us, mislead us, and actively try to harm us. Too, as we make our way we have experiences that overwhelm us and can even defeat us. We experience losses, disappointments, painful failures, and exhausting challenges. We have plans and expectations for our lives—certain hopes and dreams—but they can quickly evaporate if our lives are visited by unexpected misfortunes. That can come by sudden illness, the loss of a job, the end of a relationship, or the death of someone we love. It can happen any time life seems too much for us, so that instead of flourishing, we feel as if our lives are shutting down. If we are not to be destroyed by the inevitable challenges and setbacks of life, we need to be skilled in virtues such as courage, hope, patience, and perseverance. No one moves through life unscathed. If we are to reach the goal of the journey, we absolutely need the virtues because they enable us "to respond creatively to new situations or unanticipated difficulties."[31] Without the virtues our quest for the good will fall short. With them we can take up life with energy and hope, confidence and joy.

How We Acquire the Virtues

As we have seen, any person may be kind, just, patient, generous, and forgiving occasionally, but doing those things not only consistently but also insightfully, skillfully, and even joyfully takes time, effort, and repeated practice. Because virtues are habits, they are firm, stable, and predictable ways of being and acting. Too, because such habits are deeply rooted in us and genuinely express who we have become, they are not easily changed.

But we do not come to possess such habits quickly or easily. Acquiring the virtues takes time because it is a matter of forming a capacity into a disposition and a disposition into a habit.[32] A capacity is nothing more than a potential to act or be a certain way. Each of us has a capacity or potential for virtue, but in order for us to become virtuous that capacity or potential has to be acted upon and developed. We begin to acquire the virtues when we practice certain acts of goodness often enough that we have honed and shaped a potential for kindness or justice or perseverance into a true disposition to perform those actions. But being generally disposed to act a certain way does not yet make us virtuous. We become virtuous only when, through repeating certain acts often enough, we have formed those dispositions into something deeper, firmer, more stable, and predictable. We are virtuous when through a long process of habituation our disposition to think, act, and feel in certain ways becomes our regular and expected way of being.

And so one act does not a virtue make. Acquiring virtues takes time—and much work, practice, and patience—because it is a matter of taking a tendency and strengthening it into a habit. All of us do good from time to time, but if we are good only by chance and not by habit, then we have not yet become virtuous persons.[33] A virtuous person is so practiced at goodness that not only does doing the good seem second nature to her, she also seems unusually adept at doing what needs to be done in exactly the way it needs to be done. But she achieved this expertise not because she was more gifted than the rest of us in the ways of justice, love, courage, and mercy, but because she worked at those different ways of being good often enough until the various expressions of goodness became enduring qualities of herself.

This is why we are not surprised when such persons do what is right and good even when it is costly and difficult. Virtuous people are experts at goodness. And because repeated actions of justice, love, compassion, and kindness made both who they are and what they do good, they do what is right and good not out of fear or even duty but out of love. In sum, developing the virtues requires a history of acting a certain way long enough until the quality of the virtuous act becomes a characteristic of a now virtuous person. We become good, not instantly, but with practice, with the painstaking repetition of the kinds of actions capable of transforming us from people who can be good to people who truly are good.[34]

Growing in the virtues can be painstaking precisely because developing a virtue often means overcoming a contrary vice. When he was writing about the virtues, Thomas Aquinas observed that one reason it is hard to grow in virtue is because our wills are turned "to many incompatible things." Consequently, he reasoned, often the initial work of virtue is to "gradually erode the opposing conditions" to goodness.[35] Taken together, the vices represent "opposing conditions to goodness," and all the ways these unfortunate tendencies can take hold of our lives.

Virtue's opposite, vices, are "poor moral habits, affections, attitudes and beliefs which hinder human fulfillment or perfection, both personally and socially."[36] Vices hinder human development because they instill in us the attitudes, intentions, feelings, and behavior that turn us away from the good, and thus leave us morally and spiritually malformed. For instance, if I allow the vice of cowardice to take hold of me, I will never be able to stand up for what I believe or for a person I love, on account of fear. I will have no integrity because instead of following my conscience, I will be constantly swayed by the views and expectations of others. Too, being controlled by fear will weaken my relationships (who could have confidence in me?) and destroy any semblance of self-respect. Without courage, I will lose the relationships I need for a healthy and happy life and lack the sense of self I need to live at peace with myself.

Or, what if instead of hope, which gives us energy for life, I cultivate the vice of sloth. Sloth is habitual lethargy or listlessness—a chronic state of inactivity —that leaves us continually disengaged with life. Sloth works against our well-being because when it dominates our lives we become passive and uninvolved; nothing stirs us, nothing moves us, and ultimately nothing matters to us. Sloth dissolves hope because once I see the world as uninteresting or uninviting, why bother to do anything? Trapped in the fetters of sloth, I gradually withdraw from life because I no longer care enough about anything to act, but simply move aimlessly from one thing to the next.

The philosopher John Casey describes sloth as "an intrinsically joyless condition," and says it "involves a shrinking from activity, a melancholy, a lack of attachment."[37] If I cultivate the vice of sloth instead of, for example, virtues such as gratitude and hope, I cannot possibly have a good life because I will see no purpose in trying to achieve anything. Like cowardice, sloth illustrates how the vices make us incapable of recognizing, much less pursuing, ways of being and acting that are truly good for human beings. This is why they impair, and ultimately prevent, happiness and fulfillment. Contrary to what we sometimes suspect, the vices are the truly oppressive habits because they form us into people whose most distinctive expertise is being skilled at working against our own good.

Acquiring the virtues can be difficult and discouraging because oftentimes doing so initially means trying to uproot an already attained vice. We may find it hard to be just or generous toward others because we have too frequently looked out for ourselves first. Or we may experience a strong distaste for forgiveness because while we may expect it from others, we're more inclined to nurture resentment toward those who wrong us rather than offer them mercy.

Virtues seldom take root in us without first having to combat our ingrained tendencies toward their opposing vices. None of us is immediately courageous because we can only grow in courage when we have first allowed the fledgling virtue to weaken our tendencies to cowardice, on the one hand, or recklessness, on the other hand. And this is not easy because vices such as cowardice or recklessness are like the virtues in one important way: they are habits, ingrained tendencies to think, feel, or act a certain way. And because they are habits (firm, stable, and predictable ways of acting), they cannot be quickly or easily changed. To establish virtue, good habits must overcome bad habits, and bad habits do not easily die.[38]

This is why acquiring and growing in the virtues is not something we can single-handedly achieve, but something that requires the company of others, whether our families, spouses, friends and mentors, our churches, or other moral communities. "We learn the virtues," Kotva reminds us, "by imitating worthy role models, listening to the advice of virtuous friends and teachers, hearing the stories of virtuous people, and following rules of virtuous behavior."[39] The same is true in Buddhism. In *Living Buddha, Living Christ*, the Vietnamese Buddhist monk Thich Nhat Hanh says Buddhists best learn what it means to follow the teachings of the Buddha in a *Sangha*, which he describes as "a group of monks, nuns, laymen, and laywomen who practice together" the ways of the Buddha, and who encourage one another in the virtues and practices of Buddhism. "When we live as a Sangha, we regard each other as brothers and sisters," he writes, "and we practice the Six Concords—sharing space, sharing the essentials of daily life, observing the same precepts, using only words that contribute to harmony, sharing our insights and understanding, and respecting each other's viewpoints."[40]

Thich Nhat Hanh's comments underscore that we need others to acquire, grow together in, and embody the virtues. And we absolutely depend on others in order to acquire the virtues because virtues are essentially relational activities. They are not isolated practices, but things we do together. Alasdair MacIntyre says we acquire the virtues in a "network of relationships of giving and receiving," relationships in which "others make our good their good by helping us . . . to become ourselves the kind of human being . . . who makes the good of others her or his good."[41]

We can understand this in two ways. First, if acquiring the virtues requires "relationships of giving and receiving," then I cannot even begin to possess a virtue apart from the relationships that make it possible. For instance, I can hardly acquire the virtue of justice, a virtue that requires sustained attentiveness to the needs of others, without other persons whose presence in my life calls me out of myself in order to care for them. Or I am not likely to grow in the virtue of perseverance without others in my life who care enough about me to encourage and support me.

Certain kinds of relationships, whether in our families, with our spouses, or in our best friendships, and certain kinds of communities, not only make acquiring the virtues more pleasing; rather, they make acquiring the virtues possible. We cannot possess the virtues, much less know what they genuinely entail, apart from certain kinds of relationships and communities because they provide the very form of life that attaining the virtues requires.[42] A life of virtue is inherently a cooperative enterprise, never a solitary one, because we grow in goodness only by spending time with good people and by seeking what is best together with them.[43]

But MacIntyre's comment also suggests that we cannot grow in virtue unless there are persons who know us well enough—and who care enough about us—to help us understand where we go astray in our lives and where we need to grow.[44] Sometimes other people know us better than we know ourselves—or want to know ourselves. We are not always the best judges of our character. And our self-knowledge is not only limited but sometimes deliberately cloudy.

A spouse can remind us that our rightful anger toward someone has morphed into a toxic bitterness. A friend can recognize that what others perceive as careful planning by me is nothing more than calculated self-interest. A community can help me see that I have nursed a hurt long enough, and that if I want to move forward and be healed, I have to be willing to forgive. We cannot grow in the virtues without the guidance, counsel, and insight of others. But we also cannot grow in the virtues without people who are willing to be truthful with us—perhaps especially when it is a truth we do not want to hear—challenge us, and even correct us. We need people—and communities—who will encourage our best qualities and help us to wrestle with our worst. As Hauerwas and Pinches remind us, "good people help keep each other good."[45]

The Cardinal Virtues

Traditionally, four virtues have been seen as most essential for the moral life: prudence, justice, fortitude or courage, and temperance. These are customarily called the "cardinal" virtues (from the Latin *cardo,* meaning hinge) because every other virtue can be seen as parts or components of one of these four virtues, and because having the kind of life human beings ought to have "hinges" on possessing each of these virtues. No matter when I live or where I live, no matter what my cultural or religious background might be, I need to know how to make thoughtful and wise decisions (prudence). I need to know how to live well with others (justice). I need to know how rightly to balance and integrate the various desires, appetites, and attractions of my life (temperance). And I need to know how to confront and overcome my fears, as well as how to curb any tendencies toward being reckless (fortitude or courage). We cannot succeed at life unless we acquire the qualities of character and skills involved with each of these virtues.

Prudence
The first cardinal virtue is *prudence.* Often described as "practical wisdom," prudence is the skill of making right judgments about things to be done; or, as Josef Pieper observes, it is the "perfected ability to make right decisions."[46] Making right decisions is not as easy as we sometimes expect. A virtuous person wants to do the good; however, actually achieving the good in a particular situation requires insight, thoughtfulness, a keen assessment of circumstances, careful deliberation and reflection, and a moral imagination healthy enough to enable us to judge different possibilities for appropriate action. That is what prudence provides, and it explains why it ranks first among the cardinal virtues. Unless prudence informs each of our actions, we cannot possibly be just, temperate, or courageous because we will not know how rightly to enact each virtue's distinctive good amid the disparate situations we encounter in our lives.

For instance, we are obliged to treat others justly, but what it means to act justly toward others will vary depending on who the recipient of justice is. We owe everyone justice, but acting justly to our parents will in some significant ways be different than what it means for us to show justice to our friends. Similarly, we owe those distantly removed from our lives justice, but it will be different than the justice we owe to our children. We would hardly do the good in the way it needs to be done if, in our attempts to be just, we treated our parents as if they were anyone or our friends as if they were strangers. This is why if our desire to do what is right and good is not to misfire, our actions have to be informed and guided by the "intelligent goodness" that prudence provides.[47]

When writing about the virtue of prudence, Thomas Aquinas said, "Prudence is necessary not merely that a person may become good, but so that he may lead a good life."[48] Aquinas knew that as we move through life we encounter all kinds of people and all sorts of situations and experiences. At every moment we are called to bring goodness to life, but knowing how to do so can confound us. Prudence helps us discern not what appears to be good, but what in fact actually is good. It is the ability to choose and act wisely based on an accurate perception of reality.

Put differently, prudence reminds us that good intentions are never enough. I can always intend to do the good, but without prudence—without clearly distinguishing the true good from the apparent good—my actions will do harm. Anyone who has shown affection to someone she loves, but done so at the wrong time or in the wrong way, knows this to be true. Or anyone who has spoken the truth, but done so thoughtlessly and clumsily, knows the hurt that can result if our good intentions are not accompanied by the careful deliberation, attention to detail, and astute insight that accompany prudence. Prudence guides the acts of each of the virtues because it enables us to do the good in the most fitting way possible. In short, it is the perfected ability to reason well about what needs to be done, along with the foresight that enables us to judge, as best as we can, the possible consequences of our actions.

This discussion of prudence reminds us that we cannot rely solely on moral principles and rules to give us sufficient guidance for doing good. Rules and principles call our attention to fundamental moral obligations and basic moral values, but they cannot always show us exactly what we ought to do and how we should best do it in a particular situation. Rules and principles are necessary—and they should never be casually ignored—but they are not always sufficiently illuminating or adequately instructive. As John Casey explains, "Practical wisdom is not just the unproblematic applying of rules to a situation. It is an ability to 'see' what is at stake where the application of rules may not be at all obvious, and to know how to respond."[49]

Moral rules and principles are not enough for us to know how to do good because they are necessarily general. Designed to apply to a wide variety of circumstances and situations, they cannot give us the precision and acuity that doing the good requires, but which prudence helps our actions to achieve. Rules and principles are essential components to moral decision-making, but by themselves cannot tell us everything we need to know about the situations and challenges we face. As Kotva observes, "good moral judgment requires a kind of perceptive ability: an ability to recognize and respond to the specific and contextual features of often complex situations. Such perception is . . . a sensitivity to the concrete particulars of life. It is the flexibility to give attention to the particular features, relationships, and issues relevant to a specific situation."[50]

Parents who strive to love each of their children equally, but also in ways that respect each child's uniqueness, certainly know this to be true. Both love and justice demand sensitivity and attentiveness to the unique features of persons and a keen eye for the morally relevant features of situations. This is the work of prudence. As Diana Cates summarizes,

> the person of practical wisdom is able to discern the most salient aspects of a situation and deliberate finely about what virtue requires of him with respect to those aspects. . . . There is no formula for computing what is . . . best in a given situation. There is no mathematical equation for solving moral problems or, more generally, for constituting humanly good living.[51]

That is why there is no virtue apart from prudence, and why prudence and goodness are substantially the same.[52]

Lastly, prudence ranks first among the cardinal virtues because besides helping us judge the best way to bring about the good in particular instances, it also works to make sure that everything we do contributes to a life that is truly excellent for human beings. In this respect, prudence counsels us on how to live in such a way that the actions of our everyday lives contribute to our understanding of what overall would count as a good life for us. Prudence gives us moral wisdom not only about the particular situations confronting us, but also about our lives taken as a whole. It assures that all of our actions accord with, and serve, the overall ideal of our lives.[53]

Put differently, prudence aims to make everything we do contribute to what we take to be the ultimate good (*summum bonum*) of our lives. Prudence envisions the future. It looks ahead to the ultimate end or purpose of our lives, and shapes our everyday behavior in light of that goal. The immediate purpose of prudence is to help us discover the right means for doing the good amid the ordinary situations of our lives. But the ultimate purpose of prudence is to show us how to act today in order to attain "the final good for the whole of human life." This is why truly prudent persons are able to "think things out" well, not just for today, but "for the whole of the good life."[54] As Aquinas observed, "Prudence is of good counsel about matters regarding a man's life in its entirety, and its last end." Only those "who are of good counsel about what concerns the whole of human life" are, in the most complete sense of the word, truly prudent.[55]

Justice

Although we prize our individuality, human beings are thoroughly social creatures who from the first days of their lives to the last are enmeshed in networks of relationships that, far from being superfluous, are absolutely essential for a healthy human life. And despite how hard we may try to deny or ignore it, we are also radically dependent beings who need others not only to flourish but also even to survive. If the virtues show us how to live in ways that are truly good for the kind of creatures we are, that cannot be done apart from *justice*, the second of the four cardinal virtues, because justice teaches us how to live well with others. Unless we become experts in justice, we cannot know *eudaimonia* because we will not have acknowledged a most fundamental truth about ourselves: we are social animals that can only thrive and prosper together.

Justice helps us see that we depend on, and continually benefit from, the care, generosity, and goodness of others, just as they continually depend on and benefit from us. It helps us realize that our well-being is intricately linked to, and always inseparable from, the well-being of others. This is why becoming a person of justice is in our own best interest. If I know what is best for me, I will treat others with respect, contribute to the good of society, and live with others in mind, because I know being that kind of person will make possible the best kind of life for me, as well as for everyone else.

There is no contradiction between a healthy self-love and justice; indeed, one absolutely implies the other. If I rightly love myself and seek what is best for me, I will be a person of justice because I shall have realized that it is impossible for me to flourish apart from living in right relationship with other persons.[56] Similarly, a right understanding of justice underscores that we should not see our individual good as opposed to the common good. Rather, justice teaches us that "the well-being of individual and community are interrelated in such a way that what promotes one promotes the other, and what harms one harms the other as well."[57]

Justice begins in the discovery that something other than our self is real *and* has value. Justice opens our eyes to the reality of the other, whether a parent, a sibling, a fellow student, a stranger coming my way, persons oceans away, or another species. And in opening our eyes it teaches us to see that other people (and other creatures) have a claim on us, and that we have duties and responsibilities toward them, precisely because there is a dignity and sacredness to them that we neither create nor bestow but are called to acknowledge and respect. Justice is a matter of vision, of learning to see the world a certain way. A person of justice sees the sacredness and holiness of all life, whether human or nonhuman, and acknowledges that the respect owed other persons (and species) does not depend on one's mental or physical ability, one's status, wealth, or achievements, but rather is due them because of the goodness bestowed on all beings by God.

Furthermore, a person of justice sees the bond that exists among ourselves and every other person and creature, and strives to live in ways that honor and strengthen that bond. He or she knows we cannot be indifferent to others because we are all members one of another and collectively form one family. Today this vision of radical interdependence is often spoken of as *solidarity*. Justice is impossible apart from solidarity because solidarity sustains the moral vision by which we realize that we are all "members of one and the same household," and thus both beholden to one another and responsible for one another.[58]

How should we think of justice? How should we describe it? Aquinas famously spoke of justice as "the constant and steadfast willingness to give to each person what is his or hers by right."[59] Aquinas's definition suggests that justice turns us outward by focusing our attention away from the self and toward the needs and well-being of others. There is, of course, a justice we owe ourselves and that others owe us; however, the core energy of justice is to direct our concern and attention to the good of others.

Moreover, as a virtue of the will, justice not only disposes us to live with others in mind, but also teaches us how to fulfill our obligations and responsibilities to the various people who make up our lives, as well as those far removed from us. In this respect, acquiring the virtue of justice entails a fundamental reorientation of our lives away from the egotism, selfishness, and anxiety that narrow and restrict our world. As we grow in justice the horizons of our world expand, because we realize that to be human is to care for and attend to others, and that we should do so not occasionally or whenever it is convenient for us, but continually.

This suggests that a person of justice is not only characteristically attentive to the good of others, but also that there is never a moment when the needs of others should not call us out of ourselves in compassionate response. Too, even though our responsibilities in justice differ according to the particular circumstances of our lives and the key relationships that constitute our lives, justice cannot afford to be overly selective or provincial. We are called to live with others in mind, and this includes not only those most closely associated with us, but also those far away whose needs are often more urgent than our own, as well as those of future generations.

Given the needs of human beings and all the ways we depend on one another, justice should not be determined by strict calculations of what one person owes another; rather, justice should be magnanimous, liberal, and generous. If we too rigidly equate justice with fairness, justice can quickly become overly calculating. To counter the inevitable temptation to narrow the parameters of justice, Alasdair MacIntyre developed the notion of "just generosity," and described it as "what is needed to sustain relationships of uncalculated giving and graceful receiving." As a virtue, "just generosity" demands "the education of the affections, sympathies, and inclinations," and insists that acts of justice should be accompanied by an "attentive and affectionate regard" for persons in need. MacIntyre reminds us that our justice is less likely to shrivel if it is inspired by genuine feelings of compassion and sympathy for the plight of others, and acknowledgement of our own enduring dependency.[60]

MacIntyre also reminds us that human beings are given to one another—truly entrusted to one another—and therefore have responsibilities for one another, especially those members of society who are least able to provide for themselves. "Just generosity" recognizes that to be human is to be enmeshed in networks of giving and receiving; indeed, a person of "just generosity" acknowledges that giving and receiving are the very core of our being.[61] We can and should give to others because we have first received from others. We received our lives from others and are continually sustained in them by a multitude of persons. We can give love only because we have first received love, just as we are summoned to be generous because we are so richly indebted.

Giving and receiving is the ongoing dynamic of life and the logic behind "just generosity." A person skilled in the virtue of "just generosity" recognizes that a fundamental impediment to justice both in ourselves and in our world is a refusal to be grateful and a refusal to acknowledge indebtedness. A person of just generosity gives liberally and extravagantly because he or she understands how much they have been given. Formed in this vision, they are ready to give—indeed, it is their fundamental stance toward life—and look for opportunities to do so. Not surprisingly then, communities characterized by "just generosity" are distinguished by "the importance that they attach to the needs of children and the needs of the disabled."[62] MacIntyre summarizes beautifully the moral awareness (and imagination) that guides communities of "just generosity":

> What matters is not only that in this kind of community children and the disabled are objects of care and attention. It matters also and correspondingly that those who are no longer children recognize in children what they once were, that those who are not yet disabled by age recognize in the old what they are moving towards becoming, and that those who are not ill or injured recognize in the ill and injured what they often have been and will be and always may be.[63]

Temperance

Human beings are creatures of powerful appetites and inclinations, and powerful passions and emotions. Driven by hungers and desires, we want food and drink, sex, money and possessions, and sometimes power and fame. We cannot help loving things that are good for us, and we cannot help wanting them in our lives. We are bodily creatures who cannot live without food and drink, and who cannot help but enjoy the pleasures of sex. We are creatures who need at least some possessions to enjoy a good and healthy life, and at least enough money to have security and to plan for the future. We should never ignore the fundamental drives, appetites, and inclinations of our lives because they signal to us that we have needs we cannot afford to neglect.

But if we are honest, we also know that these same appetites, drives, and inclinations can become so strong that they begin to dominate our lives in dangerous and destructive ways; as Aquinas pithily expresses it, they "render us unreasonable."[64] If we are honest, we know that we can slip into patterns of acting that "render us unreasonable" because they work against what truly is good for us and sabotage our well-being. We can love good things in the wrong way, allowing important but partial goods to have an inordinate place in our lives. We can become obsessed with making money, obsessed with material things (consumerism encourages us to be so), or obsessed with status and reputation. When this happens, instead of allowing these fundamental drives and inclinations to direct us to the good, we allow them to rule over us, and thus lose our freedom (and our happiness) to desires we can no longer control.

This is why we cannot live a life that is good for human beings—a truly healthy and reasonable life—without *temperance*, the third cardinal virtue.[65] Temperance is the virtue that governs and directs our desires, particularly our physical appetites, to make sure that they assist us in living well. Temperance does not fear or repress the desires, passions, and hungers of our lives, but it does order and regulate them lest they begin to rule over us. In this respect, temperance reflects a very honest and realistic assessment of our human nature. It counsels us to be honest about our weaknesses, honest about areas in our lives with which we continually struggle, and honest about how certain desires can be pursued in patently destructive ways.

For example, we have an undeniable need for intimacy in our lives and for close and enduring relationships. But without temperance, our need for love and intimacy can be expressed in very destructive ways. Think of relationships crippled by infatuation, manipulation, or possessiveness. Similarly, God made us to enjoy sexual relationships, but we can pursue those pleasures in healthy and constructive ways, or in ways that bring tremendous harm both to ourselves and to those we claim to love. Sexual relationships that are guided by the virtue of temperance will be characterized by fidelity and commitment, while intemperate sexual relationships are commonly characterized by selfishness, hedonism, promiscuity, and betrayal.

Without temperance we can neither have good lives nor become good persons. And the reason is that without temperance we will do a lot of harm, to ourselves for sure, but certainly to others as well. People possessed by an intemperate desire for money become greedy, materialistic, and often dishonest. Their obsession with wealth easily blinds them to the needs of others and tempts them to dismiss other important goods of life such as friendship, giving ourselves to others, and simplicity. Anyone who has ever had his life taken over by alcohol or drugs learns quickly that a lack of temperance, far from bringing him freedom, enslaves him to a desire that exerts so much mastery over him that everything else in his life becomes expendable for its sake. Marriages end, families are torn apart, relationships are sacrificed, and jobs are lost all for the sake of desires we've allowed to become sovereign in our lives. This is why a lack of temperance is not only a moral defect, but can also make us evil.[66]

This may seem overstated, but consider the harm a person can do who lacks temperance in his or her sexual relationships. Or think of a person who can never control her anger even if the anger is justified. A lack of temperance in regard to anger can make her malicious and hateful, at which point her anger becomes toxic not only for the person to whom it is directed, but also for herself.[67] Alcohol can bring out the worst in us, leaving us saying and doing things that can be tremendously harmful to others. If our lack of temperance becomes habitual instead of occasional, then not only will we find ourselves doing evil things, but we will also, at least in certain respects, become evil persons.

We typically think of temperance as subduing and redirecting appetites and desires that have become too strong. But just as our appetites and desires can become excessive, they can also become too weak. Both excessive and uncontrollable desires, and limp, flimsy desires represent failures in temperance, and both prevent us from leading good and healthy lives. As our earlier reflections on sloth illustrated, when we lack passion or desire for anything, we lose energy for life. Nothing interests or attracts us; nothing engages us. We do not care enough about anything to pursue any good, to nurture any relationships, or to become involved with something that would connect us to other people and to life. Our world shrivels because our interests and cares disappear; consequently, our normal state is one of apathy.

This is a dangerous condition of soul because if we care about nothing and are engaged by nothing, our life shuts down. We no longer move to the good because nothing attracts us as good. In such instances, we need the virtue of temperance to help us recover passion and interest and energy for life. Likewise, there are times when we can develop an unhealthy abhorrence for goods without which we cannot live. This happens when people who are obsessed with being thin are unreasonably scrupulous about eating, or when people are so focused on living simply that they can no longer enjoy life. Whether when our desires are excessive or when they are insufficient, such a lack of temperance, as Aquinas noted, "renders us unreasonable."

There are two parts to temperance: shame and honor. To speak of shame can sound quaint because we have, for the most part, lost a concept of shame. But the language of shame reminds us that there are ways of living and acting that are beneath us. Put more positively, to speak of shame actually reflects a very high estimation of ourselves and a keen appreciation of our dignity as human beings. Shame only makes sense if we believe there is a goodness, dignity, and even a nobility to being human that can be easily lost and that certain ways of life and certain kinds of behavior destroy.

A component of temperance, shame calls our attention to ways of life and patterns of acting that truly are beneath us, ways of life and behavior that drag us down by turning us further away from what is best for us. Some things should not be done because they are repugnant to the nobility we have as creatures made in the image of God. This is why Aquinas said, "Intemperance is shameful . . . for it debases a man and makes him dim. He grovels in pleasures well-described as slavish . . . and he sinks from his high rank."[68]

Aquinas's comment illustrates that shame is connected to self-respect, to a genuine love and appreciation for one's self, and cannot be rightly understood apart from it. Thus, shame is a very valuable quality to have because it helps restrain us from pursuing some of our more destructive tendencies by alerting us to behavior that can cost us our integrity and reputation, as well as do great harm to others. As Aquinas wrote, "Sentiments to shame, when repeated, set up a disposition to avoid disgraceful things."[69] The second component of temperance, honor or beauty, reminds us that for human beings true honor comes not from wealth, celebrity, fame, or power but from goodness and virtue.[70] And it tells us that a life of virtue is a truly beautiful life and that a virtuous person, resplendent in goodness, shines with beauty too.

Courage

Life is hard. But with courage it can be lived. The final cardinal virtue, *courage* or *fortitude*, is the virtue that strengthens us so that we can overcome the fears, difficulties, setbacks, and dangers that challenge us in life and sometimes can almost defeat us. As we move through life, we inevitably encounter sorrow and suffering, adversity and disappointment, and times of intense discouragement. In fact, every stage of life is accompanied by fear.[71] It may be the fear of leaving home and going out on our own. It can be the fear that comes when we face an uncertain future, when we begin a new job, or when a change in circumstances means we have to leave the security of family and friends behind. As people enter the later years of their lives, they are faced with fear of illness, fear of diminishment and decline, and fear of their inevitable deaths.

As the story of Santiago in *The Alchemist* memorably illustrates, we cannot succeed at life without being brave, and courage teaches us what it means to be brave by giving us the fortitude and resolve we need to overcome the fears and dangers that beset us. And like Santiago, without courage we cannot progress in life because we will continually be stymied by the things we fear, or defeated by the sufferings and hardships that periodically come our way. Without a virtue that helps us subdue fear, confront danger, and persevere through hardship and suffering, we will shrink from the challenges that are part of life and never reach the goals by which we have defined our lives.

We cannot flourish and grow without courage because, lacking it, we will habitually sacrifice the most important goods and aspirations of life for the fears we cannot overcome. Anyone who has let an opportunity pass because he was too timid to grab it knows this to be true. Anyone who has failed to respond to invitations to love because of fear knows how cowardice and anxiety rob us of life. Lacking courage, our life becomes a chronicle of endless regrets and missed opportunities.

A courageous person is not someone who denies fear and danger, but someone who knows how to confront and overcome them. A courageous person knows there are times when we ought to be afraid; a soldier in battle certainly knows this is true. In fact, not to be afraid in situations of danger is not courageous but foolish.

The two vices that most directly oppose courage are cowardice and recklessness. They are both inappropriate ways to respond to fear. The coward is paralyzed by fear—truly rendered inactive by fear—while the reckless person foolishly denies there is any reason for fear, and thus places himself or others in unnecessary danger. A courageous person does not deny the reality of fear and danger; rather, he or she knows how to confront it thoughtfully, carefully, and skillfully. They know that there are times when we have to be brave, when we have to persevere and be steadfast, and realize that even though confronting fears, difficulties, and dangers is not easy, it is absolutely essential if our lives are not to shut down in dejection and defeat. There are always situations and persons we would rather flee from than confront, but if we make a practice of that we will have spent our lives allowing fear to stand between us and what we truly desire.

There are two parts to courage: perseverance or patient endurance, and attacking or daring. It is not hard for us to recognize times in our lives when we need to persevere. An aspect of courage, perseverance gives us the resolve we need to stand firm in our convictions when we are tempted to betray or abandon them because of fear or pressure, or because we know being faithful to them will be costly. Perseverance helps us to "be steadfast and not turn away from what is right"[72] at those moments when we know honoring our convictions could lead to misunderstanding, rejection, or even suffering. It is the courage that we see in persons who are willing to die rather than betray their deepest commitments and convictions.

Also, perseverance supplies the resolve we need to achieve worthwhile goals, whether finishing a challenging task or fulfilling the promise of a marriage. It is not easy to remain committed to worthwhile goals because the pursuit of anything good involves adversity, trials, and difficulties. With perseverance we are able to remain steadfast in our pursuit of what is best and most promising when we are perhaps most tempted to abandon it.

Similarly, sometimes there are sorrows in life we cannot avoid but can only suffer through, and courage gives us the fortitude, resolve, and patience we need to bear them valiantly and hopefully, lest they defeat us. The sorrow can come in the form of a debilitating illness, the divorce of parents, or the death of a loved one without whom we cannot imagine our life. As patient endurance, courage helps us enter into the sorrow and grieve the loss but not be destroyed by them. The danger of any sorrow, suffering, or immense loss is for the pain and sadness that come from them to become so debilitating that they effectively shut down our lives by snuffing out hope. Expressed as patient endurance, courage enables us to be honest about the sorrow and the loss, but not so consumed by them that we give up on life.[73]

The second part of courage, attacking or daring, gives us the energy, insight, and determination we need to battle the challenges, setbacks, and obstacles of life in order hopefully to overcome them. Our first response to difficulty, whether from another person, an institution, or a situation, should not be to surrender, but to attack; otherwise, we resign ourselves too quickly or allow adversity to prevail when perhaps it can be conquered.

Without this component of courage we risk allowing unjust persons and unjust situations to weaken the love and respect we owe ourselves. A courageous person does more than persevere and endure. She uses her imagination, wisdom, and heartfelt resolve to eliminate difficulties and to conquer adversity. We see courage at work when people refuse to remain in abusive and destructive relationships, or refuse to allow others to intimidate and control them. We see it at work when people are daring enough to challenge persons and institutions that perpetuate injustice. We see it expressed in the boldness of people who speak dangerous truths or expose comfortable but costly falsehoods; Dr. Martin Luther King, Jr., like all the prophets, certainly exemplified this dimension of courage. Without this second component of courage, we can easily grow complacent with evil by accepting wrongs we ought to denounce and attack.

Virtues in Other Traditions

The four cardinal virtues come out of a Western philosophical and theological tradition. However, we can find in other philosophical and religious traditions virtues that function in similar ways to the cardinal virtues. In his celebrated analysis of theories of virtue and understandings of courage in Thomas Aquinas (1225-1274) and the Confucian philosopher Mencius (390-310/305 b.c.e.), Lee Yearley notes that for Mencius there were four key virtues that were essential for human flourishing: benevolence, righteousness, propriety, and intelligent awareness. Mencius described benevolence (*jen*) as an abiding sensitivity to others, especially to their sufferings, and a commitment to do what one could to alleviate suffering. Akin to compassion, a person suffused with benevolence habitually shows concerns for the needs of others, has pity for the distress of others, and extends sympathy to them. Mencius also identified three levels of benevolence: "a special regard for family [*ch'in*], benevolence [*jen*] to all human beings, and a general regard [*ai*] for all beings or at least living creatures."[74]

The virtue of propriety (*li*) is rooted in reverence and respect for others. Mencius taught that reverence and respect are best demonstrated through certain ritual practices. But for him the rituals of *li* or propriety covered every area of life, extending from solemn religious rituals, such as funerals, to practices comparable to what today we would call etiquette or good manners. The rituals of *li* governed ordinary social interactions and were designed to express and protect reverence for others. They provided the "social forms" by which one could show appreciation for others, whether to a cook for a good meal, to a friend, or especially to one's parents.[75] Too, the virtue of propriety both safeguarded and strengthened human interactions by teaching one how to engage with others in ways that fostered concord and amity instead of discord and divisiveness. In this way, the rules of propriety were seen not to stifle human interactions but to enhance them. Indeed, the rituals of *li* guarded against the dissolution of relationships and the breakdown of society, especially by teaching people how to yield to others.

A central component of propriety, the willingness to yield, guarded against tendencies to self-aggrandizement and tendencies to see the needs, interests, and desires of the self as sovereign. Too, a willingness to yield weakened the disposition to always have to prevail or always to have one's way. In summary, according to Mencius, one demonstrated his or her respect for others by following "the conventional rules of propriety." "A person observes these rules," Yearley explains, "as an expression of reverence for people, their roles, and even the social organism that they embody and help preserve."[76]

In many respects, the virtue of righteousness (*yi*) is similar to justice because it guides our relationships with others by assuring that we acknowledge our debt to others and the responsibilities we have toward them. At the same time, it differs from our conventional understanding of justice because righteousness also deals with shame (*hsiu*) and aversion (*wu*). Shame is "an awareness of falling short of some standard, a repugnance manifested in shame about one's own actions"; and aversion focuses on attitude, actions, and ways of being one ought to avoid.[77] Shame and aversion serve the virtue of righteousness because sensitivity to both helps us remain in right relationship with others.

Lastly, the virtue of intelligent awareness (*chih*) resembles the cardinal virtue of prudence because it is the skill to make right judgments about what ought to be done in particular situations. A person of intelligent awareness is able to see or discern the most important features of a situation and shape her action accordingly. Instead of simply following rules or moral guidelines, she can rightly evaluate what is at stake in a situation and, in light of that judgment, act to achieve the good.[78]

In Buddhism we likewise find certain habits that function as "cardinal" or "core" virtues because they enable one to pursue the Noble Eightfold Path, sometimes called the Middle Path, which leads to enlightenment and nirvana. The virtues of the Eightfold Path are: right understanding, right thought, right speech, right action, right livelihood, right effort, right mindfulness, and right concentration. The three most directly associated with ethical conduct are right speech, right action, and right livelihood. Right speech not only concerns a commitment to speak truthfully, but also "to use words that are friendly and benevolent, pleasant and gentle, meaningful and useful." Moreover, right speech means refusing to tell lies, refraining from gossip, slander, and backbiting, as well as harsh, rude, or malicious language. Overall, right speech commits one to avoiding any "talk that may bring about hatred, enmity, disunity and disharmony among individuals or groups of people."[79]

Describing this virtue, Walpola Rahula says, "One should not speak carelessly: speech should be at the right time and place. If one cannot say something useful, one should keep 'noble silence.'" Right action "aims at promoting moral, honourable and peaceful conduct. It admonishes us that we should abstain from destroying life, from stealing, from dishonest dealings, from illegitimate sexual intercourse, and that we should also help others to lead a peaceful and honourable life in the right way." And by right livelihood one vows not to make a living through a profession that would bring harm to others.[80] More recently, the Vietnamese Buddhist monk Thich Nhat Hanh has called attention to four central virtues that need to be cultivated for a hopeful future to be possible: compassion, loving kindness, mindful speech, and mindful consumerism.[81]

VIRTUES IN THE CHRISTIAN LIFE

Thus far we have suggested that it is through the virtues and a virtuous way of life that we achieve the distinctive promise of human life. But our account of the virtues remains too general because in order to know what truly counts as a virtue we need to ask, What do we take to be the ultimate goal of our lives? Virtues fulfill their purpose only if they enable us to achieve the greatest possible good of our lives. Is that greatest possible good love, happiness, and prosperity in this world or is it, as Christianity contends, everlasting beatitude with God?

How we answer that will determine the meaning, purpose, and substance of the virtues for us, as well as the form the virtues must take in our lives. Virtues take their meaning from different understandings of life. Different ends, different purposes, and different accounts of human excellence result in correspondingly different accounts of the virtues. This is why we can talk about the virtues, but what we ultimately mean by them hinges on how we understand the most fitting and complete purpose of our lives.

Christians believe that human beings are perfected in love and communion with God. As Therese Lysaught writes, "God longs for our love and invites us to become his friends. God does so, the Christian tradition holds, because to love God and be friends with God is the fulfillment of who we are, of what it means to be human."[82] But how can we reach an end that infinitely surpasses us? How can we be united in intimate friendship and communion with a God whose goodness forever exceeds anything we could possibly achieve on our own?

Our analysis of the virtues has to go beyond the "natural" virtues that can be acquired and developed through our own moral agency alone. Because God calls us to a *telos* that completely transcends us—God's own life, goodness, and happiness—Christianity has to offer a more extensive account of the virtues, one that never sees the virtues as our own singular achievement but as acts that are rooted in grace, accompanied by grace, and perfected by grace. In the Christian life something is truly and completely a virtue *only* if it helps us achieve our supernatural destiny of friendship and communion with God. But, as William Mattison explains, "This is a destiny that far transcends our unaided created nature and unaided powers of reasoning. We could not 'get there' on our own. In fact, we cannot even begin to comprehend this invitation, let alone live it out, without the assistance of God's grace."[83] In the Christian life, we receive the "assistance of God's grace" through the theological virtues of faith, hope, and charity, and through the "infused" moral virtues.

Theological Virtues

If the ultimate goal of our lives is the supernatural destiny of communion with God, we cannot achieve that *telos* without the theological virtues. How should we understand them? What distinguishes them from the acquired natural virtues? First, the theological virtues directly concern God and direct us to God. As Mattison says about them, "We believe in God (faith). We love God above all else, and all things in God (charity or love). We yearn for union with God, experienced fully only in the next life but tasted in this one (hope). When one engages in such activities well, one is said to have these 'theological virtues.'"[84]

Second, if the acquired virtues direct us to a "natural human happiness proportionate to human powers,"[85] theological virtues direct us to a supernatural happiness that is utterly disproportionate to our human powers and thus only achievable by God's assistance. No amount of effort can produce the theological virtues in us; rather, each of them must be given to us by God. They are "habits that are infused by God, 'entirely from without,' and cannot be acquired by means of deliberate human activity (I-II 62.1, 63.1)."[86] In sum, God is the object or focus of the theological virtues; their singular purpose is to direct us to our ultimate destiny with God. And they are obtained by grace and always remain the work of grace because we cannot give ourselves the capacity for such actions and we cannot perform them without God's help.[87]

Nonetheless, we not only can but also must nurture and deepen each of the theological virtues through our everyday behavior and practices. For instance, only God can give me the theological virtue of faith. But aided by God's grace, I am called to deepen and strengthen that faith through regular habits of prayer and reflection, through membership in a faith community, and through good works.

There are many ways to describe the theological virtue of faith, but perhaps the heart of faith is an abiding assent to truths about God, truths that surpass our reason. A person of faith does not comprehend God, but he or she is habitually disposed to accept certain beliefs about God, and to discern what ought to be believed about God from what ought not to be believed about God. Moreover, faith provides us with a particular vision or perspective on life. A person of faith sees the world a certain way. People of faith view reality in light of what God has revealed; therefore, they see the world as blessed, see creation as a gift, and see other persons as neighbors they are called to love.[88]

The theological virtue of hope also focuses our lives on God, but specifically on our future happiness or beatitude with God. Hope fixes our attention on God so that as we move through life we do not turn away from God to lesser goods, but continually tend to God as our greatest possible good. Too, with hope we do not lower our expectations for our lives; rather, we steadfastly cling to God, confident that God accompanies us and assists us, and will provide what we need to reach the greatest possibility for our lives, the unsurpassable good of everlasting beatitude with God.[89]

Charity is both a particular virtue and a comprehensive way of life. Thomas Aquinas defined charity as a life of friendship with God based on the communication or sharing of God's happiness and life with us.[90] And for Aquinas, as Jean Porter emphasizes, "the claim that charity makes us friends of God is no metaphor."[91] Aquinas maintained that, thanks to the infusion of God's grace, love, and happiness into our lives in charity, we could, however incompletely, share in God's life now. Charity means that God's trinitarian life dwells within us, so that just as friends are of "one heart and soul," God too is one with us.

Just as friends seek one another's good, in charity we seek God's good as God works for and seeks our good. And just as friends are of "one will" regarding what they seek and desire in life, through charity we strive to will what God wills and to seek what God wills in everything we do. As Diana Cates observes, "in friendship with God, as Thomas conceives of it, the believer begins to share in the very life of God, and in this shared life, he begins to know and to love as a participant in the knowing and loving of God."[92]

Moreover, charity so completely transforms our lives that everything about us is oriented toward the attainment of supernatural happiness with God. Through charity we seek God in all things inasmuch as charity directs our thoughts, feelings, and attitudes to God and makes everything about our lives serve our overriding desire for God. This is why Aquinas held that "charity, rather than prudence, functions as the supreme organizing principle in the personality of the justified, by which not only all their actions but all their desires and impulses are directed toward God (II-II. 23.3.7)."[93]

Aquinas captured the special role of charity in the Christian life by speaking of it as the "form" of all the virtues. For Aquinas, if our sovereign desire in life is for friendship and communion with God, then this desire will inspire, inform, shape, and guide everything we do so that even the most ordinary activities of our lives move us toward our greatest possible good. Charity directs everything we do, and thus brings every other virtue to its utmost possible perfection, so that all our actions, no matter how small, have supernatural bearing.[94]

We can see, for example, how charity brings a different "form" to the virtues by considering its impact on prudence. Charity enlarges the activity of prudence by ensuring that we not only are able to make right judgments about what needs to be done today, but also know how to make our everyday actions and decisions serve our overall good of attaining union with God. The immediate purpose of prudence is to show us the best means for doing the good now. But when prudence is born from charity, we also know how to live today in order to attain "the final good for the whole of human life."[95]

Infused Moral Virtues

The infused moral virtues are like the theological virtues insofar as they are given to us or "infused" in us by God. Like the theological virtues, they cannot be acquired by human agency. And, like the theological virtues, the infused moral virtues are always matters of grace, dynamic expressions of how God's spirit is actively at work in our lives. But unlike the theological virtues, the immediate concern of the infused moral virtues is not God but the "inner-worldly activities" that make up our lives.[96] In this respect, they share something in common with the acquired moral virtues.

For instance, both the acquired moral virtues and the infused moral virtues govern our relationships with others (justice), help us deal with fear (courage), steer us toward the right way to respond to fundamental human needs and inclinations (temperance), and guide us in doing what is right and good (prudence). But they differ from the acquired virtues, not only because they are infused in us by God, but also because they bring to all the activities of our daily life a different perspective and goal, and thus "different understandings of what constitutes truly just, temperate, brave, and prudent action." Mattison captures well the distinctive function of the infused moral virtues when he suggests that "they incline us to do inner-worldly activities well in the larger perspective of our supernatural destiny. They give a different *meaning* to those activities, commonly leading to different particular actions."[97]

For instance, if the acquired virtue of courage helps us persevere through the trials and challenges of our lives, the infused virtue of courage (in partnership with the theological virtue of hope) helps us persevere in our quest for the reign of God. Or if the exemplar of "natural" or acquired courage is the soldier in battle, because our greatest fear is death, the exemplar of the infused virtue of courage is the martyr for whom not even the threat of death weakens her faithfulness to God.

Similarly, if the acquired virtue of justice leads us to fulfill our obligations toward others, the infused virtue of justice summons us to practice a generosity that exceeds our ordinary sense of what we owe others. Again, different accounts of excellence and different understandings of the greatest possible good will lead to different accounts of the virtues. If the goal of the moral life is to grow in the love and goodness of God, then how we think about each of the virtues will change. As Mattison explains, we need the category of infused virtues to remind us that "Christian faith transforms not just a person's relationship with God, but also a person's inner-worldly activities."[98]

Nonetheless, the relationship between the acquired moral virtues and the infused moral virtues can be confusing if we picture them as two parallel tracks of virtues at work in our lives—one set that was acquired by our own agency, and another that was infused in us by God. The infused moral virtues do not parallel the acquired moral virtues; rather, they elevate, transform, and perfect those virtues so that through the most ordinary actions of our lives we can attain our goal of everlasting beatitude with God.

Like the theological virtues, the infused moral virtues endow us with a different capacity for action; in this respect, they are principally the work of grace. But, also like the theological virtues, they need to be exercised, deepened, and developed by us. As Michael Miller notes, "The use of the term 'infused' should not imply that they are suddenly poured into us by God against our human nature, as some mistakenly suggest. Rather, God complements and perfects our very nature with these infused virtues, for these dispositions bring us both to our fulfillment as human beings and to life with God."[99] Miller's comment underscores that the infused moral virtues imply an ongoing and dynamic partnership between God and ourselves. We can neither acquire nor "perform" the infused moral virtues without God's assistance, but they are still our acts inasmuch as they "complement and perfect," not override, violate, or ignore, our nature.

Such virtues are indispensable in the Christian moral life because with them we can make all our "worldly" activities contribute to our life of friendship with God. Through them our daily acts of thoughtfulness, kindness, patience, courage, and compassion not only do good for ourselves and others now but help us share in and attain the perfection of our lives that is unwavering beatitude with God and the saints. As Cates summarizes, "Whereas acquired virtue aims at the perfection of human nature and the enjoyment of natural human flourishing, infused virtue aims at the perfection of a supernaturally elevated human nature and the enjoyment of a supernatural human flourishing in fellowship with God."[100]

Jesus and the Christian Moral Life

We cannot grow in the Christian moral life "unless we possess models of moral excellence, exemplars that we can look to and imitate as examples of a life well lived."[101] Christians have models of moral excellence in the saints, the holy ones who have gone before us, and the holy ones in our midst. From them we can learn much about what it means to grow in, and increasingly be conformed to, the goodness of God. But the saints are fitting mentors for us because they devoted themselves wholeheartedly to following and learning from Christ. Christ must be our principal mentor, guide, and exemplar in the Christian life because he is "the unsurpassable revelation and embodiment of the transcendent, comprehensive goodness that is God."[102] He is the goodness we seek and the goodness in which we are fulfilled. He is the ideal and perfection of what God created us to be.

Still, it is hard to pattern our lives after Christ because he calls us to a way of life that not only challenges our ordinary understanding of goodness, but in many respects explodes it. Jesus is the incarnation of the "scandalous" goodness of God, a goodness defined through unnerving humility, exquisite self-giving, lavish mercy and compassion, and a love that not even death can stop. If Christians are called to have the same mind or attitude that we see in Christ (Phil 2:5), then they are to witness in their own lives the costly, but truly life-giving, goodness of Jesus. They are to bring that goodness to life in the world. Doing so is not a matter of slavishly imitating the actions and examples of Jesus, as if any of us could return to first-century Palestine.

Rather, Christians bring Christ's goodness to life in the world through *improvisation*—that is, by discerning how to creatively re-present Jesus to others. In this respect, we can learn much from the saints, the most gifted improvisers of all, and from the other members of our faith communities, who show us what being faithful to Jesus really means. As Frederick Bauerschmidt explains, "If in Jesus we are offered the human exemplar of unrestricted goodness, in the saints we can perceive the Spirit's improvisation upon that exemplar; we might say that the saints are our exemplars of the kind of Spirit-filled improvisation that is required if we are to be faithful imitators of Jesus."[103] Ultimately, such "Spirit-filled improvisation" is the heart of the Christian moral life. Christians "improvise" on the story of Jesus in all the ways they try to bring the love, justice, truthfulness, obedience, mercy, and faithfulness of Christ to life in the world through their own manifold virtues.

CONCLUSION

In this chapter we have argued that we grow in the distinctive potential and excellence of human beings through the virtues, because the virtues are the habits of being and acting by which we become "good" at being human. They are not optional elements to a life of human well-being but constitute such a life, because apart from them we cannot undergo the transformation of self that genuine happiness requires. What that transformation entails depends on how one understands the unsurpassable good available for us. In the Christian moral life the transformation is forever incomplete because the goodness we seek is the transcendent beauty and goodness of God.

At the same time, our journey toward that goal is full of hope because, thanks to grace and the infused theological and moral virtues, we can partake now in a happiness we could never give ourselves. Jesus shows us the way to the happiness that is found in God. This is why the center of the Christian moral life is not a theory or an ideal, but a person to be observed, followed, imitated, and truly taken to heart. Christians grow in the virtues that lead to lasting beatitude when they apprentice themselves as disciples to Jesus. And they excel in the Christian moral life when they are skilled and daring improvisers who, like Jesus, bring God's love to life in the world in surprising and wonderful ways.

KEY POINTS

1. A desire for the good is rooted in our human nature.
2. Our happiness depends on participating in and achieving the best possible life (*eudaimonia*) for human beings.
3. The virtues are the habitual ways of being and acting by which we become good persons who lead genuinely good lives.
4. Four virtues that are believed to be especially important in the moral life are the cardinal virtues of prudence, justice, temperance, and fortitude.
5. In the Christian life, one cannot reach everlasting happiness with God without the theological virtues of faith, hope, and charity, and the infused moral virtues.
6. In order to grow in goodness, we need mentors and models. Jesus is our principal mentor and model in the Christian moral life. But we also have exemplary models to follow in the saints.

QUESTIONS FOR REFLECTION

1. How would you define *eudaimonia,* or the "best possible life," for human beings? What would it include?
2. Do you believe only good people are truly happy? Why or why not?
3. What are the virtues? Why do we need them? And why can it be difficult to acquire virtues?
4. Is there an "advantage" to being virtuous? Who are examples of virtuous persons for you?
5. Which of the cardinal virtues do you think is most important? Why?
6. What are the theological virtues? Why is charity considered the most important of the theological virtues?
7. What would it mean for you to "improvise" the life of Christ in your life today?

SUGGESTIONS FOR FURTHER READING AND STUDY

Casey, John. *Pagan Virtue: An Essay in Ethics.* Oxford: Clarendon, 1990.
Devettere, Raymond J. *Introduction to Virtue Ethics: Insights of the Ancient Greeks.* Washington, D.C.: Georgetown University Press, 2002.
Hauerwas, Stanley, and Charles Pinches. *Christians among the Virtues: Theological*

Conversations with Ancient and Modern Ethics. Notre Dame, Ind.: University of Notre Dame Press, 1997.

Kotva, Joseph J., Jr. *The Christian Case for Virtue Ethics.* Washington, D.C.: Georgetown University Press, 1996.

MacIntyre, Alasdair. *After Virtue: A Study in Moral Theory.* Notre Dame, Ind.: University of Notre Dame Press, 1981.

Mattison, William C., III. *Introducing Moral Theology: True Happiness and the Virtues.* Grand Rapids: Brazos, 2008.

McCarthy, David Matzko, and M. Therese Lysaught, eds. *Gathered for the Journey: Moral Theology in Catholic Perspective.* Grand Rapids: Eerdmans, 2007.

Meilaender, Gilbert C. *The Theory and Practice of Virtue.* Notre Dame, Ind.: University of Notre Dame Press, 1984.

Pieper, Josef. *The Four Cardinal Virtues,* trans. Richard Winston, Clara Winston, Lawrence E. Lynch, and Daniel F. Coogan. Notre Dame, Ind.: University of Notre Dame Press, 1966.

Porter, Jean. *The Recovery of Virtue: The Relevance of Aquinas for Christian Ethics.* Louisville: Westminster/John Knox, 1990.

Wadell, Paul J. *The Primacy of Love: An Introduction to the Ethics of Thomas Aquinas.* New York: Paulist, 1992.

6

Conscience—Exploring a Gift Too Precious to Lose

"Your Conscience Bears Witness" (Romans 2:15)

W HAT HAPPENS IF our conscience stops bearing witness? What happens to ourselves, to our communities and societies, and to the larger world, when men and women neglect their conscience, betray their conscience, or ultimately kill it? What is the cost to ourselves and to others if we flee the call of conscience on account of fear, pressure, moral laziness, or simply because it is profitable for us to do so? Ignoring the call of conscience is a habit we can easily—and oftentimes quite casually—develop. But it is a dangerous quality of character to acquire because it contradicts the deepest dynamism of our nature as moral beings oriented to and fulfilled in what is true, beautiful, and good. To be human is to be called to responsibility and nowhere do we hear this summons more powerfully than in the depths of our conscience. It is conscience that reminds us that to be human is to be moral and that to ignore this fundamental dimension of our being is to misunderstand ourselves in inevitably disastrous ways. Conscience is a gift too precious to lose.

Few literary works capture the importance of conscience as well as Robert Bolt's *A Man for All Seasons*. The play tells the story of Sir Thomas More, the sixteenth-century lawyer and nobleman who became Lord Chancellor to King Henry VIII. Thomas More was a friend of the king; indeed, he is the only one in the play who honors Henry by being truthful with him. But the truth More speaks is the truth of his conscience, and it is not a truth Henry wants to hear. A devout Catholic, More will not support the king's divorce from Catherine of Aragon. While everyone else surrounding Henry beguiles him with a chorus of support, More holds out because he cannot *in conscience* affirm something he believes is wrong, even if loyalty to his conscience ultimately costs him his life.

In one scene, Cardinal Wolsey, a devious and dangerously ambitious ecclesiastic, pressures More to surrender his conscience for the sake of supporting the king. "If you could just see facts flat on, without that horrible moral squint; with just a little common sense," he tells More, "you could have been a statesman." And he argues that what More believes in the privacy of his conscience is his "own affair," but not something that should ever interfere with his responsibilities to the king or the larger business of the state. To this More responds: "Well . . . I believe, when statesmen forsake their own private conscience for the sake of their public duties . . . they lead their country by a short route to chaos."[1]

For More, loyalty to his conscience takes precedence over loyalty to his king. The king may be sovereign of England, but for More conscience is the sovereign of his soul. Honoring and being faithful to his conscience is the utmost way for him to honor and be faithful to God. But it was a costly commitment to uphold because choosing to follow his conscience, instead of abandoning it to stand beside everyone else who supported Henry's divorce, led to his death. Threatened by More's integrity, Henry imprisons him in the Tower of London and soon after has him beheaded. But the man Henry hoped to erase from history today lives on in the collective memory of the community—the church—that named him a saint, one whose life is worthy of imitation.

The "horrible moral squint" that is our conscience can be a heavy burden. Even today we hear of persons whose fidelity to conscience brings them misunderstanding and estrangement from others, ridicule and loss of opportunity, great suffering, and sometimes even the loss of their lives. But what happens to us if we forsake the "horrible moral squint" that reminds us that we are creatures created from the love and goodness of God who are called to pursue that love and goodness through the everyday decisions and actions of our lives? What happens if we follow the advice of the wily Cardinal Wolsey and replace the "horrible moral squint" of conscience with the decidedly safer perspective that allows us to "see facts flat on"?

Conscience is the clearest—and oftentimes most troublesome—indicator that we are moral beings called to accountability, moral beings who live and grow and flourish only when we answer the call to responsibility that distinguishes us from every other creature on the earth. To be human is to be called into being by God. But it is also to be called to responsibility. Conscience comes to life as we hear and respond to the call to be responsible. As the liberation theologians Antônio Moser and Bernardino Leers write: "Very slowly, gradually, obscurely and vaguely at first, we come to know that we exist, that we are someone and that we can and must *become*: we begin to perceive our responsibility for our own destiny and for that of the world around us. This is the dawning of conscience."[2]

As Moser and Leers suggest, the most basic human imperative is to grow and to develop. It is to recognize that we are not just to exist, but to become more than we already are. Morally speaking, the fundamental human command is the summons to transcend ourselves in justice, goodness, and love to others, and that is the call of conscience. Or, as the Irish theologian Sean Fagan says, conscience is "an invitation and a summons, commanding us *to become* and *to be* what we are meant to be, to continually grow into our better selves."[3] In its most exquisite expression, conscience is both the summons and the capacity to share in the creative and redemptive activity of God by participating in and furthering God's goodness and love in our everyday lives.[4]

Put differently, conscience is both a *gift* and a *call*. As creatures fashioned in the image and likeness of God, conscience is the gift of moral awareness and discernment that enables us to recognize opportunities for goodness, justice, compassion, and love in our daily lives. But because we are creatures fashioned in the image and likeness of God, conscience is equally the call to moral responsibility. We are not just to see opportunities for goodness, justice, compassion, and love, but to act on them. Through the gift of personal conscience, we are to bring goodness and love more fully to life in the world. In more biblical language, we are to use the gift of conscience to share in and contribute to Christ's mission of building the reign of God.[5] And we do this not when we follow the corrupting calculations of the Cardinal Wolsey's of the world but when, like Thomas More, we strive to put on the "mind of Christ" (1 Cor 2:16) and seek to make our conscience one with it.

In this chapter then we will first consider what we mean when we speak of conscience. Is conscience nothing more than the proverbial "little voice" that whispers to us that we ought to do something and troubles us when we don't? What is the connection between a person's conscience and her character? And do our feelings and emotions have anything to contribute to our conscience? Second, in trying to understand why some people are more conscientious than others, we will look at some of the things that shape and influence our consciences for better or worse. This includes the most formative relationships of our lives, the cultures and societies in which we live, and the communities with which we most identify ourselves.

Third, we will attend to what it might mean to take responsibility for developing our conscience. If the formation of one's conscience is a lifelong task and process, how can this best be done? What must happen to us if we are to be confident about our decisions of conscience? And what role might other persons or communities have in the development and formation of our conscience?

Finally, we will conclude the chapter by sketching an account of a specifically Christian conscience. Christians are baptized into Christ so that their lives might be conformed to Christ. How does living in, from, and for Christ shape a Christian understanding of conscience? If a goal of the Christian life is to be of one mind and heart with Christ, how does this impact what it means for us to live and to act in "good" conscience? Answering these questions will put the "horrible moral squint" that is conscience in a different light.

WHAT IT MEANS TO HAVE A CONSCIENCE

The Bible and Conscience

Although the Bible does not offer a fully developed theory of conscience, it is a helpful place to begin for understanding what it means to have a conscience. The Old Testament does not explicitly use the word conscience, but "the reality of conscience is not missing from its pages." If we think of conscience as a call to do what is both good and right, a pervasive theme of the Old Testament is how the Israelites were continually called "to hear and respond to the word of God."[6]

In the Old Testament the most common metaphor for conscience is the heart, an image that captures how conscience is not something extraneous to who we are but something that lives and beats at the very center of who we are. Just as the heart is the center of life in men and women, the Old Testament scriptures "locate the human sensitivity to good and evil in the heart of the human person. (Ps 95:7, Jer 11:20, Eccl 7:22, 1 Sm 24:6, Job 27:6, Mt 15:11-17, and 1 Jn 3:19-21 are but a few of many examples.)"[7] Contrary to the modern tendency to associate conscience primarily with our minds, the Bible places conscience at the very core of our being; in fact, as the location for our deepest convictions, commitments, and desires, the heart symbolizes a person in her or his totality. This is why, as we shall later suggest, it is perhaps better to say that *we are our conscience* rather than that we have a conscience. Thus, far from being a mere ornament to our human personality, our conscience is the deepest and most genuine articulation of who we are. And just as we die if our hearts stop beating, the Old Testament hints that we decline morally and spiritually if we fail to nurture our consciences.

Moreover, the Old Testament upholds an explicitly religious understanding of conscience. Conscience is not our private possession. It is God's gift to us—part of our created being—and represents how God's spirit is at work in our lives, guiding us, summoning us, challenging us, and sometimes reproving us. Thus, while our conscience may be the most personal or "heartfelt" thing about us, the Bible suggests that it is not a purely individual or autonomous reality. To the contrary, the scriptures claim that conscience always entails a dialogue between God and ourselves.

> Conscience is "an invitation and a summons, commanding us to become and to be *what we are* meant to be, to continually grow into our better selves."

The word *conscience* literally means "knowing with" or "knowing together," and from the Bible's point of view conscience describes a "knowing" that takes place between God and ourselves. Our conscience is where we encounter God and listen for the voice of God in order to discern the will of God. In what has become a famous passage, a document from the Second Vatican Council echoes this biblical understanding of conscience when it speaks of conscience as "people's most secret core and their sanctuary," where "they are alone with God whose voice echoes in their depths."[8]

Our conscience is a holy place where we, in the silence of our hearts, listen attentively for the word of God and open ourselves to receive it. There, in a most personal encounter with God, we strive to learn the will of God in order to put it into practice. In the Old Testament fidelity to conscience is fidelity to God. Too, the prophets suggest that our conscience is not an empty space that is periodically invaded by the commands and promptings of God; rather, from the beginning our "hearts" have been inscribed with the laws and ways of God—they are stitched into our very being—so that to attend to our conscience is to seek to know how God's ways oblige us and what faithfulness to God might require of us:

> But this is the covenant that I will make with the house of Israel after those days, says the LORD: I will put my law within them, and I will write it on their hearts; and I will be their God, and they shall be my people. (Jer 31:33)

> I will give them one heart, and put a new spirit within them; I will remove the heart of stone from their flesh and give them a heart of flesh, so that they may follow my statutes and keep my ordinances and obey them. Then they shall be my people, and I will be their God. (Ezek 11:19-20)

In this respect, the Old Testament prophets suggest that conscience signals our ability to know and to do not just any good but God's good. It is from our hearts that God calls, guides, illumines, and sometimes accuses.[9]

In the New Testament the writings of Paul provide the most explicit analysis of conscience. Paul speaks of conscience in two ways.[10]

> When Gentiles, who do not possess the law, do instinctively what the law requires, these, though not having the law, are a law to themselves. They show that what the law requires is written on their hearts, to which their own conscience also bears witness; and their conflicting thoughts will accuse or perhaps excuse them on the day when, according to my gospel, God, through Jesus Christ, will judge the secret thoughts of all. (Rom 2:14-16)

> I do not understand my own actions. For I do not do what I want, but I do the very thing I hate. . . . For I do not do the good I want, but the evil I do not want is what I do. (Rom 7:15, 19)

For if others see you, who possess knowledge, eating in the temple of an idol, might they not, since their conscience is weak, be encouraged to the point of eating food sacrificed to idols? So by your knowledge those weak believers for whom Christ died are destroyed. But when you thus sin against members of your family, and wound their conscience when it is weak, you sin against Christ. (1 Cor 8:10-12)

First, there is the *antecedent* conscience. This describes the moral awareness that we possess prior to acting and deciding. Antecedent conscience refers to a person's grasp of the most basic moral principle, namely, that good is to be done and evil avoided. A dimension of conscience, it is knowledge that precedes, guides, and informs our actions, and it is knowledge that we intuitively grasp, not something we need to be taught. It is in light of antecedent conscience that we know human beings are to seek the good and to avoid what is wicked.

Second, there is *negative* or *consequent* conscience. This second dimension of conscience accounts for the remorse and regret we feel after having knowingly done something that was wrong or after having failed to do what we know we ought to have done. Our remorse and regret are a consequence of having behaved in ways that contradict the deepest moral law of our being, and realizing that our conscience accuses us. Too, we have consequent conscience only because we first have antecedent conscience. We feel sorrow and regret for some of our actions precisely because they violated something that every human being instinctively knows: we are to embrace the good and turn away from what is evil.

Overall, Paul's distinction between antecedent and negative or consequent conscience confirms the biblical view that the "whole person is called by God, for God and for the good. We can be at peace only if we respond with our whole heart to this call."[11] As the Catholic moral theologian Bernard Haring wrote, "We are created for wholeness biologically, psychologically and spiritually. The deepest part of our being is keenly sensitive to what can promote and what can threaten our wholeness and integrity."[12] This is why caring for and developing our conscience is crucial, and why neglecting or ignoring it is morally and spiritually fatal. If human beings are oriented to wholeness, it is the well-formed conscience that attunes us to the convictions, commitments, loyalties, desires, and decisions that result in genuine human well-being and alerts us to those that do not. We are created for wholeness, primed for what promotes well-being and life, and it is through a sensitive and astute conscience that we can best decipher the behavior that will lead us to wholeness and the behavior that will begin our decline.

Conscience in the Theology of Thomas Aquinas

In the Christian tradition one of the more systematic analyses of the biblical presentation of conscience is found in the writings of the great medieval theologian Thomas Aquinas (1225-1274). Aquinas spoke of conscience both as a capacity and as an action or decision. Akin to the biblical antecedent conscience, Aquinas believed that men and women by their very nature recognized that they were moral beings alive in a world that was given a moral order by God, one that they were obliged to respect. Aquinas declared not only that human beings were endowed with knowledge of the most fundamental or first principles of morality, but they were also innately inclined to live according to them. Thus, in speaking of conscience as a naturally endowed human capacity, Aquinas argued that men and women not only recognized the truth of fundamental moral principles, but also recognized that they were bound by them.[13] This first dimension of conscience is a "habitual, intuitive grasp of the first principles for action, the precepts of the law of nature, which 'prompts us to good and complains at what is bad,'" John Mahoney writes. It is "a habitual grasp of the basic rules of morality."[14]

The second part of conscience refers to the actual decisions of conscience that flow from our capacity for conscience. As Aquinas saw it, conscience acts by applying the fundamental principles of morality to the actual circumstances of our lives. Our capacity for conscience tells us that we ought to do what is good and avoid what is evil; but conscience is completed in a concrete moral judgment that brings that knowledge to bear in our daily actions and behavior.[15] For example, my capacity for conscience tells me that I ought to tell the truth, and it is through my act of conscience that I apply that knowledge or principle to the specific circumstances of my life. This is why an "action of conscience, then, is no more and no less than an ordinary act of human reason applying the various principles of morality to individual situations."[16]

But this can make acting in good conscience sound much easier than it actually is. Everyone knows that we ought to tell the truth. But it can be notoriously difficult to know how to do so in a way that good actually results. In order to act, our conscience must move from general moral principles to specific, and oftentimes highly complex, moral situations. And Aquinas emphasized that the more we move from the universal principles of morality into the detailed and often sticky circumstances of our lives, the less certainty we have about precisely what it means to do what is right.[17] I know I should tell the truth, but I do not always know how or when it is best to tell the truth. I know I should treat every human being fairly, but I am much less certain about what this practically entails when I consider all the different people in my life.

Put differently, we are never mistaken in our awareness that we ought to do what is right; however, we may often be mistaken in determining what this would actually mean when applied to the various persons, situations, and circumstances that compose our lives. The absolute certainty we enjoy in our knowledge that good should be done often fades when we wrestle with how to implement this knowledge in the challenging and frequently murky moral situations of our lives. Does treating a student respectfully and fairly mean I should always give her a second chance? If I make an exception for one student, does fairness demand that I do so for every student?

These reflections explain why we can make decisions in "good conscience" that, in retrospect, we recognize were flawed. We made them with the best of intentions and, we thought, with adequate insight and knowledge, but later realized that our judgment and, therefore, our action, were mistaken. Are we morally culpable for decisions of conscience that we later recognize were erroneous? For Aquinas, it all depends on whether we should have known something that we failed to know. In his language, was our ignorance "vincible" or "invincible"? Vincible or "conquerable" ignorance refers to something we did not know but should have known. My ignorance is vincible if with reasonable efforts I could have known something about the relevant facts of a matter that would have changed the decision I eventually made.

Put perhaps more clearly, I not only could have known otherwise but should have known otherwise; therefore, I am responsible for my erroneous conscience.[18] Too, Aquinas noted that sometimes we choose to remain ignorant of the relevant facts—we choose not to know—lest that knowledge reveal something about our proposed actions that we do not want to see. I know I can "conquer" my ignorance if I study the matter further or consider facts I have hitherto ignored; but precisely because I do not want to change what I have already decided I want to do, I deliberately fail to examine the issue further.

By contrast, invincible ignorance refers to decisions of conscience that were ultimately shown to be wrong, but for which a person is not held responsible because he or she could not have reasonably been expected to know the most relevant facts about the situation. The late Pope John Paul II described invincible ignorance as "an ignorance of which the subject is not aware and which he is unable to overcome by himself."[19] With invincible or "unconquerable" ignorance, I do not realize that I do not know something that is pertinent to the decision I eventually make. What I do not know changes the moral meaning of my proposed act and, in this respect, makes it flawed or mistaken.

Nonetheless, because I do not intentionally choose to remain ignorant of these relevant facts, my act may be flawed but I am not morally blameworthy. As James Bretzke summarizes, "But if this ignorance could not be overcome even by a person's sincere efforts, then the ignorance was called 'invincible' and the person was *not* held morally accountable for his or her actions, even though the actions themselves were still judged to violate the objective moral order."[20] For Aquinas, then, whether an erroneous conscience makes a moral agent culpable all depends "on why conscience was mistaken in the first place, and on the degree of negligence or guilt which might accompany such a state. If conscience acts from a lack of knowledge which one ought to possess, then the error is culpable and so also is the conscientious behaviour resulting from it."[21]

These reflections call to mind a very important point: a good person acting in good conscience can still do wrong. But wrong acts are not necessarily sinful acts. If a person sincerely tries to do what is right and honestly seeks to discern what ought to be done, then even if the act turns out to be mistaken it is not sinful because it was done with a good and responsible conscience. This is why many theologians today—perhaps most notably James Keenan—distinguish between good persons and wrong actions.

Good people do not always act rightly, not because they have bad intentions, but because they sometimes misjudge how the good needs to be done. Their intentions are good, but their actions may be flawed, misguided, and mistaken. If someone consistently tries to live a good life and consistently strives to do what is right, then they remain good even if their concrete judgments about particular actions sometimes miss the mark. As Keenan writes, such a person "errs in good faith" because their intention was to do what was both right and good, even though their action fell short of what needed to be done.[22] Good people acting in good conscience can do the wrong thing. If their actions sometimes fall short of the good, because they are good people who want to do good, they will learn from the experience so that they do not make the same mistake again. Although the distinction between good persons and wrong actions can be overdrawn, it is a healthy reminder of why we may vigorously disagree with something someone did without questioning her goodness. A person may do something we are convinced is wrong, but that does not necessarily make her a bad person.

Contemporary Accounts of Conscience

Over the past several decades Catholic ethicists have expanded Aquinas's analysis of conscience by speaking of three distinct but closely related dimensions of conscience. There is first our capacity for conscience; second, the process by which we make decisions of conscience; and third, the actual judgment of conscience.[23] The first dimension of conscience refers to a person's awareness that life is a moral matter and that men and women are moral beings who are called to seek the good and to live responsibly. Timothy O'Connell calls this "conscience/1" and says that it consists in "a general sense of value, an awareness of personal responsibility, which is utterly characteristic of the human person."[24]

Moreover, this first element of conscience captures humans' awareness of fundamental moral principles, their recognition that these moral principles have a claim on them as moral beings, and their ability to evaluate and decide about moral matters. In its second dimension, conscience describes the process a person employs in coming to particular judgments or decisions. Among other things, this would include reasoning or deliberating about what a situation involves, recognizing and applying pertinent moral principles, looking for the most crucial moral values and goods at stake, and being attentive to the morally relevant circumstances of a situation. Finally, the third dimension of conscience is the actual judgment of conscience by which one determines, in light of one's deliberations, what ought to be done and does it.

Josef Fuchs, a German moral theologian whose writings were highly influential in the years both before and after the Second Vatican Council (1962-1965), offers further insight into the meaning of conscience. Fuchs distinguished between *subjective* and *objective* conscience in order to emphasize that "conscience obviously involves so much more than just making right (or wrong) judgments."[25] For Fuchs, to imagine conscience as something that rather mechanically discloses appropriate solutions to moral dilemmas is to embrace a truncated and impersonal view of conscience. If we equate conscience solely with concrete moral decisions, we forget that every decision of conscience comes from a subject who is a moral being, and who "exists as a moral being before, during, and after" his or her individual decisions of conscience.[26] This is why Fuchs contends that we cannot rightly understand objective decisions of conscience without first reckoning with the subjective or personal dimension of conscience.

Sometimes described as "fundamental conscience," subjective conscience underscores that human beings are ineluctably moral creatures, creatures who know they are moral beings called to responsibility.[27] More generally, subjective conscience discloses the fundamental human urge to fulfill oneself as a human being through responsible goodness, as well as the urge to achieve one's authentic being by "ultimately seeking to be faithful and true to ourselves, being who we are made to be by God."[28] In this respect, subjective conscience points to the importance of personal integrity and character and of personal vocation.

The authenticity and wholeness sought by subjective conscience is achieved through one's objective conscience. This is why we cannot think of subjective and objective conscience as two completely separate dimensions of conscience, but must see them as reciprocally connected.[29] Objective conscience represents what people, after studying and examining a situation, are sincerely convinced they must do if they are "to be ethically 'good'" human beings, and thereby fulfill their subjective conscience.[30]

What are we as moral subjects objectively called to do in order to achieve what is both good and right? This question guides the objective dimension of conscience. Or, in more religious language, "when individuals discern and respond to what they honestly (objectively) believe God is asking of them, then they are responding to this objective pole" of conscience.[31] In this way, one grows and develops as a moral subject, and as a person of goodness and integrity, through their objective decisions of conscience.

What Does This Tell Us about Conscience?

This examination of various understandings of conscience allows us to make certain conclusions about what we mean when we speak of conscience. First, Fuchs's account of subjective conscience suggests that it is better not to think of conscience as a special moral faculty but to envision it as encompassing our whole selves as moral beings. A popular view of conscience is to picture it as a little inner voice, sometimes encouraging, sometimes illuminating, sometimes nagging, that calls us to do some things but to avoid other things.

And yet, if we think of conscience in this way we fail to recognize that conscience involves not only our minds but also our convictions and commitments, our passions, desires, and feelings, our creativity and imagination, and indeed the whole moral history that has shaped us as personal subjects. As Richard Gula notes, "a contemporary approach to conscience focuses on the whole person. Conscience includes not only cognitive and volitional aspects, but also affective, intuitive, and somatic ones as well. We understand the moral conscience holistically as an expression of the whole self as a thinking, feeling, intuiting and willing person." In light of this, Gula defines conscience as "*the whole person's commitment to value and the judgment one makes in light of that commitment of who one ought to be and what one ought to do or not do.*"[32] Thus, as Gula intimates, every decision of conscience grows from a person's more fundamental commitment to be and to become a certain kind of person through the core moral commitments of his or her life.

Moreover, if we think of conscience as that inner voice that speaks to us, we can assume that it works the same in everyone. But that clearly is not the case. Some people are obviously more conscientious than others. Some people have very sensitive and astute consciences, while others exhibit little moral awareness at all. This is why Vincent MacNamara is right to claim, "It is not so much that I have a conscience—a special piece of equipment—as that I am a conscience."[33] We are our conscience because conscience is nothing more than a way of talking about ourselves as moral beings, as creatures called to responsibility, and about the more or less adequate ways that we live in the world as moral beings. People of "good conscience" know that life is a moral matter and that to be human is to be responsible and accountable for ourselves as well as for others. They hear the moral call that speaks to us from the diverse situations of our lives and they answer it. They acknowledge the obligations we have toward others and are regularly compelled by what is true, right, and good.

By contrast, people of poor conscience may know that there is a moral dimension to life, but they readily ignore it, especially if heeding it is inconvenient or costly. They may recognize the difference between right and wrong, but it has little practical impact in their lives. Rather than nurture the conscience that makes and keeps us human, they habitually ignore it, sometimes to the point that they lose what little conscience they had.

Second, our conscience is intimately linked to our character. Our character is the unique moral identity we have given ourselves through our most habitual actions and decisions, through our most consistent attitudes, perceptions, values, feelings, convictions, loyalties, and commitments. Our conscience is a reflection of our character because it is essentially the moral self with which we relate to others and engage life. If a person has acquired virtues such as gratitude and generosity, justice and courage, loyalty and patience, compassion and love, they are likewise persons of good conscience, precisely because they have grown in the qualities of character that best enable us to live thoughtful and responsible lives.

On the other hand, if someone has grown in vices such as selfishness and insensitivity, arrogance and carelessness, bitterness and coldness, infidelity and cowardice, they can hardly exhibit traits of a good conscience because they have formed themselves into persons who will regularly ignore the moral dimension of life. Conscience cannot rescue a person from a poorly formed character; rather, our conscience will always express the character we have acquired. This is why it is impossible to have an insightful and responsible conscience without also having grown in the virtues that give us excellence and expertise in goodness. Put differently, we can hardly be trusted to have a highly developed conscience when the time comes to make important moral decisions in our lives if we have not all along fostered in ourselves the qualities of character that would enable us to do so.

Third, as mentioned above, while reason and intelligence play an obvious role in matters of conscience, so do our emotions, intuitions and feelings, and our imagination. We do not typically consider the role that our feelings and emotions play in matters of conscience because we are accustomed to think of coming to decisions of conscience as an essentially rational activity. Indeed, some hold not only that our feelings and emotions are irrelevant to the work of conscience but also that they impede it and, therefore, need to be ignored or suppressed. In this view, our feelings are too unstable and untrustworthy to contribute anything helpful to the work of conscience. Because they mislead and deceive, they must be constantly held in check by and seen as subordinate to our reason. We should, this view holds, be wary of our emotions and always choose instead to follow the clear and more trustworthy light of reason.[34]

Instead of contrasting reason and the emotions, it is better to see attending to our feelings and intuitions, as well as our imaginations, as a core part of the rationality of conscience. Although there is a tradition that has held that our emotions and feelings are essentially irrational, the truth is that our decisions of conscience can be fully reasonable only when we have taken into account what our intuitions, feelings, and imaginations might be telling us about the decisions we are considering. Many times it is through our intuitions, feelings, and our imaginations that we glean a clearer sense of what truly matters in a decision. And even though we can be led astray by our emotions, they can also take us right to the heart of an issue by alerting us to the goods and values that are most at stake.

Obviously, we need to use our reason and intelligence when coming to good decisions of conscience; however, we cannot neglect our feelings and imaginations because they too are indispensable sources for moral insight and awareness. They can, for example, remind us of what we care most about or help us to see things more keenly and perceptively. Our imaginations can challenge us to see new and better possibilities or to think more creatively.

Likewise, the messages we get from our hearts may not be infallible moral guides, but they can offer important intimations of the truth. This is why when making decisions of conscience we need to take seriously feelings of uneasiness, anxiety, or uncertainty, on the one hand, and peace, assurance, and confidence, on the other hand. This more holistic and integrated view of conscience is reflected in Sidney Callahan's definition of conscience. She defines conscience as "a personal, self-conscious activity, integrating reason, emotion, and will in self-committed decisions about right and wrong, good and evil."[35]

WHAT SHAPES OUR CONSCIENCE—FOR BETTER OR WORSE

In *Liberating Conscience* Anne Patrick says that the authentic development of conscience involves "freeing persons from whatever inhibits a full response to the divine invitation to love God, neighbor, and self in ways that are recognizably good."[36] But there are many things that inhibit the full development of our consciences and prevent us from enjoying the kind of "liberated" conscience Patrick describes.

We do not—and sometimes cannot—always respond to the divine invitation to love in ways that are truly good for ourselves or for others. As the above analysis suggested, we may be given a capacity for conscience, but we are hardly given a fully developed and mature conscience. Our conscience is a living thing, and like anything else that lives it can grow and develop; but it can also be weakened and diminished. We cannot take our consciences for granted, because they are not static, fixed realities, but dynamic, living realities that either grow or decline, and that are unmistakably influenced by multiple factors in our lives.

As James Hanigan observes,

> There is growth in conscience, growth which can be made more or less difficult or even stifled altogether. For conscience to develop, conscious and careful nurture is required. It does not just happen. It is not simply a matter of luck or fate or destiny. Like physical development, the development of conscience can be retarded by personal choice or neglect, by physical, chemical and biological deficiencies in one's own body, and by factors in the social environment.[37]

How Relationships and Communities Shape Our Conscience

It can be helpful to reflect on what has formed and shaped our conscience. Obviously, the choices we make every day, especially our most characteristic ways of being and acting, are a pivotal element. But if we were to do an inventory of what has contributed to the state of our conscience, we would have to acknowledge many other factors as well. In recent years feminist philosophers and theologians have emphasized the role relationships have in forming our moral identity and conscience. For example, our family background impacts our moral identity and conscience. Similarly, the friendships we develop shape us morally and spiritually, as well as the communities and institutions of which we are a part.

Conscience is always a "social phenomenon" because every human being is "always a self-in-relation to others," someone whose being and identity is formed, shaped, and influenced by the most significant persons in one's life.[38] As Anne Patrick writes,

> We carry our relationships with us whether we attend to them or not, and we are influenced by them especially when we confront a difficult decision. The very brain cells we use to weigh the pros and cons of a course of action are affected by the persons we have known and loved, and whom we carry in these cells or, to use the more traditional metaphor, in our hearts.[39]

If the relationships of our lives have such a lasting effect on the formation of our conscience, then our moral development hinges on having healthy relationships and being part of healthy communities. Bernard Haring speaks of "reciprocity of conscience" or "a mutuality of consciences" to underscore the ways in which "persons are a source of identity, integrity, and authenticity for each other."[40] We shape and influence one another in ways we may not suspect. Indeed, we "rub off" on one another because each of us adds something to the moral personality, character, and conscience of the "others" who constitute our lives. This is one reason that friendships matter in the moral life, especially in the formation of our character. Teachers "rub off" on students and students "rub off" on teachers. The attitudes, perceptions, convictions, and behavior of parents surely rub off on their children, just as those of religious leaders rub off, for better or worse, on their followers.

As the word *conscience* suggests, in the moral life we truly do "know together" because the kind of consciences we have, the principles and convictions that guide them, as well as the perceptions and affections that influence them, are socially acquired. Even though each of us ultimately is responsible for his or her conscience, our conscience is hardly the work of our hands alone. But it is precisely because "our conscience comes to its fullness only in reciprocity with other consciences" that we need exemplary persons (and exemplary moral communities) in our lives, persons of truly "good" conscience who can guide, inspire, and challenge us in our own moral development.[41]

How Our Social and Cultural Contexts Shape Our Conscience

In addition to relationships and communities, our consciences are also impacted by the social, cultural, and historical contexts of our lives. One reason conscience does not operate the same way in everyone is because in large measure our consciences will reflect the social, cultural, and economic contexts in which we have lived. This is one reason, for example, that people whose lives have been ravaged by war or oppression or economic deprivation will see the world differently—and reason and deliberate differently—than those who have known freedom and prosperity and abundance. The "moral knowing" of a person who lives on the margins of society will typically be markedly different from someone who has enjoyed power and status and prestige in that same society. Our consciences will reflect, and sometimes be seriously distorted by, our social, cultural, and economic locations.

A tremendous contribution of liberation theology has been not only to draw our attention to how one's social and cultural location impacts his or her conscience but also, perhaps even more importantly, to stress the moral blind spots that can exist in our conscience. The Latin American theologian Enrique Dussel offers a provocative example. He notes that how one understands the moral injunction, "You shall not steal!" often depends on his or her social and economic status. If I am wealthy, Dussel argues, I may readily acknowledge that "the theft of property that is the private possession of someone else is a moral offense, and conscience indicates it to me. But my own private property, which may well constitute, in its origin, the (objectified) *dispossession of others of their labor*—although that dispossession may have occurred imperceptibly as far as my own consciousness, my own conscience, is concerned—presents itself as legitimate and good. All other persons, 'Hands off!'"[42]

As Dussel illustrates, we may easily recognize the moral shortcomings of other persons, cultures, and societies, but be utterly blind to our own, particularly in their impact on our conscience. We have no trouble recognizing the injustice of theft when we or others like us are the victims, but can be confoundedly oblivious to how our own way of life might unjustly deprive a multitude of others of what is rightly their own. We can, as Dussel's example indicates, so thoroughly absorb the dominant ethos of a society that we regularly do things in "good conscience" that in reality are thoughtless and unjust.

The Jesuit theologian James Bretzke calls this "cultural invincible ignorance." We can be so thoroughly, albeit unconsciously, morally malformed by the principles and practices of a society or culture that we cannot see what is glaringly obvious to someone standing outside our social, cultural, and economic context. As Bretzke writes, in order to judge the adequacy of our conscience, we must first "detect any cultural logs that might be lodged in our own eyes and therefore make it very difficult for us to see the moral situation for what it truly is." He cites "serious cultural blind spots that people at the time did not clearly see, for example, racism, slavery, Jim Crow segregation legislation, the practice of child labor, exploitation of poor immigrants and so on."[43] How could so many people endorse practices that are indisputably wrong?

Consider the story of *Huckleberry Finn*, a novel that makes us question whether conscience should always be our guide. We are tutored to believe that our conscience trumps any other moral authority. But as the novel powerfully illustrates, sovereignty of conscience is a dangerous claim if our conscience has been formed by highly defective understandings of right and wrong. Mark Twain's novel tells the story of a young boy and a slave in flight. Renegades on a raft, they navigate the Mississippi in search of a freedom and hope life has denied them. Huck flees the Widow Douglas and Miss Watson's attempts to "sivilize" him because he finds their understanding of civility and goodness suffocating. A slave, Jim runs from these good Christian women, too, because in a society that embraces slavery, Jim is not a human being but another person's property. For Jim, their conventional understanding of goodness has not only been deficient—it has also been killing. Hidden inside the accepted moral notions and practices of the society Twain depicts is an injustice of which the more "respectable" members of that society are blind but whose effects are felt keenly by Jim.

A pivotal scene in the novel occurs when Huck and Jim approach Cairo, Illinois, the town where Jim knows he can go free. It's here that Huck's conscience starts to itch. The nearer they get to Cairo, the more Jim talks of his impending freedom. And the more Jim talks, the more Huck feels he's been an accomplice to something wrong. If slaves are not human beings but someone else's property, then to help Jim go free is to be involved in taking what rightly belongs to another. According to the moral canons of St. Petersburg, Huck's hometown, Jim's life is not his own; it's Miss Watson's property. This is why Huck's tender conscience is troubled. In fact, he has so fully absorbed the moral values and convictions of his world that his conscience suggests the more serious injustice is not Jim's slavery, but his helping Jim get free. As Huck recounts,

> Jim said it made him all over trembly and feverish to be so close to freedom. Well, I can tell you it made me all over trembly and feverish, too, to hear him, because I begun to get it through my head that he *was* most free—and who was to blame for it? Why, *me*. I couldn't get that out of my conscience, no how nor no way. It got to troubling me so I couldn't rest; I couldn't stay still in one place. It hadn't ever come home to me before, what this thing was that I was doing. But now it did; and it stayed with me, and scorched me more and more. I tried to make out to myself that *I* warn't to blame, because *I* didn't run Jim off from his rightful owner; but it warn't no use, conscience up and says, every time, "But you knowed he was running for his freedom, and you could 'a paddled ashore and told somebody." That was so—I couldn't get around that no way. That was where it pinched.[44]

Huckleberry Finn is a poignant reminder that before we crow about the supremacy of conscience, we need to examine carefully the moral notions that have informed our consciences. As the novel suggests, what we take to be an impeccable conscience may actually be a dangerously corrupt conscience, one so perversely formed that it leaves one "unable to recognize his deed or his situation for what it is, even when it is pointed out to him." As Alan Donagan elaborates, "And it is not necessarily confined to individuals. A whole society may refuse to face plain facts, not only about its own actions as a society, but about its institutions."[45]

Donagan's point—and one of the novel's great achievements—is to show how societies can blind us to what is obvious. It ought to be patently obvious that slavery is wrong. But a society can encourage all sorts of strategies to shield us from the obvious by teaching us to divert our attention from anything that would call its moral vision and practices into question.[46] Put differently, our consciences are corrupted when we allow ourselves to remain continually inattentive to the very evils we ought to be confronting. By training ourselves not to look, we eventually become unable to see.

The story of *Huckleberry Finn* reminds us that our "consciences are not pristine moral guides safe from the prejudices of our world; they are affected by those prejudices and often work to sustain them. They do not reason infallibly, but historically and socially."[47] Indeed, sometimes our consciences can be so thoroughly informed by defective moral visions, values, and practices that, instead of illuminating the good, they persistently conceal it. The Widow Douglas and Miss Watson did not see what Jim and Huck saw because they profited from a selective moral vision. But we are hardly different. We craft selective consciences for ourselves. We teach ourselves not to see the impact of our behavior or our way of life on others; consequently, we are able to enjoy a peaceful conscience when instead we ought to be experiencing a troubled and unsettled conscience.

If our consciences sometimes approve the very things we ought to be questioning, what should we do? How do we break through the well-fortified deceptions of a distorted conscience in order to live more justly and truthfully? One way is through an experience of *conscientization*, a term that grew out of the liberation theology of Latin America, but that has now become a central element in Christian ethics. Originally, conscientization referred to oppressed people's "waking up" or becoming aware of their oppression, seeing it for the injustice it truly is, and committing themselves to addressing it by becoming active agents in their own liberation.

As Gustavo Gutiérrez, the "father" of liberation theology, writes, "In this process, which Freire calls 'conscientization,' the oppressed person rejects the oppressive consciousness which dwells in him, becomes aware of his situation, and finds his own language. He becomes, by himself, less dependent and freer, as he commits himself to the transformation and building up of society." Thus, through conscientization the oppressed reject the oppressor's definition of themselves, they reject their unjust situation as acceptable or inevitable, and they pledge themselves to being the agents or "protagonists of their own liberation."[48] At its core, conscientization results in a radically "new social consciousness" that provides "a springboard for deep changes in the political, economic, social and religious fields."[49]

Obviously, victims of injustice are not the only ones who need to "wake up" to the reality of injustice. If our consciences all too often shield us from what we need to see, and thus foster the blindness and complacency that allow injustices to proliferate, then we too must undergo conscientization; we must realize that it is an ongoing process, and not something limited to a single instance. In fact, apart from conscientization, we ought to doubt our consciences more than we have been trained to trust them. Oftentimes, conscientization begins when we open ourselves to experiences that draw us out of the comfort and security of our own world and into the world of the poor, the world of the victims and the dispossessed. Once we are "de-centered" by entering their world, a change of consciousness can occur, because we are challenged to see the world through their eyes and thus rethink our customary assumptions.

Such experiences call into question our ordinary attitudes and perspectives, and typically reveal them as lacking.[50] Our most trustworthy guides in conscientization are the very people who suffer most from our deficient moral awareness. As Vincent Cosmao notes, "The victims of a badly twisted world are in a good position to point up its mistakes and effects."[51] Conscience needs a corrective, but perhaps the best way of correcting a malformed conscience is to make ourselves available to learning from, and being challenged by, those who can call us to a more truthful and just goodness.

And this is exactly what happens in *Huckleberry Finn*. When we left Huck on the raft, he was suffering the pangs of a troubled conscience. Given his background, his conscience told him that he was doing wrong in aiding Jim's escape from slavery; consequently, heeding the voice of his conscience, he decides to turn Jim over to those who are searching for him. But at that moment Jim begins to talk. Anticipating his freedom, he thanks Huck for helping him, and thanks him not only for being the best friend he ever had but also for being the only white man who had ever been faithful to him.

Jim's narration of their time together on the raft, the friendship that had formed between them, and his heartfelt indebtedness to Huck puts a salutary crack in Huck's conscience. Jim, the slave, becomes the agent of Huck's conscientization. Huck is not the person he was when he first boarded the raft with Jim. Having opened himself to friendship with Jim, having been helped by Jim and having learned from him, Huck has come to see Jim differently, not as property that must be returned to its owner, but as a fellow human being and as a friend. Thus, if Jim finds freedom in reaching Cairo, Huck finds freedom when he allows his friendship and experience with Jim to get the better of his conscience. In his decision not to turn Jim in, Huck renounces his former "good" conscience for one that will surely get him into more trouble—the kind of trouble that people who are not afraid of real goodness always cause.

THE DEVELOPMENT AND FORMATION OF CONSCIENCE

Despite the many things that can shape our conscience, and that either facilitate or hinder our moral development, we remain responsible for the formation of our conscience. In fact, what becomes of our conscience is largely up to us. We cannot blame our upbringing, the relationships of our lives, or our society, culture, or communities for what ultimately becomes of our conscience. Our conscience is our own creation insofar as we develop it every day through the feelings we foster, through the attachments we make, through the goods and values we endorse, through the friendships we develop, and through the choices we make or fail to make.

As human beings we are given the necessary materials for the development of our consciences (intelligence, free will, moral awareness, imagination), and it is our task to use these materials in nurturing a healthy, mature, and trustworthy conscience. And even though there may be things that have impeded our moral development, it is our responsibility not to succumb to them but to recognize and work to overcome them. As Vincent MacNamara stresses, "A genuine personal conscience is not presented to us by life as a gift and is not by any means an automatic attainment. It has to be forged in the smithy of the individual's soul."[52]

Five Steps to Consider

But if "forming our conscience is a lifelong task, an ongoing process of conversion" to "what is true and good," where should we begin?[53] If our goal is to use the gift of our freedom to choose consistently what is right and good, to what do we need to attend? What are the quintessential elements in the formation of personal conscience? There are many ways to answer this, but five things seem most important.

Although it can be easily overlooked, if we are to acquire the conscience of a responsible adult we must first *develop in ourselves a desire for and attraction to the good*.[54] In writing about conscience, Sidney Callahan argues that "the overarching ideals of goodness, rightness, and truth have to be felt as magnets attracting and exerting an overriding obligatory moral force" on us.[55] Human beings are born with a natural desire for and attraction to the good. But we must work to deepen this love for the good—to make it more resilient—because we are easily lured away by multiple counter-attractions. If the work of conscience is to enable us to choose and to do what is both right and good with insight, skill, ease, and delight, then we must move from being occasionally attracted to the good to finding it irresistible. We can fully trust our conscience only when we find what is right and good too alluring to resist. We reach this apex in our moral development when we find the good so captivating, so enchanting and alluring, so beautiful and compelling, that we cannot fathom ourselves being attracted to anything else.

Obviously, such steadfast devotion to the good can never be taken for granted. It is something we must continually nurture and develop. But it is the essential first step in the formation of conscience because, without cultivating in ourselves an abiding love for goodness, we will lack the resolve needed for doing what is right and good when it is costly or difficult. As Richard Gula suggests, "We can give all the moral instruction we want, or provide the best moral mentors we know, and create an environment where it is easy to be good, but if the person does not care about being good, nothing will happen to produce a morally good person."[56]

We can best cultivate a love for the good by *striving to live good and virtuous lives*, which is the second dimension to the formation of conscience. If our conscience is not an isolated faculty but is, rather, our whole moral self or character, then it is impossible to separate the formation of conscience from our formation in the virtues. Put differently, we should not be surprised that the persons of most astute, sensitive, and insightful consciences are likewise persons of virtue, individuals who can be counted on to be prudent, just, compassionate, thoughtful and loving, honest, caring, and loyal.

If conscience is a matter of recognizing, appreciating and apprising, and skillfully responding to the good, then men and women who are resplendent in the unique goodness captured by each of the virtues will likewise be most skilled in matters of conscience. "Virtuous practices become the exercises for the formation of conscience," James Keenan writes, because those who have achieved moral excellence through the practice of virtues such as justice, love, kindness, generosity, patience, and especially prudence, will be best equipped, when the time comes, to make good decisions of conscience.[57]

And yet, even though each of us is ultimately responsible for what we make of our consciences, the development and formation of our consciences is much too important to be entrusted to ourselves alone. If for no other reason, "our own sinfulness, our own propensity to rationalize, to call attention to ourselves, to see things as we would like them to be rather than as they really are," indicates our need for the guidance of others.[58] Moreover, given the complexity of some moral issues, none of us alone possesses the wisdom, experience, knowledge, and insight necessary for seeing clearly what ought to be done.

This is why a third very important element to the formation of our conscience is to *seek the counsel and advice of others*. These could include friends who want what is best for us and will not fail to be truthful to us, and who often know us better than we know ourselves. It could be those trustworthy mentors in our lives (parents, pastors, teachers, colleagues, community members) from whom we have learned much and whose lives exhibit a goodness, wisdom, and integrity we want to embody in our own. We can also be mentored by those who have gone before us, whether they be the saints of our communities whose goodness is recognized as exemplary, family members whose wisdom and goodness we continue to recollect, or people from our past who guided us through difficult times.

To seek counsel is to open ourselves to the viewpoints, opinions, experiences, and insights of others. To seek counsel is to be willing to listen, but not only to people who think exactly as we think or who will tell us what we want to hear. In the formation of our consciences we must not only be open to seeking counsel from persons or groups who may see things quite differently from ourselves, but we must also actively seek their advice. We cannot be reluctant to be mentored by those whose experiences, perceptions, and viewpoints conflict with our own.[59] In other words, without "hospitality to the stranger," without vulnerability to the "other" whose sense of goodness and rightness might be unsettlingly different from our own, we risk reducing conscience to being little more than a reflection of our carefully calculated preferences.[60] Such assaults on our egotism are painful to endure, but they are morally salutary because they bring us to a richer and truer understanding of goodness.

In light of this, it is especially important to avail ourselves of being mentored by the poor, the marginalized, the oppressed, and all the other forgotten members of our world. Hospitality to the victims of injustice is crucial in the development of our conscience because only when we hear "the voices of those adversely affected by the systems we live by" do we attain the moral vision and sensitivity adequate for living justly and effecting true goodness.[61] Or, as the Argentinean theologian Enrique Dussel eloquently reminds us, we must be willing to listen to the voices we find most disturbing precisely because they are the most subversively challenging.

> But in all cases it is precisely the capacity to hear the voice of the other that constitutes *ethical* conscience. In the Bible the supreme sign of goodness is to have "a heart that can *listen*" (1 Kgs 5:9—*Biblica Latinoamericana*). . . . In this case *conscience* is not so much the application of principles to concrete cases, but a listening, a hearing the voice calling to me from outside, from beyond the horizon of the system: the voice of the poor calling for justice, calling from deep within their absolute, sacred right, the right of the person as person.[62]

The Role of Prayer in the Formation of Conscience

Of course, in the Christian moral life one must also seek the counsel and advice of God. This is why prayer, a fourth element in the formation of conscience, must be embraced as an ongoing practice in the moral life. Two theologians who recently have given attention to the place of prayer in the formation of conscience are Dennis Billy and James Keating. In *Conscience and Prayer*, they follow early Christian writers in speaking of prayer as "'keeping company with God.'"[63] We have suggested that family, friendships, and other relationships play an important role in shaping our consciences; but this is especially true in our relationship with God. Christians must make a practice of "keeping company with God" if they are to attend to, participate in, and further God's goodness in the world, which is the primary goal of the Christian moral life.

Prayer keeps us mindful of God because it not only focuses our lives on God as the supreme good and final goal of our lives but also helps us to seek God's good in everything we do. Without prayer, God can easily slip to the margins of our lives so that our own interests take precedence over the desires and interests of God. But prayer brings our relationship with God from the margins to the center of our lives and helps us, Billy and Keating write, "to orient everything we do in life toward it. The more we pray, the more God becomes the focus of all we do."[64] When this occurs what we seek in any act of conscience is to discern as well as we possibly can what God is both calling and enabling us to do.

Prayer can also be described as "rapt listening, a listening that trains the heart to hear the truth," particularly the truth that comes to us in Christ.[65] Prayer creates a space for us to listen for and to receive the guidance and illumination that come from Christ and the Spirit. We can think of prayer as a dialogue between God and ourselves; but it may be better to picture it as actively listening for a word of God to guide and assist us.

Decisions of conscience can be difficult because our hearts can be cluttered with so many cares and concerns. Or they can be filled with a cacophony of voices that not only leave us confused and uncertain but also make it difficult for us to hear what God may be speaking to us. Sometimes our hearts can be filled with so much noise—so many conflicting desires and emotions—that it is impossible for us to listen for what really matters. This is why the Second Vatican Council spoke of conscience not as that sacred place in which we hear many voices, but as a sanctuary where we listen attentively for the word of God.[66]

In order to nurture in ourselves a conscience truly attuned to the will of God, we need to be humble enough to make room in our hearts for a voice other than our own, especially the voice of Christ.[67] If conscience does not mean "knowing alone" but "knowing with," then Christians aim to "know together" with Christ, and such knowledge is gained through a regular life of prayer. As Billy and Keating conclude, prayer is indispensable in the formation of conscience because ultimately the best guide in the moral life is, not a list of rules, but Christ. "In times of urgency or during childhood one may simply resort to following rules in the moral life but over the long run of Christian maturation it is the work of paying attention to Christ that truly seals the contents of one's conscience," they explain. "This is true because over time Christ becomes the content of the conscience."[68]

The primary place where Christians "keep company with God" is at the Eucharist, the central prayer of the church. This is why in addition to personal prayer and meditation on the scriptures, regular participation in the Eucharist is an essential practice for forming one's conscience according to the goodness of God. In a provocative essay, Tissa Balasuriya, a theologian from Sri Lanka, speaks of the Eucharist as a sacrament that should imbue us with a new consciousness, a conscience that is inspired by, and conforms to, the values of the reign of God.[69] Too, repeated participation in the Eucharist, he suggests, should expand the moral horizons of our lives so that we see beyond our own needs to the needs of others, particularly the destitute. And, as a sacrament of unity, the Eucharist should inform the conscience of a community so that it works to overcome the inequalities and divisions, as well as the widespread individualism, so characteristic of our Western world today and so at odds with the solidarity necessary for justice.

Of course, whether or not any of this occurs depends on how the Eucharist is celebrated. The Eucharist should lead to conversion by making us more aware of how self-interested our consciences can be, of how they can shield us from what we need to see and blind us to some of the more dangerous inconsistencies between what we profess and how we actually live. But this does not always happen.

Sometimes the Eucharist is celebrated in ways that aim to soothe consciences that ought to be uneasy or to reinforce patterns and practices that need to be exposed and overcome. As Balasuriya pointedly observes, "We go to church on Sunday; we say, 'Give us this day our daily bread,' but our social and economic options deprive the hungry of food, the multitudes of remunerative work."[70] If the Eucharist is to transform our consciences so that we really can further the goodness of God in the world, we have to allow it to subvert our ordinary ways of seeing, thinking, imagining, and acting. If we allow it to remake our consciences according to the vision of the reign of God, they can be liberated from distorted and self-serving perversions of the good, and instead help us to recognize and to work for the justice and love we are called to by God.

The Role of the Church in the Formation of Conscience

A fifth requirement in the development of a healthy and responsible conscience is to know, consult, and attend to the moral teachings and traditions of the primary communities of which we are a part, especially our faith communities. Because our consciences are too important to be left to ourselves, moral responsibility demands that we give the moral teachings of our faith communities a privileged role in the formation of our consciences. Even if we initially disagree with a church's moral teaching, as a member of that faith community we are responsible only if we are open to it, only if we strive to understand the reason for the teaching and the goods and values it seeks to protect, and only if we allow ourselves to be challenged, and possibly changed, by the teaching.

Church moral teachings ought to represent the wisdom of the community. If the formation of conscience is truly a "knowing together," then we cannot dismiss a teaching simply because we might disagree with it. Rather, in the formation of our consciences we must approach church teachings with openness, respect, and receptivity. And our initial presumption should be in favor of the teaching, not against it. We must allow the teaching to instruct us, to enlighten us, and to challenge us. As Josef Fuchs writes, "ethical prudence demands that one should not reject an ethical ordinance that is widely accepted or prescribed by a high authority, but that one should have great openness and should attempt to understand it or indeed to accept it, since it can contain great experience and lofty wisdom—even if it is not infallible."[71]

Thus, for "the believing Catholic," Fuchs says, "a moral utterance of the church's magisterium is an extremely significant element that must be taken into consideration in the responsible formation of conscience." Moreover, because Catholics believe that the magisterium or teaching authority of the church is guided by the Spirit, "the spirit of fidelity which is required in the church obliges one to be receptive to them in the internal discourse that is the formation of conscience, and to attempt to give them a certain preference over against other considerations—even one's own—that arise; this is required by the responsible conscience itself."[72]

Nonetheless, even though "one is glad to take hold of the helping hand that is offered," responsibility to conscience means that each person must ultimately decide what he or she believes is good and right and, therefore, what ought to be done.[73] We must not allow the church, or any other authority, to replace responsibility to conscience by deciding for us, but must instead accept the "creative responsibility" that comes with being an adult.

Anne Patrick says "creative responsibility involves being conscientious in preventing harm and promoting good through realistic appraisal of the likely consequences of our decisions, and it entails the willingness to act without absolute assurance of being right." Moreover, such creative responsibility suggests that "instead of relying entirely on others' formulas for behavior, one does one's own interpreting of what is going on and one's own analysis of how to prevent or minimize harm and contribute to the betterment of life for oneself and one's neighbors. This by no means rules out benefiting from the wisdom of others," she notes, "but it does rule out abdicating one's judgment to outside authorities." Patrick goes on to explain that embracing "creative responsibility" to conscience is not easy. "One risks being mistaken, being criticized, losing approval and status," she writes. "But the rewards are high, including an enhanced sense of self-esteem that comes from using one's powers, and a sense

of being a full adult participant in life rather than a minor who is only margin-
ally involved in shaping one's self and the contexts of one's life."[74]

A perduring temptation in the moral life is to shirk responsibility by sur-
rendering our consciences to persons in authority, who are all too often eager
to seize them. Part of becoming an adult is having the courage to be one's own
person. Unlike a child who unquestionably submits to the authority of her
parents, persons of responsible conscience care enough about their integrity
to commit themselves to what they honestly believe is true and good, and do
not abdicate that responsibility to others. No authority can take the place of
personal conscience.

This is not to encourage an individualism that would close a person to the
guidance of others. But it is to stress that the morally mature person does
something not because someone in authority tells her it is what she ought to
do. Rather, she makes her decision because, after having taken time to inform
her conscience, she is convinced that it is the right thing to do. As Bernard
Haring warns,

> Some people do not want to be allowed to live according to their own con-
> science; they want to be guided by others, to be told what to do. They do not
> want to take the risk inherent in living one's own life in creative liberty and
> fidelity. There is a widespread security complex among immature people,
> and this complex is constantly endorsed by authoritarian people who do
> not so much search for truth as for conformism and, through conformism,
> power over others.[75]

The proper role of the magisterium—or any teaching authority—is to be
always "at the service of conscience" and "to help the faithful to be faithful
to their own conscience."[76] Its aim should not be to dominate conscience,
much less to demand rigid conformity to its teachings, but to guide, facilitate,
and assist people in the formation of conscience.[77] Otherwise, we make the
mistake of equating fidelity to conscience with "ecclesiastical conformism,"
a move that contradicts the very meaning of conscience because it encourages "legalistic scrupulosity" rather than a true and responsible liberty of conscience.[78] At its best, the Catholic moral tradition has encouraged the creative
responsibility that allows persons to search for the truth in freedom and love.
And it has recognized "that too many laws, and an all too strict interpretation
of them, could stifle the creativity and joy of Christians."[79]

Too often persons in authority create a "mystique of obedience" that so
elevates the importance of obedience that it becomes the defining virtue of
a good and faithful Christian. But, as Sean Fagan observes, this leaves "little
room for personal responsibility and creativity in moral decision-making,"
and suggests that the only thing required "for the formation of conscience"

is "giving information and rules."[80] A teaching authority is necessary for a church, but it should never "foster passivity," "look more for submission and uniformity than for growth in moral responsibility," or "stifle initiative and creative liberty."[81]

Moreover, the "mystique of obedience" thwarts healthy moral development by equating conscience with the superego. The word *superego* literally means that "the ego of another" is "superimposed on our own to serve as an internal censor to regulate our conduct by using guilt as its powerful weapon." Based in our need for love and approval, under the power of the superego we allow an authority figure (parents, civil authorities, the church) "to become a kind of psychic parent or police officer keeping eye on our behaviour and giving us commands and setting out prohibitions." Too, the superego "tells us that we are good when we do what we have been told to do, and it tells us that we are bad and it makes us feel guilty when we do not do what we should."[82]

Obviously, if we never move beyond the superego to conscience, we remain morally infantile. Like children, we submit to those in authority rather than commit ourselves to what we genuinely believe is right and good. This is why the superego counsels conformity and submission, whereas the conscience is always a call to grow—a call to transcend ourselves in goodness and love, rather than aim for nothing higher than what might be pleasing and acceptable to others.[83] As Richard Gula observes, "The superego acts out of the obligation to be obedient. The moral conscience, by contrast, exercises responsible freedom—the freedom of wanting to do what we ought to do as virtuous persons because we own the values that we are expressing." Moreover, Gula argues, "For moral maturity one must be one's own person. It is not enough to follow what one has been told. The morally mature person must be able to perceive, choose, and identify oneself with what one does. In short, we create our character and give our lives meaning by committing our freedom, not by submitting it to someone in authority."[84]

Therefore, in order to facilitate the development of a mature and responsible conscience, the church must become a true fellowship (*koinōnia*) in which the gifts, insights, and wisdom of all the members of the community contribute to the moral teachings of the community.[85] Since the church teaches that all of the baptized receive the Spirit and are led by the Spirit—and that the Spirit gifts each of the baptized in unique and important ways—those who lead the church must excel at listening to the voices of its members and must envision the church as a Spirit-led community in which each member can both teach and learn from every other member.

In *Liberating Conscience*, Anne Patrick calls the church to become "a community of moral discourse," a community that together "searches, in dialogue, for moral wisdom."[86] Such a community will obviously have moral teachers and a tradition of moral authority. But it will also understand that authentic

---

The Five Steps in Conscience Formation

1. Develop in ourselves a desire for and attraction to the good
2. Strive to live good and virtuous lives
3. Seek the counsel and advice of others
4. Seek the counsel and advice of God
5. Know, consult, and attend to the moral teachings and traditions of the primary communities

---

teaching and authentic authority require genuinely listening to the insights, questions, and even disagreements of others (both inside and outside the community) in order to appraise more clearly how God's spirit might be speaking to and leading the community.

Referring to the Catholic Church's magisterium, Haring observes, "Their authority for the conscience of all open-minded people grows if they are outstanding observers and listeners, able to learn from the example of the saints and from the voices of the prophets and of men and women competent to speak by their learning and by their spirit of prayer."[87] Patrick echoes Haring's view when she says that "the church does not supply the perfect answer to all our moral questions, but it gives us a community where faithful moral reasoning can go on, always with attention to the values Jesus cherished and with confidence in his continued presence in our midst."[88]

Fostering Healthy Moral Communities

In order to become moral communities that are adept at the formation of persons of keen, responsible, and courageous consciences, three things seem essential. First, church leaders must see thoughtful and responsible dissent not as acts of pernicious disloyalty whose only aim is to confuse and to foster division. Rather, in humility, and trusting in the Spirit, they must be willing to accept those who dissent as at least potentially prophetic voices that God can inspire to guide the church to a greater understanding of the truth. As Haring notes, "Nobody possesses a monopoly of truth, and nobody can hope to be inspired by the Spirit unless he honors the Holy Spirit who works in all and for all," including in those who dissent.[89]

In this way, instead of viewing dissent as rare and as always harmful for the church, it should be seen as an ordinary part of the life of a pilgrim church whose members together strive to grow more deeply in the wisdom and goodness of God. Moreover, instead of threatening those who conscientiously disagree, leaders of the church must recognize that since "all non-infallible teaching is fallible, liable to be incomplete, imperfect or even mistaken, those who discover such mistakes contribute to the health of the church, of the whole body of believers, by making it known."[90]

Second, church leaders must recognize that their teaching authority is weakened if they insist on the truthfulness of a teaching that many persons, having given it due consideration, continue to find unpersuasive. Sometimes people cannot assent to a particular church teaching because the reasons given for the teaching are neither convincing nor compelling.[91] Sometimes they cannot assent because arguments given against the teaching seem more reasonable and coherent. And sometimes they cannot assent because the teaching conflicts with the moral wisdom they have gained from experience.

When people dissent from a moral teaching of the church, one should assume that their aim is not to be stubborn or difficult or disobedient. Rather, in the responsibility of conscience they have concluded "that the truth about what is good lies elsewhere and truth summons" them "to act in a different way."[92] In fact, James Hanigan insists, "for the individual who sees—or is sincerely convinced that he or she sees—that the truth about the good lies elsewhere than authority proclaims, conscientious dissent is not only a possibility; it is an obligation."[93]

Third, in order to encourage people in the development of an astute and responsible conscience, church leaders must not hesitate to affirm freedom of conscience. But we must be careful in how freedom of conscience is understood. Freedom of conscience does not mean that I can casually (or carelessly) pursue whatever I want. Freedom of conscience is both nonsensical and dangerous apart from a steadfast responsibility to my conscience. Freedom of conscience does not absolve me of the duty to seek counsel and guidance from others, and to know, learn from, and consistently attend to the teachings of the church; in fact, it makes doing so all the more important. And freedom of conscience is a dangerous right to proclaim apart from an ongoing commitment to love and to seek what is right and good, and to live a virtuous and responsible life. This is why freedom of conscience must be thought of as "more a privilege earned than a right to be casually assumed." It is "the well-earned prerogative" of persons who have taken responsibility for forming their conscience.[94]

But assuming that one has been responsible to his or her conscience, freedom of conscience is a precious right that we should never surrender to another and that no one should ever deny us. If our conscience represents, not so much what we might want to do, but what we sincerely believe God is calling us to do, then freedom of conscience, far from being a warrant for solipsistic individualism, is required for us to follow the summons of God in our lives. This is why the Catholic Church holds that it is a sin *not* to follow one's conscience and a sin to try to persuade someone to act against her conscience.[95]

In fact, freedom of conscience is rightly grasped only if its connection to obedience to conscience is acknowledged. We have freedom of conscience precisely in order that we can obey the summons of conscience; indeed, freedom of conscience is fulfilled in obedience to conscience. The Catholic moral tradition captures the intimate connection between freedom of conscience and obedience to conscience in the idea of being "bound in conscience." This means that once we are convinced in conscience that something ought to be done or ought not to be done, "we are absolutely not free to violate our conscience."[96]

If the link between freedom of conscience and obedience to conscience is broken, one could interpret freedom of conscience to imply that I can just as easily follow my conscience as ignore it. But if conscience is best understood as a response to God's call to do what is right and good, then it is more accurate to say not that I am free to follow my conscience, but that I must follow my conscience.[97] It is only in light of these reflections that we can understand and affirm the Catholic Church's resolute claim that there is no higher moral authority than the authority of personal conscience.[98]

But our consciences also "bind" us because acting against them weakens them, and doing so frequently ultimately deadens them. Every betrayal of conscience weakens the voice of conscience, sometimes to the point where it is silenced. A single instance of not heeding our conscience may seem trifling; however, repeatedly ignoring the call of conscience eventually numbs us to the appeal of goodness in our lives. Too, every betrayal is accompanied by a corresponding loss of our integrity. We cannot flee the call of conscience without compromising ourselves and gradually being alienated from ourselves. If to be human is to be called to recognize and respond to the good, then failing to do so by refusing the commands of conscience is to live at odds with our most authentic selves. "When we ignore or refuse to do what we know we should," Sean Fagan explains, "the tension remains, so we lose our basic oneness, we are torn within ourselves, separated from our better self, and we experience alienation and guilt. When there is inconsistency between our knowing and doing we become divided within ourselves." But when we do "what conscience commands" we "experience peace and wholeness, a sense of at-one-ness with ourselves. This is the peace of a 'good conscience.'"[99]

Being of One Mind and Heart with Christ

In the Christian life of discipleship, a well-formed conscience belongs to the person who "seeks to view all things with the mind of Christ."[100] As we have insisted throughout this chapter, conscience is not knowing alone, but knowing together, and for Christians formation of conscience always aims for knowing together with Christ, or a kind of "thinking with Christ" as we move through life. This is because Christians believe that our true selves are found only in and through a relationship with Christ. It is through a life of faithful discipleship that we learn, come to see more clearly, and are able to respond to what is genuinely true and good.

Put more strongly, Christians believe that the "word" spoken by conscience is ultimately the "Word" who is Jesus, the "Word in whom we are created" and in whose truth and goodness we are fulfilled.[101] The voice we hear in conscience is not our own, but Christ's, and this is why Christian formation of conscience is absolutely inseparable from a life of discipleship. Just as the disciple learns only by listening and attending to the teachings and example of her mentor, one comes to "think with Christ" only through the practice of continually attending to Christ, particularly the attitudes and actions of Christ.[102]

In his classic *Free and Faithful in Christ*, Bernard Haring beautifully expresses the absolute dependence of our consciences on Christ. As he testifies, in the Christian life acquiring a well-formed and trustworthy conscience hinges on listening to and receiving the Word that is Christ; even more, it hinges on embodying and enacting that Word in our everyday lives. To live with a Christian conscience is to re-present Christ to the world through our decisions and actions.

> Although conscience has a voice of its own, the word is not its own. It comes through the Word in whom all things are made, the Word who became flesh to be with us. And this Word speaks through the inner voice which presupposes our capacity to listen with all our being. Of itself, conscience is a candle without a flame. It receives its truth from Christ who is Truth and Light; and through him it shines forth with his brightness and warmth.[103]

Haring's point is that a Christian's conscience ought to be different because it is formed through a lifelong encounter with Jesus and marked by the awareness of "being a new creation in Christ."[104] Having died to a former way of life in baptism and risen to a new way of life in Christ, the Christian formation of conscience requires one's ongoing initiation into the attitudes, values, perspectives, and goals of the gospel. A Christian's conscience is different because he lives in the world with the distinct and abiding knowledge that he has put on Christ at baptism and promised to live in Christ and according to the ways of Christ. Far from seeing his or her "baptismal identity" as something that resides "in the background of decision-making," Christians must allow that identity to inform every decision of conscience, and must constantly measure those decisions in light of whether or not they were faithful to that identity.[105] Thus, for Christians, freedom of conscience is given for, and fulfilled in, creative fidelity to Jesus; and a well-formed conscience is one that is imbued with the values and virtues of the gospel and is skilled in implementing them.

What practically would this mean? How would one recognize a Christian conscience "at work"? Did Thomas More in his confrontation with King Henry VIII (and Huck Finn in his confrontation with his society's practice of slavery) exemplify a Christian conscience? In his *Jesus Christ Liberator*, the Brazilian theologian Leonardo Boff describes Jesus as a person of extraordinarily creative imagination and originality. He depicts the imagination in much the same way we did in chapter 2. For Boff, the imagination is not akin to "a daydreamer's flight from reality" but a "confrontation with reality and established order," and entails "having the courage to think and say something new and to take hitherto untreaded paths that are full of meaning for human beings."[106]

Boff contends that in his proclamation of the reign of God, Jesus epitomized a person of daring and conscientious imagination. Instead of conforming to the established order, Jesus radically subverted it by envisioning a social and political order characterized by justice, freedom, and inclusiveness. Indeed, in his life, his ministry, and his death and resurrection, Jesus is the creative and liberating imagination of God at work in our world on our behalf.

If Boff is right to claim, "Perhaps in the whole of human history there has not been a single person who had a richer imagination than Jesus," then Christians are called to conform their consciences to the moral imagination of Jesus.[107] Symbolized in the reign of God, the capacious imagination of Jesus envisioned a new community—indeed, a new way of humans being together—characterized by respect for the dignity and equality of persons, passionate commitment to justice, and denunciation of anything that threatens the well-being of persons. If this was the fundamental goal of Jesus' mission and ministry, Christians are of "one mind and one heart" with Christ when their consciences are inspired by, and formed according to, Jesus' vision of the reign of God.

CONCLUSION

That "horrible moral squint" that is conscience is the heart and soul of what makes and keeps us human. To be human is not to dim that "horrible moral squint," but to refine it so that we come to recognize and respond to the call of goodness in every circumstance of our lives. As the story of Thomas More—as well as Huckleberry Finn—testifies, sometimes heeding the moral squint that is conscience can be considerably risky and costly. On the other hand, if we ignore it, skew it, or completely repress it, we relinquish the one thing that sustains our humanity and keeps our world from sinking further into the chaos of evil. In an ethics of discipleship, to be of good conscience is to be of one heart and one mind with Christ, and thus to bring the goodness and compassion and mercy and justice of God more fully to life in our world. That is never an easy task to accomplish, but it is one worth doing. And it reminds us of why conscience is a gift too precious to lose.

KEY POINTS

1. Conscience reminds us that men and women are moral beings who are called to live and act responsibly.
2. Conscience represents what God is calling and enabling us to do.
3. Our conscience is a reflection of our whole self. This is why acting in good conscience involves not only our minds, but our feelings, imagination, and intuitions as well.
4. Our conscience is formed and shaped by a variety of factors, including our families, relationships, and communities, our culture and society, and our religious traditions.
5. Responsible formation of conscience includes reading and study of important moral issues, consulting others for advice, regular practices of prayer, and knowing and attending to the moral teachings of our communities.
6. In the Christian life, a well-formed conscience is one that seeks to conform to the teachings and example of Jesus.

QUESTIONS FOR REFLECTION

1. What is conscience? How would you describe it?
2. Why can a good person acting in good conscience still go wrong?
3. What are some of the things that have formed and shaped your conscience?
4. Why is it easy to ignore our conscience? Why is it costly to ignore our conscience?
5. Should we ever not follow our conscience?
6. What is conscientization? Have you ever experienced it?
7. How do you understand the role of church teaching in forming a responsible conscience?
8. How would you explain freedom of conscience?

SUGGESTIONS FOR FURTHER READING AND STUDY

Billy, Dennis J., and James F. Keating. *Conscience and Prayer: The Spirit of Catholic Moral Theology.* Collegeville, Minn.: Liturgical Press, 2001.

Bretzke, James T. *A Morally Complex World: Engaging Contemporary Moral Theology.* Collegeville, Minn.: Liturgical Press, 2004.

Callahan, Sidney Cornelia. *In Good Conscience: Reason and Emotion in Moral Decision Making.* New York: HarperCollins, 1991.

Curran, Charles E. *The Catholic Moral Tradition Today: A Synthesis.* Washington, D.C.: Georgetown University Press, 1999.

Fagan, Sean. *Does Morality Change?* Dublin: Gill & Macmillan, 1997.

Gula, Richard M. "Conscience." In *Christian Ethics: An Introduction.* Edited by Bernard Hoose, 110-22. Collegeville, Minn.: Liturgical Press, 1998.

Hanigan, James P. *As I Have Loved You: The Challenge of Christian Ethics.* New York: Paulist, 1986.

Haring, Bernard. *Free and Faithful in Christ: Moral Theology for Clergy and Laity.* Vol. 1, *General Moral Theology.* New York: Seabury, 1978.

Keenan, James F. *Moral Wisdom: Lessons and Texts from the Catholic Tradition.* Lanham, Md.: Rowman & Littlefield, 2004.

MacNamara, Vincent. *Love, Law and Christian Life: Basic Attitudes of Christian Morality.* Wilmington, Del.: Michael Glazier, 1988.

Mahoney, John. *The Making of Moral Theology: A Study of the Roman Catholic Tradition.* Oxford: Clarendon, 1987.

Patrick, Anne E. *Liberating Conscience: Feminist Explorations in Catholic Moral Theology.* New York: Continuum, 1997.

Twain, Mark. *The Adventures of Huckleberry Finn.* New York: Bantam, 1981.

7

Love—The Only True Path to Life

"Whoever Does Not Love Remains in Death" *(1 John 3:14)*

JAMES JOYCE'S NOVEL *ULYSSES* is rightly described as one of the most complex and challenging novels ever written. But its primary theme is straightforward and simple. Chronicling one day in the life of Leopold Bloom, a Jew adrift in the very Catholic world of Dublin, Joyce, through a variety of elaborate and ingenious means, testifies that the "word" known to all is the four-letter word love.

A memorable scene in the novel occurs in Barney Kiernan's Pub when Bloom, the perpetual outsider, says about himself and the Jews: "And I belong to a race too . . . that is hated and persecuted. Also now. This very moment. This very instant. . . . Robbed. . . . Plundered. Insulted. Persecuted. Taking what belongs to us by right." But after acknowledging that much of the history of the world is a story of hatred, persecution, animosity, and bloodshed, Bloom nonetheless proclaims: "But it's no use. . . . Force, hatred, history, all that. That's not life for men and women, insult and hatred. And everybody knows that it's the very opposite of that that is really life." When his barmate Alf asks what he means, Bloom announces: "Love . . . I mean the opposite of hatred." Some of those gathered mock Bloom's testimony and cynically dismiss his claim about the fundamental necessity of love. But Joyce affirms Bloom's brief soliloquy when he writes: "Love loves to love love. . . . You love a certain person. And this person loves that other person because everybody loves somebody but God loves everybody."[1]

"Love loves to love love." Nothing better expresses the most fundamental law of our nature. Created from love, we are made to love because nothing else will fulfill us, nothing else will content us, nothing else will bless us with life. Loving well may not be easy, and we may often confuse good loves for bad loves and wise loves for foolish loves. But no matter how many mistakes we make in loving, we cannot escape our call to be skilled and faithful lovers because love, as all the religions of the world attest, is the only true path to life.

But we don't need novels to convince us that the words of 1 John 3:14 are true: "Whoever does not love remains in death." We know it from our own experience. We know it from the twisted and often painful stories of our lives. We know it in our bones when the need to love and to be loved cries out to us, reminding us that we will be broken and bereft unless we are connected to others through love. Daniel Day Williams said that "the fundamental human craving is to belong, to count in the community of being," and that the "will to belong is the will to communicate, to express oneself and to find a response."[2] That's love. Love is the desire to belong, to matter, to be affirmed and accepted by someone. Love is the insatiable need to offer ourselves to others and to have that offering endorsed, embraced, and received by them in return. The fundamental rhythm of life is found in the back-and-forth of love, the mutual giving and receiving of love; thus, not to love, to refuse all offerings of love, and to nurture stony and unyielding hearts instead of open ones, is to be fatally out of step with life. "Perfection for all persons," Catherine LaCugna wrote, "resides in loving and knowing another, coming to self through another, being who one is in relation to another."[3]

Learning the art of love is the central task of the Christian moral life and, to be sure, the fundamental work of our lives. In this chapter we'll explore the mystery of love first by considering why the human vocation is a vocation to love. Why is it that love is the one thing we absolutely have to learn to do well? Why must we be experts not only at offering love but also at receiving it?

In the second part of the chapter we will consider how love works by focusing on two questions: What are we doing when we love? and What does good love require? Third, we'll consider different types of love. We typically use the single word *love* to describe ways of loving that are in significant ways different. For instance, we may "love" a good wine, but hopefully not in the same way that we love our spouses and our friends. And, as we saw in chapter 3, Christians are taught that they must love their enemies if they are to be loyal disciples of Christ; however, we surely don't love an enemy in exactly the way we love those closest to our hearts. This is why it is important to think about the different kinds of love and the different ways to love.

Finally, the chapter will conclude by considering how Christians are called to extend the circle of love. An abiding danger to any love is to allow it to narrow our concern for others. But the energy of love should always enlarge our world, never shrink it, to include those we easily overlook and dismiss. If the reign of God envisions a community where all of us find our true place of belonging, then we must try to imitate in our own lives the infinitely capacious love that we see in God.

WHY THE HUMAN VOCATION IS A VOCATION TO LOVE

God doesn't ask us to love or hope that we love. God *commands* us to love. Three times in the Synoptic Gospels (Matt 22:34-40; Mark 12:28-34; and Luke 10:25-28) Jesus summarizes all the commands of the Torah in the two-fold command to love God "with all your heart, with all your soul, and with all your mind," and to "love your neighbor as yourself" (Matt 23:37-38). He tells those who question him not only that love of God and neighbor is the great-est of the commandments but also that those who fulfill that command will inherit eternal life (Luke 10:25). Too, the fact that the command to whole-hearted love of God and the command to love of neighbor find earlier expres-sions in Deuteronomy 6:5 and Leviticus 19:18 respectively, suggests that love is the key to unlocking God's will for us.[4]

But why does God place the love commands above every other command? Why does Jesus make them the cornerstone on which the Christian life is built? God doesn't issue commands to take all the joy out of life. Rather, the commands of God are our most trustworthy guides to fullness of life. Thus, when Jesus told the inquisitive scholar in Luke 10:11, "You have answered correctly; do this and you will live," he wasn't being preachy; he was being on-the-spot truthful. The man asked Jesus how he could find fullness of life, and Jesus told him he would find it in a love expansive enough to include both God and every last one of his innumerable neighbors. Practice a love that embraces all—both the God who made you and the neighbors who are joined to you—and you will have life.

Images of a God Who Is Love

Why is this so? Why is love our most perfecting and fulfilling activity? Why is giving and receiving love what we were born to do? One reason is that we are made in the image and likeness of a God whose very being is an ever-lasting communion of love. Christians believe that God is not a "lonesome figure,"[5] but a vibrant communion of love in which each person's love gives life, identity, and joy to the other. As Michael Himes has noted, "The central point of the doctrine of the Trinity is that God is least wrongly understood as a relationship, as an external explosion of love."[6] As Trinity, God is an inti-mate partnership of love—really an ongoing dance of love—in which love is forever perfectly given and perfectly received. To speak of God as Trinity is to claim that God is not three isolated individuals (for then there would be loneliness in God) but rather the absolute solidarity of unbreakable love.[7] At the heart of God we find not solitude and isolation, not alienation and discord, but the perfection of intimacy and communion that is itself the fullness of joy. Put more powerfully, the Christian doctrine of the Trinity, as Catherine LaCugna wrote, means that "being-in-relation-to-another" is not peripheral to how we think about God, but is indeed "the ultimate originating principle of all reality."[8]

We live because God loves us into being and ceaselessly seeks to be in relation with us. We live because at every moment of our lives we receive *as gift* the love by which all things are. But we are not only to receive this love; we are also to imitate it, participate in it, share it, and model our lives on it. Learning to give and to receive love is our vocation for a lifetime because as God's finely sculpted images we grow and have life only in relationships and communities characterized by mutual and generous love. If "being-in-relation" is "the ultimate originating principle of all reality," indeed, the most inescapable fact about us as well as everything else, then the core truth of God's life is the core truth of our own. We only find life through love, a love that strives to imitate the joyous and ingenious dance of love that is God.

As Elaine Storkey writes, "Love is not an option for human beings, it is a requirement. It is the most profound statement of who we are." And that is because as God's images we have an unbreakable connection between who God is and who we are called to be and an unbreakable connection between what is life for God and what alone can be life for us. We need intimacy, communion, friendship, and fellowship in life. We need relationships and communities where people care for one another, support one another, and watch out for one another. We need persons and communities to whom we can devote our lives in love and who will devote themselves to us in love because, as God's earthly images, we are created to be-in-relation-to-others. As Storkey summarizes, "There is a community between the Father, Son and the Spirit. That community is love. But this same God has designed *us*, made us, shaped us, and loved us into being. We are to be called 'God's image.' So love too is part of our own identity."[9]

We're Neighbors Whether We Like It or Not!

A second reason that the human vocation is the vocation to give and to receive love is because from the beginning to the end of our lives we are linked to everyone else who lives. In this respect, to love is to know who we truly are and to honor it. Christianity teaches that we don't choose our neighbors because the God whose love joins all of us together makes every other person brother or sister to us, members of the same universal household. We're neighbors whether we like it or not because we are part of a fellowship constituted, not by race or nationality, not by gender, and not by religious beliefs, but by the love of God that has been poured into the hearts of every person who has ever lived (Rom 5:5).

The English theologian Liz Carmichael says "the deep meaning of society is that people should 'live as friends with one another.'"[10] We are called to live as friends with one another because, thanks to God's grace, there is a way that we already are. It is not natural for us to be at odds with one another, to be alienated and polarized. It is not natural for us to let hate and

> *Learning to give and to receive love is our vocation for a lifetime because as God's finely sculpted images we grow and have life only in relationships and communities characterized by mutual and generous love.*

hurt or bitterness and resentment abide because such forces for division violate an inescapable fact about us: we are one through the power of God's love. Put differently, it is not natural for us not to love because not to love is to fail to recognize, and to act in harmony with, what we already and always are.

Thomas Aquinas used this insight to shape his understanding of charity. For him, charity is not simply love but, more precisely, the fellowship brought into being by God sharing the divine life, love, and happiness with everyone.[11] Charity creates a real and resilient fellowship (*koinōnia*) not only between God and ourselves, but also between ourselves and everyone else. Bound together by the universal love of God, we belong to a community whose membership extends to all. For Aquinas, we are not first individuals who then decide whether to have neighbors or not. On the contrary, because all of us are joined together in the love of God, charity makes us neighbors of everyone. Every human being is a neighbor to every other human being through the exorbitantly diffusive love of God. Thus, we do not have to create unity among ourselves and others because it is there from the start. Through the grace of charity we have kinship and fellowship with everyone. Indeed, charity creates a community in which no one is finally a stranger and no one can be an outsider.

But charity also summons us to love all those who are "put on the path alongside us" as we make our way through life.[12] As we take this journey we may discover that some who are "put on the path alongside us" may not be so easy to love. Some may be quarrelsome, testy, obnoxious, or simply odd. Some may be boring, irritatingly needy, or impossibly demanding. And a chosen few may be enemies. But charity, as a fellowship of grace, insists that we love them all because each is neighbor to us. We are to love the quarrelsome and the strange, the boring and the testy, and even those who insist on being our enemies because, like ourselves, they are loved and cherished by God. In the community of charity we are called to love whomever God loves, and to love them because God loves them, even if the neighbor who is loved by God is more enemy than friend.

Aquinas reasoned that if someone is our friend, we should love whomever the friend loves for the sake of our love for our friend. But when the friend being considered is God, then for the sake of our love for God we are to love everyone and everything God loves. And because God's love excludes no one, neither should our own. As Aquinas explained, "for the sake of a friend you love those belonging to him, be they children, servants or anyone connected with him at all, even if they hurt or hate us, so much do we love him. In this way the friendship of charity extends even to our enemies, for we love them for the sake of God who is the principal in our loving."[13]

Putting Others at the Center of Our Lives

Finally, a third reason we find life only through love is that human beings are fulfilled not when we feverishly work to keep ourselves at the center of our lives, but when we live for something other than ourselves. We are satisfied, usually to our surprise, not when we consistently place our own needs and desires before the well-being of others, but when we redirect our attention away from ourselves and to another.

This isn't easy—in fact, it is notoriously difficult—because the pull of self-centeredness runs deep in all of us. But if we never dislodge the self from the center of our lives we will never discover the bliss that can come from extending ourselves for others. In this respect, love is exactly the opposite of a life spent making sure that everything always works out for our own best advantage. As Vincent Genovesi writes, "True self-fulfillment, then, demands self-transcendence, and this is possible only through the sort of self-forgetfulness that allows us to put others at the center of our attention."[14]

Consequently, we will thrive and flourish only when we make space in our lives for others. But this means we must see the call coming forth from another, not as a threat or a burden, but as a potentially liberating grace. The persons standing before me are not nuisances to avoid or obstacles to overcome; rather, they are essential to my freedom because it is only in responding to them that I can be released from the prison of my anxious self-concern. It is tempting to see the persons we love as nuisances and obstacles, at least occasionally. Spouses can surely see one another that way. Parents who are trying to relax can hear the wails of a crying child that way. And even friends can sometimes view each other more as threats than as gifts. But we cannot allow such moments to estrange us from others because it is only in becoming part of worlds larger than our own—whether that be in marriage, in families, in churches or communities—that we have life. We grow only as we move from isolation to communion through love.

Are We Called to Love Ourselves?

It is often forgotten that the command to love also includes a proper love for ourselves. Yes, we are to love God and our neighbors, but we are also summoned to love ourselves. In fact, Jesus seems to assume that we do love ourselves because he tells us to love our neighbors as we already love ourselves. What would it mean for us to obey the command to love ourselves? At the very least, it means we should never love in ways that are destructive to or that do violence to ourselves. Real love is costly because to love is to expend ourselves for the sake of another. Real love is costly because to love is to give of ourselves in care and concern of others.

And there is no real love that does not demand moments of sacrifice for the sake of someone who is dear to us. Spouses make sacrifices for one another and for the good of their marriage. Parents spend years sacrificing for the sake of their children. And the depth of friendships is sometimes seen in the sacrifices that friends are willing to make for one another. But even though "we may sacrifice everything we have, we may not sacrifice everything we are."[15] Love for others should not lead to the annihilation of the self that has been given to us by God. Love calls us to give of ourselves to others, but it does not, and never should, call us to demean or diminish ourselves, or to allow others to demean or diminish us.

This is why there are limits to the sacrifices people can ask of one another in love. And it is why we can never call good—and should never tolerate—any relationship that crushes our souls, diminishes our spirits, or erases ourselves. We have likely known people whose love for another seemed to make them disappear because they were so swallowed up by the needs and demands of the other that they lost whatever self they once had. Instead of bringing them more fully to life, they increasingly lost everything that made them the unique and special beings they were. This is why "we may give everything for love of another but we may not 'sin' in so doing," and that includes sinning against ourselves.[16]

Jesus' command to love our neighbors as we love ourselves means that we have a moral obligation to love in ways that respect and affirm the unique image of God that we are. If we do not, we break the love command just as surely as when we turn away from God or become indifferent to our neighbors. As Margaret Farley reminds us, "A love will not be true or just if there is an affirmation of the beloved that involves destruction of the one who loves. I do not refer to a justifiable 'laying down of one's life' for the beloved, but rather to a letting oneself be destroyed as a person because of the way in which one loves another."[17]

How then ought we to love ourselves? A proper love for ourselves is based in God's love for us and reflects God's love for us.[18] Knowing we are precious to God enables us rightly to prize and cherish ourselves. Moreover, if a genuine love for ourselves is rooted in God's love for us, then our love for ourselves does not compete with or detract from our love for others, but is the very thing that enables us to love them. Confident of God's love for us and grateful for God's love for us, we can put aside the anxious self-concern that hinders both our love for others and a healthy love for ourselves.

We also fulfill Jesus' command to love ourselves when we live in ways that foster the unique identity entrusted to us as a child of God and strive to become what God calls us to become. Put differently, we love ourselves rightly when we care about our character and our integrity, and when we strive to grow in goodness and holiness. As Edward Vacek suggests, we fulfill Jesus' command to love ourselves when we "affirm the saint in us and we dissent from the sinner in us."[19]

HOW LOVE WORKS

There are many ways to speak of love. Daniel Day Williams says love is "spirit seeking the enjoyment of freedom in communion with the other," and claims that this description of love applies not only to ourselves, but also to God.[20] In his well-received work on love, Edward Vacek says, "love is an affective, affirming participation in the goodness of a being (or Being)," a definition that acknowledges our intense desire to share in the lives of those we love, including God.[21] Echoing Vacek, in her book *Just Love*, Margaret Farley writes: "Love, as I understand it, is simultaneously an affective response, an affective way of being in union, and an affective affirmation of what is loved."[22] And Vincent Genovesi, with the example of Christ in mind, says "the heart of true human and Christian love is found in the desire and willingness to live creatively in the service of others' fulfillment."[23] What do these descriptions of love tell us about what we are doing when we love?

What Are We Doing When We Love?

First, Farley's and Vacek's definitions of love suggest that love begins when we are touched, stirred, and moved by another thing's goodness and beauty. Something about the other person speaks to us, enters into us, and draws us out of ourselves. Something of the other person's uniqueness imprints itself on us and shapes us before we are even dimly aware of it. Isn't this why when we reflect on our experiences of love we realize we were in love before we were consciously aware of it? Isn't it why being in love is something we discover more than initiate?

If we analyze our experiences with love we recognize that love begins not with us acting but with us being *acted upon* by the soul and spirit of another. Even though at some point we choose whether to love or not, love begins not in well-calculated choices but in *active receptivity* to another's goodness. Something about them touches us or reaches us. This is why love often takes us by surprise, or why we regularly speak of "falling in love" rather than "deciding to love." The image of falling in love recognizes that love begins in openness and vulnerability, that love is stirred in us or awakened in us in response to another's value. Similarly, when we say that another person has "captured" our hearts, we acknowledge that the initial work of love is not giving but receiving. Love begins in the vulnerability that allows us to receive into ourselves something of the other.[24] That is why, at least initially, love is a spontaneous response to the goodness of another, a goodness that somehow breaks through to us and connects with us. Farley describes well this first dimension of love when she writes:

> But there is another aspect to my loving which makes it, in its beginning, not a matter of "simply choosing." That is, my love for you is "first of all" a response—a response to your lovableness, your value and beauty. This is the passive dimension of love. I must "receive" your revelation of yourself as lovable. Your self, or some aspect of it, must touch my mind and heart, awaken it, so that I respond in love.[25]

Because we reach out in response to another's unique beauty and goodness, the second dimension of love is an "affective affirmation" of the other.[26] To love someone is to be glad that they are. To love them is to want them to be and to take delight in their existence. It is to relate to them in ways that testify that the world is a richer and better place because they are in it. As Josef Pieper says, to love someone is to say, "It's good that you exist; it's good that you are in this world!"[27] When we love another person we let them know that they matter to us, that they are important to us, and that our lives are enriched because of them. In this respect, love is a conscious, deliberate, and abiding affirmation of the being of another. It is to find him or her good not just once and not just occasionally, but again and again. And it is to devote our energy, our creativity, and our time and attention to helping them be.

But love not only wants the beloved to be; it wants her to be as fully and completely as possible. All good love is inspired by a vision of what the beloved can be and is called to be. Love envisions the fullest and most fitting development of the beloved's goodness and unique identity, and commits itself to helping bring this about. Not content with partial realizations of the beloved's soul and spirit, love focuses on the utmost possible excellence for the beloved and promises to do its part to make this possible; thus, love involves us in the lives of the persons we love.

As Vacek explains, "Hence, love is directed to the fullness of value possible to the beloved. In general terms, *love is an emotional, affirming participation in the dynamic tendency of an object to realize its fullness.*"[28] When we love then we not only respond to another person's goodness, but we also commit ourselves to doing what we can to help them achieve the fullest possible realization of it. If love begins in our receiving another's goodness, it continues by our giving of ourselves for the sake of the further development of that goodness.

It is here that we encounter the incredible power and potential beauty of love. In his analysis of love, Josef Pieper says our love for another should continue what God's love began. God's love fashioned us into life. And in creating us God not only affirmed the goodness of our existence but also delighted in us. Moreover, in creating us, God had a vision of what we could become. But what God's creative love began, human love should help to complete. The supreme dignity of human love is that in loving one another we are called to carry forward what God's love began. God entrusts the handiwork of his divine love to each of us, and calls us not only to care for the persons he has created from love but also, through our own love, to help bring them to perfection. God honors us by handing over to us the persons his own love has created.

But God also depends on us to recognize the unrepeatable goodness and beauty of every person and, through our love, to help bring that beauty and goodness more fully to life. That is what we do when we love. We take what God's love began and add to it. But we do so in ways that not merely repeat or echo God's love but contribute to it in distinctively creative ways. There is something both humbling and awesome about the responsibility of human love, because the God who began the work of creation says to each one of us, "Continue what my love began." As Pieper explains, "If all goes happily as it should, then in human love something *more* takes place than mere echo, mere repetition and imitation," because that would deny the truly human and diverse ways that we love one another. "What takes place," he asserts, "is a continuation and in a certain sense even a perfecting of what was begun in the course of creation."[29]

Spouses do this when they love one another faithfully and insightfully and creatively over the years of a marriage. Called to be responsible for one another in ways no one else is, through their love they draw one another more fully to life. Like skilled artists, they help bring to light each other's goodness and beauty, and add to what God's love began. But this is true in all real love. To love their children well, parents must be able to recognize what is unique about each one of them—the goodness and promise that may be hidden away in them—and then through their loving attention and concern, bring it more fully to life.

Similarly, part of the reason we are so indebted to our friends is because we recognize we would not be the persons we have become without them. Because they often see us and know us better than we see or know ourselves, through their care and concern, through the ingenuity of their kindness, and through the artistry of their love, they make us more than we could ever have made of ourselves. So much of who we are is the handiwork of another's love, whether our parents and siblings, our spouses and partners, our lifelong friends, or simply the people we meet in passing whose attention toward us, however momentary, is marked by love.

Third, if love begins by receiving the goodness of another, and continues by affirming and helping to enhance that goodness, love aims for the fullest possible union with the beloved. We do not want to be separated from the people we love. We want to be with them. We want to spend time with them, talk with them, and do things with them. We do not want to love them from afar; rather, we want to share in their lives as completely as possible. We even want to be one heart and soul with them. And the reason is that to a certain degree we already are. To love is to take on the other. It is, as we saw above, to open ourselves to receive the other and to have our lives changed and reshaped by them. The longer we love, the more the persons we love live in us and are part of us, and the more we live in them and are part of them. Thus, our desire to be united to the persons we love originates in an intimacy and union we already have with them.

We would not be lonely for the people we love if we did not already carry them with us. We would not feel sad at their absence if there were not already some part of them in our hearts. But because it is hard for love to be content with partial unity or imperfect intimacy, we yearn to be one with the persons we love as fully and completely as possible. As Daniel Day Williams said, love is one person seeking communion with another and God seeking communion with all of us. The will to belong, to be together with, to be intimately connected to others is the fundamental energy of life and the fundamental energy of love. It is what God seeks with us in grace, Christ, and the Spirit. And it is what we are created to seek with God and one another. Created from God's love, we hunger for an intimacy and communion to complete us, to heal our loneliness, and to satisfy the deepest longings of our hearts.

What Does Loving Well Require?

What must we do to keep love alive? What must we attend to if the most promising loves of our lives are not to die? What does loving well require? First, even though love may begin in a feeling, it must be ratified by a choice. Love lives through our conscious and deliberate decision to commit ourselves to the well-being of others. Love is an act of will that is often expressed through a promise, commitment, or vow. We pledge ourselves to love others (spouses, friends, or community members) precisely because we know that feelings are fickle.

This is one reason falling in love is something quite different from genuinely loving. Anyone can fall in love—in fact, everyone does—but actually loving someone "in season and out of season" depends not on the strength of our feelings, but on our "free decision to respond to and nurture the beauty and potential" that we perceive in another human being.[30] Feelings come and go. Feelings fade. There are periods when the feelings we have for the people we love are so strong and all consuming that it is hard for us to imagine our love without them. But then, in surprising and unsettling ways, those feelings weaken and can even disappear. At such moments we love not because we feel like loving, but because we have promised to love. As Kathleen Fischer Hart and Thomas Hart wrote, "Loving someone over the years is a very different matter from being in love. It is much less an emotional state, much more a choice. Falling in love is something that *happens* to a person; loving someone is something a person *chooses* to do or not to do."[31]

Thus, no matter how much we might be touched and moved and inspired by another person's goodness, love lives only when we endorse our initial inclination to give ourselves for the sake of others. Love is subject to choice.[32] We may not be able to decide whom we fall in love with or when we fall in love; but we can and must decide how we will love them. Will we marry them, be friends with them, or simply treat them kindly?

We can think of love as an invitation that comes to us from another. We can think of love as a call spoken to us in the presence of another. But as we saw in chapter 1, we can choose to respond to that call or to ignore it. And even if we do respond to it, we then have to decide what place the love will have in our lives.

In her analysis of love, Farley says that love offers itself to our freedom. But in our freedom we must decide either to identify with the love by committing to it or to decline the offer of love by turning away from it. To love someone is to make a decision about what we will do with our freedom. To love someone is to invest our freedom, and therefore ourselves, in being actively committed to their flourishing. "At the center of ourselves where freedom is a possibility," Farley summarizes, "we can *identify* with our loves and freely ratify them—this love or that, this form of loving or that, this or that action to express love. We take responsibility for our loves, or at least we can do so. We can also repudiate, or defer, some of our loves by choosing *not to identify* with them."[33]

> *Love lives through our conscious and deliberate decision to commit ourselves to the well-being of others. Love is an act of will.*

Second, love requires fidelity. In fact, faithfulness is so important for love that we can say love lives through fidelity and is nurtured and sustained by fidelity. Fidelity gives the loves of our lives a future by giving them time to grow, deepen, and become more resilient, and by protecting us from the temptation to give up on our loves or betray them during periods of difficulty and disillusionment. We pledge ourselves to love because we know the fullness of love is not immediately reached, but something we struggle toward and grow into over time. Love envisions the fullness of communion; it envisions abiding and unbreakable intimacy. But that perfect consummation of love is something we strive for and hope for, and wait patiently for, but never fully attain.

As Daniel Day Williams says, "Love lives not only from the ecstasy of fulfillment, but from a loyalty not yet fulfilled. Love realizes itself, not only in the enjoyment of completion, but in the suffering of the Not-yet."[34] This is why, for example, even though love may be the most essential element for a marriage or a partnership or a friendship, it is not sufficient for any of them. Fidelity allows us to guide our loves from their promising beginnings to their utmost future potential. As Margaret Farley notes, "Commitment is love's way of being whole while it still grows into wholeness."[35]

But love must also live in partnership with fidelity because real love, unlike fantasy love, is hard work. Love is a full-time occupation—a lifelong assignment—that demands patience, energy, resolve, and perseverance. Real love, unlike fantasy love, does not allow us to escape the challenges of our lives, but calls us to attend to them. And real love, unlike fantasy love, involves every aspect of ourselves and impacts every dimension of our lives. What love specifically asks of us will vary according to the different relationships of our lives, but it will never be easy precisely because it unstintingly demands that we focus our lives on the needs and well-being of others, and doing that consistently and doing that well is hard.

Furthermore, love requires fidelity because none of us is given perfect persons to love. The people we love are shockingly like ourselves, persons who can be stubborn, quarrelsome, petty, and downright ornery. When it comes to being lovable, all of us are flawed objects. We can shine in goodness and kindness, and dazzle others with our thoughtfulness and generosity. But we can also stun those very same people by our outbursts of anger, our self-centeredness, our moments of maliciousness, and by our self-righteousness. We can be very good at kindness and very sensitive to another's needs. But we can also be polished at pride, at betrayal and deceit, at coldness and indifference, and even cruelty. Marriages, friendships, and life in community are all tested at those moments when our flawed and wounded humanity asserts itself. Loving one at such moments is hard, particularly when we realize that the shortcomings of those we love will never be erased. This too is why love lives only through fidelity. When our love is tested sometimes the only way it can endure is by remembering that we have promised to love. Fidelity protects love at such moments by reminding us that sometimes we love only because we have promised to do so.

Third, loving well requires that our love for others be insightful. "Each person is a whole world in herself,"[36] Margaret Farley writes, and that is why loving well demands taking time to really know persons as they are, especially everything that makes them who they are instead of someone else. We said above that love labors on behalf of the genuine good of others and seeks the most complete and perfect fulfillment of others. But we will not know what this means if we do not first attend to the distinctive needs, hopes, dreams, and ambitions of those we love, as well as their particular shortcomings and limitations. I do not love someone well if I encourage him to be a doctor when he struggled with biology and panicked at chemistry. And my love will likely do more harm than good if I tell a student she should not be so dejected when I have not taken the time to learn why she is sad. An uninformed and undiscerning love always backfires. Love targets the good of a beloved, but we will misfire in our attempts to love if we have not taken time to ascertain what is really the most fitting good of the persons we love.

Without insight, our love is not only inept but also lazy. A lazy lover treats a beloved as if he were anybody. A lazy lover does not take the time needed to discover who he is as a singular, unique human being. Good love requires perception, astuteness, and discriminating insight. Good love requires sensitivity, sympathy, and imagination. We cannot love persons graciously and thoughtfully unless we learn who they really are and have some knowledge of their distinctive desires, struggles, hopes, and fears. Thus, a skilled lover is one who has taken time to apprise the unique identity, dignity, gifts, needs, cares, and concerns of the other.

As Daniel Day Williams wrote:

> Love requires real individuals, unique beings, each bringing to the relationship something which no other can bring. The individuals must be capable of taking account of one another in their unique individuality. . . . This "taking account of the other" means that each brings to the relationship an originality which belongs to him alone and each finds in the other an originality which belongs to that other alone.[37]

Williams's comment reminds us that the persons we love truly are originals, never-to-be-repeated expressions of the goodness, creativity, and ingenious love of God. The goal of love is to uncover, affirm, and help bring more fully to life the unique image of God every man and woman is. But we cannot do this unless we continually take into account both who they are and who they are called to be by God. I don't love others well when I assume I know what they need or when I project onto them what I believe they need, want, or are called to become. No matter how sincere, such actions are failures in love because love only succeeds when it actually contributes to another's welfare.[38] Our love of others must be judged not by our intentions, nor by the intensity of our feelings, but by the actual results of our love. Are they better for us loving them or not? Does our love truly help them be who they ought to be or does it reflect a serious misperception of who they are?

Fourth, loving well requires that we affirm and accept the freedom of the other.[39] Although it is obvious, it bears mentioning that love must be void of possessiveness, manipulation, coercion, and control. Probably all of us have known people who claimed to love us but whose love was little more than a projection of their own insecurity and unquenchable needs. It does not take long for such relationships to become suffocating because instead of loving us, these people try to absorb us completely into their lives. And it does not take long for us to resent them because their love for us masks a need to control and a fear that we might leave them. When this occurs they love us, not as ends in ourselves, but merely as means for fulfilling themselves.[40]

Love must be based in a respect for other persons, particularly a respect for their freedom and legitimate autonomy. We cannot force anyone to love us. We can reach out to them in love and extend an invitation to love. But love only works if our invitation is met by their free response. And we cannot force anyone to continue to love us. Love based on manipulation and coercion, and love born from fear, are doomed because a love that is forced is no love at all. Too, respecting the freedom of the persons we love means allowing them to love and be loved by others. None of us can be everything another person needs; thus, we hardly love them if we attempt to keep them from entering into friendships and relationships with others.

Finally, loving well requires that we be willing to change and to grow with the persons we love. We can understand this in several ways. First, love changes us because when we love someone we let him or her into our lives and give them influence over us. The people we love shape us; indeed, something of them lives on in us. The people we love and who have loved us leave their mark on us because we carry something of them along with us. Through love, they become part of us and we become part of them; thus, we cannot love and not be changed.

Second, to say that we must be willing to change and grow through love underscores that love either develops or it dies. Love is not something static; rather, it is a living thing (an energy really) that seeks ongoing growth and development, and even perfection. Love strives for the fulfillment of persons in communion. But that can only occur when both lover and beloved are willing to grow together in love. Put differently, love is a partnership, a shared endeavor, and this means that none of those involved can become indifferent to their love. In order to reach the fullness of love, we must be willing to grow, change, and be transformed. We must be open to the observations and challenges of those we love, and we must realize that part of what we owe the persons we love (whether in marriages, partnerships, friendships, or communities) is a willingness to grow together with them. In more theological language, love requires the ongoing conversion of ourselves, and this is why a refusal to continue to grow in love is a violation of the faithfulness love demands.

DIFFERENT KINDS OF LOVE

What do we love? It's a simple question with almost endless possible answers. Some objects of love are obvious. We love our spouses and we love our children and we love our friends. But it's also not uncommon for us to say that we love working with our colleagues or that we love the other members of our team. We speak of loving certain artists and authors, as well as some celebrities and movie stars. We love our country and we love its ideals. We love sunsets, walks along the beach, or a quiet evening at home. We love chocolate, good wine, fine meals, and even a good night's sleep. We can love our jobs and we can love being retired from them. We love our pets and we love our projects. We love our homes and we can even love the clothes we wear. We love so many things, but we obviously don't love them all in the same way. It would be ludicrous for spouses to say their love for one another is no different from their love for a fine beer, and just as silly for friends to say that when they talk of loving one another what comes to mind is their love for chocolate. Love covers a multitude of aims, but what we mean by love depends on what we love and why we love it.

This is why philosophers and theologians have regularly distinguished between different types of love. In his celebrated book *The Four Loves*, C. S. Lewis spoke of affection, friendship, *eros*, and charity as four different ways of understanding love. But most writers have focused on three kinds of love: *agape*, which is often described as the distinctively Christian expression of love; *eros*, which typically describes love based in desire; and *philia* or friendship love.

Although philosophers and theologians have understood the relationship between these loves in different ways, it seems best to follow Edward Vacek's claim that each love is most fittingly distinguished according to the reason or intention that we love someone or something. "We may love the beloved (1) for the sake of the beloved, (2) for our own sake, or (3) for the sake of a relationship we have with the beloved," Vacek writes. "I call these love relations (1) agape, (2) eros, and (3) philia. Thus, I distinguish agape, eros, and philia by the phrase *'for the sake of.'* The one for whose sake we love determines the kind of love we have."[41]

Agape

Following Vacek's schema, the "distinguishing feature of agape is that it is directed to the beloved for the beloved's sake. The 'object' of agape is the beloved, its 'aim' is the good of the beloved, and its 'reason' is also the good of the beloved."[42] Every love is focused on a good, and the love of agape is focused on the good of the persons we love. In this respect, agape turns us away from ourselves to the needs and well-being of others.

A typical example of agape is the love parents have for their children. Parents love their children for their children's sake. They devote themselves to the good of their children, and regularly sacrifice for the sake of their children, whether their children love them or not. Infants, for example, obviously cannot return their parents' love in any way that is commensurate with the love they have been given—and adolescents stubbornly refuse to do so! But their inability or unwillingness to return love does not lessen the parents' love. Parents hope that someday their children will return the love that is offered to them, but their love is not contingent on it.

When we love someone for his or her own sake, we naturally want that love to be mutual. But even though such mutual, reciprocal love may represent the fullness of love, the love of agape does not require it. With agape, whether someone loves us or not, our attention is directed to them and our care is extended to them, because we are committed to their good for their own sake. This can even happen in marriages and friendships. There can be periods in a marriage or a friendship when the persons we love no longer seem to love us. If we continue to love them for their own sake there is love in the relationship, but it is not mutual. We may continue to love them because they are beloved to us and because we hope our steadfast love might resurrect their love for us in return. When we do, the love we practice is agape, not friendship. If our love does call forth from them a renewed love for us, the relationship can once more be described as friendship. If they fail to love us in return, but we nonetheless continue to love them for their own sake, we do so with the love of agape.

It is this fact that led agape to be embraced as the distinctively Christian love. Just as God's love for us does not depend on our love for God, agape does not require reciprocity. But some theologians went further by identifying the most perfect expression of agape to be the sacrificial death of Jesus. For them, agape is love for the sake of another; and it is, more specifically, sacrificial love for the sake of another. In this account, the quintessential element of agape is self-sacrifice. Thus, the excellence of love is directly proportionate to its cost. Heedless of cost and unmindful of reward, we love best not when we seek to be loved in return, but when we expend ourselves as completely as possible for the sake of another. As Stephen G. Post writes, "Frequently selfless love, a love utterly heedless of self and entirely one-way in its movement, rather than circular, is thought to be ethically superior to communion and alone worthy of the designation 'Christian.'"[43]

No one developed this understanding of agape more forcefully than Anders Nygren. In his 1932 study *Agape and Eros*, Nygren sought to define and delineate agape by contrasting it with eros. For Nygren, agape is everything eros is not. Essentially selfish and egocentric, eros, according to Nygren, is a grasping, acquisitive love motivated by desire. It is needy, calculating, and conditional. When we love from eros, Nygren claimed, we love only because we perceive something as good for us and want it; if our needs and wants change, we stop loving it.

By contrast, the love of agape is unconditional, unmotivated, unselfish, and universal. It is, as Nygren classically put it, "indifferent to value" because it does not depend on the goodness of the beloved, especially the good they could offer us.[44] The love Christians are called to practice, and the love by which they most fully imitate Christ, is agape. And agape, Nygren steadily maintained, is essentially disinterested love, love that is void of any concern for return, enrichment, or reward. And because agape is deliberately indifferent to the interests and concerns of the self, it is a love characterized by self-giving and self-forgetfulness. As Nygren wrote, agape is "a love that gives itself away, that sacrifices itself, even to the uttermost."[45] Nygren made agape the love by which every other love had to be measured. And as the paradigm of Christian love, the heart of agape is found in sacrificing oneself for the sake of others.[46]

But as feminist theologians have rightly warned, to make self-sacrifice not only synonymous with Christian love, but also the ideal to aspire to, is both unhealthy and dangerous. Nygren argued that any love that is marked by self-regard—and any love that seeks something in return—is not only tainted but also the complete antithesis to Christian love. To love with agape is to be totally focused on the well-being of the other with absolutely no concern for oneself. For Nygren, self-love is not only denigrated; it is condemned. There is no room for it in the Christian life. Nygren made this clear when he wrote: "Christianity does not recognise self-love as a legitimate form of love. Christian love moves in two directions, towards God and towards its neighbour; and in self-love it finds its chief adversary which must be fought and conquered."[47]

But feminist theologians have insisted that self-regard has to be part of agape not only because, as we saw above, Jesus commanded it, but also because "excessive self-surrender" is as much a failure of love as "excessive selfishness."[48] Moreover, women particularly can be harmed by Nygren's account of love because "women (by nature and/or as a result of cultural conditioning) are often prone to destructive self-abnegation." "Many women," Barbara Hilkert Andolsen argues, "live for others to a damaging degree. Largely focused upon others, such women are unable to establish a satisfying self-definition."[49] For Andolsen, Nygren's account of agape calls us to neglect our own lives and our own development to such a degree that in practicing it we diminish the self that we are meant to care for and to share.

The feminist critique of self-sacrifice as the distinguishing element of Christian love has prompted theologians to rethink how Christians should aspire to love. Even though there has been a tendency in Christian theology to elevate selfless love over mutual and reciprocal love, recent work on love has insisted that the most fitting love is "marked by mutual respect and regard." The most fitting love is not one-sided love, but love "in which all parties are confirmed as having worth and hence all the parties are benefited."[50] And this is because we not only need to love but also need to be loved in return.

Nygren was right to say that to overcome selfishness we need to be drawn out of ourselves through love, and that such love demands sacrifice, exquisite generosity, and sometimes even hardship and loss. But what he failed to see, and what feminist theologians have recognized, is that to have a self at all we must be loved, embraced, and cherished in return. We need the give-and-take of love through which each person is drawn more fully to life by the care, goodness, and affection of the other. Love meeting love is the perfection of love, not the self-emptying that can make us disappear.

As Andolsen says, "Neither self-sacrifice nor other-regard captures the total meaning of *agape*. The full expression of the Christian ideal is mutuality."[51] Moreover, contrary to Nygren, love is motivated and interested inasmuch as what it seeks is not selflessness but communion. Just as God seeks communion with us, human love is fulfilled in intimacy and communion with others. And even though growing in communion with others sometimes requires costly sacrifices from ourselves, the purpose of the sacrifice is to deepen the union.

Eros

The second love, eros, is "love for other persons or things not for their sakes, but for the lover's sake."[52] Our love is eros when we love something principally for the delight or pleasure it brings us. There is something about the thing loved that satisfies us, pleases us, or fulfills us. In this respect, as Nygren testified, eros is never disinterested love. But unlike Nygren who gave a completely negative assessment of eros, Vacek emphasizes that even though eros is self-interested, it is not necessarily self-centered because it does involve recognition of another thing's value or goodness and, in that respect, is genuinely love of the other. "As I use the term," Vacek explains, "eros is truly love for the other. Eros emotionally unites the lover with the beloved and therein affirms the beloved's value, but does so for the sake of the perfection that accrues to the lover."[53]

For instance, if we say we love a good red wine, the love is eros because we love the wine, not for its sake, but for the pleasure it brings us. Nonetheless, our love does reflect a genuine appreciation for the distinctive goodness of the wine, and that recognition saves eros from being wholly self-centered or narcissistic. In order to love something for the value it brings us, whether another person, a painting, or a poem, we have to be able to appreciate its distinctive goodness. It would not mean anything to us if we were not able to look beyond ourselves in order to appraise its own special value.

This is why Vacek rightly insists that eros is "an *objective* love, not a subjectivism that distorts reality for our own purposes. . . . Genuine eros does not distort the good to fit our own needs," which would be the case with purely narcissistic love. Rather, with eros "we want to conform to the good as it is; otherwise we will not really be fulfilled by the beloved's good."[54] In this respect, eros and agape are similar because both require the ability to perceive and to affirm another thing's special goodness. What distinguishes the two loves is that with eros the goodness is prized not primarily for the sake of the thing itself, but largely for the enrichment, pleasure, or satisfaction that it brings the self.

Friendship

Friendship (philia) is the third kind of love, and for Vacek it represents the most perfect expression of love. Contrary to those who hold that agape is the highest expression of love, if human beings are fulfilled in communion, in intimate, substantial, and abiding relationships with God and others, then friendship is the love to which we should aspire because friendships create intimacy and communion between ourselves and others. This is why, even though we love our friends for their own sake (agape), as well as for the joy and meaning they bring to our lives (eros), more than anything we love the relationship that exists between us and our friends.

Stated another way, we don't just love our friends; rather, we also love the friendship itself and the intimacy and communion it creates. Thus, even though there can be no true friendship unless we first wish for our friends' good (benevolence) and also actively seek their good (beneficence), the heart of friendship is the shared life that exists between or among the friends. We know this is true. There is nothing we want more than to be with our friends because being with them enriches and blesses our lives. We love the time we spend with our friends and we love the things we do with them because being with them is good for us. Too, time passes quickly when we are with our friends because we realize there is something about friendship that gets to the core of what it means to be a person and what it is that brings us joy.

Why is this so? Friendships begin in mutual attraction. There is something about another person that captures our attention and draws us out of ourselves in response. There is something about him or her that makes us prefer them over others. It can be their personality and temperament or their appearance. It can be their sense of humor, their outlook on life, or their beliefs, values, hopes, and aspirations. It can be their goodness, their character and integrity, or the way we see love at work in them. It can be many things, but at the deepest level friends share the same truth because they agree on what matters most to them.

What really draws us to our friends, and distinguishes friendships from other relationships in our lives, is discovering that we share something in common with them. They are "kindred souls" because of the interests, desires, hopes, and aspirations that we share with them and that enable us to connect with them in friendship.[55] It can be a common interest in sports, shared hobbies, enjoying the same kinds of movies or music, a mutual passion for justice, or a shared love for God. Whatever the common interest is will define the friendship and explain both the life of the friendship and its possibilities. In general, the deeper and more varied the goods shared between friends, the deeper and richer the friendship.

Attaining the intimacy and communion to which friendship aspires depends on three things. First, the relationship must truly be free. Intimacy with another person cannot be achieved by force or manipulation but must be freely entered into and reflect reverence and respect for the dignity of another. As Vacek explains, "A true encounter is always with someone whom we cannot control. We can influence and be influenced, but not control and be controlled. We evoke, but cannot force, personal change in one another."[56]

Second, intimacy and communion in friendships are impossible without self-communication and self-disclosure. Friendships grow and flourish to the degree that friends are able to share and to receive the ever-deepening communication of one self to another.[57] By contrast, being guarded or overly cautious hinders friendships because it prevents the openness and receptivity on which genuine friendship depends.

Third, in order to grow to deeper communion with our friends, the friendships must be "progressively involving."[58] What does this mean? The more we share the life of a friendship, the more the friendship defines and shapes our life. We begin to think of who we are and what we are about increasingly in terms of the friendship. And we recognize that the longer we are in the friendship the more obligations and responsibilities are connected to the friendship. Obviously, some friendships—such as in marriage or religious community life—will be more "progressively involving" than others. But the more we share life with others, the more deeply engaged we will be with them and the more we will understand ourselves and our lives in light of the friendship. Such relationships promise the most abiding and satisfying intimacy.

Nonetheless, there are potential dangers to friendship, perhaps especially the closest and most intimate friendships of our lives. In fact, the very things that make friendships possible can also make them morally and spiritually unhealthy. Friendships are preferential loves because with every friendship we choose to enter into relationship with some instead of others. The best friendships should never narrow our world, but extend and expand our world by teaching us how to reach out and care for more, not fewer, of our neighbors.

But this does not always happen. Sometimes friends, in turning toward one another, turn away from everyone else. Their interest and devotion to one another is matched by their indifference to everyone else. C. S. Lewis wrote, "Every real Friendship is a sort of secession, even a rebellion."[59] He meant that, at their best, friendships give us the strength and courage we need to "secede" from or rebel against conventional thinking in order to follow what we know is right and true and better. He meant that friends should help one another both imagine and respond to more hopeful possibilities for their lives.

But while Lewis recognized that it is sometimes good to be deaf "to the voices of the outer world," he also realized "that this partial indifference or deafness to outside opinion, justified and necessary as it is, may lead to a wholesale indifference or deafness."[60] A liability to any friendship, precisely because we grow so comfortable with our friends, is to become selfishly unmindful of others. But comfort amid our friends should not lead to complacency toward others. Good friendships should make us more attuned and responsive to the needs of others. But when friendships become elitist, Lewis warned, the "partial deafness which is noble and necessary encourages the wholesale deafness which is arrogant and inhuman."[61]

Extending the Circle of Love

This is why the circle of love must always grow larger, never smaller. In *The Philosophy of Mahatma Gandhi*, Dhirendra Mohan Datta wrote about the great Hindu thinker's understanding of love: "Love helps the finite individual to widen his narrow self. It breaks the barrier between himself and others and makes the life of the individual include more and more of others, and it takes him thus towards the Universal or God."[62] For Gandhi, the circle of love should always expand, resisting our tendencies to shrink the horizons of care and concern in our lives by summoning us to recognize our connections not only to all human beings but indeed to all of life. Love should always resist a narrowing of our world by challenging us to reach out and embrace more instead of fewer, and to make room for them in our lives.

This is what Jesus had in mind when he called his disciples to love not only the neighbors they like and prefer—which usually means the ones most like ourselves—but all who came their way. Like Gandhi, Jesus envisioned a love that would continually enlarge our circle of concern, that would take down barriers between ourselves and others, and that would contribute to the reign of God, that fellowship of love to which all are called. And, like Gandhi, Jesus preached that we move toward a God of universal love only in the measure that we widen the circle of love in our lives. Love marked by hospitality and inclusion brings nearness to God because such a love, in imitating God, brings likeness to God.

And yet, a persistent temptation is not to imitate the risky and radical love of neighbor that we see in Jesus but to practice "safe neighbor love," a love that is picky and selective, calculating and stingy. With safe neighbor love we do not reach out in love to every neighbor but only to those we find easy and pleasing to love. With safe neighbor love we still live in a world of insiders and outsiders, a world where some are welcomed and others are shunned, a world where practices of exclusion are still deemed acceptable. With safe neighbor love boundaries are drawn and barriers are enthusiastically erected, as we surround ourselves with persons who see, feel, think—and often look—very much like ourselves. Safe neighbor love makes it acceptable for us to ignore and neglect the very people who typically are most in need of our care.

But safe neighbor love is assiduously at odds with how Jesus taught his followers to love because safe neighbor love thrives on the assumption that not everybody counts, that many are expendable, and that it is perfectly fine to exclude.[63] Safe neighbor love may keep us comfortable, but it also keeps the world broken and divided. And in preventing *shalom*—the fullness of life and well-being that God wants for all creatures—it opposes God's dream for the world and contradicts Jesus' vision of the reign of God.

The safe neighbor love that allows us to control and narrow the circle of love has to be replaced by a vision of solidarity that continually challenges us to extend the circle of love. Solidarity opens our eyes to see and acknowledge the connections that exist between ourselves and everything else that lives, and the responsibilities that come from those connections. Solidarity teaches us that we cannot narrow the circle of love without contradicting a fundamental truth about our lives: each of us is linked to everyone else, and each of us in some way is accountable to everyone else.

The Cuban theologian Ada María Isasi-Díaz says that a love inspired by a vision of solidarity focuses on the excluded and forgotten members of the world and seeks their liberation. And liberation is fulfilled in salvation, which she describes as a community in which love flows perfectly between God and individual human beings, and from individual human beings to every other human being. "This love relationship is the goal of all life," she writes, and "constitutes the fullness of humanity."[64]

The Zakat

Because it is easy for us to shrink the circle of love in our lives, all religions encourage practices designed to deepen our awareness of others and our responsibilities to them, especially the most vulnerable members of society. One of those practices is *zakat,* one of the Five Pillars of Islam that are required of Muslims and that enable them to "walk in the straight path."[65] Instituted by Muhammed in the seventh century, the *zakat* is "a kind of religious tax" or "legal almsgiving" levied against all adult Muslims who have wealth and property sufficient enough to share with others.[66] The principle behind the *zakat* is simple: "Those who have much should help lift the burden of those who are less fortunate."[67] The tax is one-fortieth of a person's "accumulated wealth and assets, not just their income," and is paid at the end of each year.[68] The funds collected from the *zakat* are distributed to poor Muslims, to converts to Islam in need of aid, to Muslim pilgrims and prisoners of war, to debtors unable to pay their debt, to slaves needing money to buy their freedom, to Muslims engaged in spreading the teachings of Islam, and to those who collect and distribute the alms.[69]

It is important to recognize that Muslims regard the *zakat* not as an act of charity but as an obligation of justice and an expression of stewardship. Based in the conviction that God has blessed the more prosperous members of a community with wealth and resources, and that they are entrusted with them to do good, the *zakat* enjoins them to express their gratitude to God by sharing what they have with the poor. In this way the *zakat* works against the narrowing of love by instilling a sense of communal identity and responsibility, and by teaching one to recognize duties that extend beyond one's immediate family or kin.

In *Islam: The Straight Path,* John Esposito explains: "As all Muslims share equally in their obligation to worship God, so they all are duty bound to attend to the social welfare of their community by redressing economic inequalities through payment of an alms tax or poor tithe. It is an act both of worship or thanksgiving to God and of service to the community."[70] This rightly suggests that one cannot truly worship God without also attending to the needs of others, and that sharing what one has with others is itself a way of worshiping God. In this respect, the *zakat* expresses a principle that is at the heart of all religions: anytime we extend the circle of love by serving our neighbors in need, we give praise and honor to God. As Frederick Denny notes: "God has endowed his creatures with wealth, and humankind is asked to return it through works enhancing the community. To support the community by *Zakat,* then, is to worship God."[71]

Love for All of God's Creation

Human beings are not only entrusted to one another but also entrusted by God to care for God's creation. This is why the circle of love must be extended to include other creatures and species, and why when we speak of loving our neighbors, we have our nonhuman neighbors in mind as well. This does not mean our love for other creatures is identical to our love for human beings or that their moral status is equal to that of human beings; but it does mean that we are not the only creatures that matter. Other creatures count and we have duties and responsibilities toward them.

The reason is that God, who declared our creation good, declared the creation of other species and the earth good as well. Like us, other species are created out of love and, like us, reflect the goodness, generosity, and creativity of God. The handiwork of God, they are loved and valued by God and, therefore, should be loved and valued by us. Even though these other creatures and species serve human needs and contribute to human well-being, they do not exist solely for our sakes. God did not create them simply to fulfill our needs or simply because we might find them useful, which would suggest that we can do with them whatever we want. Rather, God made them because God loves them, cares for them, and delights in them, and calls us to love and care for them as well.

In Genesis 1:26 God gave men and women "dominion over the fish of the sea, the birds of the air, and the cattle, and over all the wild animals and all the creatures that crawl on the ground." But dominion does not mean domination. In granting us dominion God is not giving us license to do whatever we want to creation but entrusting us with the holy responsibility of caring for all that he created and declared good. As the only creatures gifted with conscience, we are "to serve as responsible representatives of God's interests and values," and we do this when we recognize, respect, and care for all the other creatures that God finds good.[72] We are to be, as Steven Bouma-Prediger attests, not tyrants who destroy creation and carelessly ravage the earth, but God's "earth keepers," people who have been given the task of watching over the welfare of all creatures and of being unselfishly devoted to their good.[73] At the very least, this means that the earth that God declared beautiful and good at creation should be found beautiful and good at the end of history. Other creatures should not be worse off for having had us as their neighbors.

What would it mean to practice ecological love of neighbor? How do we love other species and creatures? We love them first by acknowledging that our interests and needs are not the only ones that matter and should not always trump the interests of nonhuman creation. Human needs and interests do not have absolute priority. There are times when they must yield for the sake of other species' well-being, especially those whose existence is most threatened. This is nothing more than applying the principle of self-sacrifice, which is part of any real love of neighbor, to the love we owe other species.[74]

Second, we love other species and creatures through our willingness to change the way we live, especially the attitudes, practices, and behavior that show disregard for their welfare and that result in unjustified harm. At the very least, this conversion of lifestyle would require renouncing the gluttonous excesses of consumerism and embracing a lifestyle marked by simplicity, frugality, and restraint.[75] Living frugally does not mean never enjoying the good things of the earth, but it does mean using them sparingly so that species other than our own can flourish. Too, ecological love of neighbor requires frugality and restraint because the goods and resources of the earth are limited. Without frugality and restraint, which are elements of the virtue of temperance, our consumerist lifestyle will bankrupt the earth.

Third, we practice ecological love of neighbor when we cultivate the humility that makes us cautious and careful, reverent and respectful, in dealing with other species. Such humility counsels us not to underestimate the impact of our technology on the earth or of our interventions in the natural world. Without humility, we can assume that our interests and needs always come first and that the consequences of our actions on other species and the earth are easily predictable and manageable. But as Bouma-Prediger counsels, "We don't know everything (though we often think we do), and our fat, restless egos often get the best of us. Therefore, we should be careful, exercise caution, go slow."[76]

CONCLUSION

James Joyce was right: "Love loves to love love." The God who is love loves to love, and all of us who were born from that love, love to love too. We love to love and to be loved because, as creatures fashioned from love, we find life and joy and fullness and completion only in love. There is no other path to life, no other possible route to happiness.

But in a world that knows too well the absence of love, in a world too often marred by hatred and animosity and conflict, there needs to be a people patiently committed to embodying and enacting God's love in the world. There must be a community whose way of life testifies to the reality and credibility of love, a community that witnesses why love is the only power we have over suffering, darkness, and death. Christians believe this about love because of the paschal mystery—the mystery of Jesus' passion, death, and resurrection. There is no more eloquent revelation of love than the crucified and risen Christ, because in him we encounter a love that neither evil nor death could defeat. In the next chapter we will explore the meaning of the paschal mystery for a Christian life of discipleship, particularly as it is manifest in the virtues of patience and compassion, each exquisite, yet challenging, expressions of love.

KEY POINTS

1. The fundamental vocation of every human being is to love and to be loved. This is because we are created in the image of a God who is a communion or partnership of love.
2. We cannot love others well without first knowing what it means to love ourselves well.
3. Love may begin in a feeling, but it must be ratified by a choice. It is through the virtue of fidelity that we continually affirm our decision to love.
4. There are different kinds of love. Christian theology has traditionally distinguished between love for the sake of another (agape), love for one's own sake (eros), and the relationship created by love (friendship or philia).
5. In the Christian life, the circle of love must be extended to include not only all human beings but also other creatures and species.

QUESTIONS FOR REFLECTION

1. Why do you think Jesus commanded us to love?
2. What do you find to be most challenging about a Christian understanding of love?
3. What would it mean for you to love yourself well?
4. When you tell someone "I love you!" what do you mean?
5. Why do you think so many relationships don't last?
6. What would it mean for you to extend the circle of love? And have you ever tried to love an enemy?

SUGGESTIONS FOR FURTHER READING AND STUDY

Carmichael, Liz. *Friendship: Interpreting Christian Love*. London: T&T Clark, 2004.

Farley, Margaret A. *Personal Commitments: Beginning, Keeping, Changing*. San Francisco: Harper & Row, 1986.

Lewis, C. S. *The Four Loves*. New York: Harcourt, Brace & World, 1960.

Pieper, Josef. *Faith, Hope, Love*. Translated by Sr. Mary Frances McCarthy, Richard Winston, and Clara Winston. San Francisco: Ignatius, 1997.

Storkey, Elaine. *The Search for Intimacy*. Grand Rapids: Eerdmans, 1995.

Vacek, Edward Collins. *Love, Human and Divine: The Heart of Christian Ethics*. Washington, D.C.: Georgetown University Press, 1994.

Wadell, Paul J. *Becoming Friends: Worship, Justice, and the Practice of Christian Friendship*. Grand Rapids: Brazos, 2002.

Williams, Daniel Day. *The Spirit and the Forms of Love*. Lanham, Md.: University Press of America, 1981.

8

The Paschal Mystery and the Moral Life

"If We Die with Christ, We Live with Him"
(Romans 6:8)

THE PASCHAL MYSTERY is a passionate love story. It is the pivotal and climactic chapter in Jesus' life and ministry devoted to proclaiming the reign of God. His suffering, death on the cross, and resurrection are the completion of a life lived in faithful obedience to God's will. It was a life committed to loving not only his friends and followers, but his enemies as well. The paschal mystery is a story about death and resurrected life. It is a cycle of death and rebirth like the grain of wheat falling to the ground and dying so as to produce new life. As we know, this process of dying and rising is characteristic of all creation. Plants and flowers die in the winter and magically bloom in the spring. At certain times of the year, some animals shed their fur and mysteriously receive a full and rich new coat. A caterpillar makes a cocoon and then sheds its old body to become a beautiful butterfly. So, too, does humankind experience a process of shedding the old to make way for the new.

An injury, illness, or death of a loved one may lead us to relinquish previous attachments and to embrace a new way of living. Or we may come to see that some aspect of our vision of the world is distorted, so we need to let go of that perception in order to envision reality through a new lens. Like Heather King, we may need to die to our addictions and allow God's grace and love to work marvelous transformations in our lives. Or we may need to die to hatred and violence in order to rise to a new life of love, as Leopold Bloom, the protagonist in James Joyce's novel, wisely proclaimed. ("Whoever does not love abides in death" [1 John 3:14]).

For Christians, the human experience of dying and rising assumes theological significance with the death and resurrection of Jesus. While Jesus' earthly life has ended, God's act of love in the resurrection offers a promise of transformation, assuring us that those who enter into the passion of Jesus will become a new creation. This rebirth is not something that will occur only in the afterlife, for there can be a change in attitudes, desires, and behavior here and now that reflects resurrected life. For such transformation to occur, however, the Christian belief is that we need to embrace the suffering and death associated with the cross. How do we interpret and respond to suffering? Can suffering, which involves the loss of something good, lead to human flourishing? And if the suffering, pain, and death are not the end of the story, what is the nature of the new life promised to those faithful disciples who undergo suffering for the sake of the reign of God?

In this chapter, we will explore the implications of the paschal mystery for the moral life. Our focus is not on the resurrection of the end-time, which concerns what will happen to our personal existence after our deaths. This aspect of the resurrection has received much attention in Christian theology and doctrine. The reality of the future fulfillment of the resurrection will necessarily be the backdrop of our discussion, but our concern here is with the significance of the paschal mystery for how disciples understand and order their lives in the here and now, and the ways that they live out their callings.

We should state at the outset that our reflection relies significantly upon our capacity to think analogically and dialectically, as was presented in chapter 3. That is because we will discern ethical implications of the paschal mystery by looking at contemporary human experience to discover what is like and unlike the original event. But to do so requires that we first consider the interpretations of the paschal mystery that are embedded in the New Testament. So we begin our discussion by turning to the New Testament to glimpse how the evangelists and the apostle Paul understood and responded to the death and resurrection of Jesus. There are some key themes that recur in the biblical stories that will provide the focus of this discussion on the paschal mystery.

THE PASCHAL MYSTERY IN THE NEW TESTAMENT

In the Gospels, we find a close connection between how Jesus lived his life and the way it ended. As we discussed in chapter 3, Jesus ate with sinners and other societal outcasts; he healed and restored people to life in God's name; he associated with lepers, paralytics, and those possessed by demons; and he declared the power of God to be stronger than the power of evil. His proclamation of the reign of God clearly had consequences.

In Mark's Gospel, Jesus' passion and death on the cross is a result of his being misunderstood throughout his public ministry by almost everyone—Pharisees, scribes, members of his family, and even his own disciples who could not grasp that he is the "suffering messiah." Only a few women followers remain faithful to him and are found at the foot of the cross (15:40-41). Despite the betrayal by Judas and abandonment by the rest of the twelve, Jesus remained faithful to his mission of proclaiming God's reign in word and deed even to his death. Those who follow Jesus are also called to take up their crosses, remain faithful in the midst of suffering (8:34), and show compassion to those who suffer as he did (3:5).

Matthew and Luke, too, view suffering as an integral characteristic of discipleship. It involves a willingness to undergo hardships, humiliation, and a readiness to lose what is of utmost value to us—our very lives for the sake of the reign of God. In their account of the Beatitudes, these two Gospels include persecution as part of the blessedness of sharing in the tradition of the prophets (Matt 5:11-12; Luke 6:22-23).

Each evangelist captures a portrait of the suffering Jesus from a different angle and with a different lens. A fuller picture emerges when the divergent facets are combined, for none of the accounts exhausts the meaning of the cross. The Markan Jesus experiences abandonment only to be vindicated. The Lucan Jesus worries about others and offers forgiveness to those responsible for his suffering and death. The Johannine Jesus is in control of what is happening to him and thus reigns victoriously from the cross. The implication for the moral life is that there may be times when we feel abandoned by God and others, other times when we are able to forgive those who have caused the suffering, and yet other moments when the power of suffering does not take control of us.[1]

For Paul, the symbol of the cross reveals a reversal of values: what some in the world think is wisdom is really folly; and what appears to be weakness is really power and wisdom. So Paul can boast about his personal weaknesses and sufferings for the sake of the gospel. When Paul says that "it is no longer I who live, but Christ who lives in me" (Gal 2:20), he identifies himself totally with Christ. Paul preached the cross of Christ not just as an instrument of torture and death but as God's way of restoring right relationship with humankind. The redemption offered by Christ's sacrifice on the cross is not some necessary payment demanded by God. Rather, it is a grace and a gift of God (Rom 3:24).

It is the resurrection, however, that is the truly saving event because it is not until Jesus has received the fullness of life that his redemptive work is complete. There are several passages in Paul's letters that emphasize this point. Jesus "was put to death for our trespasses and raised for our justification" (Rom 4:25). Those who die will also rise with him to new life (6:3-11). Jesus was raised from the dead so that "we might bear fruit for God" (7:4). To be "in Christ" who is risen is to be "a new creation" (2 Cor 5:17). It is clear in the New Testament witness that Jesus' death on the cross, and the suffering associated with it, gains its full meaning within the context of his resurrection.[2]

For the New Testament authors, the acts of love and justice that Jesus performed in order to reveal what God's reign is like presented a challenge to the rulers of society and ultimately led to his death on the cross. Jesus chose love and he accepted the suffering that accompanied this choice. He loved so greatly that he would not withdraw from his mission even when it led to conflict and death. Jesus lived and taught a way of discipleship that challenged the powers at every point. In so doing, he redefined the nature of power and the value of suffering.[3] The Christian story ends as it begins, with God's abundant and extravagant love for us. That is the context in which to understand the meaning of sacrifice, suffering, redemption, and transformation. We will discuss each of these key themes, beginning with the meaning and ethical implications of sacrifice.

SACRIFICE AS AN ACT OF LOVE FREELY OFFERED

Christ's death on the cross was a sacrificial act of love that had redemptive power. It was a sacrifice offered in response to the demands of a relationship with God and others that called for love even unto death. As S. Mark Heim explains, when the New Testament uses sacrificial terminology, it is to remember Jesus as the one unjustly accused and condemned to death, the one vindicated by God, and the one who takes no retribution. Moreover, God acts not to affirm the suffering of the innocent one as the price of peace, but to reverse such a distorted practice.

Drawing from René Girard's extensive writings on sacrifice, Heim points out that ritual sacrifice has been a feature of every human civilization, a practice found everywhere in ancient religion. What happened to Jesus happened innumerable times to others. Girard's theory of sacrifice is based on an actual cause-and-effect relation in which sacrifice is used to overcome political problems. When a heightened dispute threatens to split or dissolve the community, some distinctive person or minority in the group becomes the sacrificial victim, or scapegoat, to save the community and restore peace. But Girard argues that the passion stories reveal that what God demands is not the sacrifice of Jesus, not a perfect scapegoat, but the unconditional refusal of scapegoating even if the price is death.[4] As Heim states:

> The sacrificial necessity . . . claims Jesus is a sinful mechanism for victimization, whose rationale maintains it is necessary that one innocent person die for the good of the people. The free, loving "necessity" that leads God to be willing to stand in the place of the scapegoat is that this is the way to unmask the sacrificial mechanism, to break its cycles of mythic reproduction, and to found human community on a nonsacrificial principle: solidarity with the victim, not unanimity against the victim.[5]

God lovingly and freely enters into the position of the victim of sacrificial atonement in order to break the cycle of victimization. This is what redemption is about, righting a wrong so that wholeness and right relationships can be restored among people and in society. When people are made scapegoats or victimized, then the sacrifice associated with the cross is distorted. It is the distortions, not sacrifice in itself, that thwart the process of new life promised by the resurrection. Let us consider a story of redemptive love that illustrates both the distortions of and similarities with the sacrifice associated with the cross of Jesus.

A Story of Redemptive Love

Khaled Hosseini's novel *The Kite Runner* is a story set in Afghanistan. It spans the period from the 1970s to 2001, a time that included the Soviet invasion, a civil war that ravaged the country, the rise of the *mujahideen* opposition groups, and the fall of the odious Taliban. It is a story of fierce cruelty and violence, as well as redeeming love, told through the lens of Amir, the son of Baba, a Sunni Muslim, and a Pashtun. Baba is an educated and wealthy businessman who has servants—the polio-afflicted Ali, a Shi'a Muslim, and his cleft-lipped, illiterate son, Hassan. They are Hazaras, an ethnic group persecuted because of its perceived lower status.

Amir and Hassan spent their boyhoods as friends, roaming the streets of Kabul together. While Amir would sometimes defend his friend against taunting and abuse, he could also be cruel to him. On one particular day when Amir is thirteen, Amir fails his friend in a way that will haunt him for years to come. It is the day of the much celebrated annual kite-flying contest. A kite runner is a sort of spotter in the ancient sport of kite fighting where competitors coat their kite strings in glue and ground glass in order to cut their rivals' moorings. While the fighter's kite is struggling to rule the skies, his partner chases down all their opponents' sinking kites. During the kite-running contest, Hassan is beaten mercilessly by bullies who had previously taunted him for being a Hazara. From a safe distance, Amir hides in fear, watching his friend be brutally sexually assaulted, and does nothing to defend him. He does not want other Pashtuns to know he has befriended this lowly servant. Amir lets Hassan be sacrificed to save his own skin and preserve his public image. Later, another incident occurs when Amir again betrays Hassan. He conjures up a deceitful plan based on a lie that results in Hassan and his father having to leave Baba's household. Hassan is once again the victim sacrificed for Amir's personal needs; this time to get rid of Hassan in hopes of becoming the center of his father's attention.

When a civil war begins to ravage the country, Amir and his father flee to the United States. But even though Amir later becomes successful professionally and is happily married, a troubled conscience prevents him from finding internal peace. He begins to experience redemption when he decides to return to Afghanistan to make amends for his past grievous acts and "to try to become good again."[6]

When he arrives back in Afghanistan, Amir learns that Hassan was murdered by the Taliban. But he left behind a son that Amir could save from a similar fate if he takes him back to the United States to join his family. This is more than Amir bargained for. Despite the years living in California, at heart he is still a Pashtun, a member of the superior group that does not associate with Hazaras. Yet, Amir knows what he must do in order to experience redemption.[7] Consequently, he freely risks his own safety, and relinquishes something of his ordered and peaceful existence, by opening his heart and his family to include Hassan's son. This is a sacrificial act done out of love for a relationship broken by his youthful cowardice and jealousy. Amir does what he can to repair the damage done by his betrayals of Hassan.

But he alone cannot change the societal attitudes and structures that inflict the most damaging harm upon the Hazaras. The cleft-lipped servant was the sacrificial victim in Baba's household and the Hazaras were the sacrificial victims of the Afghan society. Society influences the kind of people we are and the kind of people we become. Amir's cowardice was reinforced by a culture and system of laws that were intended to keep the Hazaras in a state of servitude, far down on the social ladder.

Loving another necessarily requires some acts of sacrifice, but it ought not to be sacrifice that demeans or diminishes the self. As we discussed in the previous chapter, the command to love our neighbor as we love ourselves places limits on the sacrifices people can ask of one another. The norm of self-sacrificial love presumes a self that has already been reconstituted in responsibility before God. There must be a self that is capable of making a deliberate but responsible gift of self-denial. However, this does not come easily for people who have been denigrated by society, who have been told in subtle and not so subtle ways that they are worthless. An overemphasis on sacrifice can actually stifle moral development by encouraging and justifying a life of subordination and servitude.

The Problem of Servitude

While all disciples of Jesus have been called to be "servants," summoned to "wash one another's feet" as Jesus exemplified with the washing of his disciples' feet at the Last Supper (John 13:1-11), this does not mean relinquishing the freedom to choose when and how to serve another. This is what happens when certain people and groups like Hassan and the Hazaras are relegated to a lower rung of society and placed in positions of servitude. This is harmful to the moral life because such persons have not been given the opportunity to freely and lovingly enter into relationship with others, relationships that can involve both service and sacrifice.

As Jacquelyn Grant points out, this distorted way of understanding the meaning of service has historically caused pain and suffering for many oppressed peoples, especially women and men of color. As Grant states, "Black people's and Black women's lives demonstrate that some people are more servant than others." African American women have been systematically relegated to being "servants of the servants." As the history of slavery and domestic service reveals, a life of service has basically been understood as servitude. This is a distortion because, as Grant points out, discipleship is about empowerment not subordination or servitude. It is about liberation from sin and eliminating the injustices of relationships that consign some people to a status that is perceived to be of lesser value.[8]

We should be clear that there is a significant difference between service and servitude. In service we do experience the many little deaths of going beyond ourselves, becoming more human, more reflective of the image of God in which we are created. When we care for a sick or dying spouse or child, we are freely offering our love to the other even though it means letting go of some of our own needs and desires. When men and women serve their country, they undergo risks and endanger their lives in order to safeguard the nation. In these and other acts of service, choices are freely made. That is not to say such choices are easily made, but that the decision to offer service is made by an uncoerced assent of the will. In service there is liberty to say "no" to those things that we perceive will not promote human or societal flourishing.

But when someone is in a position of servitude, it is not a condition freely chosen. When people become servants to others in the way that Grant describes in the history of slavery and domestic service, and that Hassan illustrates in the *Kite Runner* story, the choice is being made by those in superior positions of power to take away the freedom of others. This, however, violates the whole meaning and liberating power of the paschal mystery. The cross and resurrection of Jesus give people who suffer as a result of being relegated to servitude not only the strength and grace to confront the suffering but also the courage and power to reject its dehumanizing power.

Suffering associated with the cross of Jesus does not imply a life resigned to deprivation and unjust sacrifice. When Peter recommends that the community he is addressing "put up with suffering for doing what is right," he is not advocating servitude (1 Pet 2:20-25). Nor is he endorsing masochism or fatalism. Masochists entrap themselves in their suffering. They feel that it is deserved, and thus they not only become resigned to a life of deprivation and pain, but even expect to be treated poorly by others.

Similarly, some people are fatalists. Like Hassan and the Hazaras, they have spent so much of their lives suffering that their very humanity is defined by it. They tend to have a low sense of self-worth and lack hope that things can change for the better. When people perceive suffering as something deserved, when they feel entrapped in their suffering, or become resigned to their state of life, there tends to be low self-esteem, a sense of powerlessness, alienation, lack of hope, and loss of imagination. All too often, they are encouraged to patiently endure the suffering. However, what is commonly understood by this encouragement does not capture the genuine meaning of patient endurance.

Patient endurance in the midst of suffering, or "bearing wrongs patiently," as Sidney Callahan expresses it, does not mean passively accepting a bad situation. Patient endurance is not fatal resignation to long-term suffering, nor does it mean self-abnegation or that a person is lacking in hope. Rather, "to bear wrongs patiently is an active, enabling form of love and power. It is having the firmness to hold ourselves and others up, through strain, stress, and evil times, without causing more suffering and evil."[9] When Callahan speaks of "wrongs," she is referring to significant social ills that harm individual lives, such as racial prejudice, sexism, ageism, homelessness, and poverty. These are long-term or chronic conditions that are forms of injustice inhering within major institutions of society.

Properly understood, neither patience nor endurance is passive in nature for both are active responses to suffering. To endure means to bear, to support and move, to carry, to sustain, to hold up, to conduct oneself in a given manner, and to exercise as a power. These are all active functions that require strength of character, courage, and fortitude. Patience, too, is an active and disciplined exercise. It means to bear suffering with calmness and self-control, to resist succumbing to hatred, apathy, or despair when confronting evil.

For Christian disciples, patience is intimately linked with the virtues of faith and hope. The patient person recognizes that the reign of God, ever present yet not fulfilled, will triumph in the end. To exercise patience is to believe in the ultimate victory of good over evil; it is to live with the conviction that the fullness of love and justice shall prevail when the power of God rights all wrongs. When we consider how disciples like Dietrich Bonhoeffer, Martin Luther King, Jr., and Dorothy Day bore wrongs patiently over the long haul, we see not portraits of apathy or passivity but examples of patient endurance. These disciples had an acute grasp of the evil evident in reality, but they did not give in to hopelessness or defeatism. While bearing with suffering, they continued to admonish wrongdoers, resisted by word and deed the evils they faced, and called upon others to work with them to right what was wrong.

Borrowing an expression from Cynthia Crysdale, Bonhoeffer, King, and Day are examples of "embracing the travail," a willingness to engage the struggle involved in resisting evil. At the same time "embracing the travail" does involve an element of surrender or letting go; it is to die to the all-too-common response toward suffering, namely, to continue the violence by seeking to turn one's victimizers into a new group of victims. "Embracing the travail" leads the disciple to opt out of the cycle of violence so that suffering and evil are not simply transferred to another set of victims, but transformed into a new reality that makes victims of no one.[10]

As Crysdale points out, there are different ways to bring about such transformation. Sometimes we need to embrace the grief and be present to the pain we are experiencing. Other times we need to work on what needs to be changed. Consider the process of childbirth. At times the mother experiences great pain and all that she can do is control her agony and to breathe rhythmically. At other times, however, she needs to push, to actively work at giving birth. If the mother were only to push, or to push at the wrong time, a new life would be imperiled. Yet if she were only to engage in breathing exercises, the birth process would be unnecessarily prolonged. For Crysdale, "Embracing travail means allowing the process to take place without manipulating it, accepting the moments in the process of birth, working with them without denying the difficulties involved."[11] Just as in childbirth, the suffering connected with accepting the cross is endured patiently because of the love, hope, and expectation that new life will emerge when the moment is right. In what has been said above, the connection of patient endurance to hope and expectation should be clearer. We turn now to an exploration of the integral relationship between love and the experience of suffering.

LOVE AND SUFFERING

Most of us would like to avoid suffering at all costs, especially in matters of love. If "love makes the world go round," as poets and musicians proclaim, suffering can bring all the joy and happiness to an end. Or so it seems. Our discussion of love in the previous chapter helps us understand why suffering cannot be dissociated from love. If we love for the sake of another, whether it is a spouse, a friend, a nation, or some just cause, then we will likely experience some pain or distress. How we approach this suffering, however, matters for the moral life.

In her now classic book on suffering, German theologian Dorothee Soelle poses two primary questions: "What is the meaning of suffering and under what conditions can it make us more human?" She begins by distinguishing between meaningless and meaningful suffering. Suffering is considered to be meaningful when a person accepts the things that happen in the world, both good and bad. Life, with its joys and sorrows, is accepted and affirmed. Suffering that is meaningful impels one to act, and it can lead to a change in attitude and actions. Meaningless suffering, on the other hand, exists when a person refuses to acknowledge and confront a painful situation and, as a result, withdraws from life, sometimes even to the point of despair. Soelle considers this a sinful condition that reflects a person turned in on oneself, unable to love. In contrast, when life is accepted with all its inherent pain and suffering, there is the possibility of unlimited love for others, even amid the painful aspects of life.[12]

But what about those who seem to suffer in vain, those for whom there is no way to change the circumstances in which they live? What about people who are unable to move through the processes of suffering that lead to change? What about those people who suffer silently and are devoid of hope? What about people caught in extreme suffering that occurs through no fault of their own?

The Russian novelist Fyodor Dostoevsky tackles these questions in a fictional conversation between two brothers—Ivan and Alyosha. Ivan presents the inexplicable situation of the suffering of innocent children. He will not accept the explanation that this suffering is justified because it serves a "higher" or "future" harmony. That is "too high a price to pay for harmony; it's beyond our means to pay so much for admission. And so I hasten to give back my ticket. . . . It's not God that I don't accept, Alyosha, only I most respectfully return him the ticket."[13]

Pointing to the innocent Christ who suffered, Alyosha criticizes Ivan for his rebellious response. But Alyosha agrees with Ivan that harmony and peace cannot be purchased at the cost of the death by torture of even one person. Their different ways of responding to suffering are rooted in their divergent views of God. Ivan's God, the one against whom he rebels, is a God who causes or allows such suffering. Alyosha, on the other hand, focuses on the sufferers and places himself in solidarity with them. After listening to the many examples of suffering that Ivan presents as witnesses against the compassion of God, Alyosha goes to Ivan, the rebel and insurrectionist, and kisses him on the lips. In a gesture that resembles Christ's response to his accusers, in Dostoevsky's "Grand Inquisitor," Alyosha silently shares the suffering of others. The story offers a crucial lesson for the moral life. We can and should change the social conditions that cause needless suffering for people. But there will always be experiences of suffering that we cannot remedy, intolerable suffering that we cannot change. When this is the case, as Alyosha witnessed, we need to share in the pain of those who suffer.

This is also at the heart of the cross's significance for Soelle. It is a symbol of divine love that God has entered into solidarity with all history's victims. If we are to embrace the cross in this manner, we must be willing to experience and engage the pain and suffering that accompanies love. When we are able to do this, we are moving toward solidarity because we can better relate to other people's suffering, even to the point of entering into it with them when the suffering cannot be removed. As Soelle states:

[T]o "serve the pain of God by your own pain" is to lead suffering out of its private little corner and to achieve human solidarity. Everyone's natural reflex is flight from suffering; but even when it succeeds it is at the same time the perpetuation of universal suffering. To "strengthen oneself" through pain is, on the contrary, to be understood as the strength of those who have achieved solidarity.[14]

Similarly, David Hollenbach interprets the cross as the "revelation of divine solidarity with every human whose experience is that of forsakenness and abandonment." It is the preeminent sign of God's compassion for all who suffer, and it is this compassion that enables us to enter into solidarity with those who suffer violence and poverty in our world. The symbol of the cross opens the possibility of an ethic of compassionate solidarity that involves one in an active struggle against the conditions that produce such suffering.[15]

What Hollenbach aims to do is to push the problem of suffering to the center of the ethical agenda where it belongs. And this is an agenda not just for Christians but for our pluralistic world as well. That is because the sign of the cross raises a question that needs to be faced by all people. As members of the human community, we ought to celebrate the heights to which cultures can rise, but we also need to acknowledge, and have compassion for, the depths of suffering into which human beings can fall.[16] At the core, the cross reveals God's compassion for all who suffer and solidarity with every human being who is forsaken and abandoned. Christ's call to his disciples to take up the cross is an invitation to continue that compassionate solidarity in every generation.

THE CROSS OF COMPASSION

The cross of Jesus Christ is a call to enter compassionately into the experience of human suffering. Compassion means "to suffer with another" and "to endure pain with others." It is an emotional response to suffering or to a situation that one deems to be wrong. Compassion implies sensitivity, vulnerability, and a willingness to let oneself be affected by the suffering person's experience. Compassion begins with the acknowledgment that we are all citizens of the same earth household. We are first and foremost fellow beings, despite distinctions of race, color, creed, class, or gender. And while many things separate us one from another, we are united by the fact that suffering and death are inescapable. It is this feeling of solidarity with all humankind that makes compassion possible.[17]

We learned something of the emotional content of compassion from the Good Samaritan parable we discussed in chapter 2. It was only the Samaritan who came to the aid of a stranger in need because he did not allow himself to remain emotionally detached. He was affected by the plight of the suffering person, a fellow human being with whom he was connected and for whom he was responsible.

The rejection that Jesus experienced throughout his ministry of preaching the reign of God, which ultimately led to his death, was not returned with violence but with compassion and forgiveness. At the moment of his death, he prays for forgiveness for those who had forsaken him. And, as Monika Hellwig points out, Jesus' compassion extends to every kind of human suffering, particularly when it is the result of injustice. To speak of Jesus as the "compassion of God" is to realize that discipleship brings us into contact with human suffering not only on a personal, familial, or communal level, but also on a massive scale when we consider the suffering that is caused by sinful social structures.[18]

The fact of suffering ought to lead us to some kind of response to correct the injustice; otherwise compassion becomes just sentimental commiseration. In this way, the compassion of Jesus is redemptive of seemingly hopeless situations. Jesus is right in the midst of people's travails, offering the possibility of new life. These are the kinds of actions required of disciples as well.[19] As Hellwig states, to be a follower of Jesus means "to enter with him into the suffering and the hope of all human persons, making common cause with them as he does, and seeking out as he does the places of his predilection among the poor and despised and oppressed."[20]

Compassion is not only integrally connected with the suffering and redemptive love of the cross, but it is also an essential element of resurrected life because compassion indicates the end of one way of living and entry into another. To be compassionate requires one to let go of a sense of superiority and separateness in order to assume a new identity as a member of the human community.[21] For Buddhists, this is the vow to be compassionate to all sentient beings, a vow that flows naturally from the perception that we are all integrally connected to the web of being. Indeed, for Buddhists compassion is the essence of human existence.[22]

Compassion in Buddhism

Just as the Christian God feels compassion for the errors and sufferings of humankind, the Buddha experiences compassion for human suffering and offers a way through it. Dukkha refers to suffering, pain, and misery. It is our dissatisfied mind or troubled heart in the midst of painful conditions such as sickness or a loss of a loved one. Of all religions, Buddhism is the one that most immediately and directly focuses on suffering, although not in a pessimistic way.[23] Ultimately, Buddhists seek the extinguishing of suffering (Nirvana), but that final elimination of suffering requires striving in the present to alleviate and transform suffering for the compassionate healing of the world.

> *The cross of Jesus Christ is a call to enter compassionately into the experience of human suffering.*

In Buddhism, compassion is the virtue that embraces the pain of others. It is a desire that all living beings be free from suffering. There are many references to compassion in the teachings and stories of the Buddha and his followers, but the focus of this compassion seems to be on helping others renounce inordinate desires, especially avarice, hatred, anger, or delusion. In a collection of essays resulting from a dialogue among American Buddhist and Christian leaders, compassion emerged as one of the key qualities of living that generates peace and happiness within oneself and in one's relationships with others. Compassion motivates us to reduce the suffering of others, and it begins to break down the self-centeredness that leads to inflicting harm on others.[24]

Moreover, in Buddhist philosophy wisdom and compassion are integrally connected. As we saw in chapter 2, wisdom (enlightenment) is the shift in awareness that happens when we relinquish the illusion that we are separate entities and come to recognize our connectedness to all living beings. Compassion is the disposition that flows naturally from that change of perception. The following passage from a *bodhisattva* illustrates how compassion aids wisdom's weakening of self-centeredness by cultivating a desire to help all suffering humanity. A bodhisattva is a person dedicated to becoming a perfect Buddha, one who is motivated by compassion and seeks enlightenment not just for oneself, but for everyone.

> Thus by the virtue collected through all that I have done,
>> may the pain of every living creature be completely cleared
>> away.
> May I be the doctor and the medicine and may I be the nurse
>> for all
>> sick beings in the world until everyone is healed.
> May a rain of food and drink descend to clear away the pain
>> of thirst
>> and hunger, and during the aeon of famine may I myself
>> change into
>> food and drink.
> May I be a protector for those without one,
>> and a guide to all travellers on the way;
>> may I be a bridge, a boat and a ship for all those who wish
>> to cross (the water).[25]

The reality, however, is that we cannot extend compassion to all those in need. The needs of friends and the many suffering people in the world are enormous, so it is important to set realistic limits to our compassionate responses. Moreover, as with other virtues, we need to steer a course between extremes of excess and deficiency. Achieving the mean of compassion will involve several factors: choosing rightly what manner of compassion to have and what degree of responsibility one has to the other; considering the circumstances, intention, and motivation; and assessing the consequences the act of compassion will achieve. The excess of compassion would be to neglect legitimate self-needs. The deficiency would be apathy toward others.[26]

There is no place for apathy in the suffering love and compassionate solidarity associated with the paschal mystery. Sometimes we refuse to engage our own pain or that of others. But when suffering is rejected because it causes too much pain, it is also a refusal to open oneself to the possibility of new life. Compassion not only leads us into the sufferings of others, but it also leads us to resurrected life. In this respect, far from protecting us from pain, apathy prevents us from experiencing the fullness of the paschal mystery.

THE PROBLEM OF APATHY

When some people experience a loss of a loved one or suffer a broken relationship, the accompanying pain can be so great that they vow never to love that deeply again. In order to protect themselves from such pain in the future, they keep people at a distance, not allowing them to melt the coldness to which the heart has succumbed. Apathy sets in to guard against future suffering. Apathy derives from the ideal of a life free from suffering and a desire to be free of pain. The consequence, though, is that we are unable to feel passionate about anything. This is certainly not what the passion of Jesus was like. His experience in Gethsemane was filled with sorrow and anguish. But Jesus did not retreat in the face of suffering; nor did he become apathetic.

To reject suffering or to refuse to engage pain has harmful consequences. As Dorothee Soelle expresses it, "the consequence of this suffering-free state of well-being is that people's lives become frozen solid. Nothing threatens any longer, nothing grows any longer, with the characteristic pains that all growth involves, and nothing changes." When apathy sets in, not only does the accompanying numbness block the pain, but it also prevents experiences of joy and happiness. When suffering is approached stoically, with indifference and without emotion, the result is a "world-conquering coldness."[27]

We have an example of the harmful consequences to the moral life of such a rejection of suffering in the story of C. S. Lewis, the renowned English author and scholar. A deeply religious man and a Christian apologist, Lewis tried to reconcile the fact of suffering with a good and loving God. But in doing so, he engaged in a form of self-deceptive rationalization. The primary form of this character trait is developing a defense mechanism that makes the pain of vulnerability tolerable by suppressing need and masking other sufferings one experiences in the world. Since the loss of his own mother when he was nine years old, Lewis shielded himself from the experience of love as a protection from feelings of pain. Indeed, he did this quite successfully until Joy Davidman Gresham entered his life.

But certain experiences in Lewis's relationship with Joy occasioned a "passionate breakthrough," a transformation in his attitudes toward suffering and love.[28] The most significant change occurred when Lewis discovered that Joy had cancer and was not expected to survive. He underwent a dramatic change, from a person trapped in a carefully composed "emotional cocoon," to a vulnerable man deeply affected by the experience of love, with its inevitable accompanying pain.[29] We witness a barrage of emotions—anger, fear, doubts—that led Lewis to withdraw from others to be alone with his grief. He is moved to passion by the love of Joy and then by anger and grief at her death. He is "rocked to the depths of his being by an earthquake of emotion . . . *flensed* raw and turned inside out."[30] Lewis's transformation is sparked by an awareness of his neediness, vulnerability, and desire to be with Joy, despite the pain. His suffering brought him to a new understanding of love, recognizing in love our human incompleteness and deficiency, our need for others, and our desire for growth.

In the course of Lewis's transformation, we observe the lived experience of the paschal mystery, a series of "dyings and risings," a letting go of old habits and embracing newness and risk. There is a dying to emotional guardedness and a rising to acceptance of vulnerability. There is a dying to the fear of love and a rising to embracing love that includes pain. And there is a dying to the suppression of passion and a rising to the liberation of desire. Through his love for Joy, Lewis came to see that happiness is experienced within an ongoing relationship and is contingent upon undergoing the paschal mystery.

In the love story of C. S. Lewis and Joy Davidman Gresham, we observe two kinds of death: Joy's terminal death and Lewis's paschal death—a dying that ends one kind of life and opens him to receive a deeper and richer form of life, a resurrected life. Lewis's wife, friend, and lover is dead, but he is still alive, albeit not in the same way as he was before her death. The story teaches that love requires dying to apathy and to excessive self-control. To love, we must suffer the loss of one kind of self so that we can be formed in the goodness and love of God experienced in human love and passion. What Lewis learned is that we can avoid suffering, but only at the excessively costly price of ceasing to love. Put differently, he learned through the love and loss of Joy that it is necessary to enter the mystery of the Passion if one is to experience resurrected life.[31]

Soelle's view of suffering and C. S. Lewis's story present a stark challenge for the moral life. If we want to experience the new life promised in the resurrection of Jesus, we cannot avoid suffering. "The only choice we have is between the absurd cross of meaninglessness and the cross of Christ, the death we accept apathetically as a natural end and the death we suffer as a passion."[32] Moreover, it is the unity of the cross and resurrection, of failure and victory, of weeping and laughing, that paradoxically make hope of a better life possible. To be faithful disciples, we need to hold on to the paradox. Followers of Jesus should expect sufferings and be willing to offer their lives as a gift of love for others, trusting in God's promise of new life.

The conversion that C. S. Lewis experienced is revelatory of the new life that is made possible when one engages the suffering that accompanies love with passion, not apathy. Moreover, without uniting the cross with the resurrection, we can locate God only in relation to the darkness of human suffering, neglecting the light and hope that are promised to those who take up their cross and follow Jesus. The transformation experienced by Jesus in the resurrection is an act of God's love that believers are called to embody analogously in their lives through loving others. And so we turn now to a discussion of the transformative love of the resurrection.

TRANSFORMATIVE LOVE OF THE RESURRECTION

For the early Christian community, the resurrection was an experience of liberation from fear of persecution, rejection, and death. But they were also liberated from a stunted imagination that could not see beyond the prejudices, rivalries, and hostilities that had once consumed them. The resurrection experience changed both their worldview and attitudes. They were able to imagine new possibilities of peace, nonviolence, and reconciliation. And what was true for the first Christians on account of Jesus' resurrection is true for us as well. In proclaiming the resurrection of Jesus, the early church was also proclaiming the resurrection of humanity, and especially proclaiming that what God creates is intended to continue and to flourish beyond death.[33]

As Brian Johnstone maintains, the resurrection experience of the early Christians that led to their transformation from unbelievers to believers, and impelled them to mission in service of others, must have an impact on the way Christians today understand the moral life. He argues that the resurrection of Jesus has three important implications for the moral life.[34] First, the original experience of the resurrection contains a dynamism within history that gave new life to the disciples and to all subsequent followers of Jesus. The resurrection of Jesus transforms one's interpretation of reality, provides a way of interpreting the experience of all Christians, and radically modifies the "moral point of view."[35]

This pronounced change emerges from an ongoing relationship with the risen Jesus, a relationship of love that generates a commitment to others, especially the victims and potential victims of the world. In the encounter with the risen Christ, one sees the faces of every human being in a new way, especially the "defaced" victims of the world. The disciples who "encounter" the risen Christ in their own lives learn to encounter every other human being in light of the risen Christ. This encounter leads to a resilient moral commitment to do what one can for others, especially the victims of the world. As Johnstone notes, "Christian morality, therefore, can never yield to forgetfulness and resignation to the fate of victims: it generates a love beyond the range of death, which moves the Christian to try to change the conditions which destroyed this victim, so that others may not be similarly destroyed. The victim rises again, not in vengeful memory, but in action to create a world where others may live."[36] This new moral point of view emerges from the love and commitment to the risen Jesus that grounds our love and responsibility to others. This is a love that seeks to raise up others so that they may experience the freedom and power of resurrected life.

Second, the resurrection experience provided the disciples with a distinct moral vision that enabled a critique of culture. It gave them an understanding of the crucifixion that was decisively different from those who were responsible for Jesus' death. From one perspective Jesus proclaimed and embodied the reign of God, and his death on the cross was seen as a defeat of God's reign. But from a Christian perspective God's sovereign power was triumphantly vindicated in the resurrection when the new order of true peace founded on justice was established. This vision of peace is not farfetched but indeed something we can work toward because it has already been given in the resurrection. The resurrection assures us that the ultimate reality is peace, and that God is committed to a new order of peace. Thus, we can be sustained in our efforts to bring at least a minimum of that peace into a world riddled with violence. This vision of peace that flows from an ethic formed in light of the resurrection will be critical of a culture of violence and will impel us to seek ways to transform it.[37]

Third, the resurrection can provide us with a criterion by which to interpret and transform the virtues. Johnstone illustrates this with the virtue of justice. The resurrection reveals the injustice done to one who was a victim of suffering, oppression, and death. As such, it establishes a hermeneutic of suspicion against systems of order that may conceal violence and subvert peace. Christians believe that God's divine power, revealed in the resurrection, overcomes the unjust sentence of death. Consequently, authentic justice must always challenge and transform ideologies and structures that legitimate injustice. As Johnstone maintains, "the revelation of the in-breaking or ontological peace in the death and resurrection of Jesus radically transforms particular notions of justice."[38]

The resurrection is an act of transformative love that represents the victory of God's justice over injustice. As Jon Sobrino states, "Jesus' resurrection is thus transformed into good news, whose central content is that once and for all justice has triumphed over injustice, the victim over the executioner."[39] Analogously, the resurrection finds expressions in contemporary life when we love as Jesus did, calling forth our very best self and bringing out the best in others. Most of all, we love as Jesus did when we love without limit or without hesitation, when we act with justice on behalf of the poor and powerless, and when we can experience joy and celebrate the goodness of creation even in the midst of pain and suffering.[40]

This is the experience of many men and women as they live in the midst of poverty, war, abduction, rape, and abandonment. With a profound experience of the resurrection, they live in hope that these sufferings will be overcome. This is possible because of their ability to identify signs of the resurrection, signs of God's presence in the midst of life's travails. Focusing on women in Nicaragua, Luz Beatriz Arellano identifies some of these signs as the hunger for justice, courage, unity, hospitality, companionship, responsibility, generosity, and joy.[41] Joy is paschal for these women because it reflects something of the experience of the fullness of life that will be known completely at the end-time.

Disciples live in hope that the new creation brought about by the resurrection can be experienced, however imperfectly and incompletely, in this world. This occurs when attitudes of hate and vengeance are transformed by forgiveness and love to reconciliation, when there is less inequality between economic classes, and when men and women and societies can experience true peace. Just as God's act of transformative love is the vehicle through which injustice is overcome and a new creation brought about, so too ought we to love in a way that pursues justice in order to attain the flourishing of God's creation. What becomes a reality for Jesus in the resurrection is what God desires for all people.[42]

But there is much in the world that stands in the way of such fulfillment. Peace is possible, but it requires the transformation of institutions that embody injustice and the ideologies that legitimate it. As Thorwald Lorenzen states: "We can only 'know' that Jesus Christ is risen from the dead, when in our life the Gospel has created new life. We can only know the power of the resurrection if we have accepted the call and cost of discipleship and have become engaged in the passion of God to make human life whole."[43]

In the Eucharistic celebration, the Christian community remembers Christ's passion, death, and resurrection, and joins in this mystery by celebrating its identity as the Body of Christ and by embracing its mission of working to transform the world in light of the resurrection. The Eucharist is an eschatological meal that recalls the past event of Jesus' table fellowship with his disciples, as well as with tax collectors and sinners. It is a meal that anticipates the future messianic banquet to which all are invited. When we celebrate the Eucharist, we gather to remember the innocent victim and pledge to join him in making peace without violence.

As Patrick McCormick explains, "eucharistic living" means patterning our lives on Jesus crucified and raised from the dead. This means practicing God's justice toward neighbors, strangers, and enemies alike, showing hospitality to the poor, and welcoming sinners and outcasts as friends. Celebrating this remembrance means becoming a community that practices God's justice. This is a justice that shows compassion to the poor, offers forgiveness to those who have hurt or offended us, and extends love even to our enemies. How can we be a eucharistic people if we are not reconciled with our brothers and sisters before coming to the altar (Matt 5:23-24)? Commemorating the Eucharist in memory of Christ means that we stand in solidarity with all those people who are impoverished, marginalized, oppressed, and abused. And it means "never forgetting the faces, cries, and sufferings of the hungry, poor, displaced, discouraged, disenfranchised, and desperate millions standing outside our banquet halls."[44]

CONCLUSION

While the cross is a central symbol in the journey of discipleship, we cannot remain at the foot of the cross. We have to engage the paschal mystery, a story about death and resurrected life. In order to come to fuller life and to become a new creation, we must constantly undergo this cycle of dying and rising. Jesus shows us a paradigm for how this should happen. The promise of the death and resurrection of Jesus is that suffering is not in vain. And the paschal mystery challenges us to find freedom in relation to hardship and suffering, particularly in those things we cannot change. If our lives are inserted into the paschal mystery, then we have found a freedom that does not depend on external good fortune.

The vision of redeemed humanity, although never fully realized on this earth, is manifested in the movement from situations of domination and subordination to relationships of mutual respect, reciprocal valuing, and sharing in solidarity with the dispossessed. The resurrection finds expression in contemporary life when we love as Jesus did, when we are a forgiving people, and when we engage in acts of reconciliation. Resurrected life is most profoundly experienced when we allow God's love to transform us, and when we love others in such a way that they experience something of God's transformative love and justice. This is all made possible by the new life of the Spirit within us. The promise of Easter is that the Spirit has become manifest in history through the life, death, and resurrection of Christ. In the next chapter, we will explore the role of the Spirit in the moral life.

KEY POINTS

1. The moral life is marked by an ongoing process of "dying and rising" symbolic of the paschal mystery.
2. The paschal mystery is a story of God's abundant love that entails both sacrifice and suffering.
3. The suffering associated with the cross requires patient endurance, which is an active form of love and power.

4. The cross is a sign of God's compassionate love for and solidarity with all who suffer.
5. The resurrection is an act of God's transformative love. It is a liberating act that represents God's victory over injustice.

QUESTIONS FOR REFLECTION

1. How is Amir's or Hassan's experience similar to or different from the sacrifice and redemptive love associated with the cross of Jesus?
2. How can suffering be considered a positive value for the moral life? What are some distorted notions of suffering?
3. Do you agree or disagree that people should patiently endure their suffering?
4. What is meant by an ethic of compassionate solidarity? What concrete actions would reveal this ethic in the world?
5. How does the meaning of the resurrection proposed in this chapter support or challenge your own viewpoint?

SUGGESTIONS FOR FURTHER READING AND STUDY

Callahan, Sidney Cornelia. "To Bear Wrongs Patiently," in *From Christ to the World: Introductory Readings in Christian Ethics*. Edited by Wayne G. Boulton, Thomas D. Kennedy, and Allen Verhey. Grand Rapids: Eerdmans, 1994.

Cates, Diana Fritz. *Choosing to Feel: Virtue, Friendship, and Compassion for Friends*. Notre Dame, Ind.: University of Notre Dame Press, 1997.

Fabella, Virginia, and Mercy Amba Oduyoye, eds. *With Passion and Compassion: Third World Women Doing Theology*. Maryknoll, N.Y.: Orbis Books, 1989.

Harrington, Daniel, S.J. *Why Do We Suffer? A Scriptural Approach to the Human Condition*. Franklin, Wis.: Sheed & Ward, 2000.

Heim, S. Mark. *Saved from Sacrifice: A Theology of the Cross*. Grand Rapids: Eerdmans, 2006.

Hellwig, Monika. *Jesus, the Compassion of God: New Perspectives on the Tradition of Christianity*. Collegeville, Minn.: Liturgical Press, 1983.

Hollenbach, David, S.J. *The Global Face of Public Faith: Politics, Human Rights, and Christian Ethics*. Washington, D.C.: Georgetown University Press, 2003.

Johnstone, Brian V., C.Ss.R. "Transformation Ethics: The Moral Implications of the Resurrection." In *The Resurrection: An Interdisciplinary Symposium on the Resurrection of Jesus*. Edited by Stephen T. Davis, Daniel Kendall, S.J., and Gerald O'Collins, S.J. New York: Oxford University Press, 1997.

Lorenzen, Thorwald. *Resurrection and Discipleship: Interpretive Models, Biblical Reflections, Theological Consequences*. Maryknoll, N.Y.: Orbis Books, 1995.

McCormick, Patrick T. *A Banqueter's Guide to the All-Night Soup Kitchen of the Kingdom of God*. Collegeville, Minn.: Liturgical Press, 2004.

Soelle, Dorothee. *Suffering*. Translated by Everett R. Kalin. Philadelphia: Fortress, 1975.

9

The Spirit and Moral Discernment

"Do Not Quench the Spirit" (1 Thessalonians 5:19)

Books in Christian ethics do not typically think about the role of the Spirit, but the Spirit was prevalent in the early Christians' understanding of their lives. When Paul advised the Thessalonians not to "quench the Spirit," he employed a metaphor that identifies the concept of fire with the Spirit. That is, the Spirit must not be stopped, as a fire or lamp might be extinguished, if one is to live as a disciple of Jesus. But what or who is this Spirit?

Believers perceive the presence of the Spirit in various ways—through extraordinary healings of the sick, in mystical experiences of prayer, and through speaking in tongues. There are also particular moments when we become aware of the experience of the Spirit. Karl Rahner, the German theologian regarded by many as the foremost Roman Catholic theologian of the twentieth century, points to concrete experiences of life that are revelatory of the Spirit, such as the beauty of creation, the love between spouses, the birth of a child. Also, the presence of the Spirit is revealed when we are able to go forward in trust and in hope after the death of a loved one, when loss and grief leave us feeling desolate. In the experience of loneliness and emptiness that gives way to a peaceful and silent presence, we experience the Spirit, whether or not we are explicitly aware of it.[1] Like St. Paul, Rahner cautions against "stifling the Spirit" who moves where and as the Spirit wills.[2]

But we have to be careful about how we understand and talk about the Spirit. Some people may mistakenly believe they have special insight and knowledge because they are filled with the Holy Spirit. Mary Gordon's novel *Men and Angels* tells a story about such a person. One of the main characters, Laura, perceives herself as a chosen one of the Lord because she received the Holy Spirit.[3]

It was in her grandmother's garden that the Spirit first came to Laura. Having fled to the garden in tears after once again being denigrated by her mother, Laura found that her pain, humiliation, and anger were replaced by an experience of the Spirit's power and love. Laura had not been loved by her mother. She was always the child that was not pretty enough, not smart enough, not even considered useful in helping out with family matters. That, at least, was the message her mother conveyed again and again.

When she received the Spirit, however, Laura knew herself to be loved in a very special way. Now, Laura felt, she possessed the wisdom and peace of the Spirit. As the self-perceived chosen one of the Lord, she believed she had the truth that only the Spirit could bestow. And since the Spirit was with her, Laura also believed that she was beyond needing the love of others; rather, it was other people who were in need of her.

At a crucial point in the novel, Laura is hired by Anne Foster to serve as a caretaker for her two children. Laura, however, comes to believe that she has been led to her new position not for the sake of the children, but to save Anne. In Laura's mind, Anne had no share in the life of the Spirit, but was a material-ist preoccupied with things of the flesh. One bit of evidence was that Anne was being drawn into an adulterous relationship, an attraction that would turn out badly. Out of touch with her own human needs, Laura was convinced that Anne loved her and that only she could save Anne from her mistakes. Yet it was Laura who was mistaken as Anne did not love her, but was, in fact, uneasy around her, finding her somewhat strange.

Mired in fantasy, Laura continued to think she alone could save Anne from the path of destruction she was walking. Laura sought to show Anne that it was she who loved her with a pure love, "with the Spirit, before which all other loves must be consumed and die."[4] Only the Spirit could eradicate the errors in Anne's life, and it was left to Laura to bring this about. It would happen by Laura laying down her life for Anne. By shedding her own blood, Laura would convince Anne how much she selflessly loved her, and that realization would, in turn, shock Anne into changing her sinful ways. Laura makes her misguided decision in isolation, believing the Spirit to be leading her to a tragic ending.

The reader is forced to ask, was Laura really listening to the Spirit, or had her distorted vision and unacknowledged craving for human love actually stifled the movement of the Spirit? Mary Gordon's story . . . raises some important ques-tions for a life of discipleship guided by the Spirit. How does one know that a certain calling, or insight, or conviction is of the Spirit? Can one trust the Spirit to lead to the truth, or is it too vague a notion to be a reliable guide for the moral life? What is the role of the Holy Spirit in leading the discerning disciple to deeper insight and wisdom?

In this chapter, we consider these questions in assessing the meaning and role of the Spirit in discerning God's call and our response. We do not want to quench the Spirit, but neither should we rely solely on our personal interpreta-tion as guide to what is right and true. This is what, in part, led Laura down the road of destruction. Her images of the Spirit were drawn from a narrow and literal reading of the Bible. She relied solely on her interpretation of what the Spirit was calling her to be and to do. Also, she confused the Spirit with her own unhealthy fantasies. This led to disastrous consequences. So, before we can come to some clarity about the appropriate role of the Spirit in making moral judgments, we need to gain some insight into the meaning and function of the Spirit. Toward that end, we begin with an overview of the manifestations of the Spirit in the Bible.

MANIFESTATIONS OF THE SPIRIT IN THE BIBLE

In the Hebrew Bible, the Spirit of God is generally connected to natural phenomena such as a breath of air or wind. Sometimes the Spirit expresses God's creative, prophetic, or renewing presence to the people of Israel and to the wider world. The Spirit is the power to do mighty deeds, the "vivifying, energizing power of God."[5] In the Book of Genesis, *ruah* is used often to refer to the breath of God that enables things to live. For example, in Genesis 2:7, it is the Spirit of God that breathes life into the dust of the earth and then breathes life into the first human's nostrils. Later in Genesis, we are told that human beings remain alive only so long as they have the divine breath abiding in them (6:3). In the Psalms, the breath of God is understood as the creative and life-giving presence of God (Ps 104:30).

The prophet Ezekiel offers a spectacular image for the life-renewing breath of the Spirit in the famous account of the valley of dry bones (37:1-4). Ezekiel's vision of God's Spirit giving new life, transforming what seems to be dead, is important for the Israelites in exile, who felt they had been abandoned by God. Just as in Genesis the earth was first a formless void and God then brought order out of chaos by bringing things to life, so too does God bring this discouraged people back to life and give them hope. Moreover, Ezekiel promises that God will give them a "new heart and a new spirit" that will enable those who believe to live good and upright lives (36:26-28).

In the wisdom literature, the Spirit of the Lord is frequently identified with Lady Wisdom. As biblical scholar Roland Murphy points out, in the Wisdom of Solomon, especially, what is said about Lady Wisdom can be said about God's Spirit as well. She was present when God created the world and she "cemented creation together."[6] Israel's journey is a quest for Lady Wisdom as an outpouring of divine glory and eternal light, the mirror of divine activity, and the image of divine goodness (7:25-26). Just as the breath of God creates and renews the face of the earth, so too does Lady Wisdom renew all creation.[7] In short, both in creating and sustaining the world and in electing and saving Israel, the wisdom literature celebrates and symbolizes God's gracious goodness in female imagery of divine wisdom.[8]

In the New Testament, the Spirit is connected with the ministry of Jesus Christ and the growth of the community of disciples. The Spirit designates the power of God at work in Jesus' preaching and healing, inspiring him to bring good news to the poor and to set free the oppressed (Luke 4:18). Early Christians experienced the Spirit as the Paraclete, advocate, intercessor, counselor, protector, supporter, as well as the truth. The Spirit gives freedom and liberation from all sorts of restrictions, especially sin (Eph 4:30), and moves us toward holiness (Gal 6:1). In the Acts of the Apostles, the Holy Spirit is reported as an extraordinary phenomenon, an explosion of energy, as at Pentecost. In the Gospel of John (20:22), Jesus appeared to the disciples and, after greeting them with "Peace be with you," breathed on them and said, "Receive the Holy Spirit," thus echoing God's breath bringing things to life in Genesis.

Paul regards the Spirit as the driving force of the moral life, and love is the firstfruit of the Spirit (Gal 5:22-26). In addressing the Corinthians, Paul warns the community not to be confused by the "wisdom of the age or the rulers of the age," but to strive to understand and receive the wisdom of God (1 Cor 2:6-13). The Spirit imparts the wisdom that resides or "dwells within" believers, creating an intimate relationship that can transform the moral and spiritual life.[9]

In sum, the Spirit is manifested in the Bible as the breath and wisdom of God that renews, energizes, and transforms life. It is not a Spirit that leads to the destruction of life. And the Spirit is the power to do mighty deeds, especially to liberate the poor and oppressed. The Spirit dwells within the human heart, creating an intimate relationship with God and Jesus Christ that should affect one's character and behavior. The gifts of the Spirit enable believers to live good and upright lives, and to discern what is of God, what is the good, the true, and the beautiful. But how does this happen? What is the Spirit's role in discerning the right thing to do, particularly whether a certain choice fits with the call to discipleship? How do we know what love requires of us in a particular situation? In the next section, we will first explain the meaning of moral discernment and then turn to the Spirit's role in that process.

THE SPIRIT AND MORAL DISCERNMENT

When we think of discernment, it usually implies deciding about a vocation—to the married life, the priesthood, or to a particular ministry. For Christians, this decision essentially involves trying to understand God's will for our lives. But the word discernment can also appropriately be used of other decisions, such as choosing whether to take a new job that will lessen time to be home with family, whether to lend money to a friend who is in need, or whether to boycott a product from a company that treats its workers unjustly. Christians are called to "discern" God's will in the choices they make every day, in concrete situations, and in the midst of the relationships that constitute their lives. As followers of Jesus, we believe that every decision is an opportunity to respond to God, who is present in the here and now, inviting us to a more abundant life. Our moral decisions ought to be a graced response to God's presence and action in our lives. Discernment is the process of discovering which course of action is most fitting to our fundamental relationship with God and others.[10]

Whether we are aware of it or not, our manner of making decisions tends to flow from an ethical model or theory. An ethical model is the general way one characterizes or understands the moral life. In choosing a model, we are selecting the primary paradigm, image, or metaphor for viewing the moral life. In doing so we are not ruling out other elements, but simply bringing some aspects of morality to the foreground and placing other things in the background.

Ethical Models

Over the course of the tradition of moral theology, three general models have been proposed—teleological, deontological, and relational-responsibility.[11] A *teleological* model sees the moral life in terms of an end or goal to be reached. The teleologist asks, What is the goal or the ideal I will pursue? The moral life is viewed as a journey, pilgrimage, or quest directed toward a goal. Character is formed as choices are made and actions are taken according to what one wants to achieve and the ideal one wants to live up to.

For example, Santiago was on a quest to find the buried treasure, and all his decisions were made in light of that goal. Or one's goal could be to become a millionaire. This would lead a person to focus attention, efforts, imagination, skills, and ingenuity on accumulating wealth. A teleologist acts with a purpose or desired future state of affairs in mind. Then she or he asks, what steps need to be taken to achieve this goal? What are my short- and long-range plans? Judgments about good and evil are made with regard to whether attainment of the goal is helped or hindered by a given act or choice. St. Augustine and St. Thomas Aquinas are two prominent figures who thought of the moral life in terms of a teleological model. The morally good is whatever leads to union with God, and the ultimate end of the human person is what brings true happiness and human fulfillment.

The *deontological* model views the Christian moral life primarily in terms of duties or obligations. For most of the history of moral theology, this has been the dominant model of the moral life. In deciding what to do or what choice to make, the deontologist asks, What is my duty or what rule governs this situation? Dominant images are that of law or command, and the primary concern is with meeting the standards established by God, society, or some other acknowledged authority. Judgments about good and evil are made in accord with certain norms that govern the moral life. This leads to duties that must be satisfied. Moral knowledge is knowledge of the rules or laws.

The German philosopher Immanuel Kant was a proponent of deontological ethics. In this framework, obedience becomes a key virtue and a sinner is someone who breaks the law. An example is the police officer that stops a person who has gone through a red light and insists on writing a ticket, even though the driver of the car is on the way to the hospital with a seriously sick child. Consequences do not matter. Furthermore, in a deontological approach to the moral life, the self can be viewed in a very individualistic manner. While one cannot avoid association with others, the focus is on the individual obeying the law and fulfilling one's duties. Moral decision-making, according to this model, is understood as the application of moral norms to concrete situations or the deduction of concrete moral obligations from universal norms.

> *The gifts of the Spirit enable believers to live good and upright lives, and to discern what is of God, what is the good, the true, and the beautiful.*

The *relational-responsibility* model highlights the multiple relationships we have with God, neighbor, self, and the whole created order. Right moral action is determined in light of growth in those relationships. H. Richard Niebuhr is probably the most famous proponent of this model. He suggested that the best way to answer "What should I do?" was to ask first, "What is going on?" or "What is the fitting response to what is happening?"[12] Since this model of the moral life gives priority to relationships, the task is to discern what is asked of us in the complex set of relationships in which we live—as parent, spouse, sibling, employer, neighbor, friend, lover, colleague. The relational-responsibility model accounts for the complexity and ambiguity of human relationships. For example, if a person is offered a prestigious job that will pay a salary double what she is presently making, but will take her away from her family for ten or twelve hours a day, should she take the job? According to this model, she must decide in light of the various relationships and responsibilities of her life and, in light of them, try to discern the most "fitting" response.

Christians are called to generous service in the world from our various "places of responsibility"—family, work, church, and state.[13] Moral reflection helps clarify the appropriate choices to be made with reference to living rightly amidst others. Responsible persons are those who demonstrate certain habitual loving attitudes in relationships with others. In this way, one's actions should be a reflection of a person's character. And moral character requires the freedom to choose what kind of person one will become. Ultimately, we choose to be a person who is either open to covenant with God and the call to discipleship or one who rejects such an invitation.

The relational-responsibility model corresponds best to the call-response framework of the moral life that we outlined in chapter 1. Teleological and deontological understandings of the moral life are not rejected, because any adequate understanding of the moral life requires dimensions of each of these models. For instance, our analysis of the virtues in chapter 5 illustrated the importance of one's *telos* or goal in life, and any approach to morality that does not appreciate the role of laws and rules and duties will be seriously deficient. But each of these must be seen in service to the various relationships and responsibilities that our lives comprise.

Furthermore, the relational-responsibility model is better suited to a process of moral discernment because it requires a listening heart or an intuitive sense of what fits in a particular situation. When we speak of moral discernment, we are referring to a way of reasoning that involves something more than a simple formula of computation. Discernment entails a capacity to perceive subtleties, to make penetrating judgments or discriminating observations. In its most general sense, we refer to discernment as "seeing into more deeply." That is why good novels, plays, and film are important resources for moral discernment; the narratives enable us to consider things more deeply than we might otherwise do if we relied only on the intellect.

In moral discernment we are concerned with choosing the right action—one that is consistent with our fundamental commitment to God and with our life of discipleship. Moral discernment is concerned with the art of determining what God is asking of us, and what our life of discipleship requires in this particular time and place. This is not simply a matter of right and wrong, obeying rules, or abstractly solving problems. Technology, especially the internet, provides easy access to an abundance of information. Facts and data on just about every topic of interest are at our fingertips. When making moral decisions, gathering data is important as we strive to choose the right course of action. For the process of moral discernment, however, such information is insufficient. To discern a particular vocation, the meaning of a specific call to discipleship, or what the reign of God requires of us, demands more than purely rational knowledge or linear reasoning. As Richard Gula explains, moral discernment involves practical reasoning that requires a discerning sensibility. This is a circular process that intertwines faith, reason, emotion, and intuition. "Discernment discovers what is the reasonable thing to do by engaging not only the head but also the heart. In and around the linear flow of discursive reasoning, discernment is an experienced perception involving the back-and-forth, around-and-about movement of intuition, affective sensibility to values, and subtle assessments of the relationships of multiple factors."[14]

The Spirit is involved in this process because it is the whole person who receives the gifts of the Spirit. Yet, for much of the history of moral theology, there has been an overemphasis on the intellectual and rational aspects of moral reasoning, while neglecting the role of the Spirit. Rational discourse has gradually been disassociated from its roots in the affective and intuitive dimensions of human nature that have close experiential rapport with the

Spirit and the gifts of the Spirit.[15] In the next section, we will discuss the importance of the gifts of the Spirit, especially the gift of wisdom, which are central to Thomas Aquinas's understanding of moral discernment. While Aquinas's moral theology focuses on our journey in search of happiness, culminating in the vision of God, it is with the assistance of the Holy Spirit, particularly through the infused virtues and the gifts of the Spirit, that a sound moral choice can be made.

THE GIFTS OF THE SPIRIT

The gifts of the Holy Spirit are like the treasured gifts we receive from a loved one. They are freely offered to believers, given out of love for our happiness and for our good. Like gifts we receive from others, the effect the gifts have on us is related to the manner of reception. We may resist the gift or we may accept it graciously and gratefully. We need an open and grateful heart, as well as a willingness to cooperate with the grace given, in order to live in a manner fitting for disciples of the Lord. The gifts of the Holy Spirit (wisdom, understanding, counsel, fortitude, knowledge, piety, and fear of the Lord) make us more amenable to the interior promptings of the Spirit. They make us conscious of the attraction to goodness and love, and they enable us to operate with a certain inclination toward what is of God. The gifts augment the capacity for leading virtuous lives, discerning God's call, and making sound judgments. They do not replace ethical analysis or logic; rather, they complement and perfect the reasoning process with connatural knowing. In fact, one of the most constant elements of the inherited tradition on the gifts of the Holy Spirit is that they are rooted in connatural, intuitive, or instinctive knowing.[16]

Connatural Knowledge

The notion of connatural knowledge offers a corrective to an excessively rational approach to the moral life, for it is different from merely knowing about something. It is not just intellectual understanding that one may gain from memorizing information for an examination. Connatural knowledge is born from love, and it is experienced as a movement welling up from within, an impelling force that is not conceived as something one ought to do, but something one must do and wants to do. It is rooted in the biblical sense of invitation and attraction, of calling, of the need to leave everything to follow Jesus, not sure of the reasons but knowing one must do this.

Furthermore, *connatural* refers to knowledge that has been so deeply appropriated in our lives—has become so much a part of us—that it truly is second nature to us. We can intellectually know about moral theology but still live an immoral life. We can know about spirituality, but still neglect prayer. But knowledge that is second nature is like the musician for whom playing the piano has become so much a part of who she is that it seems an expression of herself. Or it is like the pitcher for whom pitching is so "at one" with who he is that doing so seems to emerge from the depths of his being. Similarly, when the virtues are deeply possessed by us, they make being faithful to relationships, loving others, living responsibly, and acting justly appear "connatural" to us.[17] In this respect, the gifts "perfect" the virtues because with them we almost instinctively know whether something should be done, and know without a lot of reflection or analysis. For example, the gift of fortitude perfects the virtue of courage when a person almost instinctively acts courageously in the face of physical danger or stands up for the truth of a moral principle when doing so is costly.

But there are many manifestations of connatural knowledge. For instance, if we hear something about the meaning of human existence that is authentic, we recognize its truth almost spontaneously. It rings true; it resonates within us. What is proposed is congruent with what we seem to know in an almost *a priori* way. Thus, the notion of connatural knowledge makes room for intuition in moral discernment. Intuition often tends to be distrusted as something that cannot be proved or used as a basis of argument. But when we discern something intuitively, we presume that there is some fundamental knowledge given within human existence itself.[18] That is, we have a kind of instinctive apprehension of what is the good. We are saddened, angered, or anguished by Laura's taking her own life because we know intuitively that life is inherently good and valuable; it is to be loved, respected, and cherished.

But we can lose contact with our natural moral intuitions. Some things that are self-evident injustices to most twenty-first-century people, such as slavery, torture, and the execution of heretics, were not always perceived to be wrong by many Christians. Yet, there were some people who were attuned to the wrongness of such atrocities and confronted the societal injustices, such as Dietrich Bonhoeffer. The reality is that some people are better attuned to their moral intuitions on certain matters than others.[19] There are several things that can "stifle the Spirit" or impede reception of the moral knowledge that the Spirit makes instinctively available to us, such as inadequate nurturing, moral blindness, sin, ignorance, and power.[20]

It is not possible for any of us to be totally free from the effects of all that can inhibit our ability to intuit wisely in the moral sphere. This is what Mary Gordon's novel reveals in the case of Laura. Her early moral formation within her family consisted of being denigrated and made to feel inadequate, a person without value. Hence, there were too many factors inhibiting her freedom to rightly intuit the good that ought to be done. While she thought the experience of receiving the Spirit in her grandmother's garden made her "wise as a serpent," her inadequate nurturing did, indeed, stifle the Spirit's gift of wisdom.

The Gift of Wisdom

For Thomas Aquinas, the gift of wisdom plays a crucial role in moral discernment, for it enables us to have an intuitive or instinctive sense for what is the good that leads to true happiness. As one of the gifts that dwell within each of us, wisdom is an interior experience of God, the fruit of love aroused in our hearts through the grace of the Holy Spirit. Wisdom enables Christians to recognize in situations of daily life what is the will of God. Wisdom is not merely rational or abstract knowledge, for it "tastes" the difference between love and indifference, between justice and injustice; it understands God's peace because it is immersed in that peace.

The word "wisdom" derives from the Latin word *sapientia*, which means "tasting knowledge . . . that is delightful and not merely notional or abstract."[21] It has to do with knowing something through sense or instinct, an awareness that emerges from a familiarity with the divine, like the connatural knowledge discussed above. For example, once we experience and savor what it is like to love and be loved by God, we know that no other goods such as material things or prestige can lead to true happiness. As Thomas Heath states, "Tasting knowledge occurs when a lover comes to know the beloved in a way others do not, or the poetic experience whereby a person is grasped strongly yet inarticulately by the beautiful."[22] Wisdom thus understood is linked with the mystical tradition, with a sense of beauty and wonder for the grandeur of things.

When the poet Gerard Manley Hopkins writes about "the beauty of things deep down," he is referring to an enhanced aesthetic sense, a deepened awareness and appreciation for the divine that resides within and around us. In mystical theology the focus is not so much on the use of reason, and reasoning about God and human behavior, but on an affinity with God and the things of God. Contemplation, which is an essential aspect of the mystical tradition, is attentiveness to the loveliness of God. The one beholding God is then given a profound (but not necessarily clear) grasp of God.

Wisdom as Tasting Knowledge in Sufism

This notion of "tasting knowledge" is found also in Sufism, which represents the inward or esoteric aspect of Islam, its "spiritual essence." Sufism is a quest for spiritual illumination, a way of access to divine love and wisdom. Sufis believe that when the Spirit suffuses the heart with its spiritual light, then the heart reveals itself as the "tabernacle of the Divine Mystery" in the human person.[23] Sufism is characterized by its affirmation of the essentially divine nature of knowledge or wisdom, a gift that a person cannot gain by one's own initiative. Sufism is above all a matter of "tasting" knowledge, for to quote a Sufi adage, "Only the one who has tasted knows."[24] The law is important but, in itself, law cannot lead the disciple to the divine reality. The great spiritual master Rumi summarizes the relationship between the law and the Truth.

> The Law is like learning the theory of alchemy from a teacher or a book, and the Path is (like) making use of chemicals and rubbing the copper upon the philosopher's stone, and the Truth is (like) the transmutation of the copper into gold. Those who know alchemy rejoice in their knowledge of it, saying, "We know the theory of this (science)"; and those who practice it rejoice in their practice of it, saying, "We perform such works"; and those who have experienced the reality rejoice in the reality, saying, "We have become gold and are delivered from the practice of Alchemy; we are God's freedmen."[25]

Recall the wisdom the Alchemist offered to Santiago. He taught the young boy that love is a universal language all people could understand in their hearts. And the way to truly know something is by immersing oneself in the world that God created, for it is through visible objects that we come to understand the marvels of God's wisdom. Since Santiago was in the desert, he should immerse himself in it by listening to his heart, "Because wherever your heart is," the Alchemist told him, "that is where you'll find your treasure."

In Sufism, the instrument of spiritual knowledge or gnosis is the heart, "the center of one's being." This is closely associated with the person of "subtle understanding" or wisdom who contemplates the depth of things and discovers a deeper knowledge beyond the intellect. This "discerning intelligence" is necessary in order to understand the sacred tradition and the metaphysical sense of truth. The metaphysical knowledge referred to here is a "spiritual realization" that is the "removal of the veils" that separate the person from God and from the full reality of one's true nature.[26] In Sufism then, the ultimate aim of knowledge is not to collect an abundance of data, but to reach the center within, the Sacred or the Spirit.

To receive the Spirit one's heart must be purified. There is similarity here with Aquinas's treatment of the gifts of the Spirit. Just as Sufis say that one must surrender to the commands of the Spirit, Aquinas makes a similar point when he sees the virtues perfected in the gifts and sees the fullness of freedom as our being led by the Spirit, as being instruments of the Spirit.

For Aquinas, the gift of wisdom gives us the capacity to assess the value of the present situation in light of ultimate goodness. Even when confronted by complex decisions and difficult moral situations, the gift of wisdom disposes us, under the impulse of the Spirit, to discern what is of God.[27] Wisdom is the gift that enables us to know what is the good because it is written on the heart. The wisdom that is exercised in connaturality, and in relation to the grace of the Spirit poured into our hearts, lies at the core of Aquinas's understanding of the Law of the Spirit or the Evangelical Law.[28]

THE LAW OF THE SPIRIT

Law is important in any human society. Without law, we have chaos. Without law, justice cannot be served. Without law, frail human beings lack the protection they often need. In the Catholic moral tradition, law has been given a central role. Law has had an important place in the Bible as well. Yet, within the Bible other themes ought to be seen as having even greater importance. In the sacred texts that formed the Hebrew people, the themes of God's invitation and desire, of divine calling as well as sending are paramount. And in the New Testament, the love command is primary. Jesus puts law in its proper perspective. It is always at the service of love.

Thomas Aquinas completes his systematic treatise on law by speaking of the "Evangelical Law" or "New Law" that comes with Christ and the Gospels, but that is also closely associated with the movement of the Spirit. He begins, however, by analyzing the essence of law in general, and then by distinguishing five kinds of law: the eternal law; the natural law; human or civil law; the Old Law, which is centered in the Decalogue or Ten Commandments; and the Evangelical or New Law that comes in Christ and is sometimes called the Law of the Spirit.[29] For Aquinas, each aspect of the law is meant to be an expression of the divine wisdom, an attempt to sketch the broad lines and implications of God's eternal law for our lives. Aquinas taught that the eternal law, as an expression of divine wisdom, represented God's plan for creation. As an act of the divine reason, the eternal law depicted God's intended ordering of the world.

Natural law is humankind's participation in the eternal law, and especially its ability to discern right from wrong using human reason. The basic moral truth of natural law is to do good and avoid evil. Natural law is known by all people because everyone is able to participate in the eternal law to some extent through reason. Sin has clouded our vision of the truth, but the ability of human reason to grasp God's purposes and wisdom is not completely destroyed by sin.

In his discussion of natural law, Aquinas makes an important qualification. He cautions that as one moves from the general norms that emerge from natural law reasoning to more particular judgments, one must be more tentative in making prudential judgments. Aquinas does not give to the second level of norms the same certitude he ascribes to the level of general principles.[30]

For example, as a general norm, all people should respect life; but whether we should keep Grandma connected to a respirator is another question.

Similarly, in their pastoral letters on peace and the economy, the Catholic bishops of the United States applied Aquinas's insight to issues of peace and economic justice. They noted that when Christians are making specific judgments on these issues, the movement from moral principles to specific public policy choices is complex and difficult. The soundness of prudential judgments depends not only on the moral force of principles but also on the accuracy of information and the validity of assumptions. Therefore, the specific proposals the bishops offered on dimensions of peace and economics did not carry the same moral authority as their statements of universal principles. This is why people of good will can differ on the specifics of an issue, yet hold moral judgments consistent with the gospel and the Law of the Spirit.[31]

Positive or civil law is enacted by human beings. The community makes certain laws to ensure a well-ordered society and to protect the common good. Too, civil law guards against abuse of the common good as a result of human misjudgment or malice. We need civil law because, on account of sin's effect on our ability to know what is right, we can err in judging what is right or wrong. Similarly, we sometimes need to be restrained by law when, on account of passion or ill will, we may choose not to follow the natural law. Thus, civil law can serve as both guide and sanction.

The fourth kind of law in Aquinas's schema is the Old Law, particularly the Decalogue of the Old Testament. Revealed to human beings by God, the Ten Commandments direct our relationship with God and our relationships with one another. The first three commandments both complement and enrich our understanding of the natural law by reminding us that we are religious creatures who come from God and are called to fullness of life in God. We know ourselves rightly when we remember that we live always in and from our relationship with God. The fourth through tenth commandments also extend our understanding of the fundamental requirements of the natural law by focusing on our lives with others, whether our families or in society. They call our attention to behavior (such as murder, adultery, stealing, lying) that imperils the communal living that is essential for our happiness and well-being.

Finally, the fifth kind of law is the "Evangelical Law" or "New Law," which Aquinas also speaks of as the "Law of the Spirit." As the noted Thomist Servais Pinckaers points out, Aquinas referred to the Evangelical Law as the Law of the Spirit because it is rooted in the grace of the Spirit that is given to Christians at baptism in response to their faith in Christ. Too, it is essentially an interior law because it refers primarily to the presence and power of the Spirit dwelling in those who follow Christ. As the animating principle of the Christian life, the Spirit guides our life in Christ, teaches us, and moves us to the good.[32] This is the law, foretold by the prophets (Jer 31:33; Ezek 36:26) that is inscribed on our hearts. For Aquinas, everything else in the Christian life (the Bible, the sacraments, the laws of the institutional church) is of secondary importance inasmuch as all else exists to facilitate our growth in the "law" of the Spirit.

We should be clear that the Law of the Spirit does not lead to a rigidly legalistic understanding of the moral life or of moral decision making. Rather, the Law of the Spirit is eminently a law of freedom. Far from focusing on particular laws, for Aquinas, the evangelical Law of the Spirit favored freedom over law by reducing moral precepts to what is necessary for salvation, such as love of neighbor, being kind and just, caring for the poor, respecting life. Furthermore, Aquinas held that this freedom in the Spirit emanated from a life of virtue. As one grew in the theological and moral virtues, they developed an instinct for the things of God that enabled greater freedom and spontaneity in the moral life.[33]

Linking the freedom of the Spirit with growth in the virtues underscores why Aquinas's teaching on the Evangelical Law does not support a subjective, individualistic, or overly optimistic view of the ability of the individual Christian to discern what is morally right or wrong. But a subjective, individualistic view of morality is also avoided when we remember that personal decision making, especially on complex ethical issues, must be complemented by communal discernment. Wisdom is not solely an individual or personal prerogative, but is essentially a shared experience in society. We are guided personally by the interior wisdom of the Holy Spirit that influences our thoughts and reflections. But we also need to draw on exterior resources of wisdom in scripture, in the Christian community, and in the wisdom of society that is enacted in its laws and reflected in its institutions.

COMMUNITY AND MORAL DISCERNMENT

The excessive individualism of U.S. society can mislead us into thinking that our situation is so unique that there can be no experience comparable to our own or that the truly moral person must act in isolation, unimpeded by those around him or her. We can convince ourselves that our obligations are only to ourselves and that we arc always the best judges of our situations. Aquinas's insight about the necessity of community for human well-being highlights that moral discernment must occur with a proper appreciation for the wisdom resident in the human family. We ignore the insights of others at our peril. Those who would make wise choices ought to consult broadly, listen intently, and be willing to learn from others.

Part of the faith of Catholics and other Christians is that the community of the baptized, the church, is a community of moral wisdom that must not be ignored. This point was integral to the teaching of the Second Vatican Council's "sense of the faithful" (*sensus fidelium*). This term refers to how the

Spirit of truth arouses and sustains a "sense of faith" (*sensus fidei*) in the people of God that enables them to know the good and the right.[34] Generation after generation, believers have struggled to discover what fidelity to the truth and goodness of God might mean in specific times and places. To dismiss what lessons can be learned from that epic story is to impoverish oneself and one's moral judgments by presuming that the present has nothing to learn from the past. For Catholics, especially, the role of the church in moral matters can be understood in two ways.

There is the church as the community of those with whom one shares faith in the present time: the community with whom we pray and worship, the episcopacy, and the theological community. We need to draw on the wisdom of all these members of the universal church in making moral decisions. The lived witness of faithful people should assist us in making prudential judgments. And, as we saw in chapter 6, drawing on the teaching of the church as it is expressed by the episcopacy is necessary for conscience formation. Further, the knowledge present in the community of scholars who serve the church ought not to be ignored as one seeks to understand the teaching of the church.

Besides the present church community, there is also the historical community of the church, those men and women who have gone before us and whose lives have contributed to our traditions of belief and practice. To learn from the past is not to engage in an act of nostalgia but to gain perspective and understanding for our times. Every age has its blind spots and the twenty-first century is no exception. Just as we sometimes wonder how previous generations could have accepted things we now question, we must realize that future generations will look upon us in a similar way.

We cannot predict the future, but we can gain some distance from the present by examining the tradition of the church. The assumptions of another age, the values upheld, and the norms for living a good life, may help us to see that some of the conventional wisdom of our time may not be wisdom after all. Thus, to make right moral judgments we need to engage in a process of communal discernment that draws on the wisdom of our faith tradition, as well as the resources in society that help us advance the common good. The gift of wisdom given to individuals is also a shared experience of human society. The Spirit teaches us how to search for the truth, but we need to attend to the world and be open to the Spirit's presence in the world, for the Spirit in the Wisdom tradition fills the whole world (Wis 1:7).[35]

While the communal nature of human life needs emphasis in our individualistic culture, we should not go to the extreme of denying the value of personal experience. The element of moral genius, that realm of creative response within each of us, should not be overlooked, suppressed, or denied. Nonetheless, it is important that the reflective individual examines his or her own experience to ascertain the strengths and weaknesses of character that may dispose a person to act in one fashion rather than another. Knowing what our biases are, where in the past we have made mistakes, and how we have grown—all these factors can be usefully examined to gain insight. Too, the gifts can cleanse us of illusions so that we can see more clearly our own sinfulness and need for God's grace.[36] But, as noted above, there needs to be receptivity to the gift and a willingness to cooperate with the grace offered to us.

In sum, the Spirit imparts the breath and wisdom of God that dwells within, giving us the capacity to discern what is the right thing to do. The gifts of the Spirit (especially wisdom), the notion of connatural knowledge, and the Evangelical Law all make room for intuition in moral discernment. For Thomas Aquinas, moral discernment is the exercise of wisdom rooted in the love of God and guided by the Law of the Spirit.

To receive the gift of wisdom and other gifts of the Spirit, we need to pray fervently, striving to know what is pleasing to God. Solomon describes a personal experience of wisdom that he attained through prayer (Wis 9:1-12). While he had a noble nature, this was not sufficient for him to be considered wise. Solomon prayed often to the Lord for the gift of wisdom he received, seeking it since his youth (9:10-11).[37] So, too, do disciples of Jesus need to pray ardently for the Spirit's guidance in making wise moral decisions. There are at least three ways that prayer can help us discern the way the Spirit is leading: disposing us to discern correctly, disclosing essential aspects of the issue, and confirming our decision.[38]

PRAYER AND MORAL DISCERNMENT

The first way prayer can help us to discern the movement of the Spirit in a particular decision is by disposing us to choose well. In moral discernment, we need to be as free and conscious as possible about what is going on within and around us. We hope to be liberated from any fantasies or illusory loves that claim us illegitimately. One of the insights we gained from the biblical reflection above is that the Spirit is a power to overcome sin, to free us from all restrictions. But we need to dispose ourselves to allow the life-renewing breath of God to permeate our whole being. That includes silence, for as Mahatma Gandhi said, "In the attitude of silence the soul finds the path in a clearer light, and what is elusive and deceptive resolves itself into crystal clearness."

We pray for the gifts of the Spirit to help purify our vision and to help us gain insight. We need an open heart to receive the gifts and a willingness to cooperate with the grace freely offered to us. So we begin by praying for a "new heart," a "listening heart," as did Solomon. We pray for the gift of wisdom to aid us in discerning what is of God. Prayer makes us receptive to the gifts by helping us center properly on God.

There are at least three ways that prayer can help us discern the way the Spirit is leading: disposing us to discern correctly, disclosing essential aspects of the issue, and confirming our decision.

When we focus on God and trust in God's providence, we take ourselves less seriously. We become increasingly aware of God's care and love in our lives and in those around us. When we have a setback or come to see our limitations more clearly, we will be less defensive, more accepting of the weeds that grow along with the wheat. We may be more sympathetic and patient with other people's inadequacies and rejoice with them in their gifts and successes.

Second, prayer not only disposes us to choose well but can also disclose aspects of reality that help us to see the nature of what is at stake in the moral issue we are deliberating. Often, this experience points out how we may be part of the problem, or what our role is in the issue. Rather than blame others or make excuses, prayer can lead us to assume responsibility for our role in a damaged relationship or to acknowledge the part we directly or indirectly play in societal injustice. This requires attentive listening to and contemplative reflection on what is going on inside us. Sometimes we do not reveal the love and wisdom that is within us to others because we cannot get past the demons that confront us on the inward journey. When that occurs we are blocking the movement of the Spirit and we are also unable to live and love responsibly. We need to be in touch with, and able to cope with, the negative aspects of our own personality, especially feelings of inadequacy and fear. To do that, we must be willing to go deep within the wells inside us and wrestle with what we find there.

In *Teaching a Stone to Talk*, the novelist Annie Dillard gives us an evocative description of the nature of this aspect of the spiritual life. For Dillard, the spiritual journey moves downward and inward, not upward toward abstraction. It moves downward toward the hardest concrete realities of our lives. On the way down and in, we will meet the violence and terror we have within ourselves that we project outward onto our relationships, families, institutions, and society.

> In the deeps are the violence and terror of which psychology has warned us. But if you ride these monsters deeper down, if you drop with them farther over the world's rim, you find what our sciences cannot locate or name, the substrate, the ocean or matrix or ether which buoys the rest, which gives goodness its power for good, and evil its power for evil, the unified field: our complex and inexplicable caring for each other, and for our life together here. This is given. It is not learned.[39]

Dillard is talking about our tendency to make enemies through projection, putting what we hate within ourselves onto someone else because we don't want to go down and in to meet the enemy in our own souls. So we imagine that someone out there is the enemy—people of another race, another economic class, or another religious tradition. While we perceive the other as a threat, what we are really reacting to is the shadow of ourselves. We need to go inward to find the "spot of grace," a spot of truth and love—the Spirit—deep within that issues peace. This is akin to Aquinas's understanding of the wisdom that dwells within each of us, the interior experience of God, who is truth and peace.

The third way that prayer can assist in the process of moral discernment is by validating or confirming a decision. Prayer can be an act of remembering some experience, story, or event that ratifies our decision as one that is in keeping with our faith commitment as disciples. This reinforces for us that a particular choice we make is in harmony with our character and that we are being responsible to the myriad of relationships that constitute our lives; or that we are not. If it is of the Spirit, some sense of peace tends to accompany the decision.

Moreover, when a decision is made in the power of the Spirit, it will be one that promotes justice, in the biblical sense of fidelity to right relationships. The concern of justice is not something removed from us as we pray. When we pray we are not separate from others who suffer, but should be drawn into deeper companionship with the broken people of the world. That is how Jesus prayed, seeking to do God's will and responding to the needs and hurts of others. Jesus makes explicit the attitude of petition that should permeate our whole life. As we pray in the Spirit and are open to the movement of the Spirit, we are led into deeper and deeper relationship with God, neighbor, self, and all creation. Jesus starkly points out the integral connection of prayer and right relationships. He shocks us as we are about to come before God with gestures of gratitude, or are about to kneel for prayer: "So when you are offering your gift at the altar, if you remember that your brother or sister has something against you, leave your gift there before the altar and go; first be reconciled to your brother or sister, and then come and offer your gift" (Matt 5:23-24).

We need to think about what needs reconciling in our lives—with parents, children, brothers, sisters, and friends. Or think of our nation. We are well aware that millions of Americans, as well as people around the world, live in poverty and suffer from lack of basic human needs. Do we hear the cries of the poor as we go to prayer and worship? Do we let their cries change the way we pray and worship, and therefore change the way we live? As we give our gifts, do we stop to think of those who may have few monetary gifts to bring? Do we think of ways that perhaps we have been less than generous? A believer or a religious community that is exclusive in attitude or practice along the lines of race, social class, gender, age, or sexual orientation can offer only partial prayers, only tainted gifts.

How might Mary Gordon's story have been different if Laura had been engaged in the kind of prayerful reflection we are proposing? We noted above some reasons for her misunderstanding what the Spirit was leading her to do—a literal interpretation of scripture, inadequate moral formation, and a privatized approach to decision making. Praying fervently for wisdom, for spiritual illumination, might have revealed aspects of the problem Laura could not see. From the outset, Laura was not disposed to choose well. She lived in a fantasy world, believing her employer loved her more than anyone, when in reality Anne did not even like her. Laura's moral blindness led her to perceive those around her as sinful, lacking the Spirit. Only she was "wise as a serpent." Laura did not trust in God's providence, but rather relied on her own perceived privileged knowledge. Furthermore, Annie Dillard's keen insight is one that Laura missed. She failed to see that she was part of the problem. She never looked inward to discover her own demons. By refusing to do that, Laura was unable to be in touch with the "spot of grace" within, the love that was there beneath all the pain and anger and suspicion. The "fitting" thing to do could not be taking her own life because the Spirit of God breathes life into creation. It transforms what seems to be dead—what appears to be nothing more than "dry bones"—by bringing them back to life

In summary, prayer keeps us in right relationship with the ground of our being. Because of this, it can bring about a gradual change in our lives, beginning in the innermost sanctums of the heart, eventually flowing out into other dimensions of life. By disposing us to discern correctly, disclosing essential aspects of the issue, and confirming our decision, prayer helps us choose wisely what love requires of us and what is the most fitting thing to do.

CONCLUSION

The Spirit of God is present within us and around us, active everywhere in the world. The call to follow Jesus is not just a personal matter but a vocation to bear the fruit of the Spirit in the world. In so doing, disciples witness to God's continued presence in creation. Thus, when Jesus' followers are charged to "go and make disciples of all nations," they are empowered by the Spirit to engage in the missionary or public nature of discipleship. In the final chapter, we will consider how disciples are called to be faithful citizens in this globalized and pluralistic world.

KEY POINTS

1. The Holy Spirit is a power and wisdom that dwells within and permeates all God's creation.
2. The Spirit enables believers to lead virtuous lives and to discern what is the good and the right.

3. The gifts of the Spirit, especially wisdom, complement the objective reasoning process through an intuitive or instinctive kind of knowing.
4. The Law of the Spirit is written on our hearts; it is an interior grace that emanates from the wisdom or eternal law of God.
5. We can quench the Spirit by inadequate moral formation, moral blindness, and all sorts of restrictions, especially sin.

QUESTIONS FOR REFLECTION

1. What manifestations of the Holy Spirit can you identify in your own experience and in the world?
2. How do the gifts, especially wisdom, function in the process of moral discernment?
3. What is the role of the Christian community in the process of moral discernment? How does communal discernment factor into your own process of decision making?
4. What is meant by *connatural knowledge*?
5. What is the relationship between prayer and moral discernment?

SUGGESTIONS FOR FURTHER READING AND STUDY

Billy, Dennis, C.Ss.R. "The Person of the Holy Spirit as the Source of the Christian Moral Life." *Studia Moralia* 36 (1998): 325-59.

Bouchard, Charles, O.P. "Recovering the Gifts of the Holy Spirit in Moral Theology." *Theological Studies* 63 (2002): 539-58.

Cooke, Bernard. *Power and the Spirit of God: Toward an Experience-Based Pneumatology*. New York: Oxford University Press, 2004.

Keating, Thomas. *Fruits and Gifts of the Spirit*. New York: Lantern, 2000.

Mahoney, John. *Seeking the Spirit: Essays in Moral and Pastoral Theology*. London: Sheed & Ward; Denville, N.J.: Dimension, 1982.

Michon, Jean-Louis, and Roger Gaetani, eds. *Sufism: Love and Wisdom*. Bloomington, Ind.: World Wisdom, 2006.

Murphy, Roland. *The Tree of Life: An Exploration of Biblical Wisdom Literature*. 3rd ed. Grand Rapids: Eerdmans, 1990.

O'Keefe, Mark, O.S.B. *Becoming Good, Becoming Holy: On the Relationship of Christian Ethics and Spirituality*. New York: Paulist, 1995.

Pinckaers, Servais. *The Sources of Christian Ethics*. Translated by Sr. Mary Thomas Noble, O.P. Washington, D.C.: Catholic University of America Press, 1995.

Rahner, Karl. "Experience of the Holy Spirit." In *Theological Investigations* 18. New York: Crossroad, 1983.

Warrington, Keith. *Discovering the Holy Spirit in the New Testament*. Peabody, Mass.: Hendrickson, 2005.

10

The Mission of Public Discipleship

"Go and Make Disciples of All Nations" *(Matthew 28:16-20)*

FOLLOWERS OF JESUS are called to mission. When we commonly think of mission it is in relation to the work of religious missionaries, those persons who are sent to a foreign land to spread the faith. But the concept of mission is a broader term, and one not necessarily associated with evangelization. Missionary activity includes providing medical, educational, or other assistance to people. One could be on a mission to clean up a neighborhood or to change an educational system. Understood militarily, mission can mean to capture or defend something, such as freedom and democracy. Essentially, a person on a mission seeks to accomplish a task or to discover something. Santiago was on a mission to find a buried treasure in the pyramids of Egypt that would make him a rich man. Dietrich Bonhoeffer was on a mission to protect human rights by opposing Hitler, the rise of fascism, and anti-Jewish policies. Balian, the Christian Crusader, was on a mission to establish the kingdom of heaven in Jerusalem, where Christians, Muslims, and Jews could live in harmony and peace.

Each of us has a mission or "calling" to pursue a vocation. In this book, we have focused on the mission of discipleship. We have noted that all Christians are called to follow Jesus, to grow in likeness to him, and to give witness to him through the character of their lives. Followers of Jesus are called to witness to the eschatological reign of God, to proclaim and to make more visible the presence of God in our midst. In Matthew's Gospel, Jesus sends his followers into the world to "make disciples of all nations." This missionary task requires Christians to take on a dual identity as followers of Jesus and members of society. The difficult and demanding task is discerning how to be faithful to this dual citizenship.

Throughout the Christian tradition, there have been various responses to the question of how disciples ought to interact with the wider social and political world while remaining loyal to Jesus. It is a question riddled with tensions and ambivalence, and one that we do not aim to resolve in this chapter. Rather, our goal is more modest. We will provide some insights from the biblical and theological traditions to guide the discernment process about how to be good citizens *and* disciples of Jesus. Each of us has to decide how to live faithfully and responsibly in those dual roles. We begin by considering a trajectory of responses, starting with the early Christians. While they were sent into a different world and confronted with issues very different from those contemporary believers face, nonetheless there are common and persistent tensions. Moreover, the experiences and perspectives of previous generations of disciples offer wisdom for the missionary task ahead.

TENSION AND AMBIVALENCE

Biblical Perspectives

Biblical scholar Walter Brueggemann points out that when Jesus sends disciples into the world, he is making the same claim as the God of the Old Testament. Israel's mission is to be a blessing, "to mend the world." God's vision of creation is a world of "shalom" that reflects the peace and well-being of all creation. The presence of God is known when creation functions according to the intention of the creator.

Like the Israelites called into covenant relationship, like Moses who confronted the injustice of the pharaoh, and like the prophets who challenged rulers who oppressed the poor, disciples of Jesus are called to break cycles of violence and alienation by positive acts of reconciliation, peace, and justice. Men and women are called away from the dehumanizing values of the world to follow, to obey, and to participate in Jesus' passion and mission.[1] Considering the sequence from Old Testament to New Testament to early church, Brueggemann concludes that disciples are to be an *"alternative community* in the midst of conventional communities." That requires disciples to name and confront the powers in society that are alien to the reign of God, particularly the socio-political-economic powers.[2]

Matthew, of all the Gospels, makes it clear that those who follow Jesus are sent into the world with a great commission—to share in Jesus' task of preaching, teaching, and witnessing to the reign of God. Matthew's wealthy, urban, and well-educated community experienced conflict between daily interaction with societal structures and the call to wholehearted obedience to the cause of Jesus. But clearly their missionary task demanded societal participation. The thorny question that remains is how are followers to participate in society as disciples of the Lord? Disciples live in an ambivalent relationship with society, struggling between detachment from society and participation in it. They are to participate in public life, but challenge those values and structures that are counter to the reign of God.

For the early Christians, baptism was like taking on a new citizenship; it entailed a change of primary allegiance from the empire to God's rule. The newly initiated did not totally reject the values of the surrounding culture, but they did see the culture in a new way and they did live in it differently. Baptism initiated the early Christians into a community called to witness to God's presence in the world. Put differently, the church was not to be a sect apart from the world, but Christ's body in the world.

This point is important to keep in mind when we consider the relation of discipleship and citizenship in the New Testament. There are duties of citizenship that Christians are expected to fulfill—ordinary civic duties such as paying taxes and obeying the laws of society, rendering "to Caesar the things that are Caesar's, and to God the things that are God's" (Matt 22:21). But Christians are also called to challenge some practices of society and to work to transform society. As John Coleman points out, "Christians are urged to live moral lives in accord with the highest available societal ethical codes and to transform the ethos of their societies, 'in the Lord'" (Eph 5:22-33). The challenge is to seek the appropriate relationship between discipleship and citizenship. There is no pat formula that solves this relationship once and for all.[3]

As time went on, two factors emerged that affected the moral reasoning of Christians: first, the end of the world was no longer seen to be imminent; second, the church was growing and expanding into cultures other than that of Palestinian Judaism. So the community had to reflect on how to be a Christian in a pagan world, and in a world that was not soon coming to an end. This compelled Christians to ask what it meant to be faithful to Christ amid pagan peoples in a state that was going to survive. And there were new questions of cooperation. Can Christians take oaths to Caesar in order to hold public office or military rank? How should Christians behave with regard to fashion and dress, theater and entertainment, acquiring wealth, facing martyrdom, or reconciling with people who had lapsed from the faith? New questions and new issues, along with some persistent tensions, led to a variety of theological opinions. We will highlight some of the more significant perspectives in the next section.

Theological Perspectives

In the fifth century, St. Augustine addressed the issue by contrasting two cities—the city of God, the heavenly realm where there is perfect happiness, with the earthly city founded on sin or "splendid vices." According to Augustine, the earthly city was not totally depraved. Peace and happiness were possible insofar as one's will and disposition were focused on love of God.[4] In the sixteenth century, Martin Luther addressed the issue of Christian involvement in society with his famous doctrine of the "two swords," which distinguished the spiritual and temporal realms. Luther argued that the authority of the church (the sword of doctrine) extended only to "spiritual" matters and that the church should never interfere with the running of the state (the sword of the princes).[5]

A sharper dichotomy between the earthly and heavenly kingdoms is found in Karl Barth's theology. Stressing the difference between Christian faith and the values of society, Barth sees a wide chasm between them. His "confessing Church" is one that refuses to participate in public moral discourse, thus placing real limitations to Christian participation in public moral choices. His is a radical theology of obedience to God's will, something that can only be known in the faith community. Christians can offer guidance to civic debate not by engaging the public discussion, but by witnessing to what they know in conscience before God. At the same time, they are not to claim that knowledge of God's will can be discovered through human reasoning or argumentation.[6]

The theologies of Emil Brunner and Dietrich Bonhoeffer, by contrast, develop a conception of what is required and forbidden on the basis of our human nature and experience. In this way, those who are not Christian can agree with Christians' reasons for a moral choice. This is a "realism" that allows God's will to be discerned in the "common experience of human reality." Brunner and Bonhoeffer share Barth's claim that the commandment of God is the starting point for Christian ethics. But the command is embodied in the structures of human life, in the "orders of creation," as well as in the particular understanding of the Christian church.

As ethicist Robin Lovin states: "The theological realism of Bonhoeffer and Brunner preserves the distinction between faith and culture, but it seeks to understand what might be commonly shared between people of faith and others in society toward achieving the good."[7]

Like Barth, the contemporary moral theologian Stanley Hauerwas preserves a sharp distinction between Christian faith and the values of culture. He reasserts "the social significance of the church as a distinct society with an integrity peculiar to itself."[8] Hauerwas maintains that faithfulness to the Christian story sometimes precludes full participation in public moral deliberations. The responsibility of the church is to witness to the "peaceable kingdom," showing the world to be the violent place it is. There may be points of contact where Christians can cooperate with the moral endeavors of others, but there is little common ground for moral deliberation. For Hauerwas, Christians exercise social responsibility by maintaining the church's freedom from the values of any culture.[9]

The various ways Christians try to resolve the tension and ambivalence between discipleship and culture can be seen in the five classic "types" proposed by H. Richard Niebuhr. The *Christ-against-culture* model views the reign of God in opposition to what exists at the present and serves as the basis for a radical opposition between the reign of God and cultural norms and societal institutions. The extreme opposite posture is the *Christ-of-culture* model, which tends to identify the reign of God with the present culture. It is amid the existing culture that men and women exercise faithful and responsible discipleship.

The *Christ-above-culture* type recognizes the good in culture as a gift from God. But this good needs to be properly ordered and completed by Christ, who is both discontinuous and continuous with social life and culture. The *Christ-and-culture* in paradox type finds less continuity between culture and the Christian life. It keeps a critical distance from culture, and yet sees it as useful in the Christian life if kept within its appropriate bounds. There is an irreconcilable tension experienced as Christians of this type are obedient to two different, and often conflicting, authorities.

Niebuhr's final type, *Christ-transforming-culture*, reflects a critical stance toward, but appreciation for, culture. Culture is the raw material that can be shaped by Christians according to the Christian vision of human life. Those who hold this view will form an alliance with those aspects of culture that are perceived as capable of becoming part of the ongoing work of the kingdom of God. There is a recognition that human nature is fallen or sinful, and that this perversion is not only inherent in the culture but transmitted by it. So, like the first and fourth types, Christians of the transformationist group recognize some opposition between Christ and all human institutions and cultures. But this antithesis does not lead either to separation from the world or to a posture of enduring the present reality in expectation of salvation at the end time. Rather, Christ is seen as the one who can bring about conversion in the midst of culture and society, not apart from them.

Niebuhr maintained that there was no conclusive answer as to which of these types is the right way for Christian disciples to relate to culture. He held that the five models are not wholly exclusive; rather, each model challenges, corrects, and complements each of the other models. Christians of every age tend to operate within one or another model, or a combination of models, as they try to discern how to live as free and responsible members of society and as loyal disciples of Jesus Christ.[10]

While we agree that there are a variety of valid ways for Christians to relate to culture and public life, followers of Jesus typically ought not to assume a posture of radical opposition between faith and society. As we have discussed throughout this book, disciples are called to make the world a better place—one that reflects the values of the reign of God—by assuming responsibility for one another, for the larger community and society, and for the earth. We need to discover and promote what is most like God's reign, and that will always be what most promotes human and societal flourishing. This includes loving and forgiving those we consider our enemies, offering hospitality to the stranger, extending compassion to those who suffer, feeding the hungry, sheltering the homeless, and creating just social structures and laws that protect and promote human dignity. Disciples are also called to identify

> *Disciples are called to make the world a better place— one that reflects the values of the reign of God—by assuming responsibility for one another, for the larger community and society, and for the earth.*

and correct injustices that demean or diminish humankind and the created order—those attitudes and actions that are unlike the reign of God, such as gross economic inequality, zoning laws that discriminate against racial minorities, foreign aid that favors military assistance while neglecting human needs, trade policies that ignore workers' rights, and environmental laws that contribute to ecological degradation.

Promoting the values of God's reign and creating a just society can be done most effectively by engaging in public deliberation and action, not by withdrawing from public life. Part of the problem, though, and a reason that some Christians resist such engagement, is that there is an inauthentic or distorted view of public life. Thus, in order to discern rightly how to respond to the command to "go into the world and make disciples of all nations," we need to understand what is meant by the concept of public life that we are called to as part of the missionary task and its importance for discipleship.

THE VALUE OF PUBLIC LIFE FOR DISCIPLESHIP

Before discussing the value of public life for discipleship, we need to be clear about what is meant by public life. The *res publica* includes, but is much larger than, the sphere of government. As Parker Palmer maintains, authentic public life does not happen simply in the halls of government; nor is it just the result of public policy decisions. The settings for public life are many and diverse. It occurs in city parks, sidewalk cafés, and museums where people can pause, spend time in one another's presence, and share common interests and pleasures. It happens at rallies, forums, and debates where people have an opportunity to listen and be heard, to air differences and conflicts, to influence one another's thinking, and to move toward mutual accommodation. But it also happens at carnivals, festivals, and fairs where people can be entertained and can entertain others; in the neighborhood that gives the notion of "public" a human face and human scale; and in voluntary associations in which people relate in a framework of common interests, concerns, and commitments, and are thus empowered to enter larger spheres of public activity.[11]

Parker notes several characteristic functions of public life, three of which have particular significance for the moral life. The first and most basic feature is that in public life *strangers meet on common ground*. Our individual lives are intertwined with those of strangers, and this requires us to live in ways that take them into account. In public life we are not developing relationships of intimacy. The foundation of public life "is not the intimacy of friends but the capacity of strangers to share a common territory, common resources, common problems—without ever becoming friends. . . . The public life is a place where we learn that there can—and must—be honor among strangers as well as among friends."[12] For example, this means we honor signs in public spaces that ask us to speak softly, shut off cell phones, and extend common courtesy to the stranger.

Another characteristic of public life is that it calls us *to face and to deal with our fear of the stranger*. Unlike private life, in public life we do not deal only with those who are "like us," people of the same race, economic status, and life experience. This is why when we participate regularly in public life, the experience helps to destroy, or at least challenge, some of our stereotypes and fantasies of "the stranger." Interacting with people we do not know, or know little about, humanizes them and helps us to have a more realistic perception of them. In such interaction, we can come to see that underneath all surface differences, people share a common humanity.[13] As we discussed in chapter 1, the experience of the "other" as valuable and as gift is the source of moral obligation and the primal data on which ethical reflection proceeds. Too often, though, the other is viewed as threat rather than gift. In public life, fear of the stranger needs to be faced and dealt with simply because we are often surrounded by strangers with whom we need to mingle or collaborate.

Third, in public life people are both *empowered and protected against abuses of power*. Totalitarian countries intentionally try to extinguish public life because it both empowers people to influence the government and protects them against excessive incursions of governmental power. Parker points out that in public life we have the opportunity to learn about our common interests and difficulties, and that we are not alone and vulnerable to the powers that seem to control our lives. As a result, we can be strengthened to pursue the values and goals that are important to us. In public life, we have the opportunity to join together in various ways to demonstrate the power of our collective sentiments.

Furthermore, as we undertake projects in the public realm, we *learn the skills of collective action, leadership, decision making, and conflict resolution*.[14] These skills are particularly important as disciples enter the political arena and work to make the laws and institutions of society to be more in accord with their vision of what constitutes the good life. But Christians have no special expertise in the techniques, strategies, or particular policies needed to achieve this goal. It is through a common effort with other citizens that a more just and loving society can be created, one that more clearly reflects the reign of God.

In sum, public life enriches discipleship because it is the arena where we can expand our vision of the other and correct some of the distorted images or stereotypes that create obstacles to the missionary task. In public life, we extend courtesy to the stranger and we limit or restrain our own desires in consideration of the needs of others. Moreover, in public life we can discover shared values among people of different faiths and nationalities. It is in public life, including but not limited to the political realm, that disciples can witness to and make more visible the values of God's reign. And because Christian disciples have no special expertise in creating a just society, citizenship "adds to discipleship *a humbler* service in the day-to-day reality of politics," and thus enriches the life of discipleship.[15] Despite the importance of public life, however, it remains an untapped potential in American society. This is due not only to a distorted view of public life but also to a commonly perceived dichotomy between private and public life.

The Dichotomy between Private and Public Life

There is a common perception in North American society that private and public life are two distinct and separate realms. The way an individual lives his or her personal moral life should have no bearing on what is done in public. One of the central tenets of the dominant version of modern liberal political theory is that beliefs about what is morally right or wrong are mostly relegated to the private sphere, and moral neutrality is preserved in the public arena.[16] As Michael Sandel states, "However unencumbered we may be in private, however claimed by moral or religious convictions, we should bracket our encumbrances in public and regard ourselves, qua public selves, as independent of any particular loyalties or conceptions of the good." The purpose of politics in modern liberal political theory is to offer a fair and neutral procedure for regulating claims between parties who value different things. Thus, no public official's personal values or morality should interfere with what is believed to be a neutral, unbiased administration of government affairs.[17]

However, when questions of morality are relevant only for individuals, not for larger organizations, these institutions tend to become ends in themselves and cannot be accurately described as morally neutral.[18] Examination of public scandals, whether related to government, corporations, or religious institutions, tends to focus only on the morals, values, and actions of the individuals involved. But we need to take into account ways in which the personal shapes the institutional and institutions impact persons.

But without a healthy public life, both private and political life will suffer. A community of disciples—the church—can enrich public life by helping to break down barriers between the private and public realms and between faith and citizenship. As Alexis de Tocqueville noted in the nineteenth century, habits and practices of religion and democratic participation educate citizens to a larger view than the private world allows. He saw religion as a political institution having the capacity to form persons with a certain kind of character necessary for public life, particularly the practices and demands of citizenship. In more contemporary language, this would be part of the mission of a public church.

A PUBLIC CHURCH

As defined by Martin Marty more than two decades ago, a public church is composed of believers from mainstream Protestant, evangelical Protestant, and Catholic traditions. It is more a movement than a formal institution.

> A public church is a family of apostolic churches with Jesus Christ at the center, churches which are especially sensitive to the *res publica*, the public order that surrounds and includes people of faith. The public church is a communion of communions, each of which lives its life partly in response to its separate tradition and partly to the calls for a common Christian vocation.[19]

Over the years, theologians have interpreted the notion of a public church differently. Closely aligned with Marty's definition, but more practically useful, Michael and Kenneth Himes speak of a public church to mean a community whose social mission is characterized by three things. First, there is a respect for the legitimate autonomy of other public institutions and the reality of secularization. Political, economic, and educational institutions all have something to contribute to creating a just society, in conjunction with religious institutions. Second, a public church accepts some responsibility for the well-being of society. It is not sectarian, focused simply on the spiritual well-being of its members or separated from the rest of society. Third, a public church is ecumenical; it works with other institutions for the common good of society. All believers and nonbelievers can contribute to shaping a world that respects and fosters human rights and human development for all people.[20] As defined, a public church will necessarily be involved in the political realm.

One of the concerns raised by the Catholic magisterium is how to be involved in the political realm without sacrificing the church's religious mission. How can Christians "mend the world" and make it more reflective of the reign of God without becoming just another political actor? A document of the Second Vatican Council, *Gaudium et spes* (Pastoral Constitution on the Church in the Modern World), provides a helpful insight. *Gaudium et spes* suggests that the mission of the church is to proclaim and witness to the reign of God, and that the power of God's reign is to touch every aspect of human life. There can be no fragmentation of life so as to divorce religion from other aspects of human existence.

Accordingly, as the church pursues its religious ministry of serving God's reign, it must contribute to four areas that have political and social consequences—defense of human dignity, promotion of human rights, fostering unity among the human family, and providing meaning to every aspect of human life and activity.[21] These four realms provide a role for the church that is religious in nature and aim, but with consequences that are politically significant. In short, the engagement of the community of disciples in the political realm is indirect. Because of its religious mission, the church must transcend every political system; but it must also be engaged in the political order due to its religious mission. It is a politically significant but religiously rooted ministry to the world, rooted in the dignity of the person and the reign of God. Further, as the church pursues its religious ministry, it can help to create a more authentic public life and a just political order by communicating its vision of the good life to a wider society.

A VISION OF THE GOOD LIFE

In chapter 2, we discussed the importance of vision for the moral life and the integral connection between seeing and acting rightly. The biblical vision of creation, covenant, and the reign of God moves us away from a narrow concern for private life that undercuts the disciples' missionary task. It calls us to a prophetic witness so that the church does not too easily accommodate with cultural values antithetical to the reign of God. Moreover, as we saw, the aim of the parables is to shock us into new ways of seeing. They work to reorient us to God's world by showing us that what we assume to be reasonable and sensible may not fit the vision of the reign of God, a relational state of being marked by love, justice, righteousness, compassion, forgiveness, and generosity.

It is this eschatological vision that challenges the current social order to move to greater realization of these values. Our vision of the future in some way guides and shapes our sense of the present and calls us forward. Human betterment and progress in the world are possible, but these will always be colored by finitude and sin. The values of this world are to be set against a horizon

The mission of the church is to proclaim and witness to the reign of God, and that the power of God's reign is to touch every aspect of human life.

of transcendent values and a transcendent destiny that relativizes the present. Moreover, the church can offer a prophetic stance toward issues that affect human life with its vision of a consistent ethic of life.

The consistent ethic of life, or "seamless garment ethic," as it was articulated by Cardinal Joseph Bernardin, can move religious belief away from the narrow concern for personal life that undercuts the church's missionary task. It provides an overarching vision of the public good by promoting certain values along the entire continuum of life.[22] This vision is based on the theological conviction stated above that the mission of the church is to serve as sign and safeguard of human dignity and to protect human rights. Disciples have a responsibility to support human dignity and rights in every political system. In other words, there are many threats to human life, and the church can speak to such perilous times more effectively and cogently with a comprehensive and consistent approach to the many problems that affect the dignity of human beings. This is an overarching moral vision that moves beyond ad hoc single issue agendas by promoting certain values along the entire continuum of life.

This is the stance that orients disciples toward the good life. But what is it that makes human life good? In chapter 5, we discussed the nature of the good life in relation to virtue. We said that a virtuous person knows what counts as a good human life and a good society. Virtuous people have a wisdom about life that enables them to live in ways that are truly becoming for human beings. It is through the virtues that we flourish together and grow in happiness. For a life to be considered good, it has to be one by which we can develop the characteristics, habits, and activities that best represent who we ought to become, and for men and women these are the virtues.

Each of the virtues activates a particular dimension of goodness and, therefore, is intrinsic to happiness or what we consider the good life. We have discussed the cardinal virtues of prudence, justice, temperance, and courage, as well as theological virtues of faith, hope, and charity. We examined the virtue of love and its various manifestations, along with other virtues central to the reign of God such as righteousness, compassion, and patient endurance. With all virtues, it is essential that one become involved in the activity that the virtue (the good) intends.

In the classical Greek perspective, politics represents the most complete form of such activity. It is through participation in the *polis* that citizens can acquire the moral habits necessary to achieve the common good. It is in political life that people of different religious, ethnic, and cultural backgrounds engage in some common effort to find a way to live together. A good community or society will comprise institutions and laws that foster and protect both the individual and social good. Consequently, since it is the virtuous person who knows what counts as a good human life and a good society, every virtue is in a sense a "civic" virtue. The practice of civic virtues sustains and promotes public life and the common good, while their lack leads to distrust, lack of participation and cooperation, and eventual social breakdown.[23]

The U.S. Catholic bishops, in their pastoral letter on economic justice, state that virtues of citizenship are an expression of Christian love, and are more crucial than ever in today's interdependent world. "The virtues grow out of a lively sense of one's dependence on the commonweal and obligations to it. . . . In the absence of a vital sense of citizenship among the businesses, corporations, labor unions, and other groups that shape economic life, society as a whole is endangered."[24] In the final section of this chapter, we will discuss the virtue of solidarity, which the bishops maintain is another name for the social friendship or civic commitment that makes human moral and economic life possible. It is a civic virtue integrally related to several other virtues and one that enables people to seek and willingly care for the public good.

VIRTUE OF SOLIDARITY

As a virtue, solidarity is a habit that constitutes a consistent way of deliberating, choosing, and acting that contributes toward the good life. While solidarity is an important theme found in many documents of Catholic social teaching, John Paul II gives it the most comprehensive treatment. In the encyclical *Sollicitudo rei socialis* (On Social Concern), he describes the virtue of solidarity not as a "vague compassion" but rather as "a firm and persevering determination to commit oneself to the common good . . . because we are all responsible for all."[25] As a Christian virtue, solidarity is integrally related to charity and to the Christian ideal of unity or communion, with love at its core, which reflects the intimate life of the Trinity.[26] Solidarity unites love and justice and binds us to those who are close to us, to society as a whole, and to the world community.

As it is linked with justice, solidarity requires an "option or love of preference for the poor," as John Paul II expresses it. The option for the poor embraces the immense multitudes of the hungry, needy, homeless, those without medical care, and those without hope of a better future. Solidarity necessitates, on the part of the powerful, a responsibility and willingness to share; on the part of the weaker, an active claiming of rights based on their human dignity.[27] Solidarity helps us to see the other—whether a person, people, nation, or the cosmos—not just as some kind of instrument to be exploited and discarded when no longer useful, but as a partner in the banquet of life to which all are equally invited by God. As defined by John Paul II, solidarity links the virtues of love and justice. Let us consider how these virtues are connected.

Love and Justice

Love can only be authentic when it faces honestly the conditions under which we must love in this world. Love is not fantasy; it sees the world as it is with not only the many signs of God's presence but also the injustices that reflect what is not like the reign of God. The love command calls us to love God, neighbor, and self. And if we love others, we owe them justice, which prevents us from sentimentalizing love. Christian disciples are concerned with matters of justice, such as peace or ecology, not primarily because of an interest in particular causes, but because of love for persons who are affected by institutions—legal, political, economic, educational, religious—that violate human dignity. Christian concern for justice is a necessary outgrowth of our moral call to respond lovingly to the value of persons and the integrity of creation.

The intrinsic relation between justice and charity is emphasized by Pope Benedict XVI in his encyclical *Caritas in veritate* (Charity and Truth).[28] In fact, the pope states that charity, which he defines as "love received and given," goes beyond justice because to love is to freely offer what is ours to the other. But it must include justice, which prompts us to give to the other what is due them. If we love others, then we necessarily must be just to them. Justice is the minimum measure of charity, an integral part of loving another. On one hand, charity demands justice so that the legitimate rights of individuals and peoples are acknowledged and respected. On the other hand, charity transcends justice, and completes it with the generosity and forgiveness that enable communion with others.[29]

As we saw in chapter 7, to love another is to desire that person's good and to take effective steps to secure it. But linking justice to love reminds us that there is another good that we ought to seek—that is, the good of the social community that comprises individuals, families, and intermediate groups. This is what is meant to seek the common good, and it is a requirement of justice and charity. To strive to secure a common good that corresponds to the needs of our neighbors is the best way to effectively express our love for them. To take a stand for the common good requires involvement in the juridical, civil, political, and cultural institutions that structure societal life. This is what the pope calls the "political path" of charity, and it is no less excellent and effective than the kind of charity extended to the neighbor in need.

In an increasingly globalized society, the common good ought to include the whole human family, the community of peoples and nations.[30] And here we have the integral relation with solidarity. Solidarity is a moral imperative generated by the fact of our inescapable interdependence with other persons and creatures. But for Christians it is also grounded in our belief in the fundamental unity of the human family. And like all moral imperatives, it calls for conversion of heart, mind, and will. Solidarity must be a conscious choice of people who seek ways of promoting the common good. It will require change in the way our societal and global order has been structured when some people, classes, or nations are dismissed as beyond the bounds of concern.[31] In other words, solidarity lives through justice.

The Meaning of Justice

In our discussion of the virtues in chapter 5, we said that justice is rooted in our social and relational nature. It aids in our living well because justice helps us to realize that we cannot flourish apart from living in right relationship with others. Similarly, a right understanding of justice underscores the connection between our individual good and the common good. Justice teaches us that the well-being of individual and community are interrelated in such a way that what promotes one promotes the other, and what harms one harms the other as well. A person of justice sees the bond that exists among ourselves and every other person and creature, and strives to live in ways that honor and strengthen that bond.

The biblical understanding of justice is essentially fidelity to the demands of relationships. A just society is marked by the fullness of love, compassion, holiness, and peace, each of which is a constitutive characteristic of the reign of God. Moreover, a biblical understanding of justice insists that the justice of a community must be determined in light of its treatment of the powerless in society—the widow, the orphan, the poor, and the stranger in the land. This biblical vision is the goal toward which we strive. To provide guidance on how to move toward the realization of a just society, Catholic social teaching, like much philosophical reflection, distinguishes three dimensions of basic justice: commutative, distributive, and social. These are the minimum levels of mutual care and respect that all persons owe one another in an imperfect world.[32]

Commutative justice pertains to those rights, duties, and obligations that are involved in one-to-one relations. It demands respect for the equal human dignity of all persons in economic transactions, promises, or contracts. For example, if you borrow money from me it is with the understanding that it will be repaid by a certain date. Your obligation to repay the sum under the terms of the agreement is derived from the idea of commutative justice. And in an employment situation, employers are obligated to pay fair wages in exchange for diligent work done by their employers and establish truly humane working conditions.[33] Commutative justice, as all justice, must be a loving respect extended to the other.

Distributive justice is concerned with what the community owes the individual. Distributive justice specifies the claim that all persons have to some share in the goods that are essentially public or social, such as fertility of the earth, domestic and national security, and industrial productivity. None of these goods belongs exclusively to any one class or group, for all members of society contribute, indirectly at least, to the preservation of such goods. So distributive justice establishes the right of all to share in the goods and opportunities of a community. Moreover, as the U.S. bishops state, "Distributive justice requires that allocation of income, wealth, and power in society be evaluated in light of its effects on persons whose basic material needs are unmet."[34]

In Catholic teaching, *social justice* refers to the obligation of all citizens to assist in the creation of patterns of social organization and activity that are essential both for the preservation of the common good and the protection of basic human rights that constitute the common good. In other words, social justice is a political virtue having to do with the way we organize ourselves as a society through the various social institutions we create—the state, legal system, educational system, religious organizations, and the economy. The U.S. bishops include participation as an integral component of social justice. They state that there is a reciprocal obligation between individuals and society. Individuals have an obligation to be active and productive participants in public life and society has a duty to aid in this participation.[35] Solidarity that includes justice and aims toward the achievement of the common good requires participation and collaboration in decision making.

Participation and Collaboration

The common good is a social reality that requires the active participation of all persons. This is particularly important in an interdependent, globalized society. Unless directed by a moral concern that all persons share mutually in the benefits that come from material and social advancement, interdependence can become a negative force of domination and exploitation.[36] A major threat to human dignity is that large segments of the populations of many nations are excluded from active participation in shaping the social, economic, and political structures that affect their lives. This lack of participation results in the more glaring effects of injustice, such as lack of food, housing, education, and jobs.

Collaboration is an integral part of solidarity and necessary to create a just society because it is a process that aims toward consensus in decision making. Forming relationships of mutual trust, respect, and reciprocity through dialogue is one of the most important aspects of collaboration. Only with continued dialogue can there be an opportunity to work together and find solutions. Without dialogue the collaborative effort ceases, reducing or eliminating the possibility for solidarity.

Collaboration and dialogue require the ability to listen to the other in mutual respect. And as a facet of solidarity, collaboration requires listening especially to the voices of poor people and nations. Moreover, there needs to be interreligious dialogue about the visions of the good life held by diverse religious communities. David Hollenbach calls the spirit required for such discourse about the public good "intellectual solidarity—a willingness to take other persons seriously enough to engage them in conversation and debate about what they think makes life worth living, including what they think will make for the good of the polis."[37]

This view of solidarity includes all citizens, thereby reminding Christians that God's grace exists outside church borders. It is a "wider solidarity" shown by Christian concern, neighborly love, and co-stewardship with our fellow citizens. Solidarity, thus understood, enables the Christian community to live out its ecclesial mission in the world to create a just society. And the solidarity of disciples when given expression through good citizenship can focus Christian worship of God on God's only accessible image: men and women of all religions, races, and nationalities.[38]

In sum, a community of disciples can enrich public life by joining in solidarity with other citizens for the common good. Christian disciples can indirectly overcome the trap of privatization by engaging in reasoned dialogue in collaboration with others. As members of a public church with a prophetic stance and a consistent life ethic, discipleship offers a vision of the good life that promotes human and societal well-being.

The human good is discovered and sustained in communities that practice forgiveness, mutual respect, love, and justice. A just community requires that social structures and laws facilitate the participation of all, especially the needs of the poor.

CONCLUSION

There is a vision of human life and society at the core of a life of discipleship. It includes a substantive view of the social good based on the goodness of creation. Even though sin is an inherent part of the created order, creation is fundamentally good. Sin cannot destroy the essentially graced nature of humankind. Furthermore, God called men and women into being for the purpose of "civilizing the earth" and to have dominion over it. This means that we are to be good stewards of the earth, conscious of our responsibility for creation and for its future. Because of the reality of social sin and the obligations of social justice, we are obliged to try to change those laws, institutions, and structures of society that diminish or denigrate humankind and the created order.

Moreover, while Jesus is not remembered for putting forward specific economic policies to reconstruct society in order to make it more just, he did not withdraw from society or encourage his disciples to do so. Rather, Jesus' teaching and conduct indicate considerable involvement in society. Thus, the mission of discipleship is not just about personal calling; it is a communal venture that we share with fellow disciples as well as with people of different beliefs and cultures. Witnessing to God's reign requires disciples to work to better the human situation, to render justice to the poor, and to actively seek to achieve the common good. When this happens, signs of God's presence on this earth are made more visible.

Just as Jesus could not avoid the suffering associated with the cross if he was to be faithful to his mission, neither can his followers avoid the "cost" of discipleship. And as we discussed in chapter 8, the cross of Jesus Christ is a symbol of God's love and compassion for all who suffer. If we are to embrace the cross in this manner, we must be willing to engage the pain and suffering that accompanies love. An essential aspect of the mission of disciples who take up their crosses to follow Jesus, then, will be to enter into compassionate solidarity with all those who suffer violence and poverty in our world.

But, as we know, the cross is not the last word. The resurrection was God's act of new creation and contemporary disciples are called to witness to that reality by living and loving in the present time as signs of that new creation. We are to confront the dehumanizing powers of the world with the power of the Spirit, and to bear fruits of the Spirit in the world. Part of the mission to which we are called as disciples is to embody visibly before the world the reconciliation that God desires for all of creation, and to live the fruits of the Spirit—love, joy, peace, patience, kindness, goodness, faithfulness, gentleness—as testimony to God's continued presence and work in the world.

"To go forth and make disciples of all nations" requires that we acknowledge and appreciate the values and gifts of diverse religious traditions and cultures. Non-Western Christians and non-Christians have much to contribute to our understanding of how concretely to love others, practice justice, and walk humbly with our God. For example, we learned from Latin American liberation theologians that the poor person in need is the privileged expression of God's call to humankind. The call of the poor is a call to conscience that comes primarily from the experience of the presence of Christ in suffering humanity. Thus, the perspectives and experiences of the impoverished, marginalized, and oppressed people of the world need to influence our understanding of the call and mission of discipleship.

An important insight gained from Buddhism is that if we are to become good, our vision has to be rehabilitated in order to see clearly, reverently, and compassionately. It is only when we see rightly and truthfully that we can engage in just and loving actions. For Buddhists, everyone is called to awakening or enlightenment, which is essential if humanity is to recognize and overcome the injustice that contributes to human suffering.

From Islam, we learned about the practice of *zakat* that enables Muslims who practice this virtue to "walk in the straight path." *Zakat* is not simply an act of charity but an obligation of justice and an expression of stewardship. It is based in the conviction that God has blessed the more prosperous members of a community with wealth and resources and that they are entrusted with them to do good. *Zakat* thus leads to a deepening awareness of others and one's responsibilities to them, especially the most vulnerable members of society. In this respect, the *zakat* expresses a principle that is at the heart of all religions: anytime we extend the circle of love by serving our neighbors in need, we give praise and honor to God.

An insight we gained from Sufism is the constitutive relation between spirituality and wisdom. Sufism is characterized by its affirmation of the essentially divine nature of knowledge or wisdom, a gift that a person cannot gain by one's own initiative. The heart is the center of wisdom and the core of discernment. It is the place where one contemplates the depth of things and discovers a more profound knowledge that is beyond the intellectual. The ultimate aim of knowledge is not simply to collect an abundance of data, but to reach the center within, the Sacred or the Spirit. This is where we gain the "tasting knowledge" that is associated with wisdom in the Christian tradition.

It is our hope that we have come to a better understanding of why the call of discipleship is a challenging, perilous, and rewarding adventure. It is a journey that requires an ongoing process of conversion toward the fullness of life and happiness. Discipleship is a vocation to greater and greater realization of the path God calls us to follow. But as the Alchemist pointed out,

> Unfortunately, very few follow the path laid out for them—the path to their Personal Legends, and to happiness. Most people see the world as a threatening place, and because they do, the world turns out, indeed to be a threatening place. . . . Don't give into your fears. . . . The one thing that makes a dream impossible to achieve is the fear of failure.[39]

Disciples go forward in the faith that fears can be overcome, that love conquers all, and that hope burns eternal. While we are called to mission in a world of violence, poverty, and other manifestations of sin, we believe that it is a world filled with the marvels, the glory, and wisdom of God.

KEY POINTS

1. Tensions and ambivalence accompany the missionary task of public discipleship.
2. The challenge for Christian believers of every age is to discern how to live rightly as both faithful disciples and responsible citizens.
3. Engagement in public life is an essential aspect of discipleship.
4. There is a mutually beneficial and enriching relationship between discipleship and citizenship.
5. Disciples can best respond to the missionary task in solidarity with others as part of a public church.

QUESTIONS FOR REFLECTION

1. What is the greatest tension or ambiguity that you experience in trying to live as a faithful disciple and a responsible citizen?
2. What attitudes or concrete actions reflect the Christian community as an "alternative community" in the world? Do you agree or disagree with this stance? Why or why not?
3. Does your experience of public life fit with Parker Palmer's definition? Do you experience a dichotomy between private and public life?
4. Does the concept of a public church support or challenge your understanding of the meaning and role of the Christian community?
5. How do you envision a consistent ethic of life and the virtue of solidarity helping the disciple in the missionary task to "make disciples of all nations"?

SUGGESTIONS FOR FURTHER READING AND STUDY

Brueggemann, Walter. *The Word That Redescribes the World: The Bible and Discipleship.* Minneapolis: Fortress, 2006.

Coleman, John A. "The Two Pedagogies: Discipleship and Citizenship." In *Education for Citizenship and Discipleship.* Edited by Mary C. Boys. New York: Pilgrim, 1989.

———. *An American Strategic Theology.* Ramsey, N.J.: Paulist, 1982.

Himes, Michael J., and Kenneth R. Himes. *Fullness of Faith: The Public Significance of Theology.* Mahwah, N.J.: Paulist, 1993.

Hollenbach, David, S.J. *The Global Face of Public Faith: Politics, Human Rights, and Christian Ethics.* Washington, D.C.: Georgetown University Press, 2003.

Lovin, Robin W. *Christian Faith and Public Choices: The Social Ethics of Barth, Brunner, and Bonhoeffer.* Philadelphia: Fortress, 1984.

Marty, Martin E. *The Public Church.* New York: Crossroad, 1981.

Niebuhr, H. Richard. *Christ and Culture.* New York: Harper, 1956.

Palmer, Parker J. *The Company of Strangers: Christians and the Renewal of America's Public Life.* New York: Crossroad, 1986.

Notes

PREFACE

1. Decree on the Training of Priests, *Optatam totius* 17, in *Vatican Council II: The Conciliar and Post Conciliar Documents*, ed. Austin Flannery, O.P. (Collegeville, Minn.: Liturgical Press, 1975).

1. THE CALL OF DISCIPLESHIP

1. Cotton Mather, *A Christian at His Calling* (Boston: B. Green & Allen, 1701), 38.

2. Paulo Coelho, *The Alchemist*, trans. Alan R. Clarke (New York: HarperSanFrancisco, 1998), 22.

3. Ibid., 78-79, 131.

4. Ibid., 127, 128, 131, 141.

5. Ibid., xii.

6. Biblical references are from *The New Oxford Annotated Bible with the Apocrypha, Revised Standard Version*, ed. Herbert G. May and Bruce M. Metzger (New York: Oxford University Press, 1977).

7. Bernard Haring, *Free and Faithful in Christ: Moral Theology for Clergy and Laity*, vol. 1 (New York: Seabury, 1978), 7.

8. On the prophetic movement, see Abraham J. Heschel, *The Prophets*, vol. 2 (New York: Harper & Row, 1962).

9. James D. G. Dunn, *Jesus Remembered*, vol. 1 (Grand Rapids: Eerdmans, 2003), 540-41.

10. See Frank J. Matera, *New Testament Ethics: The Legacies of Jesus and Paul* (Louisville: Westminster John Knox, 1996).

11. N. T. Wright, *Following Jesus: Biblical Reflections on Discipleship* (Grand Rapids: Eerdmans, 1994), 67-72.

12. Gail R. O'Day, "Surprised by Faith: Jesus and the Canaanite Woman," in *A Feminist Companion to Matthew*, ed. Amy-Jill Levine with Marianne Blickenstaff (Cleveland: Pilgrim, 2001), 124-25.

13. John Meier notes that although the specific term "disciple" is not used of any woman, the reality was otherwise (*A Marginal Jew: Rethinking the Historical Jesus*, vol. 3 [New York: Doubleday, 1994], 374-80).

14. Dorothy Lee, "Abiding in the Fourth Gospel: A Case Study in Feminist Biblical Theology," in *A Feminist Companion to John*, vol. 2, ed. Amy-Jill Levine with Marianne Blickenstaff (Cleveland: Pilgrim, 2003), 64-78.

15. See Paul J. Wadell, *The Primacy of Love: An Introduction to the Ethics of Thomas Aquinas* (New York: Paulist, 1992).

16. Sebastian Moore, *Jesus the Liberator of Desire* (New York: Crossroad, 1989), ix, 17.

17. Ronald Rolheiser, *The Holy Longing: The Search for a Christian Spirituality* (New York: Doubleday, 1999), 196-204.

18. Elizabeth A. Johnson, *She Who Is: The Mystery of God in Feminist Theological Discourse* (New York: Crossroad, 1992), 196.

19. See Peter J. Paris, *Virtues and Values: The African and African American Experience* (Minneapolis: Fortress, 2004), 1-4.

20. Enda McDonagh, *Gift and Call: Towards a Christian Theology of Morality* (St. Meinrad, Ind.: Abbey Press, 1975), 27-29.

21. Ibid., 34-37.

22. On the meaning and role of moral presumptions in moral decision making, see J. Philip Wogaman, *Christian Moral Judgment* (Louisville: Westminster/John Knox, 1989), 59-97.

23. Daniel C. Maguire and A. Nicholas Fargnoli, *On Moral Grounds: The Art/Science of Ethics* (New York: Crossroad, 1991), 19-25.

24. Antonio Moser and Bernardino Leers, *Moral Theology: Dead Ends and Alternatives*, trans. Paul Burns (Maryknoll, NY: Orbis Books, 1990), 131-52.

25. Gustavo Gutiérrez, *We Drink from Our Own Wells: The Spiritual Journey of a People* (Maryknoll, NY: Orbis Books, 1985), 35.

26. Francisco Moreno Rejon, "Fundamental Moral Theology in the Theology of Liberation," in *Mysterium Liberationis: Fundamental Concepts of Liberation Theology*, ed. Ignacio Ellacuría, S.J., and Jon Sobrino, S.J. (Maryknoll, NY: Orbis Books, 1993), 214-15.

27. Avery Dulles, S.J., *Models of the Church*, rev. ed. (New York: Image Books, 2002), 195-217. Dulles maintains that in light of scripture and Catholic tradition, especially in the perspectives of Vatican II, the institutional model should not be primary.

28. Elisabeth Schüssler Fiorenza, *In Memory of Her* (New York: Crossroad, 1983), esp. 213.

29. See Peter C. Phan, "Doing Theology in the Context of Cultural and Religious Pluralism: An Asian Perspective," *Louvain Studies* 27 (2002): 51-52.

30. H. Richard Niebuhr, *The Responsible Self: An Essay in Christian Moral Philosophy* (New York: Harper & Row, 1963), 86.

2. THE CHRISTIAN MORAL LIFE AND LEARNING TO SEE

1. Brian Friel, *Molly Sweeney* (New York: Penguin Books, 1995), act 1, pp. 6, 10.

2. Ibid., act 2, pp. 55-56.

3. Iris Murdoch, "The Idea of Perfection," in *The Sovereignty of Good* (London: Routledge & Kegan Paul, 1970), 37.

4. Martha C. Nussbaum, *Love's Knowledge: Essays on Philosophy and Literature* (New York: Oxford University Press, 1990), 163.

5. Robert Ellsberg, *The Saints' Guide to Happiness* (New York: North Point Press, 2003), 169.

6. Ibid., 171.

7. Arthur Sutherland, *I Was a Stranger: A Christian Theology of Hospitality* (Nashville: Abingdon Press, 2006), 78.

8. Ibid., 79.

9. Stanley Hauerwas, *Vision and Virtue: Essays in Christian Ethical Reflection* (Notre Dame, Ind.: Fides, 1974), 32.

10. Christopher Steck, *The Ethical Thought of Hans Urs von Balthasar* (New York: Crossroad, 2001), 124.

11. Hauerwas, *Vision and Virtue*, 33.

12. Iris Murdoch, "On 'God' and 'Good,'" in *Sovereignty of Good*, 59, 67.

13. Ibid., 52.

14. Iris Murdoch, *Metaphysics as a Guide to Morals* (New York: Penguin, 1992), 322.

15. William C. Spohn, *Go and Do Likewise: Jesus and Ethics* (New York: Continuum, 1999), 100.

16. Robert E. Webber and Rodney Clapp, *People of the Truth: A Christian Challenge to Contemporary Culture* (Harrisburg, Pa.: Morehouse, 1988), 23-24.

17. Steck, *Ethical Thought*, 126.

18. Frederick Franck, *To Be Human against All Odds* (Berkeley, Calif.: Asian Humanities Press, 1991), 150.

19. Paul J. Wadell, *Friendship and the Moral Life* (Notre Dame, Ind.: University of Notre Dame Press, 1989), 145.

20. Thomas W. Ogletree, *Hospitality to the Stranger: Dimensions of Moral Understanding* (Philadelphia: Fortress, 1985), 45.

21. Murdoch, *Metaphysics*, 331.

22. Murdoch, "The Sovereignty of Good over Other Concepts," in *Sovereignty of Good*, 93.

23. Murdoch, *Metaphysics*, 321.

24. Spohn, *Go and Do Likewise*, 56.

25. Murdoch, *Metaphysics*, 322.

26. Scott Bader-Saye, *Following Jesus in a Culture of Fear* (Grand Rapids: Brazos, 2007), 15.

27. Ibid., 16, 25.

28. Ibid., 28.

29. Ibid., 29.

30. John F. Kavanaugh, *Following Christ in a Consumer Society: The Spirituality of Cultural Resistance*, rev. ed. (Maryknoll, N.Y.: Orbis Books, 1992), 37.

31. Paul J. Wadell, *Becoming Friends: Worship, Justice, and the Practice of Christian Friendship* (Grand Rapids: Brazos, 2002), 47.

32. Mitch Albom, *Tuesdays with Morrie* (New York: Doubleday, 1997), 123-25.

33. Ibid., 125.

34. Kavanaugh, *Following Christ*, 18-19.

35. Murdoch, "On 'God' and 'Good,'" 56.

36. Franck, *To Be Human*, 61.

37. Thich Nhat Hanh, *Being Peace* (Berkeley, Calif.: Parallax, 1987), 65.

38. Franck, *To Be Human*, 144.

39. Hanh, *Being Peace*, 13, 14-15.

40. Leo D. Lefebure, *The Buddha and the Christ: Explorations in Buddhist and Christian Dialogue* (Maryknoll, N.Y.: Orbis Books, 1993), 36.

41. Franck, *To Be Human*, 79, 81.

42. Lefebure, *The Buddha and the Christ*, 35, 36.

43. Franck, *To Be Human*, 61

44. Steck, *Ethical Thought*, 142.

45. Ibid., 125.

46. Murdoch, "On 'God' and 'Good,'" 66.

47. Wadell, *Becoming Friends*, 127.

48. Thomas Merton, *Conjectures of a Guilty Bystander* (Garden City, N.Y.: Doubleday, 1966), 140.

49. Ibid., 141, 142.

50. Ibid

51. Steck, *Ethical Thought*, 147, 148.

52. Stephen Crites, "The Narrative Quality of Experience," in *Why Narrative? Readings in Narrative Theology*, ed. Stanley Hauerwas and L. Gregory Jones (Grand Rapids: Eerdmans, 1989), 70.

53. H. Richard Niebuhr, *The Meaning of Revelation* (New York: Macmillan, 1941), 69.

54. Ibid, 75.

55. Spohn, *Go and Do Likewise*, 67.

56. On this point see Paul J. Wadell, "What Do All Those Masses Do for Us? Reflections on the Christian Moral Life and the Eucharist," in *Living No Longer for Ourselves: Liturgy and Justice in the Nineties*, ed. Kathleen Hughes, R.S.C.J., and Mark R. Francis, C.S.V. (Collegeville, Minn.: Liturgical Press, 1991), 159.

57. George Lindbeck, *The Nature of Doctrine: Religion and Theology in a Postliberal Age* (Philadelphia: Westminster, 1984), 117.

58. Richard B. Hays, *The Moral Vision of the New Testament: A Contemporary Introduction to New Testament Ethics* (New York: HarperCollins, 1996), 76.

59. Ibid., 77.

60. Sallie McFague, "Conversion: Life on the Edge of the Raft," *Interpretation* 32, no. 3 (1978): 256.

61. Spohn, *Go and Do Likewise*, 104.

62. McFague, *Conversion*, 258.

63. Spohn, *Go and Do Likewise*, 103.

64. Ibid., 104.

65. Ibid., 105, 106.

66. William C. Spohn, *What Are They Saying about Scripture and Ethics?* (New York: Paulist, 1995), 90.

67. Allen Verhey, *Remembering Jesus: Christian Community, Scripture, and the Moral Life* (Grand Rapids: Eerdmans, 2002), 270.

68. Ibid., 271.

69. Ibid., 274.

70. Spohn, *Go and Do Likewise*, 89.

71. Ibid.

72. Ibid.

73. Ibid., 87.

74. Donald Senior, *Jesus: A Gospel Portrait*, rev. and exp. ed. (New York: Paulist, 1992), 63.

75. Elizabeth A. Johnson, *Consider Jesus: Waves of Renewal in Christology* (New York: Crossroad, 1990), 55.

76. William C. Placher, *Narratives of a Vulnerable God: Christ, Theology, and Scripture* (Louisville: Westminster John Knox, 1994), 145.

77. Elizabeth A. Johnson, *She Who Is: The Mystery of God in Feminist Theological Discourse* (New York: Crossroad, 1992), 151.

78. Ibid., 153.

79. Johnson, *Consider Jesus*, 111-12.

80. Johnson, *She Who Is*, 95.

81. Ibid.

82. Johnson, *Consider Jesus*, 112.

83. Johnson, *She Who Is*, 99.

84. Peter C. Phan, *Christianity with an Asian Face: Asian American Theology in the Making* (Maryknoll, N.Y.: Orbis Books, 2003), 117.

85. Ibid., 131, 137-39.

3. THE TREASURE WE SEEK—
THE REIGN OF GOD AND THE MORAL LIFE

1. The film *Kingdom of Heaven* is available on DVD (2005).
2. The Greek word *basileia* is sometimes translated as "kingdom," "reign," "rule," "sovereignty," or "presence." Since the "kingdom of God" is a rich symbol, not a clear concept, it cannot be exhaustively defined. See Norman Perrin, *Jesus and the Language of the Kingdom: Symbol and Metaphor in the New Testament Interpretation* (Philadelphia: Fortress, 1976), 54.
3. Rudolf Schnackenburg, *God's Rule and Kingdom*, trans. John Murray (Montreal: Palm, 1963), 18-35.
4. John Fuellenbach, *The Kingdom of God: The Message of Jesus Today* (Maryknoll, N.Y.: Orbis Books, 2002), 94.
5. Ibid., 82-93.
6. Schnackenburg, *God's Rule and Kingdom*, 85-86.
7. Fuellenbach, *Kingdom of God*, 98.
8. Joachim Jeremias, *Rediscovering the Parables* (New York: Charles Scribner's Sons, 1966), 119, 120.
9. Ibid., 47.
10. John R. Donahue, S.J., "The 'Parable' of the Sheep and the Goats: A Challenge to Christian Ethics," *Theological Studies* 47 (1986): 24-31.
11. Fuellenbach, *Kingdom of God*, 96.
12. See Carl E. Braaten, *Eschatology and Ethics: Essays on the Theology and Ethics of the Kingdom of God* (Minneapolis: Augsburg, 1974), 105-22.
13. Frank J. Matera, *New Testament Ethics: The Legacies of Jesus and Paul* (Louisville: Westminster John Knox, 1996), 44-50.
14. Schnackenburg, *God's Rule and the Kingdom*, 105-7.
15. Daniel Harrington, S.J., and James Keenan, S.J., *Jesus and Virtue Ethics: Building Bridges between New Testament Studies and Moral Theology* (Lanham, Md.: Sheed & Ward, 2002), 62-63.
16. Benedict T. Viviano, O.P., "The Gospel according to Matthew," in *The New Jerome Biblical Commentary*, ed. Raymond E. Brown, S.S., Joseph A. Fitzmyer, S.J., Roland E. Murphy, O.Carm. (Englewood Cliffs, N.J.: Prentice Hall, 1990), 640.
17. Richard M. Gula, S.S., *The Good Life: Where Morality and Spirituality Converge* (New York: Paulist, 1999), 102-5.
18. Matera, *New Testament Ethics*, 44-45.
19. Ibid., 46-47.
20. Lisa Sowle Cahill, *Love Your Enemies: Discipleship, Pacifism, and Just War Theory* (Minneapolis: Fortress, 1994), 29-31 at 29.
21. L. Gregory Jones, *Embodying Forgiveness: A Theological Analysis* (Grand Rapids: Eerdmans, 1995), 164.
22. Cahill, *Love Your Enemies*, 34-35.
23. Glen H. Stassen and David P. Gushee, *Kingdom Ethics: Following Jesus in Contemporary Context* (Downers Grove, Ill.: InterVarsity, 2003), 126-27.
24. Dietrich Bonhoeffer, *The Cost of Discipleship* (New York: Macmillan, 1963), 105-17.
25. Kenneth Morris, *Bonhoeffer's Ethic of Discipleship* (University Park: Pennsylvania State Press, 1955), 7.
26. Quoted in Stassen and Gushee, *Kingdom Ethics*, 126.
27. Daniel C. Maguire, *The Moral Core of Judaism and Christianity* (Minneapolis: Fortress, 1993), 50.

28. Josef Pieper, *Hope*, trans. Mary Frances McCarthy, S.N.D. (San Francisco: Ignatius, 1986), 27.

29. Anthony Kelly, *Eschatology and Hope* (Maryknoll, N.Y.: Orbis Books, 2006), 5-6.

30. Ibid., 17-18.

31. Quoted in *Once upon a Time in Asia: Stories of Harmony and Peace*, compiled by James H. Kroeger and Eugene F. Thalman (Maryknoll, N.Y.: Orbis Books, 2006), 25.

32. Chung Hyun Kyung, *Struggle to Be the Sun Again: Introducing Asian Women's Theology* (Maryknoll, N.Y.: Orbis Books, 2004), 23, 42, 101.

33. Quoted in C. S. Song, *Tell Us Our Names: Story Theology from an Asian Perspective* (Maryknoll, NY: Orbis Books), 40.

34. See David Tracy, *The Analogical Imagination: Christian Theology and the Culture of Pluralism* (New York: Crossroad, 1981), 386.

35. William C. Spohn, *Go and Do Likewise: Jesus and Ethics* (New York: Continuum, 1999), 50.

36. Ibid., 54-67.

37. Ibid., 59-60.

38. See Gustavo Gutiérrez, *God of Life*, trans. Matthew J. O'Connell. (Maryknoll, N.Y.: Orbis Books, 1991).

39. Jürgen Moltmann, *God for a Secular Society: The Public Relevance of Theology* (Minneapolis: Fortress, 1999), 135-52.

40. Ibid., 140

41. Ibid., 142.

42. Thomas W. Ogletree, *Hospitality to the Stranger: Dimensions of Moral Understanding* (Philadelphia: Fortress, 1985), 2.

43. Ibid., 4.

44. Moltmann, *God for a Secular Society*, 145-46.

4. STARTING OVER AGAIN AND AGAIN

1. Heather King, *Redeemed: A Spiritual Misfit Stumbles toward God, Marginal Sanity, and the Peace That Passes All Understanding* (New York: Viking, 2008), 2.

2. Ibid., 172.

3. Ibid., 2.

4. Ibid., 3, 215.

5. Ibid., 1, 172.

6. Ibid., 5.

7. Herbert McCabe, O.P., *God, Christ and Us*, ed. Brian Davies, O.P. (New York: Continuum, 2003), 29.

8. Ibid., 63.

9. Servais Pinckaers, O.P., *The Sources of Christian Ethics*, trans. Sr. Mary Thomas Noble, O.P. (Washington, D.C.: Catholic University of America Press, 1995), 41.

10. James T. Bretzke, *A Morally Complex Word: Engaging Contemporary Moral Theology* (Collegeville, Minn.: Liturgical Press, 2004), 198.

11. Vincent MacNamara, *Love, Law and Christian Life: Basic Attitudes of Christian Morality* (Wilmington, Del.: Michael Glazier, 1988), 183.

12. William C. Mattison III, *Introducing Moral Theology: True Happiness and the Virtues* (Grand Rapids: Brazos, 2008), 247.

13. Richard M. Gula, S.S., *Reason Informed by Faith: Foundations of Catholic Morality* (New York: Paulist, 1989), 91.

14. Ibid.

15. McCabe, *God, Christ and Us*, 63

16. Bernard Haring, *Free and Faithful in Christ: Moral Theology for Clergy and Laity*, vol. 1 (New York: Seabury, 1978), 386.

17. Gula, *Reason Informed by Faith*, 101.

18. Daniel Harrington, S.J., and James Keenan, S.J., *Jesus and Virtue Ethics: Building Bridges between New Testament Studies and Moral Theology* (Lanham, Md.: Sheed & Ward, 2002), 92.

19. Russell B. Connors, Jr., and Patrick T. McCormick, *Character, Choices and Community: The Three Faces of Christian Ethics* (New York: Paulist, 1998), 206.

20. Kevin F. O'Shea, C.SS.R., "The Reality of Sin: A Theological and Pastoral Critique," in *The Mystery of Sin and Forgiveness*, ed. Michael J. Taylor, S.J. (New York: Alba House, 1971), 95.

21. Ismael Garcia, *Dignidad: Ethics through Hispanic Eyes* (Nashville: Abingdon, 1997), 139, 140.

22. Mattison, *Introducing Moral Theology*, 235.

23. McCabe, *God, Christ and Us*, 30.

24. Josef Pieper, *The Concept of Sin*, trans. Edward T. Oakes, S.J. (South Bend, Ind.: St. Augustine's Press, 2001), 33.

25. Michael J. Himes, *Doing the Truth in Love: Conversations about God, Relationships and Service* (New York: Paulist, 1995), 69.

26. Connors and McCormick, *Character, Choices and Community*, 205.

27. Haring, *Free and Faithful in Christ*, 1:391.

28. Himes, *Doing the Truth in Love*, 69.

29. Pieper, *Concept of Sin*, 38.

30. Gula, *Reason Informed by Faith*, 101.

31. Peter J. Henriot, "Social Sin and Conversion: A Theology of the Church's Social Involvement," in *Conversion: Perspectives on Personal and Social Transformation*, ed. Walter E. Conn (New York: Alba House, 1978), 318.

32. Thomas P. Rausch, *Catholicism at the Dawn of the Third Millennium* (Collegeville, Minn.: Liturgical Press, 1996), 129.

33. Garcia, *Dignidad*, 138.

34. Gregory Baum, "Critical Theology," in *Conversion: Perspectives on Personal and Social Transformation*, 288.

35. Kenneth R. Melchin, *Living with Other People: An Introduction to Christian Ethics Based on Bernard Lonergan* (Collegeville, Minn.: Liturgical Press, 1998), 94.

36. Rausch, *Catholicism at the Dawn of the Third Millennium*, 129.

37. Connors and McCormick, *Character, Choices and Community*, 220.

38. Mattison, *Introducing Moral Theology*, 242.

39. MacNamara, *Love, Law and Christian Life*, 178.

40. Gula, *Reason Informed by Faith*, 115.

41. Haring, *Free and Faithful in Christ*, 1:213.

42. Mattison, *Introducing Moral Theology*, 242.

43. MacNamara, *Love, Law and Christian Life*, 177.

44. Haring, *Free and Faithful in Christ*, 1:215.

45. Connors and McCormick, *Character, Choices and Community*, 217-18.

46. Ibid., 215.

47. Gula, *Reason Informed by Faith*, 111.

48. Thomas R. Kopfensteiner, "The Theory of the Fundamental Option and Moral Action," in *Christian Ethics: An Introduction*, ed. Bernard Hoose (Collegeville, Minn.: Liturgical Press, 1998), 128.

49. Thomas Aquinas, *Summa Theologiae* (New York: McGraw-Hill, 1969), I-II, 78,2.

50. Ted Peters, *Sin: Radical Evil in Soul and Society* (Grand Rapids: Eerdmans, 1994), 31.

51. Aquinas, *ST*, I-II, 82,1.

52. Gilbert C. Meilaender, *Faith and Faithfulness: Basic Themes in Christian Ethics* (Notre Dame, Ind.: University of Notre Dame Press, 1991), 67.

53. John E. Smith, "The Concept of Conversion," in *Conversion: Perspectives on Personal and Social Transformation*, 51.

54. Wayne E. Oates, "Conversion: Sacred and Secular," in *Conversion: Perspectives on Personal and Social Transformation*, 150.

55. Bernard J. F. Lonergan, S.J., "Theology in Its New Context," in *A Second Collection*, ed. William F. J. Ryan, S.J., and Bernard J. Tyrrell, S.J. (Philadelphia: Westminster, 1974), 66.

56. William James, "The Divided Self and Conversion," in *Conversion: Perspectives on Personal and Social Transformation*, 125.

57. Smith, "Concept of Conversion," 54, 56.

58. Melchin, *Living with Other People*, 27-28.

59. Ibid., 28, 90.

60. John C. Haughey, S.J., *Should Anyone Say Forever? On Making, Keeping, and Breaking Commitments* (Chicago: Loyola University Press, 1975), 44.

61. Karl Barth, "The Awakening to Conversion," in *Conversion: Perspectives on Personal and Social Transformation*, 35, 36.

62. Ibid., 49.

63. Oates, "Conversion: Sacred and Secular," 152.

64. Each of these descriptions occurs in Book III of *The Confessions*. See Augustine, *The Confessions*, trans. Maria Boulding, O.S.B. (Hyde Park, N.Y.: New City, 1997).

65. Ibid., VIII, xxix.

66. Jacques Pasquier, "Experience and Conversion," in *Conversion: Perspectives on Personal and Social Transformation*, 191.

67. Sallie McFague, "Conversion: Life on the Edge of the Raft," *Interpretation* 32, no. 3 (1978): 260.

68. Connors and McCormick, *Character, Choices and Community*, 238.

69. Bernard J. F. Lonergan, S.J., "Natural Knowledge of God," in *A Second Collection*, 129.

70. Bernard J. F. Lonergan, S.J., "The Response of the Jesuit as Priest and Apostle in the Modern World," in *A Second Collection*, 170.

71. Ibid., 167.

72. Ibid., 168.

73. Ibid., 171, 172.

74. McFague, "Conversion," 256.

75. Leo D. Lefebure, *The Buddha and the Christ: Explorations in Buddhist and Christian Dialogue* (Maryknoll, N.Y.: Orbis Books, 1993), 35.

76. Ibid., 36.

77. Walpola Rahula, *What the Buddha Taught*, rev. and expanded ed. (New York: Grove, 1974), 45.

78. John L. Esposito, *Islam: The Straight Path*, rev. 3rd ed. (New York: Oxford University Press, 2005), 27, 88-91.

79. Peter C. Phan, *In Our Own Tongues: Perspectives from Asia on Mission and Inculturation* (Maryknoll, N.Y.: Orbis Books, 2003), 47.

80. Mattison, *Introducing Moral Theology*, 218.

81. Josef Pieper, *Faith, Hope, Love*, trans. Sr. Mary Frances McCarthy, S.N.D., Richard Winston, and Clara Winston (San Francisco: Ignatius, 1997), 25-28, 51-52.

82. Ibid., 29, 30.

83. Ibid., 40.

84. Ibid., 56.

85. Haring, *Free and Faithful in Christ*, 1:419.

86. Gustavo Gutiérrez, "A Spirituality of Liberation," in *Conversion: Perspectives on Personal and Social Transformation*, 309.

87. Phan, *In Our Own Tongues*, 49.

88. Haring, *Free and Faithful in Christ*, 1:420.

89. Garcia, *Dignidad*, 152.

90. Haring, *Free and Faithful in Christ*, 1:428.

5. THE VIRTUES—HOW TO BE GOOD AT BEING HUMAN

1. Herbert McCabe, O.P., *The Good Life: Ethics and the Pursuit of Happiness*, ed. Brian Davies, O.P. (New York: Continuum, 2005), 9.

2. Raymond J. Devettere, *Introduction to Virtue Ethics: Insights of the Ancient Greeks* (Washington, D.C.: Georgetown University Press, 2002), 37.

3. Ibid.

4. Jean Porter, *The Recovery of Virtue: The Relevance of Aquinas for Christian Ethics* (Louisville: Westminster/John Knox, 1990), 37.

5. Joseph J. Kotva, Jr., *The Christian Case for Virtue Ethics* (Washington, D.C.: Georgetown University Press, 1996), 38.

6. Ibid.

7. Devettere, *Introduction to Virtue Ethics*, 35.

8. Ibid., 43.

9. David Cloutier, "Human Fulfillment," in *Gathered for the Journey: Moral Theology in Catholic Perspective*, ed. David Matzko McCarthy and M. Therese Lysaught (Grand Rapids: Eerdmans, 2007), 136.

10. Porter, *Recovery of Virtue*, 86.

11. Ibid., 78.

12. Kotva, *Christian Case for Virtue Ethics*, 22.

13. Jean Porter, *Nature as Reason: A Thomistic Theory of the Natural Law* (Grand Rapids: Eerdmans, 2005), 160.

14. Diana Fritz Cates, *Choosing to Feel: Virtue, Friendship, and Compassion for Friends* (Notre Dame, Ind.: University of Notre Dame Press, 1997), 16.

15. Stanley Hauerwas and Charles Pinches, *Christians among the Virtues: Theological Conversations with Ancient and Modern Ethics* (Notre Dame, Ind.: University of Notre Dame Press, 1997), 13.

16. Porter, *Nature as Reason*, 154.

17. Ibid., 155.

18. Porter, *Nature as Reason*, 171.

19. Russell B. Connors, Jr., and Patrick T. McCormick, *Character, Choices and Community: The Three Faces of Christian Ethics* (New York: Paulist, 1998), 25.

20. William C. Mattison III, "Moral Virtue, the Grace of God, and Discipleship," in *Gathered for the Journey: Moral Theology in Catholic Perspective*, ed. David Matzko McCarthy and M. Therese Lysaught (Grand Rapids: Eerdmans, 2007), 199.

21. Livio Melina, *Sharing in Christ's Virtues: For a Renewal of Moral Theology in Light of Veritatis Splendor*, trans. William E. May (Washington, D.C.: Catholic University of America Press, 2001), 42.

22. Kotva, *Christian Case for Virtue Ethics*, 30.

23. Ibid., 24.

24. Mattison, "Moral Virtue," 200.

25. Gilbert C. Meilaender, *The Theory and Practice of Virtue* (Notre Dame, Ind.: University of Notre Dame Press, 1984), 9.

26. Lee H. Yearley, *Mencius and Aquinas: Theories of Virtue and Conceptions of Courage* (Albany: State University of New York Press, 1990), 68.

27. Connors and McCormick, *Character, Choices and Community*, 25.

28. Kotva, *Christian Case for Virtue Ethics*, 23.

29. Meilaender, *Theory and Practice of Virtue*, 11.

30. Melina, *Sharing in Christ's Virtues*, 51.

31. Meilaender, *Theory and Practice of Virtue*, 9.

32. Yearley, *Mencius and Aquinas*, 107.

33. Paul J. Wadell, *The Primacy of Love: An Introduction to the Ethics of Thomas Aquinas* (New York: Paulist, 1992), 116.

34. Ibid.

35. Thomas Aquinas, *Summa Theologiae* (New York: McGraw-Hill, 1964), I-II, 51,3.

36. Connors and McCormick, *Character, Choices and Community*, 25.

37. John Casey, *Pagan Virtue: An Essay in Ethics* (Oxford: Clarendon, 1990), 107.

38. Wadell, *Primacy of Love*, 118-19.

39. Kotva, *Christian Case for Virtue Ethics*, 6.

40. Thich Nhat Hanh, *Living Buddha, Living Christ* (New York: Riverhead, 1995), 63-65.

41. Alasdair MacIntyre, *Dependent Rational Animals: Why Human Beings Need the Virtues* (Chicago: Open Court, 1999), 108.

42. Nancy Sherman, *The Fabric of Character: Aristotle's Theory of Virtue* (Oxford: Clarendon Press, 1989), 127.

43. Paul J. Wadell, *Friendship and the Moral Life* (Notre Dame, Ind.: University of Notre Dame Press, 1989), 64-66.

44. MacIntyre, *Dependent Rational Animals*, 96-97.

45. Hauerwas and Pinches, *Christians among the Virtues*, 36.

46. Josef Pieper, *The Four Cardinal Virtues*, trans. Richard Winston, Clara Winston, Lawrence E. Lynch, and Daniel F. Coogan (Notre Dame, Ind.: University of Notre Dame Press, 1966), 6.

47. Casey, *Pagan Virtue*, 160.

48. Aquinas, *ST*, I-II, 57,5.

49. Casey, *Pagan Virtue*, 146.

50. Kotva, *Christian Case for Virtue Ethics*, 32-33.

51. Cates, *Choosing to Feel*, 15.

52. Pieper, *Four Cardinal Virtues*, 7.

53. Porter, *Recovery of Virtue*, 163.

54. Aquinas, *ST*, II-II, 47,2.

55. Ibid., I-II, 57,4.

56. Porter, *Nature as Reason*, 209-10.

57. Porter, *Recovery of Virtue*, 127.

58. Pope John XXIII, *Mater et Magistra* (Christianity and Social Progress), in *Catholic Social Thought: The Documentary Heritage*, ed. David J. O'Brien and Thomas A. Shannon (Maryknoll, N.Y.: Orbis Books, 192), #157.

59. Aquinas, *ST*, II-II, 58,1.

60. MacIntyre, *Dependent Rational Animals*, 121-22.

61. Ibid., 145.

62. Ibid.

63. Ibid., 146.

64. Aquinas, *ST*, II-II, 141,2.

65. For a superb account of temperance, see William C. Mattison III, *Introducing Moral Theology: True Happiness and the Virtues* (Grand Rapids: Brazos, 2008), 75-94.

66. Casey, *Pagan Virtue*, 104.

67. Ibid., 136.

68. Aquinas, *ST*, II-II, 142,4.

69. Ibid., II-II, 144,1.

70. Ibid., II-II, 145,1.

71. Casey, *Pagan Virtue*, 54.

72. Aquinas, *ST*, I-II, 61,2.

73. Yearley, *Mencius and Aquinas*, 136-37.

74. Ibid., 36, 38, 39.

75. Ibid., 36-37.

76. Ibid., 37, 41.

77. Ibid., 37, 38, 41.

78. Ibid., 37.

79. Walpola Rahula, *What the Buddha Taught*, rev. and expanded ed. (New York: Grove, 1974), 46-47; quotations from 47.

80. Ibid.

81. Hanh, *Living Buddha, Living Christ*, 90-105.

82. Therese Lysaught, "Love and Liturgy," in *Gathered for the Journey*, 27.

83. Mattison, "Moral Virtue," 207.

84. Ibid., 200. For a fuller account of the theological virtues, see Mattison, *Introducing Moral Theology*.

85. Cates, *Choosing to Feel*, 32.

86. Ibid.

87. Mattison, "Moral Virtue," 201.

88. Cates, *Choosing to Feel*, 32-34.

89. Ibid., 34.

90. Aquinas, *ST*, II-II, 23,1.

91. Porter, *Recovery of Virtue*, 170.

92. Cates, *Choosing to Feel*, 36.

93. Porter, *Recovery of Virtue*, 169.

94. Wadell, *Primacy of Love*, 127.

95. Aquinas, *ST*, II-II, 47,13.

96. Mattison, "Moral Virtue," 210.

97. Ibid., 210, 211.

98. Ibid., 210.

99. Michael R. Miller, "Freedom and Grace," in *Gathered for the Journey*, 178.

100. Cates, *Choosing to Feel*, 40.

101. Frederick Christian Bauerschmidt, "The Trinity," in *Gathered for the Journey*, 83.

102. Ibid.

103. Ibid., 85.

6. CONSCIENCE—EXPLORING A GIFT TOO PRECIOUS TO LOSE

1. Robert Bolt, *A Man for All Seasons* (New York: Vintage Books, 1990), act 1, pp. 19, 22.

2. Antonio Moser and Bernardino Leers, *Moral Theology: Dead Ends and Alternatives*, trans. Paul Burns (Maryknoll, N.Y.: Orbis Books, 1990), 19.

3. Sean Fagan, S.M., *Does Morality Change?* (Dublin: Gill & Macmillan, 1997), 106.

4. Ibid., 90.

5. Moser and Leers, *Moral Theology*, 18.

6. Charles E. Curran, *The Catholic Moral Tradition Today: A Synthesis* (Washington, D.C.: Georgetown University Press, 1999), 174.

7. James P. Hanigan, *As I Have Loved You: The Challenge of Christian Ethics* (New York: Paulist, 1986), 127.

8. "Pastoral Constitution on the Church in the Modern World" (*Gaudium et spes*), in *The Basic Sixteen Documents of Vatican Council II*, ed. Austin Flannery, O.P. (Northport, N.Y.: Costello, 1996), 16.

9. Bernard Haring, *Free and Faithful in Christ: Moral Theology for Clergy and Laity*, vol. 1, *General Moral Theology* (New York: Seabury, 1978), 226.

10. Curran, *Catholic Moral Tradition Today*, 175.

11. Haring, *Free and Faithful in Christ*, 1:227.

12. Ibid., 1:234.

13. Ibid., 1:230.

14. John Mahoney, *The Making of Moral Theology: A Study of the Roman Catholic Tradition* (Oxford: Clarendon, 1987), 188.

15. Haring, *Free and Faithful in Christ*, 1:230.

16. Mahoney, *Making of Moral Theology*, 188.

17. Curran, *Catholic Moral Tradition Today*, 151. Aquinas makes this point in his *Summa Theologiae*, I-II, 94, 4.

18. James F. Keenan, S.J., *Moral Wisdom: Lessons and Texts from the Catholic Tradition* (Lanham, Md.: Rowman & Littlefield, 2004), 38.

19. Cited in James T. Bretzke, *A Morally Complex World: Engaging Contemporary Moral Theology* (Collegeville, Minn.: Liturgical Press, 2004), 122. Pope John Paul II made this point in his 1993 encyclical *Veritatis splendor*, #63.

20. Bretzke, *Morally Complex World*, 118.

21. Mahoney, *Making of Moral Theology*, 192.

22. Keenan, *Moral Wisdom*, 41. For a much more extensive analysis of this point see idem, *Goodness and Rightness in Thomas Aquinas's Summa Theologiae* (Washington, D.C.: Georgetown University Press, 1992).

23. Dennis J. Billy and James F. Keating, *Conscience and Prayer: The Spirit of Catholic Moral Theology* (Collegeville, Minn.: Liturgical Press, 2001), 12.

24. Timothy E. O'Connell, *Principles for a Catholic Morality* (New York: Seabury Press, 1978), 89.

25. Bretzke, *Morally Complex World*, 124.

26. Ibid., 125.

27. Josef Fuchs, S.J., "Conscience and Conscientious Fidelity," in *Moral Theology: Challenges for the Future*, ed. Charles E. Curran (New York: Paulist, 1990), 111.

28. Bretzke, *Morally Complex World*, 125.

29. Ibid., 131.

30. Fuchs, "Conscience," 116.

31. Bretzke, 126, 130.

32. Richard M. Gula, "Conscience," in *Christian Ethics: An Introduction*, ed. Bernard Hoose (Collegeville, Minn.: Liturgical Press, 1998), 114.

33. Vincent MacNamara, *Love, Law and Christian Life: Basic Attitudes of Christian Morality* (Wilmington, Del.: Michael Glazier, 1988), 154.

34. Paul J. Wadell, *Happiness and the Christian Moral Life: An Introduction to Christian Ethics* (Lanham, MD: Rowman & Littlefield, 2008), 169.

35. Sidney Cornelia Callahan, *In Good Conscience: Reason and Emotion in Moral Decision Making* (New York: HarperCollins, 1991), 14.

36. Anne E. Patrick, *Liberating Conscience: Feminist Explorations in Catholic Moral Theology* (New York: Continuum, 1997), 16.

37. Hanigan, *As I Have Loved You*, 129.

38. Patrick, *Liberating Conscience*, 36.

39. Ibid.

40. Haring, *Free and Faithful in Christ*, 1:265-66.

41. Ibid., 282.

42. Enrique Dussel, *Ethics and Community*, trans. Robert R. Barr (Maryknoll, N.Y.: Orbis Books, 1988), 33.

43. Bretzke, *Morally Complex World*, 136-37.

44. Mark Twain, *The Adventures of Huckleberry Finn* (New York: Bantam, 1981), 85. For an analysis of some of the moral dimensions of *Huckleberry Finn*, see Paul J. Wadell, "Huckleberry Finn: An Adventure in Unconventional Morality," *New Theology Review* 2 (1989): 66-80.

45. Alan Donagan, *The Theory of Morality* (Chicago: University of Chicago Press, 1977), 140.

46. Ibid., 139.

47. Wadell, "Huckleberry Finn," 78.

48. Gustavo Gutiérrez, *A Theology of Liberation*, trans. Sr. Caridad Inda and John Eagleson (Maryknoll, N.Y.: Orbis Books, 1973), 91, 113.

49. Moser and Leers, *Moral Theology*, 113.

50. Wadell, *Happiness*, 238.

51. Vincent Cosmao, *Changing the World: An Agenda for the Churches*, trans. John Drury (Maryknoll, N.Y.: Orbis Books, 1984), 24.

52. MacNamara, *Love*, 156.

53. Gula, "Conscience," 115.

54. Wadell, *Happiness*, 174.

55. Callahan, *In Good Conscience*, 198.

56. Gula, "Conscience," 121.

57. Keenan, *Moral Wisdom*, 35.

58. Hanigan, *As I Have Loved You*, 140.

59. Bretzke, *Morally Complex World*, 141.

60. Thomas W. Ogletree, *Hospitality to the Stranger: Dimensions of Moral Understanding* (Philadelphia: Fortress, 1985), 35.

61. Patrick, *Liberating Conscience*, 197.

62. Dussel, *Ethics and Community*, 38-39.

63. Billy and Keating, *Conscience and Prayer*, 3.

64. Ibid., 34.

65. Ibid., 45.

66. "The Church in the Modern World," 16.

67. Billy and Keating, *Conscience and Prayer*, 59.

68. Ibid., 62.

69. Tissa Balasuriya, "The Eucharist in Contemporary Society," in *Liberation Theology: An Introductory Reader*, ed. Curt Cadorette, Marie Giblin, Marilyn J. Legge, and Mary Hembrow Snyder (Maryknoll, N.Y.: Orbis Books, 1992), 260.

70. Ibid., 259.

71. Fuchs, "Conscience," 118.

72. Ibid., 119.

73. Ibid., 120.

74. Patrick, *Liberating Conscience*, 184.

75. Haring, *Free and Faithful in Christ*, 1:290.

76. Moser and Leers, *Moral Theology*, 126.

77. Fuchs, "Conscience," 121.

78. Haring, *Free and Faithful in Christ*, 1:292.

79. Ibid., 288.

80. Fagan, *Does Morality Change?* 104.

81. Haring, *Free and Faithful in Christ*, 1:263.

82. Gula, "Conscience," 111.

83. Keenan, *Moral Wisdom*, 33-34.

84. Gula, "Conscience," 111, 118.

85. Mahoney, *Making of Moral Theology*, 344.

86. Patrick, *Liberating Conscience*, 56.

87. Haring, *Free and Faithful in Christ*, 1:283.

88. Patrick, *Liberating Conscience*, 38.

89. Haring, *Free and Faithful in Christ*, 1:283.

90. Fagan, *Does Morality Change?* 180.

91. Mahoney, *Making of Moral Theology*, 293.

92. Hanigan, *As I Have Loved You*, 141-42.

93. Ibid., 142.

94. Wadell, *Happiness*, 180.

95. Hanigan, *As I Have Loved You*, 123.

96. Keenan, *Moral Wisdom*, 36.

97. Mahoney, *Making of Moral Theology*, 291.

98. Hanigan, *As I Have Loved You*, 121.

99. Fagan, *Does Morality Change?* 109.

100. Billy and Keating, *Conscience and Prayer*, 29.

101. Haring, *Free and Faithful in Christ*, 1:224.

102. Billy and Keating, *Conscience and Prayer*, 61.

103. Haring, *Free and Faithful in Christ*, 1:224.

104. Ibid., 247.

105. Billy and Keating, *Conscience and Prayer*, 49.

106. Leonardo Boff, *Jesus Christ Liberator: A Critical Christology for Our Time*, trans. Patrick Hughes (Maryknoll, N.Y.: Orbis Books, 1981), 90-91.

107. Ibid., 91.

7. LOVE—THE ONLY TRUE PATH TO LIFE

1. James Joyce, *Ulysses*, ed. Hans Walter Gabler with Wolfhard Steppe and Claus Melchior (New York: Random House, 1986), 273.

2. Daniel Day Williams, *The Spirit and Forms of Love* (Lanham, Md.: University Press of America, 1981), 146, 221.

3. Catherine Mowry LaCugna, "God in Communion with Us," in *Freeing Theology: The Essentials of Theology in Feminist Perspective*, ed. Catherine Mowry LaCugna (New York: HarperCollins, 1993), 93.

4. Daniel Harrington, S.J., and James Keenan, S.J., *Jesus and Virtue Ethics: Building Bridges between New Testament Studies and Moral Theology* (Lanham, Md.: Sheed & Ward, 2002), 79.

5. Andre Guindon, *The Sexual Language: An Essay in Moral Theology* (Ottawa: University of Ottawa Press, 1976), 45.

6. Michael J. Himes, "Finding God in All Things: A Sacramental Worldview and Its Effects," in *As Leaven in the World: Catholic Perspectives on Faith, Vocation, and the Intellectual Life*, ed. Thomas M. Landy (Franklin, Wis.: Sheed & Ward, 2001), 98.

7. Paul J. Wadell, *Happiness and the Christian Moral Life: An Introduction to Christian Ethics* (Lanham, Md.: Rowman & Littlefield, 2008), 79.

8. LaCugna, "God in Communion with Us," 86-87.

9. Elaine Storkey, *The Search for Intimacy* (Grand Rapids: Eerdmans, 1995), 239.

10. Liz Carmichael, *Friendship: Interpreting Christian Love* (London: T&T Clark, 2004), 179.

11. Thomas Aquinas, *Summa Theologiae* (New York: McGraw-Hill, 1975), II-II, 23,1.

12. Eberhard Schockenhoff, "The Theological Virtue of Charity," trans. Grant Kaplan and Frederick G. Lawrence, in *The Ethics of Aquinas*, ed. Stephen J. Pope (Washington, D.C.: Georgetown University Press, 2002), 252.

13. Aquinas, *ST*, II-II, 23,1.

14. Vincent Genovesi, *In Pursuit of Love: Catholic Morality and Human Sexuality* (Collegeville, Minn.: Liturgical Press, 1996), 28.

15. Margaret A. Farley, *Personal Commitments: Beginning, Keeping, Changing* (San Francisco: Harper & Row, 1986), 106.

16. Ibid.

17. Margaret A. Farley, *Just Love: A Framework for Christian Sexual Ethics* (New York: Continuum, 2006), 200-201.

18. Harrington and Keenan, *Jesus and Virtue Ethics*, 87.

19. Edward Collins Vacek, S.J., *Love, Human and Divine: The Heart of Christian Ethics* (Washington, D.C.: Georgetown University Press, 1994), 242.

20. Williams, *Spirit and the Forms of Love*, 3.

21. Vacek, *Love, Human and Divine*, 34.

22. Farley, *Just Love*, 168.

23. Genovesi, *In Pursuit of Love*, 25-26.

24. Williams, *Spirit and the Forms of Love*, 117.

25. Farley, *Personal Commitments*, 31. See also eadem, *Just Love*, 168-69.

26. Farley, *Personal Commitments*, 30.

27. Josef Pieper, *Faith, Hope, Love*, trans. Sr. Mary Frances McCarthy, S.N.D., Richard Winston, and Clara Winston (San Francisco: Ignatius, 1997), 164.

28. Vacek, *Love, Human and Divine*, 44.

29. Pieper, *Faith, Hope, Love*, 171-72.

30. Genovesi, *In Pursuit of Love*, 140.

31. Kathleen Fischer Hart and Thomas N. Hart, *The First Two Years of Marriage: Foundations for a Life Together* (New York: Paulist, 1983), 13. Cited in Genovesi, *In Pursuit of Love*, 140.

32. Farley, *Just Love*, 204.

33. Ibid., 205.

34. Williams, *Spirit and the Forms of Love*, 14.

35. Farley, *Personal Commitments*, 34.

36. Farley, *Just Love*, 214.

37. Williams, *Spirit and the Forms of Love*, 114.

38. Vincent MacNamara, *Love, Law and Christian Life: Basic Attitudes of Christian Morality* (Wilmington, DE.: Michael Glazier, 1988), 69.

39. Williams, *Spirit and the Forms of Love*, 116.

40. Farley, *Just Love*, 212.

41. Vacek, *Love, Human and Divine*, 157-58.

42. Ibid., 162.

43. Stephen G. Post, *A Theory of Agape: On the Meaning of Christian Love* (Cranbury, NJ: Associated University Presses, 1990), 17.

44. Anders Nygren, *Agape and Eros*, trans. Philip S. Watson (New York: Harper & Row, 1969), 77.

45. Ibid., 118.

46. Barbara Hilkert Andolsen, "Agape in Feminist Ethics," in *Feminist Theological Ethics: A Reader*, ed. Lois K. Daly (Louisville: Westminster John Knox, 1994), 147.

47. Nygren, *Agape and Eros*, 217.

48. Andolsen, "Agape in Feminist Ethics," 149.

49. Ibid., 151.

50. Ibid., 155.

51. Ibid., 156.

52. Vacek, *Love, Human and Divine*, 247.

53. Ibid., 249.

54. Ibid.

55. C. S. Lewis, *The Four Loves* (New York: Harcourt, Brace & World, 1960), 96-97.

56. Vacek, *Love, Human and Divine*, 290.

57. Ibid.

58. Ibid., 292.

59. Lewis, *Four Loves*, 114.

60. Ibid., 115-16.

61. Ibid., 117.

62. Dhirendra Mohan Datta, *The Philosophy of Mahatma Gandhi* (Madison: University of Wisconsin Press, 1953), 76.

63. Paul J. Wadell, *Becoming Friends: Worship, Justice, and the Practice of Christian Friendship* (Grand Rapids: Brazos, 2002), 32.

64. Ada María Isasi-Díaz, "Solidarity: Love of Neighbor in the 1980s," in *Feminist Theological Ethics: A Reader*, ed. Lois K. Daly (Louisville: Westminster John Knox, 1994), 79.

65. Huston Smith, *The Religions of Man* (New York: Harper & Row, 1958), 235.

66. Frederick M. Denny, *Islam* (San Francisco: Harper & Row, 1987), 51.

67. Smith, *Religions of Man*, 240.

68. John L. Esposito, *Islam: The Straight Path*, rev. 3rd ed. (New York: Oxford University Press, 2005), 90.

69. Smith, *Religions of Man*, 240.

70. Esposito, *Islam*, 90.

71. Denny, *Islam*, 72.

72. James A. Nash, *Loving Nature: Ecological Integrity and Christian Responsibility* (Nashville: Abingdon, 1991), 149.

73. Steven Bouma-Prediger, *For the Beauty of the Earth: A Christian Vision of Creation Care* (Grand Rapids: Baker Academic, 2001), 154-55.

74. Nash, *Loving Nature*, 150.

75. Bouma-Prediger, *For the Beauty of the Earth*, 145.

76. Ibid., 147.

8. THE PASCHAL MYSTERY AND THE MORAL LIFE

1. Raymond E. Brown, S.S., *A Crucified Christ in Holy Week: Essays on the Four Gospel Passion Narratives* (Collegeville, Minn.: Liturgical Press, 1986), 68-71.

2. See Richard P. McBrien, *Catholicism*, vol. 1 (Minneapolis: Winston, 1980), 410-23.

3. N. T. Wright, *Following Jesus: Biblical Reflections on Discipleship* (Grand Rapids: Eerdmans, 1994), 18-19.

4. S. Mark Heim, *Saved from Sacrifice: A Theology of the Cross* (Grand Rapids: Eerdmans, 2006), 110-14. See René Gerard, *The Scapegoat* (Baltimore: Johns Hopkins University Press, 1986).

5. Heim, *Saved from Sacrifice*, 115.

6. Khaled Hosseini, *The Kite Runner* (New York: Riverhead Books, 2003), 226.

7. Ibid., 231.

8. Jacquelyn Grant, "The Sin of Servanthood," in *A Troubling in My Soul: Womanist Perspectives on Evil and Suffering*, ed. Emilie M. Townes (Maryknoll, N.Y.: Orbis Books, 1993), 200-216; quotation from 216.

9. Sidney Cornelia Callahan, "To Bear Wrongs Patiently," in *From Christ to the World: Introductory Readings in Christian Ethics*, ed. Wayne G. Boulton, Thomas D. Kennedy, and Allen Verhey (Grand Rapids: Eerdmans, 1994), 270-79, quotation from 272.

10. Cynthia S.W. Crysdale, *Embracing Travail, Retrieving the Cross Today* (New York: Continuum, 2001), especially 55-56.

11. Ibid., 27.

12. Dorothee Soelle, *Suffering*, trans. Everett R. Kalin (Philadelphia: Fortress, 1975), 5, 86-94.

13. Fyodor Dostoevsky, *The Brothers Karamazov*, trans. Constance Garnett (New York: Heritage, 1961), 184.

14. Soelle, *Suffering*, 45.

15. David Hollenbach, S.J., *The Global Face of Public Faith: Politics, Human Rights, and Christian Ethics* (Washington, D.C.: Georgetown University Press, 2003), 64, 66.

16. Ibid., 67.

17. Sam Keen, *To Love and Be Loved* (New York: Bantam Books, 1999), 96.

18. Monika Hellwig, *Jesus, the Compassion of God: New Perspectives in the Tradition of Christianity* (Collegeville, Minn.: Liturgical Press, 1983), 121-23.

19. Ibid., 131.

20. Ibid., 107-8.

21. Keen, *To Love and Be Loved*, 96.

22. Ibid., 99.

23. John Bowker, *Problems of Suffering in Religions of the World* (New York: Cambridge University Press, 1970), 237-40.

24. See *Transforming Suffering, Reflections on Finding Peace in Troubled Times*, ed. Donald W. Mitchell and James Wiseman, O.S.B. (New York: Doubleday, 2003).

25. Quoted in Peter Harvey, *An Introduction to Buddhist Ethics* (New York: Cambridge University Press, 2000), 124.

26. Diana Fritz Cates, *Choosing To Feel: Virtue, Friendship, and Compassion for Friends* (Notre Dame, Ind.: University of Notre Dame Press, 1997), 189.

27. Soelle, *Suffering*, 38-39, 100.

28. Rosemary Haughton, "Passionate Breakthrough—The Passionate God," in *Women's Spirituality: Resources for Christian Development,* ed. Joann Wolski Conn (New York: Paulist, 1986), 239.

29. Stefan Ulstein, "*Shadowlands* Portrays Lewis with Poignance," *Christianity Today* (February 7, 1994), 50. Both a play and a film, *Shadowlands* portrays the love story of C. S. Lewis and Joy Davidman Gresham.

30. Leonore Fleischer, *Shadowlands: A Novel* (New York: Signet, 1993), 10.

31. Patricia Lamoureux, "The Transformative Power of Love in *Shadowlands*," in *Seeking Goodness and Beauty: The Use of the Arts in Theological Ethics*, ed. Patricia Lamoureux and Kevin J. O'Neil, C.Ss.R. (Lanham, Md.: Rowman & Littlefield, 2005), 71-81.

32. Soelle, *Suffering*, 157.

33. Hellwig, *Jesus*, 104.

34. Brian V. Johnstone, C.Ss.R., "Transformation Ethics: The Moral Implications of the Resurrection," in *The Resurrection: An Interdisciplinary Symposium on the Resurrection of Jesus*, ed. Stephen T. Davis, Daniel Kendall, and Gerald O'Collins (New York: Oxford University Press, 1997), 339-40.

35. Ibid., 344-45.

36. Ibid., 346.

37. Ibid., 348-50.

38. Ibid., 351.

39. Jon Sobrino, *Jesus in Latin America* (Maryknoll, N.Y.: Orbis Books, 1988), 149.

40. Ibid., 156.

41. Luz Beatriz Arellano, "Women's Experience of God in Emerging Spirituality," in *With Passion and Compassion: Third World Women Doing Theology*, ed. Virginia Fabella and Mercy Amba Oduyoye (Maryknoll, N.Y.: Orbis Books, 1989), 146.

42. Lyle K. Weiss, "The Bodily Resurrection of Jesus and Moral Vision," in "The Public Significance of the Bodily Resurrection of Jesus Christ" (Ph.D. diss., St. Mary's Seminary and University, 2007), 133-41.

43. Thorwald Lorenzen, *Resurrection and Discipleship: Interpretive Models, Biblical Reflections, Theological Consequences* (Maryknoll, N.Y.: Orbis Books, 1995), 146.

44. Patrick T. McCormick, *A Banqueter's Guide to the All-Night Soup Kitchen of the Kingdom of God* (Collegeville, Minn.: Liturgical Press, 2004), x.

9. THE SPIRIT AND MORAL DISCERNMENT

1. Karl Rahner, "Experience of the Holy Spirit," *Theological Investigations* 18 (New York: Crossroad, 1983), 203.

2. Karl Rahner, "Do Not Stifle the Spirit!" *Theological Investigations* 7 (New York: Herder & Herder, 1971), 72-87.

3. Mary Gordon, *Men and Angels* (New York: Ballantine, 1985).

4. Ibid., 245.

5. John L. McKenzie, "Aspects of Old Testament Thought," in *New Jerome Biblical Commentary*, ed. Raymond Brown, Joseph Fitzmyer, and Roland Murphy (Englewood Cliffs, N.J.: Prentice-Hall, 1990), 1291.

6. See Roland Murphy, *The Tree of Life: An Exploration of Biblical Wisdom Literature*. 3rd ed. (Grand Rapids: Eerdmans, 1990), 118-20, 144. Murphy points out that Wisdom is described in various ways: as a tree of life, fear of the Lord, instruction for moral formation, human experience, the mysteries of creation, Law or Torah, a mysterious divine call, and a spouse.

7. Ibid., 133-49. Other key references to Lady Wisdom are Job 28; Proverbs 9; Sirach 24; and Baruch 3:9-4, 4. Lady Wisdom is: intelligent, holy, unique, manifold, subtle, agile, clear, unstained, certain, not baneful, loving the good, keen, unhampered, beneficent, kindly, firm, secure, tranquil, all-powerful, all-seeing, and pervading all spirits (Wis 7:22-23).

8. Elizabeth A. Johnson, *She Who Is: The Mystery of God in Feminist Theological Discourse* (New York: Crossroad, 1992), 86-87.

9. Keith Warrington, *Discovering the Holy Spirit in the New Testament* (Peabody, Mass.: Hendrickson, 2005), 42-43, 87-88, 109-10, 177.

10. See Mark O'Keefe, O.S.B., *Becoming Good, Becoming Holy: On the Relationship of Christian Ethics and Spirituality* (New York: Paulist, 1995), 125-28.

11. See Charles E. Curran, *The Catholic Moral Tradition Today: A Synthesis* (Washington, D.C.: Georgetown University Press, 1999), 60-83.

12. See H. Richard Niebuhr, *The Responsible Self: An Essay in Christian Moral Philosophy* (New York: Harper & Row, 1963).

13. On this way of understanding the structures of family, state, economy, church, and education as "places of responsibility," see Robert Benne, *Ordinary Saints: An Introduction to the Christian Life* (Minneapolis: Fortress, 2003), 63-79.

14. Richard M. Gula, S.S., *Moral Discernment* (New York: Paulist, 1997), 50.

15. Charles Bouchard, O.P., "Recovering the Gifts of the Holy Spirit in Moral Theology," *Theological Studies* 63 (2002): 549-51.

16. Ibid., 549.

17. Ibid.

18. Bernard Hoose, "Intuition and Moral Theology," *Theological Studies* 67 (2006): 603.

19. Ibid., 615-16.

20. Ibid., 622.

21. Thomas Keating, *Fruits and Gifts of the Spirit* (New York: Lantern, 2000), 108.

22. Thomas Heath, OP, "The Holy Spirit is Gift," available online at http://www .catholicireland.net/pages/index.php?nd=3&art=565 (April 17, 2006), 3.

23. Titus Burckhardt, "Sufi Doctrine and Method," in *Sufism: Love and Wisdom*, ed. Jean-Louis Michon and Roger Gaetani (Bloomington, Ind.: World Wisdom, 2006), 12-13.

24. Eric Geoffroy, "Approaching Sufism," in *Sufism: Love and Wisdom*, 48.

25. Quoted in William C. Chittick, "Sufism and Islam," in *Sufism: Love and Wisdom*, 32.

26. Chittick, "Sufism and Islam," 22.

27. John Mahoney, *Seeking the Spirit: Essays in Moral and Pastoral Theology* (London: Sheed & Ward; Denville, N.J.: Dimension, 1982), 67.

28. Ibid., 68.

29. Servais Pinckaers, O.P., *The Sources of Christian Ethics*, trans. Sr. Mary Thomas Noble, O.P. (Washington, D.C.: Catholic University of America Press, 1995), 181.

30. See John Macquarrie, "Rethinking Natural Law," in *Natural Law and Theology*, ed. Charles E. Curran and Richard A. McCormick, Readings in Moral Theology 7 (Mahwah, N.J.: Paulist, 1991), 221-46.

31. See U.S. Catholic Bishops, "The Challenge of Peace: God's Promise and Our Response," pars. 9-11; and "Economic Justice for All," pars. 134-35, in *Catholic Social Thought: The Documentary Heritage*, ed. David J. O'Brien and Thomas A. Shannon (Maryknoll, N.Y.: Orbis Books, 1992).

32. Pinckaers, *Sources of Christian Ethics*, 174-75.

33. Ibid., 186.

34. *Gaudium et Spes*, par. 52, in *Catholic Social Thought*, ed. O'Brien and Shannon.

35. John Paul II writes of the universality of the Spirit's presence and action in the world from the beginning; see *Dominum et vivificantem*, Lord and Giver of Life (May 30, 1986), par. 53.

36. Bouchard, "Recovering the Gifts," 551, 555-56.

37. Murphy, *Tree of Life*, 145.

38. This way of understanding the role of prayer in moral discernment is drawn from Kenneth Himes, O.F.M., "The Relationship of Religion and Morality," *Social Thought* 15 (Summer-Fall 1989): 33-41.

39. Annie Dillard, *Teaching a Stone to Talk* (New York: HarperPerennial, 1982), 19-20.

10. THE MISSION OF PUBLIC DISCIPLESHIP

1. Walter Brueggemann, *The Word That Redescribes the World: The Bible and Discipleship* (Minneapolis: Fortress, 2006), 92-99.

2. Ibid., 103-4.

3. John A. Coleman, "The Two Pedagogies: Discipleship and Citizenship," in *Education for Citizenship and Discipleship*, ed. Mary C. Boys (New York: Pilgrim, 1989), 68, 69.

4. St. Augustine, *City of God* (New York: Penguin Books, 1972).

5. Martin Luther, *Selected Political Writings*, ed. J. M. Porter (Minneapolis: Fortress, 1974).

6. Robin W. Lovin, *Christian Faith and Public Choices: The Social Ethics of Barth, Brunner, and Bonhoeffer* (Philadelphia: Fortress, 1984), 18-44.

7. Ibid., 11-16; quotation from 16.

8. Stanley Hauerwas, *A Community of Character* (Notre Dame, Ind.: University of Notre Dame Press, 1981), 1.

9. Stanley Hauerwas, *The Peaceable Kingdom: A Primer in Christian Ethics* (Notre Dame, Ind.: University of Notre Dame Press, 1983).

10. H. Richard Niebuhr, *Christ and Culture* (New York: Harper, 1956).

11. Parker J. Palmer, *The Company of Strangers: Christians and the Renewal of America's Public Life* (New York: Crossroad, 1986), 38-40.

12. Ibid., 40-41.

13. Ibid., 41.

14. Ibid., 45-46.

15. Coleman, "Two Pedagogies," 59.

16. See Jean Bethke Elshtain, *Public Man, Private Woman: Women in Social and Political Thought* (Princeton, N.J.: Princeton University Press, 1981).

17. Michael J. Sandel, *Democracy's Discontent: America in Search of a Public Philosophy* (Cambridge, Mass.: Belknap Press of Harvard University Press, 1996), 3-28; quotation from 18.

18. Kathryn E. Kuhn, "Social Values and Bureaucratic Morality," in *Values and Public Life*, ed. Gerald Magill and Marie D. Hoff (Lanham, Md.: University Press of America, 1995), 158-59.

19. Martin E. Marty, *The Public Church* (New York: Crossroad, 1981), 3.

20. Michael J. Himes and Kenneth R. Himes, *Fullness of Faith: The Public Significance of Theology* (Mahwah, N.J.: Paulist, 1993), 2.

21. Second Vatican Council, *Gaudium et spes* (Pastoral Constitution on the Church in the Modern World, 1965), in *Catholic Social Thought: The Documentary Heritage*, ed. David J. O'Brien and Thomas A. Shannon (Maryknoll, N.Y.: Orbis Books, 1992), pars. 40-42.

22. See Joseph Cardinal Bernardin, *Consistent Ethic of Life* (Kansas City, Mo.: Sheed & Ward, 1988).

23. Thomas C. Kohler, "Civic Virtue at Work: Unions as Seedbeds of Civic Virtues," in *Seedbeds of Virtue: Sources of Competence, Character, and Citizenship In American Society*, ed. Mary Ann Glendon and David Blankenhorn (Lanham, Md.: Madison, 1995), 149.

24. U.S. Catholic Bishops, "Economic Justice for All," (1986) in *Catholic Social Thought*, ed. O'Brien and Shannon, par. 66.

25. John Paul II, *Sollicitudo rei socialis* (On Social Concern, 1987), in *Catholic Social Thought*, ed. O'Brien and Shannon, par. 38.

26. Ibid., par. 40.

27. Ibid., par. 42.

28. Pope Benedict XVI, *Caritas in Veritate*, Charity and Truth (Vatican City: Libreria Editrice Vaticana, 2009), par. 5.

29. Ibid., par. 6.

30. Ibid., par. 7.

31. Himes and Himes, *Fullness of Faith*, 172-73.

32. "Economic Justice for All," par. 68.

33. Ibid., par. 69.

34. Ibid., par. 70.

35. Ibid., pars. 71, 72.

36. *Sollicitudo rei socialis*, par. 38.

37. David Hollenbach, S.J., *The Global Face of Public Faith: Politics, Human Rights, and Christian Ethics* (Washington, D.C.: Georgetown University Press, 2003), 161.

38. Coleman, "Two Pedagogies," 59-61.

39. Paulo Coelho, *The Alchemist*, trans. Alan R. Clarke (New York: HarperSanFrancisco, 1998), 131.

Bibliography

Albom, Mitch. *Tuesdays with Morrie*. New York: Doubleday, 1997.

Andolsen, Barbara Hilkert. "Agape in Feminist Ethics." In *Feminist Theological Ethics: A Reader*. Edited by Lois K. Daly, 146-59. Louisville: Westminster John Knox, 1994.

Aquinas, Thomas. *Summa Theologiae*. New York: McGraw-Hill, 1964-1975.

Arellano, Luz Beatriz. "Women's Experience of God in Emerging Spirituality." In *With Passion and Compassion: Third World Women Doing Theology*. Edited by Virginia Fabella and Mercy Amba Oduyoye, 135-50. Maryknoll, N.Y.: Orbis Books, 1989.

Augustine. *City of God*. New York: Penguin Books, 1972.

———. *The Confessions*. Translated by Maria Boulding, O.S.B. Hyde Park, N.Y.: New City Press, 1997.

Bader-Saye, Scott. *Following Jesus in a Culture of Fear*. Grand Rapids: Brazos, 2007.

Balasuriya, Tissa. "The Eucharist in Contemporary Society." In *Liberation Theology: An Introductory Reader*. Edited by Curt Cadorette, Marie Giblin, Marilyn J. Legge, and Mary Hembrow Snyder, 256-68. Maryknoll, N.Y.: Orbis Books, 1992.

Barth, Karl. "The Awakening to Conversion." In *Conversion: Perspectives on Personal and Social Transformation*. Edited by Walter E. Conn, 35-49. New York: Alba House, 1978.

Bauerschmidt, Frederick Christian. "The Trinity." In *Gathered for the Journey: Moral Theology in Catholic Perspective*. Edited by David Matzko McCarthy and M. Therese Lysaught, 68-87. Grand Rapids: Eerdmans, 2007.

Baum, Gregory. "Critical Theology." In *Conversion: Perspectives on Personal and Social Transformation*. Edited by Walter E. Conn, 281-95. New York: Alba House, 1978.

Benedict XVI. *Caritas in veritate* (Charity and Truth). Vatican City: Libreria Editrice Vaticana, 2009.

Benne, Robert. *Ordinary Saints: An Introduction to the Christian Life*. Minneapolis: Fortress, 2003.

Bernardin, Joseph Cardinal. *Consistent Ethic of Life*. Kansas City, Mo.: Sheed & Ward, 1988.

Billy, Dennis, C.Ss.R. "The Person of the Holy Spirit as the Source of the Christian Moral Life." *Studia Moralia* 36 (1998): 325-59.

Billy, Dennis J., and James F. Keating. *Conscience and Prayer: The Spirit of Catholic Moral Theology*. Collegeville, Minn.: Liturgical Press, 2001.

Boff, Leonardo. *Jesus Christ Liberator: A Critical Christology for Our Time*. Translated by Patrick Hughes. Maryknoll, N.Y.: Orbis Books, 1981.

Bolt, Robert. *A Man for All Seasons*. New York: Vintage Books, 1990.

Bonhoeffer, Dietrich. *The Cost of Discipleship*. New York: MacMillan, 1963.

Bouchard, Charles, O.P. "Recovering the Gifts of the Holy Spirit in Moral Theology." *Theological Studies* 63 (2002): 539-58.

Bouma-Prediger, Steven. *For the Beauty of the Earth: A Christian Vision of Creation Care*. Grand Rapids: Baker Academic, 2001.

Bowker, John. *Problems of Suffering in Religions of the World*. New York: Cambridge University Press, 1970.

Braaten, Carl E. *Eschatology and Ethics: Essays on the Theology and Ethics of the Kingdom of God*. Minneapolis: Augsburg, 1974.

Bretzke, James T. *A Morally Complex World: Engaging Contemporary Moral Theology*. Collegeville, Minn.: Liturgical Press, 2004.

———. "Moral Theology Out of East Asia." *Theological Studies* 62 (2000): 106-21.

Brown, David. *Discipleship and Imagination: Christian Tradition and Truth*. New York: Oxford University Press, 2000.

Brown, Raymond E., S.S. *The Churches the Apostles Left Behind*. New York: Paulist, 1984.

———. *The Community of the Beloved Disciple*. New York: Paulist, 1979.

———. *A Crucified Christ in Holy Week: Essays on the Four Gospel Passion Narratives*. Collegeville, Minn.: Liturgical Press, 1986.

Brueggemann, Walter. *The Word That Redescribes the World: The Bible and Discipleship*. Minneapolis: Fortress, 2006.

Cahill, Lisa Sowle. *Love Your Enemies: Discipleship, Pacifism, and Just War Theory*. Minneapolis: Fortress, 1994.

Callahan, Sidney Cornelia. *In Good Conscience: Reason and Emotion in Moral Decision Making*. New York: HarperCollins, 1991.

———. "To Bear Wrongs Patiently." In *From Christ to the World: Introductory Readings in Christian Ethics*. Edited by Wayne G. Boulton, Thomas D. Kennedy, Allen Verhey, 270-79. Grand Rapids: Eerdmans, 1994.

Carmichael, Liz. *Friendship: Interpreting Christian Love*. London: T&T Clark, 2004.

Casey, John. *Pagan Virtue: An Essay in Ethics*. Oxford: Clarendon, 1990.

Cates, Diana Fritz. *Choosing to Feel: Virtue, Friendship, and Compassion for Friends*. Notre Dame, Ind.: University of Notre Dame Press, 1997.

Chung Hyun Kyung. *Struggling to Be the Sun Again: Introducing Asian Women's Theology*. Maryknoll, N.Y.: Orbis Books, 2004.

Cloutier, David. "Human Fulfillment." In *Gathered for the Journey: Moral Theology in Catholic Perspective*. Edited by David Matzko McCarthy and M. Therese Lysaught, 134-52. Grand Rapids: Eerdmans, 2007.

Coelho, Paulo. *The Alchemist*. Translated by Alan R. Clarke. New York: HarperSanFrancisco, 1998.

Coleman, John A. *An American Strategic Theology*. Ramsey, N.J.: Paulist, 1982.

———. "The Two Pedagogies: Discipleship and Citizenship." In *Education for Citizenship and Discipleship*. Edited by Mary C. Boys, 35-75. New York: Pilgrim, 1989.

Congar, Yves. "'God Has Sent the Spirit of His Son into Our Hearts' (Gal 4:6)." In *I Believe in the Holy Spirit*. Vol. 2, *The Complete Three-Volume Work*, 779-99. New York: Crossroad, 2005.

Connors, Russell B., Jr., and Patrick T. McCormick. *Character, Choices and Community: The Three Faces of Christian Ethics*. New York: Paulist, 1998.

Conn, Walter E., ed. *Conversion: Perspectives on Personal and Social Transformation*. New York: Alba House, 1978.

Cooke, Bernard. *Power and the Spirit of God: Toward an Experience-Based Pneumatology*. New York: Oxford University Press, 2004.

Cosmao, Vincent. *Changing the World: An Agenda for the Churches*. Translated by John Drury. Maryknoll, N.Y.: Orbis Books, 1984.

Crites, Stephen. "The Narrative Quality of Experience." In *Why Narrative? Readings in Narrative Theology*. Edited by Stanley Hauerwas and L. Gregory Jones, 65-88. Grand Rapids: Eerdmans, 1989.

Crosby, Michael, O.F.M. Cap. *House of Disciples: Christ, Economics, and Justice in Matthew*. Maryknoll, N.Y.: Orbis Books, 1988.

Crysdale, Cynthia S. W. *Embracing Travail, Retrieving the Cross Today*. New York: Continuum, 2001.

Curran, Charles E. *The Catholic Moral Tradition Today: A Synthesis*. Washington, D.C.: Georgetown University Press, 1999.

Datta, Dhirendra Mohan. *The Philosophy of Mahatma Gandhi*. Madison: University of Wisconsin Press, 1953.

Del Colle, Ralph. "The Holy Spirit: Presence, Power, Person." *Theological Studies* 62 (2001): 322-40.

Denny, Frederick M. *Islam*. San Francisco: Harper & Row, 1987.

Devettere, Raymond J. *Introduction to Virtue Ethics: Insights of the Ancient Greeks*. Washington, D.C.: Georgetown University Press, 2002.

Dillard, Annie. *Teaching a Stone to Talk*. New York: HarperPerennial, 1982.

Donagan, Alan. *The Theory of Morality*. Chicago: University of Chicago Press, 1977.

Donahue, John R., S.J. "Discipleship and the Life of Grace." *Southwestern Journal of Theology* 28 (1986): 73-78.

Dostoevsky, Fyodor. *The Brothers Karamazov*. Translated by Constance Garnett. New York: Heritage, 1961.

Dulles, Avery Cardinal, S.J. *Models of the Church*. Rev. ed. New York: Image Books, 2002.

Dunn, James D. G. *Christianity in the Making*. Vol. 1, *Jesus Remembered*. Grand Rapids: Eerdmans, 2003.

———. *Jesus' Call to Discipleship*. Cambridge: Cambridge University Press, 1992.

Dussel, Enrique. *Ethics and Community*. Translated by Robert R. Barr. Maryknoll, N.Y.: Orbis Books, 1988.

Ellsberg, Robert. *The Saints' Guide to Happiness*. New York: North Point Press, 2003.

Elshtain, Jean Bethke. *Public Man, Private Woman: Women in Social and Political Thought*. Princeton, N.J.: Princeton University Press, 1981.

Esposito, John L. *Islam: The Straight Path*, rev. 3rd ed. New York: Oxford University Press, 2005.

Fabella, Virginia, M.M., and Mercy Amba Oduyoye, eds. *With Passion and Compassion: Third World Women Doing Theology*. Maryknoll, N.Y.: Orbis Books, 1989.

Fagan, Sean, S.M.. *Does Morality Change?* Dublin: Gill & Macmillan, 1997.

Farley, Margaret A. *Just Love: A Framework for Christian Sexual Ethics*. New York: Continuum, 2006.

———. *Personal Commitments: Beginning, Keeping, Changing*. San Francisco: Harper & Row, 1986.

Flannery, Austin, O.P. *The Basic Sixteen Documents of Vatican Council II*. Northport, N.Y.: Costello, 1996.

———. *Vatican Council II: The Conciliar and Post Conciliar Documents*. Collegeville, Minn.: Liturgical Press, 1975.

Fleischer, Leonore. *Shadowlands: A Novel*. New York: Signet, 1993.

Franck, Frederick. *To Be Human against All Odds*. Berkeley, Calif.: Asian Humanities Press, 1991.

Friel, Brian. *Molly Sweeney*. New York: Penguin, 1995.

Fuchs, Josef, S.J.. "Conscience and Conscientious Fidelity." In *Moral Theology: Challenges for the Future*. Edited by Charles E. Curran, 108-24. New York: Paulist, 1990.

Fuellenbach, John. *The Kingdom of God: The Message of Jesus Today*. Maryknoll, N.Y.: Orbis Books, 2002.

Garcia, Ismael. *Dignidad: Ethics through Hispanic Eyes*. Nashville: Abingdon, 1997.

Genovesi, Vincent. *In Pursuit of Love: Catholic Morality and Human Sexuality*. Collegeville, Minn.: Liturgical Press, 1996.

Gerard, René. *The Scapegoat*. Baltimore: Johns Hopkins University Press, 1986.

Gittins, Anthony. *Come Follow Me: The Commandments of Jesus, Invitation to Discipleship*. St. Louis: Liguori, 2004.

Gordon, Mary. *Men and Angels*. New York: Ballantine, 1985.

Grant, Jacquelyn. "The Sin of Servanthood." In *A Troubling in My Soul: Womanist Perspectives On Evil and Suffering*. Edited by Emilie M. Townes, 199-218. Maryknoll, N.Y.: Orbis Books, 1993.

Guindon, Andre. *The Sexual Language: An Essay in Moral Theology*. Ottawa: University of Ottawa Press, 1976.

Gula, Richard M., S.S. "Conscience." In *Christian Ethics: An Introduction*. Edited by Bernard Hoose, 110-22. Collegeville, Minn.: Liturgical Press, 1998.

———. *The Good Life: Where Morality and Spirituality Converge*. New York: Paulist, 1999.

———. *Moral Discernment*. New York: Paulist, 1997.

———. *Reason Informed by Faith: Foundations of Catholic Morality*. New York: Paulist, 1989.

Gutiérrez, Gustavo. *God of Life*. Translated by Matthew J. O'Connell. Maryknoll, N.Y.: Orbis Books, 1991.

———. *The Power of Poor in History*. Maryknoll, N.Y.: Orbis Books, 1985.

———. "A Spirituality of Liberation." In *Conversion: Perspectives on Personal and Social Transformation*. Edited by Walter E. Conn, 307-13. New York: Alba House, 1978.

———. *A Theology of Liberation*. Translated by Sr. Caridad Inda and John Eagleson. Maryknoll, N.Y.: Orbis Books, 1973.

———. *We Drink from Our Own Wells: The Spiritual Journey of a People*. Maryknoll, N.Y.: Orbis Books, 1985

Hanh, Thich Nhat. *Being Peace*. Berkeley, Calif.: Parallax, 1987.

———. *Living Buddha, Living Christ*. New York: Riverhead, 1995.

Hanigan, James P. *As I Have Loved You: The Challenge of Christian Ethics*. New York: Paulist, 1986.

Haring, Bernard. *Free and Faithful in Christ: Moral Theology for Clergy and Laity.* Vol. 1, *General Moral Theology.* New York: Seabury, 1978.

Harrington, Daniel, S.J. *Why Do We Suffer? A Scriptural Approach to the Human Condition.* Franklin, Wis.: Sheed & Ward, 2000.

Harrington, Daniel, S.J., and James Keenan, S.J.. *Jesus and Virtue Ethics: Building Bridges between New Testament Studies and Moral Theology.* Lanham, Md.: Sheed & Ward, 2002.

Hart, Kathleen Fischer, and Thomas N. Hart. *The First Two Years of Marriage: Foundations for a Life Together.* New York: Paulist, 1983.

Harvey, Peter. *An Introduction to Buddhist Ethics.* New York: Cambridge University Press, 2000.

Hauerwas, Stanley. *A Community of Character.* Notre Dame, Ind.: University of Notre Dame Press, 1981.

———. *The Peaceable Kingdom: A Primer in Christian Ethics.* Notre Dame, Ind.: University of Notre Dame Press, 1983.

Hauerwas, Stanley, and Charles Pinches. *Christians among the Virtues: Theological Conversations with Ancient and Modern Ethics.* Notre Dame, Ind.: University of Notre Dame Press, 1997.

———. *Vision and Virtue: Essays in Christian Ethical Reflection.* Notre Dame, Ind.: Fides, 1974.

Haughey, John C., S.J. *Should Anyone Say Forever? On Making, Keeping, and Breaking Commitments.* Chicago: Loyola University Press, 1975.

Haughton, Rosemary. "Passionate Breakthrough—The Passionate God." In *Women's Spirituality: Resources for Christian Development.* Edited by Joann Wolski Conn, 233-42. New York: Paulist, 1986.

Hays, Richard B. *The Moral Vision of the New Testament: A Contemporary Introduction to New Testament Ethics.* New York: HarperCollins, 1996.

Heath, Thomas, OP. "The Holy Spirit is Gift." Available online at http://www.catholicireland.net/pages/index.php?nd=3&art=565 (April 17, 2006).

Heim, S. Mark. *Saved from Sacrifice: A Theology of the Cross.* Grand Rapids: Eerdmans, 2006.

Hellwig, Monika. *Jesus, the Compassion of God: New Perspectives on the Tradition of Christianity.* Collegeville, Minn.: Liturgical Press, 1983.

Henriot, Peter J. "Social Sin and Conversion: A Theology of the Church's Social Involvement." In *Conversion: Perspectives on Personal and Social Transformation.* Edited by Walter E. Conn, 315-26. New York: Alba House, 1978.

Heschel, Abraham J. *The Prophets*, vol. 2. New York: Harper & Row, 1962.

Himes, Kenneth, O.F.M. "The Relationship of Religion and Morality." *Social Thought* 15 (Summer-Fall 1989): 33-41.

Himes, Michael J. *Doing the Truth in Love: Conversations about God, Relationships and Service.* New York: Paulist, 1995.

———. "Finding God in All Things: A Sacramental Worldview and Its Effects." In *As Leaven in the World: Catholic Perspectives on Faith, Vocation, and the Intellectual Life.* Edited by Thomas M. Landy, 91-103. Franklin, Wis.: Sheed & Ward, 2001.

Himes, Michael J., and Kenneth R. Himes, O.F.M. *Fullness of Faith: The Public Signifi-cance of Theology*. Mahwah, N.J.: Paulist, 1993.

Hollenbach, David, S.J. *The Global Face of Public Faith: Politics, Human Rights, and Christian Ethics*. Washington, D.C.: Georgetown University Press, 2003.

Hoose, Bernard. "Intuition and Moral Theology." *Theological Studies* 67 (2006): 54-71.

Hosseini, Khaled. *The Kite Runner*. New York: Riverhead Books, 2003.

Howard-Brook, Wes, and Sharon H. Ringe. *The New Testament: Introducing the Way of Discipleship*. Maryknoll, N.Y.: Orbis Books, 2002.

Isasi-Díaz, Ada María. "Solidarity: Love of Neighbor in the 1980s." In *Feminist Theo-logical Ethics: A Reader*. Edited by Lois K. Daly, 77-87. Louisville: Westminster John Knox, 1994.

James, William. "The Divided Self and Conversion." In *Conversion: Perspectives on Per-sonal and Social Transformation*. Edited by Walter E. Conn, 121-36. New York: Alba House, 1978.

Jeremias, Joachim. *Rediscovering the Parables*. New York: Charles Scribner's Sons, 1966.

John XXIII. *Mater et Magistra* (Christianity and Social Progress). In *Catholic Social Thought: The Documentary Heritage*. Edited by David J. O'Brien and Thomas A. Shannon, 84-128. Maryknoll, N.Y.: Orbis Books, 1992.

John Paul II. *Sollicitudo rei socialis* (On Social Concern, 1987). In *Catholic Social Thought: The Documentary Heritage*. Edited by David J. O'Brien and Thomas A. Shannon, 393-436. Maryknoll, N.Y.: Orbis Books, 1992.

Johnson, Elizabeth A. *Consider Jesus: Waves of Renewal in Christology*. New York: Crossroad, 1999.

———. *She Who Is: The Mystery of God in Feminist Theological Discourse*. New York: Crossroad, 1992.

Johnstone, Brian V., C.Ss.R. "Transformation Ethics: The Moral Implications of the Resurrection." In *The Resurrection: An Interdisciplinary Symposium on the Resurrec-tion of Jesus*. Edited by Stephen T. Davis, Daniel Kendall, S.J., and Gerald O'Collins, S.J., 339-60. New York: Oxford University Press, 1997.

Jones, L. Gregory. *Embodying Forgiveness: A Theological Analysis*. Grand Rapids: Eerd-mans, 1995.

Joyce, James. *Ulysses*. Edited by Hans Walter Gabler with Wolfhard Steppe and Claus Melchior. New York: Random House, 1986.

Kavanaugh, John F. *Following Christ in a Consumer Society: The Spirituality of Cultural Resistance.* Rev. ed. Maryknoll, N.Y.: Orbis Books, 1992.

Keating, Thomas. *Fruits and Gifts of the Spirit*. New York: Lantern, 2000.

Keen, Sam. *To Love and Be Loved*. New York: Bantam Books, 1999.

Keenan, James F., S.J. *Goodness and Rightness in Thomas Aquinas's Summa Theologiae*. Washington, D.C.: Georgetown University Press, 1992.

———. *Moral Wisdom: Lessons and Texts from the Catholic Tradition*. Lanham, Md.: Rowman & Littlefield, 2004.

Kelly, Anthony. *Eschatology and Hope*. Maryknoll, N.Y.: Orbis Books, 2006.

King, Heather. *Redeemed: A Spiritual Misfit Stumbles toward God, Marginal Sanity, and the Peace That Passes All Understanding*. New York: Viking, 2008.

Kohler, Thomas C. "Civic Virtue at Work: Unions as Seedbeds of Civic Virtues." In

Seedbeds of Virtue: Sources of Competence, Character, and Citizenship in American Society. Edited by Mary Ann Glendon and David Blankenhorn, 131-62. Lanham, Md.: Madison, 1995.

Kopfensteiner, Thomas R. "The Theory of the Fundamental Option and Moral Action." In *Christian Ethics: An Introduction*. Edited by Bernard Hoose, 123-34. Collegeville, Minn.: Liturgical Press, 1998.

Kotva, Joseph J., Jr. *The Christian Case for Virtue Ethics*. Washington, D.C.: Georgetown University Press, 1996.

Kroeger, James H., and Eugene F. Thalman, eds. *Once upon a Time in Asia: Stories of Harmony and Peace*. Maryknoll, N.Y.: Orbis Books, 2006.

Kuhn, Kathryn E. "Social Values and Bureaucratic Morality." In *Values and Public Life*. Edited by Gerald Magill and Marie D. Hoff, 139-68. Lanham, Md.: University Press of America, 1995.

LaCugna, Catherine Mowry. "God in Communion with Us." In *Freeing Theology: The Essentials of Theology in Feminist Perspective*. Edited by Catherine Mowry LaCugna, 83-114. New York: HarperCollins, 1993.

Lamoureux, Patricia A. "The Transformative Power of Love in *Shadowlands*." In *Seeking Goodness and Beauty: The Use of the Arts in Theological Ethics*. Edited by Patricia Lamoureux and Kevin J. O'Neil, C.Ss.R., 71-86. Lanham, Md.: Rowman & Littlefield, 2005.

Lee, Dorothy. "Abiding in the Fourth Gospel: A Case Study in Feminist Biblical Theology." In *A Feminist Companion to John*, vol. 2. Edited by Amy-Jill Levine with Marianne Blickenstaff, 64-78. Cleveland: Pilgrim, 2003.

Lefebure, Leo D. *The Buddha and the Christ: Explorations in Buddhist and Christian Dialogue*. Maryknoll, N.Y.: Orbis Books, 1993.

Lewis, C. S. *The Four Loves*. New York: Harcourt, Brace & World, 1960.

Lindbeck, George. *The Nature of Doctrine: Religion and Theology in a Postliberal Age*. Philadelphia: Westminster, 1984.

Lonergan, Bernard J. F., S.J. *A Second Collection*. Edited by William F. J. Ryan, S.J., and Bernard J. Tyrrell, S.J. Philadelphia: Westminster, 1974.

Longenecker, Richard N., ed. *Patterns of Discipleship in the New Testament*. Grand Rapids: Eerdmans, 1996.

Lorenzen, Thorwald. *Resurrection and Discipleship: Interpretive Models, Biblical Reflections, Theological Consequences*. Maryknoll, N.Y.: Orbis Books, 1995.

Lovin, Robin W. *Christian Faith and Public Choices: The Social Ethics of Barth, Brunner, and Bonhoeffer*. Philadelphia: Fortress, 1984.

Luther, Martin. *Selected Political Writings*. Edited by J. M. Porter. Minneapolis: Fortress, 1974.

Lysaught, Therese. "Love and Liturgy." In *Gathered for the Journey: Moral Theology in Catholic Perspective*. Edited by David Matzko McCarthy and M. Therese Lysaught, 24-42. Grand Rapids: Eerdmans, 2007.

MacIntyre, Alasdair. *After Virtue: A Study in Moral Theory*. Notre Dame, Ind.: University of Notre Dame Press, 1981.

———. *Dependent Rational Animals: Why Human Beings Need the Virtues*. Chicago: Open Court, 1999.

MacNamara, Vincent. *Love, Law and Christian Life: Basic Attitudes of Christian Morality.* Wilmington, Del.: Michael Glazier, 1988.

Macquarrie, John. "Rethinking Natural Law." In *Natural Law and Theology.* Edited by Charles E. Curran and Richard A. McCormick, 221-46. Readings in Moral Theology 7. Mahwah, N.J.: Paulist, 1991.

Maguire, Daniel C. *The Moral Choice.* New York: Winston Press, 1978.

―――. *The Moral Core of Judaism and Christianity.* Minneapolis: Fortress, 1993.

Maguire, Daniel C., and A. Nicholas Fargnoli. *On Moral Grounds: The Art/Science of Ethics.* New York: Crossroad, 1991.

Mahoney, John. *The Making of Moral Theology: A Study of the Roman Catholic Tradition.* Oxford: Clarendon, 1987.

―――. *Seeking the Spirit: Essays in Moral and Pastoral Theology.* London: Sheed & Ward; Denville, N.J.: Dimension, 1982.

Marty, Martin E. *The Public Church.* New York: Crossroad, 1981.

Matera, Frank J. *New Testament Ethics: The Legacies of Jesus and Paul.* Louisville: Westminster John Knox, 1996.

Mattison, William C., III. *Introducing Moral Theology: True Happiness and the Virtues.* Grand Rapids: Brazos, 2008.

―――. "Moral Virtue, the Grace of God, and Discipleship." In *Gathered for the Journey: Moral Theology in Catholic Perspective.* Edited by David Matzko McCarthy and M. Therese Lysaught, 198-215. Grand Rapids: Eerdmans, 2007.

McBrien, Richard P. *Catholicism.* Vol. 1. Minneapolis: Winston, 1980.

McCabe, Herbert, O.P. *God, Christ and Us.* Edited by Brian Davies, O.P. New York: Continuum, 2003.

―――. *The Good Life: Ethics and the Pursuit of Happiness.* Edited by Brian Davies, O.P. New York: Continuum, 2005.

McCormick, Patrick T. *A Banqueter's Guide to the All-Night Soup Kitchen of the Kingdom of God.* Collegeville, Minn.: Liturgical Press, 2004.

McDonagh, Enda. *Gift and Call: Towards a Christian Theology of Morality.* St. Meinrad, Ind.: Abbey Press, 1975.

―――. *The Making of Disciples.* Wilmington, Del.: Michael Glazier, 1985.

McFague, Sallie. "Conversion: Life on the Edge of the Raft." *Interpretation* 32, no. 3 (1978): 255-68.

McKenzie, John L. "Aspects of Old Testament Thought." In *New Jerome Biblical Commentary.* Edited by Raymond Brown, Joseph Fitzmyer, and Roland Murphy, 1284-1315. Englewood Cliffs, N.J.: Prentice-Hall, 1990.

Meier, John. *A Marginal Jew: Rethinking the Historical Jesus.* Vol. 3. New York: Doubleday, 1994.

Meilaender, Gilbert C. *Faith and Faithfulness: Basic Themes in Christian Ethics.* Notre Dame, Ind.: University of Notre Dame Press, 1991.

―――. *The Theory and Practice of Virtue.* Notre Dame, Ind.: University of Notre Dame Press, 1984.

Melchin, Kenneth R. *Living with Other People: An Introduction to Christian Ethics Based on Bernard Lonergan.* Collegeville, Minn.: Liturgical Press, 1998.

Melina, Livio. *Sharing in Christ's Virtues: For a Renewal of Moral Theology in Light of*

Veritatis Splendor. Translated by William E. May. Washington, D.C.: Catholic University of America Press, 2001.

Merton, Thomas. *Conjectures of a Guilty Bystander.* Garden City, N.Y.: Doubleday, 1966.

Michon, Jean-Louis, and Roger Gaetani, eds. *Sufism: Love and Wisdom.* Bloomington, Ind.: World Wisdom, 2006.

Miller, Michael R. "Freedom and Grace." In *Gathered for the Journey: Moral Theology in Catholic Perspective.* Edited by David Matzko McCarthy and M. Therese Lysaught, 177-97. Grand Rapids: Eerdmans, 2007.

Mitchell, Donald W., and James Wiseman, O.S.B., eds. *Transforming Suffering, Reflections on Finding Peace in Troubled Times.* New York: Doubleday, 2003.

Moltmann, Jürgen. *God for a Secular Society: The Public Relevance of Theology.* Minneapolis: Fortress, 1999.

Moore, Sebastian. *Jesus the Liberator of Desire.* New York: Crossroad, 1989.

Morris, Kenneth. *Bonhoeffer's Ethic of Discipleship.* University Park: Pennsylvania State Press, 1955.

Moser, Antônio, and Bernardino Leers. *Moral Theology: Dead Ends and Alternatives.* Translated by Paul Burns. Maryknoll, N.Y.: Orbis Books, 1990.

Murdoch, Iris. *Metaphysics as a Guide to Morals.* New York: Penguin, 1992.

———. *The Sovereignty of Good.* London: Routledge & Kegan Paul, 1970.

Murphy, Roland. *The Tree of Life: An Exploration of Biblical Wisdom Literature.* 3rd ed. Grand Rapids: Eerdmans, 1990.

Nash, James A. *Loving Nature: Ecological Integrity and Christian Responsibility.* Nashville: Abingdon, 1991.

Niebuhr, H. Richard. *Christ and Culture.* New York: Harper, 1956.

———. *The Meaning of Revelation.* New York: Macmillan, 1941.

———. *The Responsible Self: An Essay in Christian Moral Philosophy.* New York: Harper & Row, 1963.

Nussbaum, Martha C. *Love's Knowledge: Essays on Philosophy and Literature.* New York: Oxford University Press, 1990.

Nygren, Anders. *Agape and Eros.* Translated by Philip S. Watson. New York: Harper & Row, 1969.

Oates, Wayne E. "Conversion: Sacred and Secular." In *Conversion: Perspectives on Personal and Social Transformation.* Edited by Walter E. Conn, 149-68. New York: Alba House, 1978.

O'Connell, Timothy E. *Making Disciples: A Handbook of Christian Moral Formation.* New York: Crossroad, 1998.

———. *Principles for a Catholic Morality.* New York: Seabury, 1978.

O'Day, Gail R. "Surprised by Faith: Jesus and the Canaanite Woman." In *A Feminist Companion to Matthew.* Edited by Amy-Jill Levine with Marianne Blickenstaff, 114-25. Cleveland: Pilgrim, 2003.

Ogletree, Thomas W. *Hospitality to the Stranger: Dimensions of Moral Understanding.* Philadelphia: Fortress, 1985.

O'Keefe, Mark, O.S.B. *Becoming Good, Becoming Holy: On the Relationship of Christian Ethics and Spirituality.* New York: Paulist, 1995.

O'Shea, Kevin F., C.Ss.R. "The Reality of Sin: A Theological and Pastoral Critique."

In *The Mystery of Sin and Forgiveness*. Edited by Michael J. Taylor, S.J., 91-112. New York: Alba House, 1971.

Palmer, Parker J. *The Company of Strangers: Christians and the Renewal of America's Public Life*. New York: Crossroad, 1986.

Paris, Peter J. *Virtues and Values: The African and African American Experience*. Minneapolis: Fortress, 2004.

Pasquier, Jacques. "Experience and Conversion." In *Conversion: Perspectives on Personal and Social Transformation*. Edited by Walter E. Conn, 191-200. New York: Alba House, 1978.

Patrick, Anne E. *Liberating Conscience: Feminist Explorations in Catholic Moral Theology*. New York: Continuum, 1997.

Perrin, Norman. *Jesus and the Language of the Kingdom: Symbol and Metaphor in the New Testament Interpretation*. Philadelphia: Fortress, 1976.

Peters, Ted. *Sin: Radical Evil in Soul and Society*. Grand Rapids: Eerdmans, 1994.

Phan, Peter C. *Christianity with an Asian Face: Asian American Theology in the Making*. Maryknoll, N.Y.: Orbis Books, 2003.

———. "Doing Theology in the Context of Cultural and Religious Pluralism: An Asian Perspective." *Louvain Studies* 27 (2002): 51-52.

———. *In Our Own Tongues: Perspectives from Asia on Mission and Inculturation*. Maryknoll, N.Y.: Orbis Books, 2003.

Pieper, Josef. *The Concept of Sin*. Translated by Edward T. Oakes, S.J. South Bend, Ind.: St. Augustine's Press, 2001.

———. *Faith, Hope, Love*. Translated by Sr. Mary Frances McCarthy, S.N.D., Richard Winston, and Clara Winston. San Francisco: Ignatius, 1997.

———. *The Four Cardinal Virtues*. Translated by Richard Winston, Clara Winston, Lawrence E. Lynch, and Daniel F. Coogan. Notre Dame, Ind.: University of Notre Dame Press, 1966.

———. *Hope*. Translated by Mary Frances McCarthy, S.N.D. San Francisco: Ignatius, 1986.

Pinckaers, Servais, O.P. *The Sources of Christian Ethics*. Translated by Sr. Mary Thomas Noble, O.P. Washington, D.C.: Catholic University of America Press, 1995.

Placher, William C. *Narratives of a Vulnerable God: Christ, Theology, and Scripture*. Louisville: Westminster John Knox, 1994.

Porter, Jean. *Nature as Reason: A Thomistic Theory of the Natural Law*. Grand Rapids: Eerdmans, 2005.

———. *The Recovery of Virtue: The Relevance of Aquinas for Christian Ethics*. Louisville: Westminster/John Knox, 1990.

Post, Stephen G. *Spheres of Love: Toward a New Ethics of the Family*. Dallas: Southern Methodist University Press, 1994.

———. *A Theory of Agape: On the Meaning of Christian Love*. Cranbury, N.J.: Associated University Presses, 1990.

Rahner, Karl. "Do Not Stifle the Spirit!" In *Theological Investigations* 7. New York: Herder & Herder, 1971, 72-87.

———. "Experience of the Holy Spirit." In *Theological Investigations* 18. New York: Crossroad, 1983, 189-210.

Rahula, Walpola. *What the Buddha Taught.* Rev. and expanded ed. New York: Grove, 1974.

Rausch, Thomas P. *Catholicism at the Dawn of the Third Millennium.* Collegeville, Minn.: Liturgical Press, 1996.

Rejon, Francisco Moreno. "Fundamental Moral Theology in the Theology of Liberation." In *Mysterium Liberationis: Fundamental Concepts of Liberation Theology.* Edited by Ignacio Ellacuría, S.J., and Jon Sobrino, S.J., 210-21. Maryknoll, N.Y.: Orbis Books, 1993.

Rolheiser, Ronald. *The Holy Longing: The Search for a Christian Spirituality.* New York: Doubleday, 1999.

Sakenfeld, Katharine. *Faithfulness in Action.* Philadelphia: Fortress, 1985.

Sandel, Michael J. *Democracy's Discontent: America in Search of a Public Philosophy.* Cambridge, Mass.: Belknap Press of Harvard University Press, 1996.

Schnackenburg, Rudolf. *God's Rule and Kingdom.* Translated by John Murray. Montreal: Palm, 1963.

Schockenhoff, Eberhard. "The Theological Virtue of Charity." Translated by Grant Kaplan and Frederick G. Lawrence. In *The Ethics of Aquinas.* Edited by Stephen J. Pope, 244-58. Washington, D.C.: Georgetown University Press, 2002.

Schüssler Fiorenza, Elisabeth. *In Memory of Her.* New York: Crossroad, 1983.

Second Vatican Council. *Gaudium et spes* (Pastoral Constitution on the Church in the Modern World, 1965). In *Catholic Social Thought: The Documentary Heritage.* Edited by David J. O'Brien and Thomas A. Shannon, 393-436. Maryknoll, N.Y.: Orbis Books, 1992.

Senior, Donald. *Jesus: A Gospel Portrait.* Rev. and expanded ed. New York: Paulist, 1992.

Sobrino, Jon. *Jesus in Latin America.* Maryknoll, N.Y.: Orbis Books, 1988.

Segovia, Fernando F. *Discipleship in the New Testament.* Philadelphia: Fortress, 1985.

Sherman, Nancy. *The Fabric of Character: Aristotle's Theory of Virtue.* Oxford: Clarendon, 1989.

Smith, Huston. *The Religions of Man.* New York: Harper & Row, 1958.

Smith, John E. "The Concept of Conversion." In *Conversion: Perspectives on Personal and Social Transformation.* Edited by Walter E. Conn, 51-61. New York: Alba House, 1978.

Soelle, Dorothee. *Suffering.* Translated by Everett R. Kalin. Philadelphia: Fortress, 1975.

Spohn, William C. *Go and Do Likewise: Jesus and Ethics.* New York: Continuum, 1999.

———. *What Are They Saying about Scripture and Ethics?* New York: Paulist, 1995.

Stassen, Glen H., and David P. Gushee. *Kingdom Ethics: Following Jesus in Contemporary Context.* Downers Grove, Ill.: InterVarsity, 2003.

Steck, Christopher. *The Ethical Thought of Hans Urs von Balthasar.* New York: Crossroad, 2001.

Storkey, Elaine. *The Search for Intimacy.* Grand Rapids: Eerdmans, 1995.

Sutherland, Arthur. *I Was a Stranger: A Christian Theology of Hospitality.* Nashville: Abingdon Press, 2006.

Tracy, David. *The Analogical Imagination: Christian Theology and the Culture of Pluralism* New York: Crossroad, 1981.

Twain, Mark. *The Adventures of Huckleberry Finn.* New York: Bantam, 1981.

Ulstein, Stefan. "*Shadowlands* Portrays Lewis with Poignance." *Christianity Today* 3/2 (February 7, 1994): 50.

U.S. Catholic Bishops. "The Challenge of Peace: God's Promise and Our Response" (1983). In *Catholic Social Thought: The Documentary Heritage*. Edited by David J. O'Brien and Thomas A. Shannon, 492-571. Maryknoll, N.Y.: Orbis Books, 1992.

———. "Economic Justice for All" (1986). In *Catholic Social Thought: The Documentary Heritage*. Edited by David J. O'Brien and Thomas A. Shannon, 572-681. Maryknoll, N.Y.: Orbis Books, 1992.

Vacek, Edward Collins, S.J. *Love, Human and Divine: The Heart of Christian Ethics*. Washington, D.C.: Georgetown University Press, 1994.

Verhey, Allen. *The Great Reversal: Ethics and the New Testament*. Vancouver: Regent College Publishing, 1984.

———. *Remembering Jesus: Christian Community, Scripture, and the Moral Life*. Grand Rapids: Eerdmans, 2002.

Viviano, Benedict T., O.P. *The Kingdom of God in History*. Wilmington, Del.: Michael Glazier, 1988.

Wadell, Paul J. *Becoming Friends: Worship, Justice, and the Practice of Christian Friendship*. Grand Rapids: Brazos, 2002.

———. *Friendship and the Moral Life*. Notre Dame, Ind.: University of Notre Dame Press, 1989.

———. *Happiness and the Christian Moral Life: An Introduction to Christian Ethics*. Lanham, Md.: Rowman & Littlefield, 2008.

———. "Huckleberry Finn: An Adventure in Unconventional Morality," *New Theology Review* 2 (1989): 66-80.

———. *The Primacy of Love: An Introduction to the Ethics of Thomas Aquinas*. New York: Paulist, 1992.

———. "What Do All Those Masses Do for Us? Reflections on the Christian Moral Life and the Eucharist." In *Living No Longer for Ourselves: Liturgy and Justice in the Nineties*. Edited by Kathleen Hughes, R.S.C.J., and Mark R. Francis, C.S.V., 153-69. Collegeville, Minn.: Liturgical Press, 1991.

Warrington, Keith. *Discovering the Holy Spirit in the New Testament*. Peabody, Mass.: Hendrickson, 2005.

Webber, Robert E., and Rodney Clapp. *People of the Truth: A Christian Challenge to Contemporary Culture*. Harrisburg, Pa.: Morehouse, 1988.

Weiss, Lyle K. "The Bodily Resurrection of Jesus and Moral Vision." In "The Public Significance of the Bodily Resurrection of Jesus Christ," 115-55. Ph.D. dissertation. St. Mary's Seminary and University, 2007.

Williams, Daniel Day. *The Spirit and the Forms of Love*. Lanham, Md.: University Press of America, 1981.

Wogaman, J. Philip. *Christian Moral Judgment*. Louisville: Westminster/John Knox, 1989.

Wright, N. T. *Following Jesus: Biblical Reflections on Discipleship*. Grand Rapids: Eerdmans, 1994.

Yearley, Lee H. *Mencius and Aquinas: Theories of Virtue and Conceptions of Courage*. Albany: State University of New York Press, 1990.

Index